Britain's Maritime Empire

Britain's Maritime Empire explores the maritime gateway to Asia around the Cape of Good Hope and its critical role in the establishment, consolidation and maintenance of the British Empire in the late eighteenth and nineteenth centuries. Situated at the centre of a maritime chain that connected seas and continents, this gateway bridged the Atlantic and Indian Oceans. Its commercial and strategic links formed a global web that reflected the development of the British Empire in the period. The book examines how contemporaries perceived, understood and represented this area; the ways in which it worked as an alternative hub of empire, enabling the movement of people, goods, and ideas, as well as facilitating information and intelligence exchanges; and the networks of administration, security and control that helped to cement British imperial power.

John McAleer is a lecturer in history at the University of Southampton.

Britain's Maritime Empire

Southern Africa, the South Atlantic and the
Indian Ocean, 1763–1820

John McAleer

University of Southampton

CAMBRIDGE
UNIVERSITY PRESS

University Printing House, Cambridge CB2 8BS, United Kingdom

Cambridge University Press is part of the University of Cambridge.

It furthers the University's mission by disseminating knowledge in the pursuit of education, learning and research at the highest international levels of excellence.

www.cambridge.org
Information on this title: www.cambridge.org/9781107100725

© John McAleer 2017

First published 2017

Printed in the United Kingdom by Clays, St Ives plc

A catalogue record for this publication is available from the British Library

Library of Congress Cataloguing in Publication data
McAleer, John, author.
Britain's maritime empire : Southern Africa, the South Atlantic and the Indian Ocean, 1763–1820 / John McAleer.
Cambridge, United Kingdom : Cambridge University Press, [2016]
LCCN 2015036419 | ISBN 9781107100725 (hardback : alkaline paper)
LCSH: Cape of Good Hope (South Africa) – History – 1795–1872. | Cape of Good Hope (South Africa) – Politics and government – 1795–1872. | British – South Africa – Cape of Good Hope. | Great Britain – Colonies – Africa – History. | Great Britain – Colonies – Asia – History. | Great Britain – Colonies – Administration – History. | Great Britain – Foreign relations. | BISAC: HISTORY / Europe / Great Britain.
LCC DT2042 .M33 2016 | DDC 909/.097124107–dc23
LC record available at http://lccn.loc.gov/2015036419

ISBN 978-1-107-10072-5 Hardback

Contents

Acknowledgements

In the course of writing this book, I have accrued a great many personal and professional debts and it is a pleasure to acknowledge and thank those people and institutions on which I have relied so heavily.

This book began its long voyage at a workshop held at the University of Sussex in July 2007. I would like to thank the organisers – Huw Bowen, Elizabeth Mancke and John Reid – for inviting me to contribute and Trevor Burnard for hosting the event. The intensive discussions around the question 'British Asia and the British Atlantic: Two Worlds or One?' encouraged me to explore some of the ideas and themes presented in the pages that follow. Serendipity is a crucial part of all research and I had the good fortune to share a train carriage back to London with Stephen Conway and Peter (P. J.) Marshall, which gave me the opportunity to benefit from their collective wisdom. For their advice, encouragement and support over a number of years, I owe a great deal to Huw Bowen, John MacKenzie and John Oldfield.

At the National Maritime Museum, Greenwich, I was fortunate to have the privilege to work with the extraordinary collections and archives in that institution. The NMM also afforded me the opportunity to present and refine my ideas on Atlantic and Indian Ocean history in a range of fora and for that I am grateful. Most importantly, it gave me the chance to work with some great colleagues. My colleagues in History at the University of Southampton were similarly generous with their time and advice. Beyond that, the eclectic band of philosophers, historians, linguists, geographers and wine merchants comprising the Cavaliers football team helped to keep academic problems in perspective by putting the *Monty Python* sketch into practice – sometimes rather too accurately – every week.

Writing this book would not have been possible without the help and assistance of a variety of libraries, librarians and archivists. I am particularly grateful to Nick Graffy at the Hartley Library and to his colleagues in the Inter-library Loan Department at the University of Southampton. The staff at the Caird Library of the National Maritime Museum were equally helpful. I would also like to thank Penny Brook, Margaret Makepeace and all of their colleagues in the India Office Records for their generous assistance and guidance. In the UK, I relied heavily on the staffs of the British Library, London, the Bodleian Libraries at the University of Oxford and the Hartley Library at the University of Southampton. My research trips to South Africa would have been immeasurably less productive and much less enjoyable without the warm welcome and assistance that I met everywhere there. In Cape Town, I was helped by Erika le Roux and her colleagues at the Western Cape Archives and Records Service and by Melanie Geustyn, Laddy McKechnie and their colleagues at the National Library of South Africa. Jennifer Kimble, Sally MacRoberts and their colleagues at the Brenthurst Library made my stay in Johannesburg a real pleasure. Similarly, I would like to thank Michele Pickover, Zofia Sulej, Gabriele Mohale and their colleagues in the Department of Historical Papers at the University of the Witwatersrand, Johannesburg. Their unfailing good cheer as I requested yet another dusty box of archives only enhanced my admiration for librarians and archivists everywhere. A Small Research Grant awarded by the British Academy and the Leverhulme Trust made these archival visits possible and for that I am very grateful.

For their assistance and for permission to quote from collections in their care, I would like to thank the following: Arquivo Histórico Ultramarino, Lisbon; Bodleian Libraries, University of Oxford; the Brenthurst Library, Johannesburg; the British Library; Cadbury Research Library, University of Birmingham; Cambridge University Library; Cumbria Record Office, Carlisle; Department of Historical Papers, William Cullen Library, University of the Witwatersrand, Johannesburg; Department of Manuscripts and Special Collections, Nottingham University Library; Devon Record Office, Exeter; East Sussex Record Office, Lewes; Foyle Special Collections Library, King's College, London; Hampshire Record Office, Winchester; Hertfordshire Archives & Local Studies, Hertford; the National Archives, Kew; National Archives of Scotland, Edinburgh; National Library of Scotland, Edinburgh; Plymouth and West Devon Record Office, Plymouth; Public Record Office of Northern Ireland, Belfast; Royal Botanic Gardens, Kew; Western Cape Archives and Records Service, Cape Town.

Elements of this book, in the form of conference papers and research seminars, were presented at a number of institutions: the Institute of Historical Research; the National Maritime Museum, Greenwich; the National Museum of the Royal Navy, Portsmouth; the University of Greenwich; the University of Hull; the University of Kent; the

University of Lisbon; the University of London; the University of Mauritius; the University of Plymouth; and the University of Southampton. I am grateful to the organisers of these events and to the participants and attendees for their comments and suggestions. Some of the ideas presented in Chapter 5 initially appeared in my article, '"The Key to India": Troop Movements, Southern Africa and Britain's Indian Ocean World, 1795–1820', *International History Review* 35 (2013).

One of the most rewarding things about this project was the opportunity it gave me to observe and engage with a variety of academic, disciplinary and historiographical traditions and perspectives. With that in mind, I am grateful to the two anonymous readers for Cambridge University Press who were generous in offering their respective expertise, advice and scholarly perspectives.

I am also particularly grateful – and it is a real pleasure to acknowledge – the advice, suggestions, encouragement and friendship of the people who contributed in all sorts of ways to the research and writing of this book: Seema Alavi, Clare Anderson, Anyaa Anim-Addo, Tim Barringer, Maxine Berg, Robert Blyth, Huw Bowen, Trevor Boyns, David Brown, Phil Buckner, Gwyn Campbell, Isabelle Charmentier, Helen Clifford, Quintin Colville, Stephen Conway, Helen Cowie, Nigel Dalziel, James Davey, Lizelle de Jager, Richard Drayton, Lindsay Doulton, Richard Dunn, Nick Evans, Ellen Filor, Margot Finn, Robert Fletcher, Douglas Fordham, Gillian Forrester, Steven Gray, Douglas Hamilton, Rachel Herrmann, Rebekah Higgitt, Vinesh Hookoomsing, Gillian Hutchinson, Richard Huzzey, Charlie Jarvis; Claire Jowitt, Stephanie Jones, Roger Knight, David Lambert, Don Leggett, Margarette Lincoln, Sarah Longair, Jane McDermid, Philip McEvansoneya, John MacKenzie, Margaret Makepeace, Peter (P. J.) Marshall, Maria Newbery, Marianne O'Doherty, Miles Ogborn, John Oldfield, Kendrick Oliver, William O'Reilly, Sarah Palmer, Helen Paul, Sarah Pearce, Christer Petley, Chris Prior, Katherine Prior, Geoff Quilley, Jesse Ransley, John Reid, Giorgio Riello, Nigel Rigby, Lissa Roberts, Johanna Roethe, Simon Schaffer, Suzanne Schwarz, Sujit Sivasundaram, Crosbie Smith, Kate Smith, David J. Starkey, Phil Stern, Ian Talbot, Patrick Walsh, Chris Ware, Claire Warrior, Martin Wilcox, Charlie Withers, Zoë White, Glyn Williams, Mary Wills, Chris Woolgar, and Nigel Worden.

I am particularly grateful to those friends who voluntarily subjected themselves to reading parts (or indeed all) of the manuscript. The shortcomings and inadequacies of the book are, of course, my sole responsibility but they would be immeasurably more extensive without the forbearance, good counsel and academic acuity of these people: Robert Blyth, Huw Bowen, David Brown, James Davey, Douglas Hamilton, Sarah Longair, John MacKenzie, John Oldfield, Johanna Roethe and Zoë White. Finally, I would like to thank Michael Watson, Amanda George, the copy-editor Martin Barr and all their colleagues at Cambridge University Press for their encouragement and support in helping to make this book a reality.

Abbreviations

The following abbreviations are employed throughout the text:

Add. MS	Additional Manuscripts
AHU	Arquivo Histórico Ultramarino, Lisbon
BL	British Library
Bodl.	Bodleian Library Special Collections, University of Oxford
B'hurst	Brenthurst Library, Johannesburg
CA	Western Cape Archives and Records Service, Cape Town
CRL	Cadbury Research Library, University of Birmingham
CRO	Cumbria Record Office, Carlisle
CUL	Cambridge University Library
Diaries	*The Cape Diaries of Lady Anne Barnard, 1799–1800*, edited by Margaret Lenta and Basil Le Cordeur, 2 vols. (Cape Town: Van Riebeeck Society, 1999)
DRO	Devon Record Office, Exeter
ESRO	East Sussex Record Office, Lewes
HALS	Hertfordshire Archives & Local Studies, Hertford
HRO	Hampshire Record Office, Winchester
IOR	India Office Records, British Library
Journals	*The Cape Journals of Lady Anne Barnard, 1797–1798*, edited by A. M. Lewin Robinson with Margaret Lenta and Dorothy Driver (Cape Town: Van Riebeeck Society, 1994)
KCL	Foyle Special Collections Library, King's College, London, Foreign and Commonwealth Office Historical Collections
Letters	*The Letters of Lady Anne Barnard to Henry Dundas*, edited by A. M. Lewin Robinson (Cape Town: A. A. Balkema, 1973)

Londonderry	*Correspondence, Despatches and other Papers of Viscount Castlereagh, Second Marquess of Londonderry*, edited by Charles William Vane, Marquess of Londonderry, 12 vols. (London: William Shoeberl, 1851)
Minto	*Lord Minto in India: Life and Letters of Gilbert Elliot, First Earl of Minto, from 1807 to 1814*, edited by Emma Eleanor Elizabeth, Countess of Minto (London: Longmans, Green, and Co., 1880)
NAS	National Archives of Scotland, Edinburgh
NHM	Natural History Museum, London
NLS	National Library of Scotland, Edinburgh
NMM	National Maritime Museum, Greenwich
NUL	Nottingham University Library, Department of Manuscripts and Special Collections
OUMNH	Oxford University Museum of Natural History
PRONI	Public Record Office of Northern Ireland, Belfast
PWDRO	Plymouth and West Devon Record Office, Plymouth
RBG	Royal Botanic Gardens, Kew
RCC	*Records of the Cape Colony*, edited by George McCall Theal, 36 vols. (Cape Town: Government of the Cape Colony, 1897–1905)
RH	Bodleian Library of Commonwealth and African Studies, Rhodes House, University of Oxford
Spencer	*Private Papers of George, Second Earl Spencer*, edited by Julian S. Corbett and H. W. Richmond, 4 vols. (London: Navy Records Society, 1913–24)
TNA	National Archives, Kew
Two Views	*Two Views of British India: The Private Correspondence of Mr Dundas and Lord Wellesley, 1798–1801*, edited by Edward Ingram (Bath: Adams and Dart, 1970)
US	University of Southampton Library, Special Collections
UWits	Department of Historical Papers, William Cullen Library, University of the Witwatersrand, Johannesburg
WRO	Worcestershire Record Office, Worcester

Map

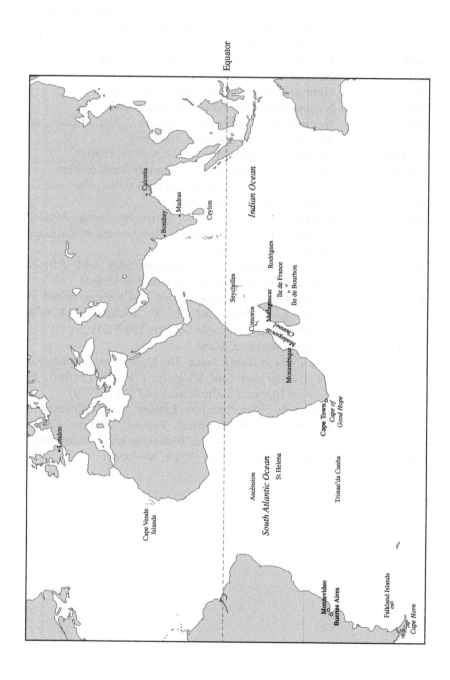

1   Introduction: 'the master link of connection'

On 4 May 1797, after a voyage of seventy-one days, Lord Macartney finally arrived at the Cape of Good Hope, one of Britain's newest colonial possessions.[1] The following day, after a brief ceremony in Cape Town, he assumed the latest in a long series of diplomatic and administrative appointments stretching back over thirty years.[2] In taking the oaths of office, this stalwart servant of the Crown was now entrusted with the custodianship of this recently acquired colony at the southern tip of Africa, a place at a crucial crossroads in Britain's maritime channels of communication and commerce. After several months at sea, journeying southwards in HMS *Trusty*, Macartney must have been relieved finally to disembark his gouty frame and survey the place that British troops had captured only two years previously. They had done so in the name of the Dutch House of Orange. Ostensibly, Britain claimed to be protecting the colony, its settlers and its institutions from the nefarious depredations of the republican Dutch government, with its revolutionary principles and French sympathies, rather than aggrandising its own position in this part of the world. Others, however, saw less altruistic motivations behind the British capture.[3] Whatever the reality, this did not alter the fact that, as Diogo de Souza, the Portuguese governor of Mozambique, put it, the British were now 'masters of the Cape of Good Hope'.[4]

As the first British civilian governor of the Cape, Macartney recognised that this recent turn of events meant that the future required careful consideration. Writing to Henry Dundas in London, he made a shrewd

---

[1] J. L. McCracken, 'The Cape of Good Hope, 1796–98', in Peter Roebuck (ed.), *Macartney of Lisanoure, 1737–1806* (Belfast: Ulster Historical Foundation, 1983), pp. 266–77, p. 267.

[2] Maurice Boucher and Nigel Penn (eds.), *Britain at the Cape, 1795 to 1803* (Johannesburg: Brenthurst Press, 1992), p. 69.

[3] See, for example, 'Extract from a Proclamation of General Dumoriez to the Batavians', February 1793, *RCC*, vol. I, p. 3.

[4] AHU, Conselho Ultramarino (CU), Moçambique (Moç.), CX75/62, Diogo Rodrigo de Souza Coutinho to Luis Pinto de Souza, 28 September 1796. The phrase in the original document is 'Senhors do Cabo di Boa Esperanza'.

assessment of his new bailiwick. Its 'geographical situation' was vital, he observed. In fact, it 'formed the master link of connection between the western and eastern world'. It was 'the great outwork of our Asian commerce and Indian Empire'.[5] Macartney was not the first person to consider the geopolitical consequences of the British presence in (or, indeed, absence from) the region. Nor was he alone in regarding the capture of the Cape as crucial to Britain's commercial and political empire in Asia. Nevertheless, his statement raises a number of interesting questions. First, what were the geographical boundaries of Macartney's 'western' and 'eastern' worlds? Second, what sort of 'master link' did Macartney have in mind when he suggested the Cape could unite them? Third, what motivations might individuals, trading companies or countries have for connecting these seemingly disparate maritime and political spaces? And, finally, was the Cape the only place that could connect these worlds? In other words, was the 'master link' centred on one place, or was its strength, like a chain, in the binding together of many links to make a stronger whole?

This book explores these issues, arguing for the need to see beyond the boundaries of oceanic basins and suggesting the flexible, overlapping and interdependent nature of the various maritime worlds comprising Britain's late eighteenth-century empire.[6] Key components of that empire – such as the East India Company in Asia, which encompassed complex, interconnected networks of people, places and resources – stretch beyond the confines of traditional historiographical and geographical frameworks.[7] Although many might have agreed with Macartney that the Cape formed part of the 'Indian World', the precise definition as well as the extent and boundaries of that world were much less clear.[8] The discussion that follows, then, offers a differently imagined geography of empire. It is one viewed from the southern hemisphere. It comprises places as diverse and geographically distant from each other as Río de la Plata and Mauritius, St Helena and the Cape of Good Hope, Tristan da Cunha and the Indian Ocean coastline of Southern Africa, and links them in the same frame of historical analysis. In adopting this perspective and approach, the book demonstrates how the British Empire evolved in

---

[5] TNA, WO 1/329, p. 17, Lord Macartney to Henry Dundas, 10 July 1797.

[6] This point mirrors ideas outlined in Philip J. Stern, 'Politics and Ideology in the Early East India Company-State: The Case of St. Helena, 1673–1696', *Journal of Imperial and Commonwealth History* 35 (2007), pp. 1–23, and Gerald Groenewald, 'Southern Africa and the Atlantic World', in D'Maris Coffman, Adrian Leonard and William O'Reilly (eds.), *The Atlantic World* (Abingdon: Routledge, 2015), pp. 100–16.

[7] Richard B. Allen, *European Slave Trading in the Indian Ocean, 1500–1850* (Athens, OH: Ohio University Press, 2014), p. 61.

[8] NAS, GD51/1/530/5, Macartney to Dundas, 9 March 1798.

the second half of the eighteenth century and into the early nineteenth, through the challenges of global wars and political revolutions.

Macartney's correspondent, Henry Dundas, needed little explanation of Britain's place in the wider world. As Secretary of State for War, and President of the Board of Control (the governmental body which oversaw the British East India Company), Dundas was a central figure in much of the political rhetoric and logistical realities that connected distant parts of the British Empire to Britain and to each other in the period.[9] As a confidant of William Pitt, the Prime Minister, he was one of the most significant architects of Britain's wartime strategy and imperial policy during the long years of the Revolutionary and Napoleonic Wars.[10] As Dundas recognised in a memorandum circulated among his cabinet colleagues in 1800, the regions beyond Europe, acquired in the crucible of war, were 'objects essential to the permanent interests of Great Britain'.[11] And, like many politicians in London, Dundas had shown himself to be keenly interested in the Cape as the gateway to India.[12]

Indeed, there is evidence that Dundas also tried to work out where the Cape sat in this reoriented British Empire. His evolving thoughts are laid out in a series of 'Suggestions respecting the Cape of Good Hope', which were appended to a larger document on the region and which Dundas presumably presented to his cabinet colleagues. Should the Cape under the British follow the Dutch model, he wondered, and be considered 'in no other light but as subservient to their Indian trade'? Dundas felt this would simply result in government 'upon those principles of grievous and oppressive monopoly which has always marked the policy of the Dutch in India'.[13] Instead he advocated a different approach: 'I lay it down as a fundamental principle that Great Britain must never attempt to hold possession of the Cape on the principles of strict colonial connexion.'

---

[9] By the end of the eighteenth century, the Secretaryship of State for War had also come to embrace the colonies, although the official change of name only occurred in 1801.

[10] There is a copious literature on Dundas. The most helpful sources include: Michael Fry, *The Dundas Despotism* (Edinburgh: Edinburgh University Press, 1992); Holden Furber, *Henry Dundas, First Viscount Melville, 1742–1811* (Oxford: Oxford University Press, 1931); Cyril Matheson, *The Life of Henry Dundas, First Viscount Melville, 1742–1811* (London: Constable, 1933).

[11] TNA, PRO 30/8/243, p. 91, Henry Dundas, 'Memorandum for the consideration of HM's Ministers', 31 March 1800.

[12] Dundas received many letters and suggestions with regard to the Cape and its strategic position. One George Forster of the Madras Civil Service, for example, discussed the strength of the garrison at the Cape and the oppressive nature of the government there. UWits, A154, George Forster to Dundas, 22 January 1786.

[13] KCL, DT2042 [Henry Dundas], 'Suggestions respecting the Cape of Good Hope' [*c.*1796], unpaginated. For details on the authorship of the 'Suggestions' and further thoughts on the attached 'Sketches', see accompanying correspondence in the DT2042 file.

More pointedly, he continued: 'The important benefit we must look to from this possession is the immense security it gives to our Indian Empire, which would not exist if it was in the hands of any other powerful European nation.'[14] His musings reflect the wider backdrop against which the events and opinions discussed in this book were played out. Should the Cape, and the ports and islands in the surrounding region, form part of the commercial empire of the East India Company? Or, alternatively, should they be subsumed into the Westminster-controlled colonial framework of the British Atlantic?[15]

Few disagreed with either Macartney or Dundas about the importance of this fulcrum between Britain's Atlantic and Asian empires. The Cape lay along the principal oceanic arterial route that sustained the long-distance maritime trade plied by the ships of the East India Company. Within three years of its capture, it was being touted as politically and strategically vital for Britain's global interests, particularly those centred on the Indian subcontinent. Richard Wellesley, governor general in India, alerted Sir George Yonge, Macartney's successor at the Cape, to the importance of this foothold in Southern Africa. Harking back to Yonge's more conscientious predecessor, Wellesley extolled the wider imperial benefits of an efficient exchange of information between Calcutta and Cape Town:

My correspondence with the Earl of Macartney furnishes abundant proof of the advantages to be derived to the Public Service in India by the speedy communication from the Cape of Good Hope of intelligence affecting the interests of this empire.[16]

Wellesley's grand views of Britain's empire in India, and his place in it, are well known.[17] And he had a troubled relationship with Yonge, whom he considered to be a martinet of the most dissolute kind. This impression was not improved, it should be said, by Yonge's performance at the Cape: he was described by Sylvester Douglas as 'having bedeviled himself there so as to make it necessary to recall him'.[18] However, it appears that, on

---

[14] *Ibid.*

[15] For more on this, see UWits, A88/20, Notes from Meeting of the Privy Council, 23 December 1795; A88/31a, 'Queries submitted by Mr David Scott to the Court of Directors [of the East India Company] relative to the Cape of Good Hope, with proposed answers thereto, July 1796'.

[16] BL, Add. MS 13784, f. 82, Richard Wellesley to Sir George Yonge, 15 September 1800.

[17] The most comprehensive account is still P. E. Roberts, *India under Wellesley* (London: G. Bell and Sons, 1929).

[18] ESRO, AMS5440/354, Sylvester Douglas to Lord Sheffield [October 1800]. For alternative, more sympathetic, interpretations of Yonge's governorship, see *Diaries*, vol. I, p. xxiii; Hermann Giliomee, *Die Kaap Tydens die Eerste Britse Bewind, 1795–1803* (Cape Town: HAUM, 1975), pp. 117, 344.

this point at least, Yonge needed little guidance. In November of the same year, he wrote to Henry Dundas along the same lines as Wellesley had adopted when writing to him:

The situation of the Cape makes it the Gibraltar of this part of the world, and it is so acknowledged by France, Holland, America, & by the East India Company, by the unanimous concurrent voice of all these it is admitted & confessed, that an active power possessed of the Cape will command all communication between the Eastern & Western World.[19]

The importance of the Cape to British imperial interests continued to be acknowledged into the first decade of the nineteenth century. Robert Percival, an army officer who served both at the Cape and in India, was adamant about its importance:

The situation of the Cape of Good Hope, however, placed as it is directly in the middle between the two great divisions of the British empire, forces itself upon the attention of Great Britain, as a possession which would not only contribute to her prosperity, but which seems almost essential to her safety.[20]

And an anonymously authored document in the Lowther family papers, carrying the suggestive title 'The Importance of the Cape of Good Hope Considered', reminded its readers that:

When the Cape of Good Hope was first captured by Sir Alured Clarke, it was considered of the utmost importance to the British Empire, and its advantages as a military as well as a naval station were so impressively described in the discussion upon the Peace of Amiens that it was almost unanimously designated the physical guarantee or the Key of India.[21]

Quite apart from its importance and significance for the subsequent history of South Africa, the capture of the Cape cemented the British position in the maritime region comprising the southern Atlantic and Indian oceans. By 1815, and along with St Helena and Mauritius, the Cape formed a chain of British way stations on the route to India, acting as a 'sub-network' within the wider British Indian Ocean world that was (and, in many ways, still is) being defined.[22] The area was lauded, by a variety of people with diverse interests and concerns, as a critical part of Britain's Asian empire. By the middle of the nineteenth century, the

[19] Yonge to Dundas, 15 November 1800, *RCC*, vol. III, p. 358.
[20] Robert Percival, *An Account of the Cape of Good Hope* (London: C. & R. Baldwin, 1804), p. 329.
[21] CRO, D LONS/L13/1/91, 'The Importance of the Cape of Good Hope Considered' (*c.* 1815–16), p. 2.
[22] Megan Vaughan, 'Foreword', in Shawkat Toorawa (ed.), *The Western Indian Ocean: Essays on Islands and Islanders* (Port Louis: Hassam Toorawa Trust, 2007), pp. xv–xix, p. xv.

Indian Ocean had come to be regarded as a 'British lake' in the anglo-phone world, and a fundamental part of this dominance was control over the maritime gateway connecting the Atlantic and Indian oceans.[23] When Britain captured the Cape, it was already part of a sophisticated maritime system of strategic and commercial interests sustained by the Dutch. But the first decades of British rule in Southern Africa facilitated the development of another set of connections and exchanges, as political, military and scientific links were forged. As such, the region, with its commercial maritime links and strategic military requirements, was woven into the fabric of the British Empire as it developed in the late eighteenth and early nineteenth centuries.

It would be misleading, however, to suggest that the Cape was the only place on the route to India to be described in such fulsome and compli-mentary terms. In fact, the encomia bestowed on the Cape should alert us to the importance attached by contemporaries to securing the entire maritime route to the East, rather than any specific part of it. The Cape was only one stepping stone among many potential way stations in the southern reaches of both the Atlantic and Indian oceans, as well as along the southern coastline of Africa. Invariably, these places were seen in terms of their utility to broader British strategic and commercial interests. For example, Lady Anne Barnard, the wife of the resident colonial secretary at the Cape, recorded some thoughts about Algoa Bay in her diary entry for 27 October 1799. This inlet, some 425 miles east of Cape Town, had neither settlers nor infrastructure. But this did not prevent some people from imagining a great future for it. Lady Anne recalled that Major-General Francis Dundas, the military commander at the Cape and a nephew of Henry Dundas, resolved 'to make Algoa Bay a second Gibraltar', guarding the entrance to the Indian Ocean in the same way as Gibraltar stood sentinel to protect the Mediterranean.[24] Thomas Brooke, author of one of the first histories of St Helena, suggested that this South Atlantic island had similar potential: 'This little spot, with congenial prosperity, may continue to protect and facilitate our

[23] Kavalam Madhava Panikkar, *India and the Indian Ocean* (London: Allen & Unwin, 1945), p. 9. For more on British hegemony in the region in the eighteenth and nineteenth centuries, see Milo Kearney, *The Indian Ocean in World History* (London: Routledge, 2004), pp. 118–35. See also Sugata Bose, *A Hundred Horizons: The Indian Ocean in the Age of Global Empire* (Cambridge, MA: Harvard University Press, 2006); Thomas R. Metcalf, *Imperial Connections: India in the Indian Ocean Arena, 1860–1920* (Berkeley, CA: University of California Press, 2007).

[24] *Diaries*, vol. I, p. 314. For an introduction to Lady Anne's life and career, see Madeleine Masson, *Lady Anne Barnard: The Court and Colonial Service under George III and the Regency* (London: Allen & Unwin, 1948). For more on Lady Anne's writings, see Margaret Lenta (ed.), *Paradise, the Castle and the Vineyard: Lady Anne Barnard's Cape Diaries* (Johannesburg: Wits University Press, 2006).

commerce with the East, and, by participating in its success, be always regarded as an important and essential part of the British Empire.'[25] And from the middle of the eighteenth century, the Ile de France (present-day Mauritius) was referred to as the 'star and the key of the Indian Ocean'.[26] In 1807, Félix Renouard de Sainte-Croix described the island as occupying 'a central geographical point between every other place in the world'.[27] This book integrates the various histories and historiographies of these places, arguing for their individual and collective importance in the development of Britain's maritime empire and providing a new way of conceptualising the region that straddled the worlds of the Atlantic and Indian oceans.

When Macartney took office in 1797, Britain's command of this important maritime gateway was relatively negligible. The Cape was only supposed to be in British hands temporarily; the adjacent coastlines of Africa were either uncharted or in the hands of the Portuguese; and the Ile de France and a clutch of other islands in the south-western Indian Ocean were French, and harboured the pirates and privateers who wreaked such havoc on British shipping coming from Asia. And while the East India Company controlled St Helena, and despite Brooke's opinions to the contrary, this was hardly a major boon, either for company or country. The island was geographically remote and isolated, '1200 miles distant from the nearest land', and far removed from other British settlements.[28] By virtue of prevailing sailing patterns, it was only useful for homeward-bound ships coming from the East, and it relied almost entirely on imported foodstuffs and other supplies to sustain it. Just over a decade later, by the start of 1811, the position had changed dramatically and British power in the region had expanded considerably. All of the major southern ports in the Atlantic and Indian oceans – Cape Town, St Helena, Mauritius and Rio de Janeiro – were in British hands or guarded by British ships.[29] By the end of the war in 1815, and together with other British-controlled locations like

[25] Thomas H. Brooke, *A History of the Island of St Helena: From its Discovery by the Portuguese to the Year 1806* (London: Black, Parry and Kingsbury, 1808), p. 428.

[26] Auguste Toussaint, *La Route des Iles, contribution à l'histoire maritime des Mascareignes* (Paris: SEVPEN, 1967), p. 95. Contemporary British writers tend to refer to this island by a number of different names, often in the same document: 'Ile de France', 'Isle de France', 'Isle of France', 'Mauritius'. The collective name for the group of islands east of Madagascar – consisting of Mauritius, Réunion and Rodrigues – is derived from the Portuguese navigator Pedro Mascarenhas, who first visited them in the early sixteenth century.

[27] Quoted in Lissa Roberts, '"*Le centre de toutes choses*": Constructing and Managing Centralization on the Isle de France', *History of Science* 52 (2014), pp. 319–42, pp. 319–20.

[28] BL, Add. MS 30097, f. 108, 'Memorandum on the Island of St Helena, by Robert Wilson' (1806).

[29] James Fichter, 'The British Empire and the American Atlantic on Tristan da Cunha, 1811–16', *Journal of Imperial and Commonwealth History* 36 (2008), pp. 567–89, p. 568.

Tristan da Cunha, Ascension and the Falkland Islands, the British maritime sphere of influence at the gateway to the Indian Ocean was considerable. Studying this maritime region as a whole, and considering the rhetoric surrounding its acquisition and the practical connections that subsisted within it, provides a powerful illustration of the symbiotic nature of maritime and imperial activities and enterprises in this period.

In considering the nature of Britain's presence in the South Atlantic and southern Indian Ocean, the maritime context in which all eighteenth-century European empires operated is essential. As N. A. M. Rodger reminds us, 'the use of the sea was an indispensable precondition for the existence of these empires'.[30] Access to sea routes and commercial opportunities mattered more than territorial control. This was an age in which islands played crucial roles in commerce, navigation and defence.[31] Britain's imperial power rested on its maritime strength. It was, in the words of Simon Bolívar, the 'mistress of the seas'.[32] In reflecting on the route to the East, the Chairman and Deputy Chairman of the East India Company stated the glaringly obvious in a letter to the Secretary of State for the Southern Department, the Earl of Hillsborough, in 1781. 'No fleet can possibly sail to, or return from, India', they declared, 'without touching at some proper place for refreshment, and, in time of war, it must be equally necessary for protection'.[33] Consequently, the ability to establish a network of island bases and mainland trading stations, tied together commercially and strategically by communication routes connected to Europe, was vital for any country with significant overseas trade interests. The ability to maintain such a network, especially those southern-hemisphere stations on the route to India, was fundamental to British global power. In fact, the British became so good at this that, as the Victorian author and wit Sydney Smith observed in the late nineteenth century, they maintained garrisons 'on every rock in the ocean where a cormorant could perch'.[34] Henry Dundas was fully aware of the

---

[30] N. A. M. Rodger, 'Seapower and Empire: Cause and Effect?', in Bob Moore and Henk Van Nierop (eds.), *Colonial Empires Compared: Britain and the Netherlands, 1750–1850* (Aldershot: Ashgate, 2003), pp. 97–111, p. 97.

[31] John R. Gillis, 'Islands in the Making of an Atlantic Oceania, 1500–1800', in Jerry H. Bentley, Renate Bridenthal, and Kären Wigen (eds.), *Seascapes: Maritime Histories, Littoral Cultures, and Transoceanic Exchanges* (Honolulu: University of Hawai'i Press, 2007), pp. 21–37.

[32] Quoted in Barry M. Gough, 'Sea Power and South America: The "Brazils" or South American Station of the Royal Navy, 1808–1837', *American Neptune* 50 (1990), pp. 26–34, p. 27.

[33] BL, IOR, H/154, p. 281, Laurence Sulivan and Sir William James to the Earl of Hillsborough, 25 October 1781.

[34] Quoted in James Morris, *Pax Britannica: The Climax of an Empire* (Harmondsworth: Penguin, 1979), p. 429.

connection, explaining to Lord Spencer, First Lord of the Admiralty, with admirable confidence in 1796: 'Home will take care of itself ... In the present war ... there can be no real injury done to this country but in its distant possessions ... the Eastern World is their [the enemy's] only rational object'.[35] Others concurred. Sir Hugh Christian, on station at the Cape, agreed that 'India must be their highest object'.[36] In 1799, Dundas explained to Richard Wellesley that 'Great Britain can at no time propose to maintain an extensive and complicated war but by destroying the colonial resources of our enemies and adding proportionately to our own commercial resources, which are, and must ever be, the sole basis of our maritime strength'.[37] In 1800, Dundas told his cabinet colleagues in no uncertain terms:

I need not remark, because it is obvious, that the present strength and pre-eminence of this country is owing to the extent of its resources arising from its commerce and its naval power which are inseparably connected. They must stand and fall together.[38]

The connection may have been self-evident but it was never inevitable. The acquisition and maintenance of maritime nodes of empire was fraught with logistical, military and political problems. It attracted considerable jealousy from, and outright conflict with, European rivals, while the connections forged by and between these places created new networks of economic, cultural and scientific exchange that required careful management, scrutiny and control.

In re-examining and reappraising Britain's oceanic empire, this book focuses on the maritime arc stretching from the islands of the South Atlantic, around the coastline of Southern Africa, and into the south-western corner of the Indian Ocean.[39] It explores the rhetoric and the reality of this oceanic space, and the various maritime 'keys' that defined it and guarded the route to the East. The discussion considers how this region, its islands and its contiguous land masses were represented, and the vital role they played both in cementing Britain's Asian empire and in frustrating its European rivals. Taken together, they enabled the

[35] Dundas to Lord Spencer, 24 March 1796, *Spencer*, vol. I, p. 240.
[36] UWits, A88/292, Hugh Christian to Macartney, 29 April 1798.
[37] Dundas to Wellesley, 31 October 1799, *Two Views*, p. 206.
[38] TNA, PRO 30/8/243, p. 94, Dundas, 'Memorandum'.
[39] Some scholars have described the south-western Indian Ocean (or, more precisely, its islands) as 'a regional cultural corridor'. See Pamila Gupta, 'Island-ness in the Indian Ocean', in Pamila Gupta, Isabel Hofmeyr and Michael Pearson (eds.), *Eyes Across the Water: Navigating the Indian Ocean* (Pretoria: UNISA Press, 2010), pp. 275–85, p. 282, n. 16. The phrase is Sarah Nuttall's. The image of a maritime 'arc' better describes the trajectory and movement inherent in the maritime connections that characterised the wider region in the period under discussion here.

movement of people, goods and ideas, as well as facilitating information and intelligence exchanges. Individual, often insular, bases formed part of a dense network of administration, security and control that helped to buttress the burgeoning British Empire in the early nineteenth century. Contemporaries frequently dubbed these 'Gibraltars of India'. The book explores places that laid claim to the title of, or were proposed as, crucial 'gateways' to or 'outposts' of India.[40] The chapters that follow explore the deployment of these monikers in different contexts, the rhetorical baggage that accreted around them, and the practical and logistical connections that enfolded the region into Britain's wider maritime empire.[41] The book posits the region as a crucial hub in understanding the character and workings of the late eighteenth-century British Empire as it struggled to redefine itself following the loss of thirteen colonies on mainland North America. And it also examines the connections that were said to exist both within the region and between constituent parts of the region and India, investigating how these worked in practice.

Throughout the period, speculation, debate and disagreement abounded, as a whole host of soldiers, sailors, businessmen, governors, administrators and others offered their views on the place of the southern Atlantic and Indian oceans in Britain's overlapping commercial, political and imperial interests. The first reference to the word 'strategy' in the Oxford English Dictionary dates from 1810; before then, ministers, politicians and commentators considered 'policy towards the outside world'. This was a subject, therefore, which took on 'diplomatic, political, commercial, ideological, financial, military and naval expression according to the circumstances'.[42] Discussion and deliberation about the place of the Cape, and the surrounding islands and seas in the wider British Empire extended far beyond the upper echelons of government in London. As a result, the cast of characters that informs this history ranges widely. We will encounter the opinions of monarchs, merchants and politicians. But those of prospectors, prophets, profit-mongers, and even the proprietor of a remote island also have a role to play in the story that follows. It includes the views of hoary old governors, men of science and ladies of

---

[40] The discussion that follows does not deal with the Comoros, the Seychelles, or any of the myriad 'stepping stones' to India north of the Equator. However, the ways in which the British state and the East India Company approached these places, with their indigenous, Arabic and other Asian connections, deserves serious scholarly attention.

[41] For other uses of these terms in similar or analogous contexts, see Frank Broeze, *Gateways of Asia: Port Cities of Asia in the 13th–20th Centuries* (London: Routledge, 1997), and Philip Henshaw, 'The "Key to South Africa" in the 1890s: Delagoa Bay and the Origins of the South African War', *Journal of Southern African Studies* 24 (1998), pp. 527–44.

[42] Rodger, 'Seapower and Empire', pp. 98, 99.

letters, all of whom provide insights into the consolidation of British power in the region, and the development of the British Empire more generally. It draws on the evidence of people like Richard Wellesley, governor general of Fort William, and Robert Percival, an army officer who served both in Africa and Asia, to show the ways in which this region was bound together in a trans-oceanic relationship with India and Britain. By bringing together the views of this disparate group of people, and demonstrating how these connections worked in practice, the book reveals how the region fitted into the nascent British Indian Ocean world increasingly identified by scholars.[43] It deals with high-flown political rhetoric and prospectuses that promised much. But the development of British power in the region was not just about abstract policy-making; it also responded to the practical realities on the ground (and on the waves). Thus, the book also considers the more workaday, diurnal realities that connected the region to the wider British world: the transmission and exchange of intelligence and information through nodes of empire; the recruitment of troops and the movement of these men on ships over vast distances; and the mobility of scientific specimens and expertise. Ultimately, all of these connections resulted from, and were dependent on, the maritime spaces and oceanic geographies of the route to India.[44]

[43] See Michael Pearson, *The Indian Ocean* (London: Routledge, 1992); K. N. Chaudhuri, *Trade and Civilisation in the Indian Ocean: An Economic History from the Rise of Islam to 1750* (Cambridge: Cambridge University Press, 1985); K. N. Chaudhuri, *Asia before Europe: Economy and Civilisation of the Indian Ocean from the rise of Islam to 1750* (Cambridge: Cambridge University Press, 1990); Kenneth McPherson, *The Indian Ocean: A History of People and the Sea* (Oxford: Oxford University Press, 1993); Devleena Ghosh and Stephen Muecke (eds.), *Cultures of Trade: Indian Ocean Exchanges* (Newcastle-upon-Tyne: Cambridge Scholars Press, 2007). Specifically in relation to Southern Africa, see Nigel Worden, 'VOC Cape Town as an Indian Ocean Port', in Himanshu Prabha Ray and Edward A. Alpers (eds.), *Cross Currents and Community Networks: The History of the Indian Ocean World* (Oxford: Oxford University Press, 2007), pp. 142–62.

[44] The evidence used to piece this history together is drawn from an extensive and eclectic selection of archival and primary sources. The voluminous official papers of the East India Company, held at the British Library, form a strong spine running through the work. This is complemented by the copious archives of key organs of state found in the National Archives at Kew. All scholars of the region, and of South Africa in particular, are indebted to George McCall Theal's monumental 36-volume compilation, *Records of the Cape Colony*, published between 1897 and 1905. Complementary caches of papers can be found at the Cape Archives, the University of the Witwatersrand, Rhodes House Library, the National Archives of Scotland, and the Public Record Office of Northern Ireland. Weaving together public and private papers produces interesting juxtapositions, highlighting prejudices and uncovering agendas in both. The people whose views and opinions are represented in the Admiralty and the Colonial Office papers, for example, offer different perspectives on the British position in the Indian Ocean to those held by their contemporaries in Leadenhall Street, the headquarters of the East India Company. The study also relies on the private and personal correspondence of a wide assortment

Viewed from a terrestrial perspective, a focus on the islands and out-posts of the southern Atlantic and Indian oceans might seem to be a study on the historiographically traditional 'edge' of empires. And yet, the pulse of the ocean can often be felt better here than anywhere else.[45] These locations 'marked the historical destiny' of the ocean by playing signifi-cant roles as stepping stones, fulcra and bases for trade and conquest.[46] Janet Abu-Lughod's evocative phrase 'an archipelago of cities' is sugges-tive of the ways in which these physically insular pieces of land shared much in common with other ports and settlements in the region and were vitally connected to them by the sea.[47] And recently, there has been increasing interest among scholars of the British Empire in the islands of the Indian Ocean and their strategic import for a developing British maritime hegemony in the region.[48]

The 'pulse' foregrounded in the chapters that follow is the flow of commercial and political interest between Britain and Asia. They explore the development and evolution of the British Empire at one of the great fault lines of imperial and maritime history – the region that connected the Atlantic and Indian oceans. But the discussion also questions our ideas about the importance of location. It situates 'peripheral' regions at the heart of the story of a developing and evolving empire. Although in many respects Britain was at its hub, the trans-global nature of the British Empire meant that the boundaries of the imperial 'centre' were remark-ably permeable.[49] Historians now recognise the diversity and dynamism of the so-called periphery, acknowledging that regions considered as

of individuals. People like Henry Dundas, George Macartney and Lady Anne Barnard generated huge amounts of material, while the influence of less well-known figures, like George Baldwin, Henry Pemberton and William Dalrymple, can be retrieved through their correspondence with policymakers and politicians. Yet others, such as Robert Percival, James Prior, Thomas Brooke and Charles Telfair, are best accessed through the publications by which they sought to present their views on this part of the world to a wider audience. Taken together, these sources tell us much about this maritime region, and contribute to our understanding of the forces that shaped the Indian Ocean world and wider British Empire in this period.

[45] Auguste Toussaint, *History of the Indian Ocean*, translated by June Guicharnaud (London: Routledge & Kegan Paul, 1966), pp. 3–5.

[46] See Jacques Auber, *Histoire de l'Océan Indien* (Antananarivo: Société Lilloise d'imprim-erie de Tananarive, 1955), pp. 16–29. Quoted in Roxani Margariti, 'An Ocean of Islands: Islands, Insularity, and Historiography of the Indian Ocean', in Peter N. Miller (ed.), *The Sea: Thalassography and Historiography* (Ann Arbor, MI: University of Michigan Press, 2013), pp. 198–229, p. 220, n. 12.

[47] Janet L. Abu-Lughod, *Before European Hegemony: The World System, A.D. 1250–1350* (New York: Oxford University Press, 1989), p. 13.

[48] See, for example, Sujit Sivasundaram, *Islanded: Britain, Sri Lanka and the Bounds of an Indian Ocean Colony* (New Delhi: Oxford University Press, 2013).

[49] Alan Lester, 'British Settler Discourse and the Circuits of Empire', *History Workshop Journal* 54 (2002), pp. 24–48, p. 25.

peripheral in one sense may, in fact, occupy a central role in other instances.[50] Local or regional centres such as Sydney and Calcutta or, in this context, Cape Town, Jamestown and Port Louis, took on a measure of autonomy and authority while remaining within a framework of empire.[51] In this understanding, then, the supposedly liminal positions of the regions under discussion are superseded by their roles as pivotal locations, mediating between maritime worlds, oceanic systems and imperial networks. The Cape was a place, as Kerry Ward points out, at both an oceanic and historiographical crossroads.[52] Similarly, the places considered in this book were at the centre of a maritime chain that linked Europe and Asia. Far from being isolated or remote, the Cape and the surrounding maritime region was, as Keletso Atkins observes, 'strategically positioned at the southernmost end of a great commercial and information highway'.[53] This was a region at the centre, subject to rival European empires and their covetous glances, and buffeted by changing political sentiments as settlers and colonists increasingly played their part in determining the fate of the region's constituent parts.

This is neither a work of Atlantic history nor Indian Ocean history; it does not present an international history or a comparative history in the traditional sense.[54] Rather, the approach adopted here has been to take a large but defined geographical and maritime space, preserving the specificity of individual places and yet allowing for historical comparisons which overcome traditional barriers of geography and historiography. Taken together, the book offers new perspectives on Britain's maritime

---

[50] On this point, see Clare Anderson, 'Introduction to Marginal Centers: Writing Life Histories in the Indian Ocean World', *Journal of Social History* 45 (2011), pp. 335–44; Sujit Sivasundaram, 'Sciences and the Global: On Methods, Questions and Theory', *Isis* 101 (2010), pp. 146–58.

[51] See Roy MacLeod, 'On Visiting the "Moving Metropolis": Reflections on the Architecture of Imperial Science', in Nathan Reingold and Marc Rothenberg (eds.), *Scientific Colonialism: A Cross-Cultural Comparison* (Washington, DC: Smithsonian Institution Press, 1987), pp. 217–49. Lissa Roberts reminds us that Dutch Cape Town was 'a veritable centre on the periphery'. Lissa Roberts, 'Centres and Cycles of Accumulation', in Lissa Roberts (ed.), *Centres and Cycles of Accumulation in and around the Netherlands during the Early Modern Period* (Zurich: LIT, 2011), pp. 3–27, p. 7.

[52] See Kerry Ward, '"Tavern of the Seas"? The Cape of Good Hope as an Oceanic Crossroads during the Seventeenth and Eighteenth Centuries', in Bentley, Bridenthal, and Wigen (eds.), *Seascapes*, pp. 137–52.

[53] Keletso Atkins, 'The "Black Atlantic Communication Network": African American Sailors and the Cape of Good Hope Connection', *Issue: A Journal of Opinion* 24 (1996), pp. 23–25, p. 23.

[54] Sivasundaram, *Islanded*, pp. 323, 336. For more on overlaps between historical approaches which take a 'comparative' approach and those which offer 'entangled' or transnational perspectives, see Jürgen Kocka, 'Comparison and Beyond', *History and Theory* 42 (2003), pp. 39–44.

empire. By shifting the sea to the centre of the analysis, we also move this region to the heart of our understanding of the British Empire. Viewed from the perspective of the sea, shipping routes and the maritime connections these facilitated, different interpretative possibilities are uncovered. Rather than the southern periphery of the Northern Atlantic world, or the outer edge of the bustling Indian Ocean world, the region is situated at a pivotal point in interpretations of the ways in which those maritime spaces and their overlapping imperial and commercial concerns operated. What was once a marginal space suddenly occupies the centre of the analysis.[55]

The route to Asia: geographies and chronologies

Historians have long understood the vital importance of geographical facts for the development of history.[56] For Gerald S. Graham 'the geography of the sea ... shaped Britain's destiny'.[57] The political, strategic and commercial contexts of the southern Atlantic and Indian oceans suggest that this region needs to be regarded as an interconnected whole. It was, as this book sets out to demonstrate, a crucial gateway to the Indian Ocean world, a term that encompasses the entire region from the Cape of Good Hope to Cairo to Calcutta and Canton.[58] This is not to deny, of course, the importance of individual locations, or the specific local circumstances and conditions pertaining to them. On the contrary, by assessing the connections linking (or perceived as linking) these places to Britain's defence of its Indian empire, the value of somewhere like Mauritius or St Helena to the preservation of Britain's global position in the early nineteenth century becomes even more apparent. The southern reaches of these interrelated and interdependent maritime spaces may be physically distant from Britain but they were at the very heart of Britain's commercial calculations and, ultimately, its political and national interest. As with many of Britain's important trading spheres, fears over its vulnerability and anxiety about its defence went in tandem with an

[55] For a discussion of the importance of a focus on 'locality' to counterbalance the emphasis on the power of the centre and the submission of the periphery, see Sivasundaram, *Islanded*, p. 175.
[56] Panikkar, *India and the Indian Ocean*, p. 17.
[57] Gerald S. Graham, *The Politics of Naval Supremacy* (Cambridge: Cambridge University Press, 1965), p. 10.
[58] Gwyn Campbell, *An Economic History of Imperial Madagascar, 1750–1895: The Rise and Fall of an Island Empire* (Cambridge: Cambridge University Press, 2005), p. 5. For more on the geographical peculiarities of the region, see Panikkar, *India and the Indian Ocean*, pp. 19–23. For more on the idea of 'gateways' to the Indian Ocean, see Toussaint, *History of the Indian Ocean*, p. 3.

acknowledgement of its utility. Just as there were a number of keys that could unlock the commercial potential of Asia, so they could just as easily become – within a short space of time and with limited military intervention (so the argument ran) – important bases from which to attack British shipping passing through the region.

The route to India had grown in importance as British commercial links with Asia had strengthened and its political commitments in the Indian subcontinent deepened in the second half of the eighteenth century. The great engine for this expansion was the East India Company, founded in London in 1600 and reaching the height of its profit-making powers in the early nineteenth century. It was one of the bulwarks of Britain's commercial empire.[59] In 1780, for example, the homeward-bound convoy from India was said to comprise 'the greatest mass of wealth that ever was destined at any one time into the Thames' with the result that 'the actual possession of so much riches must enhance the public credit of the State'.[60] The Company was responsible, among other things, for introducing commodities like tea, silk and printed cottons to British consumers. And it did so in such huge quantities that it changed the British way of life in the process. In 1798, for example, it imported nearly £5 million worth of tea.[61] But the Company's importance involved much more than merely introducing cups of Chinese tea or printed textiles from India to people back in Britain. Commerce was at the heart of the country's rise to global dominance, and its preservation and expansion was vital to Britain's continued success. The Company straddled the maritime worlds of the Atlantic and Indian oceans, connecting their port cities, their trading systems, and their overlapping and interconnected British imperial and commercial interests. For example, St Helena and Cape Town, key locations for the Company, are situated in the Atlantic Ocean.[62]

[59] The literature on the East India Company is prodigious and growing. For useful introductions, see John Keay, *The Honourable Company: A History of the English East India Company* (London: Harper Collins, 1993); Philip Lawson, *The East India Company: A History, 1600–1857* (London: Longmans, 1993); K. N. Chaudhuri, *The Trading World of Asia and the English East India Company, 1660–1760* (Cambridge: Cambridge University Press, 1978).

[60] TNA, SP 89/87/158, p. 434, W. Macintosh to John Undny at Leghorn, dated Cape of Good Hope, 29 September 1780. My thanks to Helen Paul for bringing this reference to my attention.

[61] B. R. Mitchell, *Abstract of British Historical Statistics* (Cambridge: Cambridge University Press, 1971), p. 289. The exact figure was £4,487,000.

[62] St Helena is located on the mid-Atlantic ridge, while the Cape Peninsula is some 94 miles west of Cape Agulhas, the southern-most point of the African continent and thus the geographical meeting place of the Atlantic and Indian oceans. See Groenewald, 'Southern Africa and the Atlantic World', p. 103. The importance of these locations in the early years of the eighteenth century can be gauged by the fact that,

As Lakshmi Subramanian points out, the 'East India Company was the principal conduit between two related but divergent worlds, the Asian and the Atlantic'.[63] Historians of the East India Company, therefore, might usefully heed H. V. Bowen's enjoinder not to forget about East Indiamen when they enter the waters of the Atlantic.[64] The East India Company conducted its business using huge vessels, all of which had to pass around the Cape of Good Hope on their way to and from the lucrative markets of India and China. Ships were dependent on clear seaways and safe routes. It was only with the opening of the Suez Canal in 1869, and the development of steam technology, that the stranglehold of the monsoon system was broken.[65] Before that, this circuitous route – down the west coast of Africa into the South Atlantic, around the Cape, and into the Indian Ocean – was the only feasible way of accessing the bustling commercial emporia of Asia. It was little wonder then that the critical gateways to India and China were feared and coveted in equal measure. British merchants and politicians feared them as potential weak links in the British commercial chain to Asia, harbouring imperial rivals, fomenting piratical activity, and disrupting trading connections. Henry Dundas was painfully alive to this threat, as he told Lord Spencer, 'I mean the route which trading ships from India are obliged to take, the course of which makes them an easy prey to a hostile squadron stationed at the Cape'.[66] But these places – from ports such as Buenos Aires, Rio de Janeiro and Cape Town to whole islands such as St Helena or Mauritius – were also coveted as the potential means to secure British traffic to Asia and, consequently, the country's economic and imperial power. The importance of the region to politicians and policymakers might be adduced from the overseas expeditions mounted by the British state in wartime. In the first decade of the nineteenth century, only one

in November 1732, St Helena and Cape Town were chosen as subjects for two of the 'six pictures of the Forts' commissioned by the Company to adorn the Directors' Court Room in East India House on Leadenhall Street, London. See Brian Allen, 'The East India Company's Settlement Pictures: George Lambert and Samuel Scott', in Pauline Rohatgi and Pheroza Godrej (eds.), *Under the Indian Sun: British Landscape Artists* (Bombay: Marg, 1995), pp. 1–16.

[63] Lakshmi Subramanian, 'Seths and Sahibs: Negotiated Relationships between Indigenous Capital and the East India Company', in H. V. Bowen, Elizabeth Mancke and John G. Reid (eds.), *Britain's Oceanic Empire: Atlantic and Indian Ocean Worlds, c. 1550–1850* (Cambridge: Cambridge University Press, 2012), pp. 311–39, p. 311.

[64] H. V. Bowen, 'Britain in the Indian Ocean Region and Beyond: Contours, Connections and the Creation of a Global Maritime Empire', in Bowen, Mancke and Reid (eds.), *Britain's Oceanic Empire*, pp. 45–65, p. 46.

[65] For more on the ways in which the monsoon system of winds and currents dictates the navigation of vessels in the Indian Ocean, see Pearson, *Indian Ocean*, pp. 13–26.

[66] Dundas to Spencer, 5 November 1797, *Spencer*, vol. II, p. 215.

large expedition sailed from Britain with a colonial objective: the 6,500-strong force sent to seize the Cape in 1805.[67]

It is only by approaching the region from a maritime perspective that the geographical extent (and limitations) of this study can be comprehended. Even here, difficulties abound. Kären Wigen has noted the inherent problems associated with determining the precise spatial boundaries of studies that focus on maritime matters and which are, almost by definition, fluxive, fluid and indeterminate.[68] Oceans are intrinsically transnational phenomena: the history of one sea or ocean quickly becomes the history of others.[69] The study of maritime spaces requires an expansive spatial vision extending across horizons, and even oceans, making it difficult to demarcate closely defined and self-contained areas of analysis. This study suggests that the maritime space that encompassed the 'gateway' to the British Asian empire needs to be similarly broad and expansive, effectively extending from the Ile de France to Río de la Plata. Indeed, in some instances, the geography of the region and the places within it remained a fictional one – based on rumour and hearsay, vision and chimera – and reflecting what people wanted to see rather than on the reality.

Whatever visions abounded for strategically important keys to India, it is important, however, that the place of Africa, particularly sub-Saharan Africa, is included in this maritime analysis. Too often, the continent plays only a tangential role in studies of the Atlantic. This is even more pronounced in relation to the study of the Indian Ocean. In her study of European imperial rivalry in South-Eastern Africa, Mabel Jackson Haight identified deficiencies in the way that historians traditionally conceive of the region. The limits within which the history of Southern Africa are studied 'have been too narrowly drawn' for a place that is 'inextricably linked with the other parts of that great amphitheatre' of the Indian Ocean.[70] As Gwyn Campbell has noted, southern, eastern and north-eastern Africa – as well as the numerous islands lying off the coast of the continent – had strong historical and cultural ties to the Middle East, South and Southeast Asia, and the Far East. They formed an integral part of 'the Asia-Indian Ocean economy'.[71] This book continues the work of

---

[67] Christopher D. Hall, *British Strategy in the Napoleonic War, 1803–15* (Manchester: Manchester University Press, 1992), p. 95.

[68] Kären Wigen, 'Introduction', in Bentley, Bridenthal, and Wigen (eds.), *Seascapes*, pp. 1–18, p. 12.

[69] John Mack, *The Sea: A Cultural History* (London: Reaktion, 2013), p. 20.

[70] Mabel V. Jackson Haight, *European Powers and South-East Africa: A Study of International Relations on the South-Eastern Coast of Africa, 1796–1856* (London: Routledge & Kegan Paul, 1967), p. 2.

[71] Campbell, *Imperial Madagascar*, p. 5.

rectifying this imbalance by reintegrating the history of Southern Africa with the contiguous maritime regions.

The chronological period covered by this study covers the rise of the East India Company and its transformation from a relatively small trading concern to a powerful territorial sovereign entity. It stretches from the end of the Seven Years War to the end of the long Revolutionary and Napoleonic Wars in 1815, when Britain was confirmed as 'masters' of the Cape of Good Hope, Mauritius and many of the other 'keys to India' discussed in this book. Such chronological divisions need to be seen as indicative rather than definitive. Nevertheless, the end of the Seven Years War had significant ramifications for British overseas activities around the globe. The 1760s witnessed the East India Company's rise to power and prominence in India, as it acquired the *Diwani*, or the right to collect taxes in Bengal, effectively becoming a territorial power in the subcontinent. The commercial and political balance of Britain's maritime empire responded to these circumstances, as we will see. But these shifts also brought major challenges, not least of which was defending, protecting and potentially extending Britain's maritime connections with this increasingly important part of the globe. A major focus of the work, therefore, is on the consolidation and extension of these connections in the approximately twenty-year period between the first capture of the Cape in 1795 and its ultimate cession to Britain following the signing of the Convention of London (1814) and the Congress of Vienna (1815).

The whole period is one of great upheaval and seismic shifts in the international political landscape. Events in western Europe and North America – revolutions and rebellions, wars and constitutional conflicts – had truly global consequences, sending shock waves that lapped at a host of distant shores and powerfully affected the story that follows. As one contemporary put it, 'during the Great War that agitated all Europe the cannon roar was heard to the very extremity of the earth on the Indian Ocean'.[72] And the outcomes were never inevitable; as another author cautioned, 'who can tell where the revolutionary principle that now makes such gigantic strides throughout the continent of Europe, will stop at last?'.[73] The British Empire alone went through a series of extraordinary changes and metamorphoses, from the unprecedented expansion following the Treaty of Paris in 1763, to the shock of the American Revolution and the eventual consolidation of a global empire after victory at Waterloo. The astonishing British successes in Asia and the wider

[72] NUL, Mi 2F 4, 'An Account of Operations off Isles of France and Bourbon' [1809–10], p. 1.
[73] Benjamin Stout, *Narrative of the Loss of the Ship Hercules*, edited by A. Porter (1798; revised edition, Port Elizabeth: Historical Society of Port Elizabeth, 1975), p. 17.

Indian Ocean during the Revolutionary and Napoleonic Wars were particularly remarkable. As Henry Dundas put it to Robert Brooke, the governor of St Helena, 'the East seems to be the only quarter from which we are always to look for good news'.[74] At the outset of the war, 'dread of a French invasion of India haunted the imagination of statesmen'. By its conclusion, France had lost all its possessions east of the Cape. Territorial gains and the fact that the French fleet was swept 'from the Indian seas' left Britain 'without a rival in the eastern hemisphere'. It was only with slight exaggeration, therefore, that Lady Minto could pronounce that: 'The conquests of England in one hemisphere redressed the balance of power in the other. Every fresh gain by France in Europe was followed by a corresponding loss in Asia.'[75] And the importance of this history for our understanding of the development, expansion and consolidation of the British Empire does not end with the Congress of Vienna and the confirmation of Britain's dominance in the South Atlantic, Southern Africa and the south-western Indian Ocean. As Barry Gough has pointed out, there were clear continuities in policy-making in the century *after* Waterloo. Before the outbreak of the Great War in 1914, Britain's interests – whether they encompassed trade or territory or both – were still secured and defended through maritime supremacy.[76]

But this chronology needs to be qualified. In October 1805, the name 'Horatio Nelson' resonated around the British world. The naval commander who won the Battle of Trafalgar, dying in the cockpit of HMS *Victory* at the moment of triumph, was lauded in Britain and beyond. But off the coast of South Africa, it was the fate of the *Horatio Nelson*, 'the stoutest ship coming out this season', that preoccupied British naval personnel. The ship was less successful than its namesake, however, as Captain Ross Donnelly reported that she had fallen prey to the French privateers that infested the waters in the southern Indian Ocean.[77] The coincidence is noteworthy in so far as it reminds us that similar

---

[74] B'hurst, MS.062/3, Dundas to Robert Brooke, 30 October 1795.

[75] Emma Eleanor Elizabeth, Countess of Minto, *Lord Minto in India: Life and Letters of Gilbert Elliot, First Earl of Minto, from 1807 to 1814* (London, Longmans, Green, and Co., 1880), p. 239.

[76] Barry Gough, *The Falkland Islands/Malvinas: The Contest for Empire in the South Atlantic* (London: Athlone Press, 1992), p. 137. One might even push the discussion beyond the early twentieth century and consider Britain's imperial role in Antarctica and the South Atlantic. For more on this, see Klaus Dodds, *Pink Ice: Britain and the South Atlantic Empire* (London: I. B. Tauris, 2007).

[77] Ross Donnelly to Home Popham, 30 October 1805, *RCC*, vol. V, p. 248. Although Donnelly mentions the *Horatio Nelson* by name six times in his letter, and gives extensive details about the action, the incident remains obscure. He may be referring to a 'country ship' of that name as no records exist for a British East Indiaman named the *Horatio*

concerns – in this case, a global conflict with France over access to trade and colonies – affected different parts of the British world in different ways at the same time. Bearing this in mind, this book follows the chronological contours of political developments in European and world affairs, as well as great changes in the British domestic state and overseas empire. Yet it should be understood that the events and incidents analysed here need to be seen in conjunction with the specific geographical and historical contexts in which they occurred.[78] As the example of Nelson illustrates, grand military battles and high politics, conducted in the salons of Europe, were not the sole driving forces behind historical change in the region in the period. Nor, indeed, do these dates denote watersheds in which everything changed. There were, in fact, powerful continuities with earlier periods. But they do correspond, however vaguely, to the shifting British presence in, and priorities towards, this region.

The route to Asia: historiographies

The study of this geographically broad, interconnected, maritime space raises a number of methodological and historiographical questions. It draws together places not usually studied in conjunction with each other, encouraging us to think about historiographies that are traditionally separate: from the British interest in Spain's South American empire, to the acquisition of the Cape in Southern Africa, to the capture of Mauritius and consolidation of Britain's place in the wider Indian Ocean. These cover a broad range of distinct contexts and tend to be situated in wider but divergent historiographical traditions: the development of Latin American nationalisms and independence; the growth of free-trade sentiment in Britain; the balance between formal and informal empire; the development of the British interest in sub-Saharan Africa leading, eventually, to the Scramble later in the nineteenth century; the expanding British Empire in Asia. By bringing these together, this book contributes to new directions in imperial, oceanic and maritime history. Situated at the confluence of these, it foregrounds oceanic approaches in the writing of imperial histories. In so doing, it offers a reappraisal and

---

Nelson. In any case, it should not be confused with the East Indiaman *Lord Nelson,* which was captured by the French privateer, *Bellona,* off the south coast of Ireland in August 1803. For details of that action, see Evan Cotton and Charles Fawcett, *East Indiamen: The East India Company's Maritime Service* (London: Batchwood Press, 1949), p. 165.

[78] For a similar approach in relation to another part of the Indian Ocean, Ceylon, see Sivasundaram, *Islanded,* pp. 321–2.

recalibration of the distinctions between oceanic and maritime, political and imperial, cultural and scientific histories and approaches.

Before considering its structure, it is useful to pause and consider some of the historiographical debates to which this book seeks to contribute. These can be bracketed under three broad headings. First, it attempts to integrate maritime and imperial historiographies of the British Empire in order to provide a more comprehensive picture of the development of that empire. It suggests that maritime and oceanic approaches, which have long been adopted in other contexts to great success, can contribute significantly to our understanding of the region. Second, the study adds to new comparative approaches in the shared history of the Atlantic and Indian oceans. Third, by exploring the extent and practical operation of networks of movement and communication, the book contributes to our knowledge of the development of the early modern British Empire and the place of this region within it.

Imperial and maritime histories

For a variety of practical and intellectual reasons, the history of the British Empire has often been neatly compartmentalised according to chronology or geography or perceived purpose. The 'first' empire of maritime trade and commerce is succeeded by a 'second' focusing on settlement, colonisation and 'civilising' values; the North Atlantic axis of early English (and later British) settlement around the oceanic littoral is frequently juxtaposed with the 'Eastern' empire of the nineteenth and twentieth centuries. Few studies attempt to synthesise or analyse these by situating them in a global perspective. There are exceptions to this rule, of course. Vincent T. Harlow and, more recently, P. J. Marshall and Alan Frost, have provided magisterial works on the global nature of the British Empire at this time.[79] As Marshall has shown, the evolution of the British Empire was significantly more complex than the simple dichotomy between 'first' and 'second' empire allows. Frost's book offers a grand, sweeping and largely convincing interpretation of globalisation in the late eighteenth century and Britain's imperial role in those processes. This work has more modest ambitions: to interrogate the creation and consolidation of empire, as well as the patterns of connections forged by those processes, in a much more geographically limited space.

[79] See Vincent T. Harlow, *The Founding of the Second British Empire, 1763–1793*, 2 vols. (London: Longmans, 1952–64); P. J. Marshall, *The Making and Unmaking of Empires: Britain, India and America c. 1750–1783* (Oxford: Oxford University Press, 2007); Alan Frost, *The Global Reach of Empire: Britain's Maritime Expansion in the Indian and Pacific Oceans, 1764–1815* (Carlton: Miegunyah Press, 2003).

As William Innes Pocock reminded readers of his *Five Views of the Island of St Helena*, 'considerable skill in navigation is requisite to make this island to a certainty'.[80] Analogous intellectual skills are required to reorient our thinking from its 'habitual terrestrial location' and reposition it 'off-shore'.[81] In attempting to write a history that straddles such geographical and chronological boundaries, this work adopts a consciously maritime perspective. This has not always been the case when writing histories of empire. All too often, in general histories of the British Empire, as in those of the East India Company, 'the sea disappears from view from about the mid-eighteenth century' to be replaced by a resolutely land-locked focus on individual colonies or territories.[82] As Kären Wigen points out 'on the mental maps of most scholars, oceans are oddly occluded': 'Geographically marginal to the grids of academic inquiry, the watery world seems to fall between our conceptual cracks as well'. Maritime topics are relegated to footnotes; ocean basins are sliced in half on standard maps, and many fields of inquiry are conceived in 'terrestrial terms'.[83] For a long time, it seems, historians had less interest or experience in imagining how oceans connect rather than divide people and places.[84]

Recently, however, oceans have 'swung insistently into view'.[85] They have been 'rediscovered' by historians, and identified as crucial spaces for the gestation of globalisation in the early modern world. Ocean-centred approaches offer the chance to conceptualise geographies and histories that move beyond the categories of the local and the national; they provide opportunities to understand the interrelationships between the human and natural worlds.[86] They offer a means of thinking 'beyond the landlocked nation-state and beyond the terra firma that has been its presumptive ground'.[87] By viewing continents and places through the lens of maritime history, we can reconsider the ways in which peripheries

[80] William Innes Pocock, *Five Views of the Island of St Helena from Drawings taken on the Spot* (London: S. and J. Fuller, 1815), p. 1.
[81] John Mack, 'The Land viewed from the Sea', *Azania* 42 (2007), pp. 1–14, p. 3.
[82] Bowen, 'Britain in the Indian Ocean Region', p. 45.   [83] Wigen, 'Introduction', p. 1.
[84] David Igler, *The Great Ocean: Pacific Worlds from Captain Cook to the Gold Rush* (Oxford: Oxford University Press, 2013), p. 8.
[85] For some recent interventions in ocean history, see Rainer F. Buschmann, *Oceans in World History* (New York: McGraw-Hill, 2007); Jerry H. Bentley, 'Sea and Ocean Basins as Frameworks of Historical Analysis', *Geographical Review* 89 (1999), pp. 215–24.
[86] David Lambert, Luciana Martins and Miles Ogborn, 'Currents, Visions and Voyages: Historical Geographies of the Seas', *Journal of Historical Geography* 32 (2006), pp. 479–93, p. 479. See also Bernard Klein and Gesa Mackenthun (eds.), *Sea Changes: Historicizing the Ocean* (New York: Routledge, 2004); Philip E. Steinberg, 'Of Other Seas: Metaphors and Materialities in Maritime Regions', *Atlantic Studies*, 10 (2013), pp. 156–69.
[87] Antoinette Burton, 'Sea Tracks and Trails: Indian Ocean Worlds as Method', *History Compass* 11 (2013), pp. 497–502, p. 497.

and centres were connected by the ability to operate on the seas. It also permits an examination of the role of sea power in forging maritime empires, patrolling trade routes and protecting strategic objectives. Auguste Toussaint regarded this people-centred approach to history as an under-researched, under-represented 'middle way between economic history and nautical archaeology'.[88] The 'ability to operate on the seas' was what, as Alan Frost points out, 'linked peripheries to the centre, what underwrote imperial activity'.[89] Such approaches, applying oceanic frameworks to the histories of empires, can lead to interesting and unexpected connections.

The pioneering work of Fernand Braudel has inspired nearly all scholarship of this kind. By taking the entire Mediterranean basin as his subject of study, his seminal work, *The Mediterranean and the Mediterranean World in the Age of Philip II*, helped to define all subsequent work in the field.[90] As Nile Green has observed, in focusing on an enclosed and interacting sphere of human activity – at once geographic, economic and cultural – Braudel's conception of 'the maritime "worlds" model has been tremendously productive in shifting spatial conceptions of history from the land-based (and national) to the sea-based (and transnational)'.[91] Although the direct relationship between the two is contentious, one of the most successful and influential branches of history to draw on Braudel's work is Atlantic history, where the ocean is posited as a bridge rather than a barrier, connecting people and places.[92] For many years, the Indian Ocean was the Atlantic's (and the Pacific's) poor relation.[93] Recently, the Indian Ocean has also seen rising interest in its status as an interconnected maritime space, becoming a preoccupation for scholars from a wide variety of disciplinary and institutional backgrounds.[94] K. N. Chaudhuri, Michael Pearson and others have put the ocean at the centre of their analyses of the region and its littoral.[95]

---

[88] Toussaint, *Route des Iles*, p. 99, n. 2.   [89] Frost, *Global Reach of Empire*, p. 1.

[90] Fernand Braudel, *The Mediterranean and the Mediterranean World in the Age of Philip II*, 2 vols. (London: Collins, 1972–73).

[91] Nile Green, 'Maritime Worlds and Global History: Comparing the Mediterranean and Indian Ocean through Barcelona and Bombay', *History Compass* 11 (2013), pp. 513–23, p. 513.

[92] Useful introductions to the subject may be found in David Armitage and Michael J. Braddick (eds.), *The British Atlantic World, 1500–1800* (Basingstoke: Palgrave Macmillan, 2002), and Bernard Bailyn (ed.), *Atlantic History: Concept and Contours* (Cambridge, MA: Harvard University Press, 2005).

[93] See Toussaint, *History of the Indian Ocean*, pp. 1–3.

[94] For analysis of the Indian Ocean as a historiographical method, see Markus Vink, 'Indian Ocean Studies and the "New Thalassology"', *Journal of Global History* 18 (2007), pp. 41–62.

[95] See n. 43 above.

Yet, there has been relatively little work on the southern extremities of these oceans, and even less on the ways in which they are connected to other parts of their respective oceanic basins. While the historiography of the British Atlantic is a well-developed area of academic enquiry, it is strongly rooted in the northern hemisphere. Few historians of the British Atlantic venture south of the Equator. There are, of course, very good reasons why this should be so.[96] However, it is not the complete picture of British interest in the Atlantic, as this book sets out to demonstrate. Similarly, studies of the Indian Ocean have often ended at the Cape (or even well before). As a region, or geographical space of analysis, the area covered in this study has, as Isabel Hofmeyr observes, often been omitted from 'canonical' scholarship on 'the monsoon-driven early modern trans-oceanic trading system of the western Indian Ocean'.[97] Some historians, notably P. J. Marshall and H. V. Bowen, have tried to remedy this situation, arguing for a more holistic approach to maritime history (and one more in keeping with the experiences of contemporaries, it might be added). Philip Stern has attempted to extend the boundaries of the Indian Ocean with his work on St Helena.[98] This study attempts to continue this work by reinserting that maritime context back into the story of the British Empire in the Indian Ocean world, focusing on the connections it facilitated, and the relationships it forged, in the South Atlantic and southern Indian Ocean. These oceans do not isolate; on the contrary, they are a binding medium, intimately connecting the region with both Europe and Asia.[99]

Connecting oceans

Oceans flow into each other, physically and culturally.[100] They are not blank spaces on the global map, nor are they gaps in the histories of a world consisting of continents. Like the continents around them, as Megan Vaughan has observed, they are 'human creations in the sense that their limits are not naturally given'.[101] As long ago as 1940, Boise Penrose pointed out that many of the leading figures in the early history of the East India Company and of the Virginia colony took part in the activities of both

[96] Alan Villiers, *The Western Ocean: Story of the North Atlantic* (London: British Museum Press, 1957), pp. 13–15.
[97] Isabel Hofmeyr, 'South Africa's Indian Ocean – Notes from Johannesburg', *History Compass* 11 (2013), pp. 508–12, p. 508.
[98] Stern, 'Politics and Ideology in the Early East India Company-State'.
[99] Haight, *European Powers and South-East Africa*, p. 4.
[100] Rainer F. Buschmann, 'Oceans of World History: Delineating Aquacentric Notions in the Global Past', *History Compass* 2 (2004), pp. 1–5.
[101] Vaughan, 'Foreword', p. xv.

enterprises. Penrose described people like Christopher Newport and Sir Thomas Dale – veterans of the Elizabethan wars with Spain and in Ireland, and founding fathers of the Virginia Company who subsequently died in Banten and Masulipatam respectively.[102] While this may be axiomatic for the sixteenth and seventeenth centuries, historians have long held a different view with regard to the eighteenth-century empire. The prevailing historiography for this period has frequently abrogated any links between the hemispheres. As early as 1846, Leitch Ritchie wrote about the remarkable 'eastern march of England'.[103] Much subsequent scholarship is, of course, inflected with echoes of Vincent Harlow's great work and its central, driving tenet of a 'swing to the East', which he used to describe 'a diversion of interest and enterprise from the Western World to the potentialities of Asia and Africa', and which he detected throughout the eighteenth century.[104] Debate on the origins, chronology and descriptive accuracy of the term has proved remarkably durable.[105] While Harlow's work has been fundamental to understanding the diverging priorities and changing nature of the British Empire over the period, however, it has often had the effect of driving a historiographical wedge between those who work on the Atlantic and those who do not. There are sound intellectual, methodological, practical and historical reasons for dividing these spaces. There is, for example, evidence to suggest that contemporaries envisaged Britain's imperial activities in the Atlantic and Asian worlds as fundamentally different.[106] However, this should not blind us to the fact that, in some cases, connections and intersections were powerfully present and helped to shape the development of this global empire. Emma Rothschild warns us not to assume that the distinction was complete: 'The British Empire in the Atlantic and the British Empire in the Indian Ocean were far less disconnected, in the minds even of mid-eighteenth-century officials, than they became in the post-revolutionary world.' The maritime routes protected by

---

[102] Boise Penrose, 'Some Jacobean Links between America and the Orient', *Virginia Magazine of History and Biography*, 48 (1940), p. 289.

[103] Leitch Ritchie, *The British World in the East: A Guide Historical, Moral and Commercial to India, China, Australia, South Africa, and the other Possessions and Connexions of Great Britain in the Eastern and Southern Seas*, 2 vols. (London: W. H. Allen, 1846), vol. I, p. viii.

[104] Harlow, *Second British Empire*, vol. I, p. 62.

[105] See, in particular, P. J. Marshall, 'The Eighteenth-Century Empire', in Jeremy Black (ed.), *British Politics and Society from Walpole to Pitt, 1742–1789* (Basingstoke: Macmillan, 1990), pp. 177–200; P. J. Marshall, *'A Free though Conquering People': Eighteenth-Century Britain and its Empire* (Aldershot: Ashgate, 2003); C. A. Bayly, *Imperial Meridian: The British Empire and the World, 1780–1830* (London: Longman, 1989).

[106] See P. J. Marshall, *Remaking the British Atlantic: The United States and the British Empire after Independence* (Oxford: Oxford University Press, 2012), p. 126.

the way stations of empire in the South Atlantic and southern Indian Ocean connected lives and experiences, as well as places and ports, making these two worlds 'blur even in the lives of individuals or families'.[107] This study is part, then, of this process of interrogating and investigating the fundamentally interconnected nature of the early modern British Empire. The 'skeins of maritime connection', as Kären Wigen suggests, 'quickly transcend the confines of a single ocean'.[108]

As the fulcrum around which two maritime systems operated, the spatial relationship between this part of the world and the northern hemisphere nodes of Britain and the Indian subcontinent has been at the heart of the historiography of European involvement in the region.[109] For Mabel Jackson Haight, the southern part of Africa was a 'tricontinental frontier'.[110] Charles Boxer speculated on who first gave Cape Town the appellation of *de Indische Zeeherberg* ('tavern of the Indian Ocean'), a phrase already in common usage by the eighteenth century when the Swedish surgeon-botanist Carl Peter Thunberg described it as 'an inn for travellers to and from the East Indies, who, after several months' sail may get here refreshments of all kinds, and are then about half way to the place of their destination, whether homeward or outward bound'.[111] Similarly, in the southern Indian Ocean, Mauritius has often been identified as a focal point.[112] For Megan Vaughan, Mauritius has always been 'a profoundly cosmopolitan place ... the product of multiple influences, multiple sources, which to differing degrees merge, take root, and "naturalize" in this new soil'.[113] And these places were part of an even wider hinterland of connections. Places like Batavia and Cape Town were hubs linked to regional economies beyond them. The Ile de France connected Madagascar, Rodrigues, and the Ile de Bourbon, as well as more disparate India Ocean islands, such as Agalega, Diego Garcia, the Comoros and the Seychelles.[114] One of the most successful ways of

---

[107] Emma Rothschild, 'The Atlantic Worlds of David Hume', in Bernard Bailyn and Patricia L. Denault (eds.), *Soundings in Atlantic History: Latent Structures and Intellectual Currents, 1500–1830* (Cambridge, MA: Harvard University Press, 2009), pp. 405–48, p. 438.

[108] Wigen, 'Introduction', p. 1.

[109] Robert Ross, 'Cape Town (1750–1850): Synthesis in the Dialectic of Continents', in Robert Ross and Gerard J. Telkamp (eds.), *Colonial Cities: Essays on Urbanism in a Colonial Context* (Dordrecht: Martinus Nijhoff, 1985), pp. 105–21, p. 107.

[110] Haight, *European Powers and South-East Africa*, p. xii.

[111] See Ward, '"Tavern of the Seas"?', p. 139.

[112] Rosabelle Boswell, 'Islands in the (Global) Stream: The Case of Mauritius and Seychelles', in Gupta, Hofmeyr and Pearson (eds.), *Eyes Across the Water*, pp. 286–303.

[113] Megan Vaughan, *Creating the Creole Island: Slavery in Eighteenth-Century Mauritius* (London: Duke University Press, 2005), p. 2.

[114] James R. Fichter, *So Great a Profit: How the East Indies Trade Transformed Anglo-American Capitalism* (Cambridge, MA: Harvard University Press, 2010), pp. 158, 334, n. 1. For more on Diego Garcia, see Frost, *Global Reach of Empire*, pp. 190–1.

further interrogating how this maritime arc of empire worked in practice is by considering the networks it sustained, cultivated and extended.

Networks, connections and empire

This study uses the connections and connectivities forged across the region, and with the wider world beyond, in order to integrate and analyse the South Atlantic and southern Indian Ocean in the broader geographical context of Britain's oceanic and maritime empire. By the early eighteenth century, the idea of networks as 'intricate systems of circulation' was beginning to gain wider currency.[115] People, places and ideas were interconnected by personal networks that were increasingly 'fluid, fragile and geographically expansive'.[116] And these were also inflected and imbricated by the official, institutional and commercial networks which evolved during the course of the century.[117] The use of networks as analytical tools in exploring global and transnational phenomena has long been advocated by scholars.[118] For example, Steven Harris has highlighted ways in which networks can help to explain the workings of global corporations, such as the East India Company, and their involvement in large-scale commercial, logistical and scientific enterprises.[119] Historians have similarly recognised the value of using such concepts to describe the interrelatedness of empire. Natasha Glaisyer has argued that empire can be understood as 'a set of networks through which knowledge was exchanged, trust was negotiated, people travelled (sometimes against their will), and commodities were traded'.[120] And in her magisterial study

On the Seychelles, see William McAteer, *Rivals in Eden: The History of Seychelles, 1742–1827* (Mahé: Pristine Books, 2002).

[115] See Lindsay O'Neill, *The Opened Letter: Networking in the Early Modern British World* (Philadelphia: University of Pennsylvania Press, 2015), p. 3.

[116] In this, they bear more resemblance to those networks of interest identified by historians of science and knowledge as opposed to the concept of networks – often employed by social historians – as deeply embedded social structures tied to a single location. For an enlightening discussion of the distinction between networks of interest and broad social networks, see O'Neill, *Opened Letter*, pp. 4–7.

[117] *Ibid.*, pp. 18, 140–68.

[118] This approach is not unproblematic. For a summary of the origins of the term, and a consideration of its merits and relative usefulness for historians, see David Hancock, 'The Trouble with Networks: Managing the Scots' Early Modern Madeira Table', *Business History Review* 79 (2005), pp. 467–91, pp. 470–3. As Nicholas Purcell has noted, it is of course 'social relations and processes which render people and things mobile ... rather than the mere fact of the connectivity'. See Nicholas Purcell, 'Tide, Beach, and Backwash: The Place of Maritime Histories', in Miller (ed.), *The Sea*, pp. 84–108, p. 86.

[119] Steven J. Harris, 'Long-Distance Corporations, Big Sciences, and the Geography of Knowledge', *Configurations* 6 (1998), pp. 269–304.

[120] Natasha Glaisyer, 'Networking: Trade and Exchange in the Eighteenth-Century British Empire', *Historical Journal*, 47 (2004), pp. 451–76, p. 474. See also Douglas Hamilton,

of the place of South Africa in the Dutch Indian Ocean world of the seventeenth and eighteenth centuries, Kerry Ward points out that empires are intersections of material and discursive networks that exist simultaneously as 'paths of circulation' for people, goods and information, and as 'nodal regulatory points' in regional centres.[121] Imperial experiences were characterised and fundamentally shaped by the personal, material and information exchanges made possible by ships and the sea. The complexities and ambiguities of the British Empire were preserved, recreated and reshaped by maritime circuits of communication and exchange.

As part of this process, the study of oceans and sea basins offers new perspectives on the political, economic, cultural and scientific networks that defined imperial connections.[122] They provide ways of understanding the contingency and fluidity of these processes of exchange and interaction. In her work on the circulation of scientific material in the Atlantic World, for example, Londa Schiebinger asserts that the networks created by such exchanges were far from fixed. On the contrary, they were 'rich and multicentred ... multivariate and complex', offering fertile grounds for diversification and innovation.[123] For Durba Ghosh and Dane Kennedy, the British imperial experience created 'multiple networks of exchange'. The resulting connections linked colonies and other areas of British imperial activity to each other, as well as to Britain.[124] Tony Ballantyne has also identified the ways in which local centres of knowledge helped to create 'webs of empire', which complicate monolithic definitions of 'periphery' and 'centre'.[125] The existence of such diverse and overlapping connections suggests that it is more appropriate to view the maritime basis of the early modern British Empire as a 'polycentric communications network' rather than simply as a centripetal phenomenon, drawing things to politicians in Westminster,

---

'Local Connections, Global Ambitions: Creating a Transoceanic Network in the Eighteenth-Century British Atlantic Empire', *International Journal of Maritime History* 23 (2011), pp. 1–18.

[121] See Kerry Ward, *Networks of Empire: Forced Migration in the Dutch East India Company* (Cambridge: Cambridge University Press, 2008), pp. 8–10.

[122] See Lambert, Martins and Ogborn, 'Currents, Visions and Voyages', p. 480.

[123] Londa Schiebinger, 'Scientific Exchange in the Eighteenth-Century Atlantic World', in Bernard Bailyn and Patricia L. Denault (eds.), *Soundings in Atlantic History: Latent Structures and Intellectual Currents, 1500–1830* (Cambridge, MA: Harvard University Press, 2009), pp. 294–328, pp. 322, 327.

[124] Durba Ghosh and Dane Kennedy, 'Introduction', in Durba Ghosh and Dane Kennedy (eds.), *Decentring Empire: Britain, India and the Transcolonial World* (London: Sangam Books, 2006), p. 2.

[125] Tony Ballantyne, *Orientalism and Race: Aryanism in the British Empire* (Basingstoke: Palgrave, 2002), pp. 13–15.

or the East India Company's Court of Directors in Leadenhall Street.[126] These crucial points underline the fact that connections facilitated by sea power and maritime empire were more complicated, often bypassing imperial metropoles, linking nodes at the so-called 'peripheries' to each other.

This emphasis on the fluid and the fluxive results in a more complex and nuanced spatial and political geography of empire. And it suggests the value of conceiving of imperial relations as matrices of interconnections in which those that link the metropole with colonies are certainly critical, but are by no means the only ones.[127] In addition to these bilateral links binding the centre to the periphery, then, we have become much more aware of the relationships that linked various colonies with one another. Specifically in this regard, Clare Anderson has reminded us of the need to think about the Indian Ocean context of the East India Company's activities and spheres of influence.[128] In doing so, we might approach the kinds of 'connected' Indian Ocean histories for which Sanjay Subrahmanyam has called.[129] This book uses these insights, and the multi-centric approach to empire, in the context of the southern Atlantic and Indian oceans. It attempts to contribute to a recalibration of imperial networks and their circuits of exchange by exploring the ways in which geographically disparate places were linked and consolidated using the maritime connections of the burgeoning British Empire.

In doing so specifically in relation to this region, this study builds on some important and valuable existing work. The Cape of Good Hope, and Southern Africa more generally, has been better served by its historians in terms of situating the late eighteenth- and early nineteenth-century

[126] This phrase is borrowed from David Wade Chambers and Richard Gillespie, 'Locality in the History of Science: Colonial Science, Technoscience, and Indigenous Knowledge', in Roy MacLeod (ed.), 'Nature and Empire: Science and the Colonial Enterprise', *Osiris* 15 (2000), pp. 221–40. They use it specifically in relation to early modern science. For more on the implications of examining different regions of empires in 'a single analytic field', see Ann Laura Stoler and Frederick Cooper, 'Between Metropole and Colony: Rethinking a Research Agenda', in Frederick Cooper and Ann Laura Stoler (eds.), *Tensions of Empire: Colonial Cultures in a Bourgeois World* (Berkeley, CA: University of California Press, 1997), pp. 1–56 (quote on p. 4).

[127] Much of the paragraph that follows is based on the ideas outlined in Douglas M. Peers and Nandini Gooptu, 'Introduction', in Douglas M. Peers and Nandini Gooptu (eds.), *India and the British Empire* (Oxford: Oxford University Press, 2012), pp. 1–15, pp. 1–2.

[128] See Clare Anderson's contribution in a roundtable review of Kerry Ward's *Networks of Empire*, *International Journal of Maritime History* 21 (2009), pp. 297–340, p. 299.

[129] See Sanjay Subrahmanyam, 'Connected Histories: Notes towards a Reconfiguration of Early Modern Eurasia', *Modern Asian Studies* 31 (1997), pp. 735–62. For a similar approach focusing on commercial activities, see Pedro Machado, *Ocean of Trade: South Asian Merchants, Africa and the Indian Ocean, c.1750–1850* (Cambridge: Cambridge University Press, 2014).

colony in wider historical contexts. The Cape in particular has a long and complex relationship with the history of European maritime empires. Before the advent of British control at the end of the eighteenth century, a century and a half of Dutch colonial activity had enveloped the Cape into a range of commercial, political and military networks that spanned the Indian Ocean. Some important research has identified the archival traces of the Cape's connections with the Indian Ocean world of the East India Company in the period covered by this study.[130] Marcus Arkin's excellent studies locate the economic history of the Cape in a wider regional context, shedding valuable light on its commercial relationship with the Company and its activities in India.[131] More recently, a number of historians have recognised the need to situate the history of Southern Africa in a broader global context.[132]

Kerry Ward's work on Cape Town as a port city also provides clear evidence of how networks connected Southern Africa with the wider world. She remarks on the necessity of considering the connectedness of this port:

Cape Town emerged within the [Dutch East India] Company period as a littoral society fundamentally engaged with the intersections of multiple imperial networks of trade, information, and migration across the Atlantic and Indian oceans.[133]

This book similarly attempts to reintegrate the history of Southern Africa into a broader geographical context and network of connections that

---

[130] See Jill Geber, 'The East India Company and Southern Africa: a guide to the archives of the East India Company and the Board of Control, 1600–1858', Ph.D. dissertation, University of London, 1998.

[131] See, for example, the following by Marcus Arkin, 'John Company at the Cape: A History of the Agency under Pringle (1794–1815)', *Archives Year Book for South African History 1960* (Pretoria: Government Printer, 1961), pp. 177–344; 'Supplies for Napoleon's Gaolers: John Company and the Cape-St Helena Trade during the Captivity, 1815–21', *Archives Year Book for South African History 1964* (Cape Town: Government Printer, 1965), pp. 167–225; *Storm in a Teacup: The Late Years of John Company at the Cape, 1815–36* (Cape Town: Struik, 1973).

[132] Saul Dubow, 'How British was the British World? The Case of South Africa', *Journal of Imperial and Commonwealth History* 37 (2009), pp. 1–27; Nigel Worden (ed.), *Contingent Lives: Social Identity and Material Culture in the VOC World* (Cape Town: University of Cape Town Press, 2007); Nigel Worden, 'VOC Capetown as an Indian Ocean Port', in Ghosh and Muecke (eds.), *Cultures of Trade*, pp. 31–46; Kerry Ward, *Networks of Empire*; Kirsten McKenzie, *Scandal in the Colonies: Sydney and Cape Town, 1820–1850* (Carlton: Melbourne University Press, 2004); Gerald Groenewald, 'Entrepreneurs and the Making of a Free Burgher Society', in Nigel Worden (ed.), *Cape Town between East and West: Social Identities in a Dutch Colonial Town* (Hilversum: Uitgeverij Verloren, 2012), pp. 45–64; Groenewald, 'Southern Africa and the Atlantic World'.

[133] Ward, '"Tavern of the Seas"?', p. 146.

spanned oceanic spaces. Like that colonial settlement, the wider region was 'shaped by forces beyond its immediate geographical confines'; it was 'part of a much wider network of interchanges of people, material goods and ideas'.[134] One of the central objectives of this book, therefore, is to trace these exchanges and connections, and to consider the entire maritime spaces as an interlinked whole. It responds to Nigel Worden's call to investigate the Cape (and, in the context of this present study, other places in the region) in a 'transmarine and transcontinental context'.[135] In doing so, it follows the work of people like Worden, Metcalf and Ward in assessing the place of the Cape from the perspective of the Indian Ocean.[136] But, where Worden and Ward focus primarily on the Dutch Indian Ocean world, and Metcalf concentrates on the post-East India Company period, this study explores the perceived value of the Cape to British Indian Ocean interests and the ways in which these segued into British activities in the South Atlantic.

Structure of the book

The book is divided into two sections. After this introduction, the first two chapters explore the notion of a 'key' to India and examine the term's rhetorical and representational purchase in a range of political, diplomatic and commercial debates. They consider the related themes of Britain's interest in the region and the competition it faced from rival European empires. The second half of the book explores some of the ways in which this maritime space worked in practice, the connections that subsisted within it, and the links that were formed between it and other parts of the British Indian Ocean world, principally the Indian subcontinent. These concluding chapters move the chronological focus of the book forward to the period of the Revolutionary and Napoleonic Wars, when the region became ever more deeply entwined with the fate of various European empires. They analyse the practicalities of the British control of this gateway to Asia, the movement and networks that this control sustained, and the effect of this movement of people, information and ideas on the development of the British Empire in Asia.

The discussion in Chapter 2 explores the claims of various places in the southern Atlantic and Indian oceans to the title of 'key' to the East, assessing their individual and collective political and strategic value. In 1801, barely six years after it was first taken by his troops, George III

---

[134] Nigel Worden, 'Introduction', in Worden (ed.) *Cape Town between East and West*, pp. ix–xxii, p. xiii.
[135] *Ibid.*, p. xi.
[136] Metcalf, *Imperial Connections*, p. 1; Ward, *Networks of Empire*, pp. 8–10.

remarked that he thought not enough benefit had been derived from the Cape of Good Hope following its capture.[137] The question of what 'benefit' could be derived or even expected from a British presence in the region was one that exercised politicians, military men and East India Company officials long before George Keith Elphinstone conquered the Cape in 1795. Most agreed that colonies here were never going to be economically advantageous. On the contrary, they were more to be valued as strategic and military links in the chain of the Indian Ocean world in which Britain was becoming increasingly dominant. They were the agents that unlocked connections, and the catalysts that changed the nature of this maritime space and Britain's relationship with it. They offered possibilities for refreshing and repairing ships on the long journeys to and from the lucrative markets of Asia. And, because it offered essential bases from which to control the commerce of three continents and as many oceans, this gateway to the Indian Ocean became an arena of European power politics. This chapter interrogates the deployment of monikers such as 'key', 'gateway', 'Gibraltar' and 'half-way house' in contemporary descriptions and discourse. It asks what this tells us about these locations as individual places, about the region as a whole, and, ultimately, about the ways in which it functioned as part of Britain's global maritime empire. Assessing the rhetorical baggage that accreted around the region by the use of such language and images helps us better to understand the practical and logistical connections that, by the early nineteenth century, had enfolded the entire region into Britain's wider maritime empire.

But this accounts for only part of the story. Edward Thompson, on his expedition to South Atlantic waters to survey the coasts of Southern Africa in 1785, commented on 'the superior advantage the Dutch, Portuguese & French have reaped over us in their Indian Navigation & commerce'. He attributed this squarely to 'their having more convenient ports of refreshment in their passages'.[138] Chapter 3 argues that the British interest in the South Atlantic and southern Indian Ocean cannot be understood without considering rival European empires or issues of intensifying settler identity, both of which influenced the tone and extent of British activity in the region.[139] There were indigenous groups, such as those Malagasy

---

[137] The king's remarks were recorded in Sylvester Douglas's diary entry for 29 January 1801. See Francis Bickley (ed.), *The Diaries of Sylvester Douglas, Lord Glenbervie*, 2 vols. (London: Constable, 1928), vol. I, p. 151.

[138] TNA, CO 267/9, Memorandum of Edward Thompson, 9 March 1785.

[139] See Eliga H. Gould, 'Entangled Histories, Entangled Worlds: The English-Speaking Atlantic as a Spanish Periphery', *American Historical Review* 112 (2007), pp. 764–86.

kingdoms highlighted by Gwyn Campbell, with grand ambitions too. Governments in Europe, and their military forces in the field, had to contend not only with each other but also with 'the dynamics of indigenous imperial interests'.[140] But, for many contemporaries, the fate of the British Empire was linked, in an inverse proportion, to that of its European rivals. In a memorandum of December 1779, for example, John Dalrymple told Lord Sandwich that the capture of the Cape or Buenos Aires or Mauritius would be 'equally advantageous to this country and detrimental to our enemies'.[141] The apparent decay of rival empires presented opportunities for consolidating and expanding British sea routes in the region. Reports about the dissatisfaction of settlers are widespread in the archives. There was much talk about 'the state of the Spanish possessions' in Latin America, for example, which were apparently constantly teetering on the brink of open rebellion.[142] Francis Baring, in advocating the British capture of the Cape, observed the fact that the local inhabitants were 'very ill disposed towards their own government'.[143] Lord Macartney reported that affairs at Mauritius were 'in a very disturbed state'.[144] From dealings with the Dutch at the Cape and the Spanish at the River Plate, to fear of the French and anxiety about the Americans, this chapter reinserts rival empires into the analysis of the British presence across this maritime gateway to India. In doing so, it argues for the importance of seeing Britain's role as a destroyer, as well as a builder, of empire in the region. And enemy empires, principally the French, posed another, altogether more dangerous threat: the prospect of establishing and exploiting their own strategic hubs or even acquiring British ones. In 1777, a certain Morice, a former *Compagnie* surgeon turned slave supplier to the Mascarenes proposed the formation of a French empire in the western Indian Ocean stretching from Surat, on the west coast of India, to Mozambique, on the south-east coast of Africa.[145] A range of sources, from the archives of the East India Company and the correspondence of sailors and naval officers to the private letters and diaries of people like Lady Anne Barnard and Samuel Eusebius Hudson, provide striking evidence of the persistent hazards posed by the presence of other

---

[140] Gwyn Campbell, 'Imperial Rivalry in the Western Indian Ocean and Schemes to Colonise Madagascar (1769–1826)', in Laurence Marfaing and Brigitte Reinwald (eds.), *Afrikanische Beziehungen: Netzwerke und Räume* (Hamburg: LIT Verlag, 2001), pp. 111–30, p. 111.

[141] NMM, SAN F/22/97, Memorandum [of John Dalrymple] [December 1779].

[142] Roger Curtis to Spencer, 19 December 1800, *Spencer*, vol. VI, p. 244.

[143] Sir Francis Baring to Dundas, 4 January 1795, *RCC*, vol. I, p. 18.

[144] RH, MSS.Afr.t.3, Macartney to Brooke, 4 May 1798.

[145] Campbell, 'Imperial Rivalry', p. 117.

European empires in the region.[146] Furthermore, the triangular relationship between Britain, rival empires and various settler colonists further illuminates the complex interplay of political forces shaping the region in the late eighteenth century, subverting any notions of a simple and clear rise to British dominance in the area. Focusing on a number of incidents and examples, drawn from across the geographical scope of the maritime region, this chapter demonstrates how closely entwined the British presence there was with other competing empires of trade and settlement.

The second half of the book explores how this maritime 'world' at the southern reaches of the Atlantic and Indian oceans operated in practice, the ways in which it was increasingly incorporated into the British Empire in Asia, the limits and possibilities for exercised British power, and the practical connections that linked it with the Indian subcontinent. Building on models developed by scholars of the Atlantic world, and being increasingly explored by those interested in Britain's Indian Ocean world, these chapters concentrate on the movement of people, information and ideas within and beyond this region. As many scholars have identified, the oceanic networks that sustained the East India Company's trade and, ultimately, the British presence in Asia relied on the movement of people, goods and objects. In many ways, Britain's interest in the entire route to the East was predicated on the movement of goods: the successful and regular return of large shipments of Asian commodities to sell in western markets. But the southern arc of this maritime route was also associated with such movements and exchanges. Objects, people and ideas moved within the region, and between the region and the Indian subcontinent. Everything from goods, like rice and teak, to botanical specimens, organised troop movements, sensitive political intelligence and military men on furlough, circulated around this region, creating patterns of exchange and networks of interdependence. On St Helena, for example, paddy rice shipped from India was the principal cereal consumed by the inhabitants, while livestock, forage and wine came mainly from the Cape.[147] The island was also subject to less welcome imports from Southern Africa: Robert Brooke, governor in the late eighteenth century, remarked that 'unfortunately most of all the peach trees, mulberry trees and some other sorts have been destroyed by an insect said to

---

[146] See, for example, UWits, A88/49, Evan Nepean to Thomas Pringle, 23 January 1797. On Hudson, see Kirsten McKenzie, *The Making of an English Slave-owner: Samuel Eusebius Hudson at the Cape of Good Hope, 1796–1807* (Rondebosch: University of Cape Town Press, 1993).

[147] Arkin, 'Supplies for Napoleon's Gaolers', p. 174.

have been introduced from the Cape'.[148] And the island was supplied with slaves from Bengal and Madagascar, further emphasising and strengthening its connections with the Indian Ocean.[149] The French Mascarene Islands had links as far afield as the Philippines in the east and Río de la Plata in the west. One of the islands' principal points of contact was Madagascar, and there was a lively trade from the Cape, chiefly in butter, wheat, pork, lard, candles and tobacco.[150] And scientific specimens also circulated in the holds of the merchant ships plying the trade routes and the naval vessels protecting them. Just as these places occupied strategic hubs, so they also sat at botanical and scientific crossroads. The Persian traveller Mirza Abu Taleb Khan advised readers of his account that, on St Helena, one met with 'the trees and fruits both of Europe and Asia'.[151] And at the governor's country house, 'hedges of myrtle and roses' and 'English vegetables and every kinds of fruits' could be seen in juxtaposition with 'plants and trees of the east': 'The produce of such different climates growing altogether is curious and wonderful, when at one view is beheld the oak, the bamboo, beetle and coffee tress.'[152] For the traveller, such a sight might have appeared incongruous but, for the places of this region, it was a function of their location at the crossroads of oceanic trading systems and reflected the patterns of commerce and maritime movement these networks produced.

Chapter 4 focuses on the circulation of ideas, information and intelligence, which have long been understood as forming the staple diet of imperial states.[153] It explores the ways in which information arrived in the region, the channels through which it flowed, and the effects that it had on the British presence there. Much of this approach will be particularly familiar to historians of the Atlantic. But the specific contexts are different. The discussion investigates the role of the region as an information nodal point, conveying intelligence from India to Britain and vice versa. Lord Wellesley, as we have seen, acknowledged the importance of such 'a

---

[148] BL, IOR, G/32/165, p. 3, Robert Brooke, 'Account of St Helena with Various Observations Annexed' [1792].

[149] See Alexander H. Schulenburg, 'Transient observations: the textualizing of St Helena through five hundred years of colonial discourse', Ph.D. thesis, University of St Andrews, 1999, pp. 201–4.

[150] Toussaint, *Route des Îles*, pp. 95, 132–3, 135, n. 2.

[151] Mirza Abu Taleb Khan, *Travels of Mirza Abu Taleb Khan in Asia, Africa, and Europe, during the years 1799, 1800, 1801, 1802, and 1803*, translated by Charles Stewart (London: Longman, Hurst, Rees, Orme, and Brown, 1814), p. 97.

[152] HALS, DE/B472/25930c, 'Account of the Island of St Helena' (1789).

[153] See Thomas Richards, *The Imperial Archive: Knowledge and the Fantasy of Empire* (London: Verso, 1993); C. A. Bayly, *Empire and Information: Intelligence Gathering and Social Communication in India, 1780–1870* (Cambridge: Cambridge University Press, 1996).

constant and unreserved correspondence on every question affecting the mutual interests of India' with British settlements in the southern Atlantic and Indian oceans.[154] And there was a constant circulation of information, intelligence and expertise *within* the maritime space itself, creating an intra-regional network of exchange. Information about the progress of wars, news of naval victories, and tidings about a whole host of other matters regularly reached the region on its way to and from India. The interpretation and effect of this forms the basis of this chapter. But less welcome information also arrived, coming in the form of false intelligence spread by rivals in an effort to destabilise the nascent British presence, as well as subversive sentiments of mutiny from home. By exploring the physical distribution and dissemination of information and ideas, as well as their effects, the chapter emphasises the *central* location of this 'peripheral' space in the circulation of such information.

Chapters 5 explores the region's role as a hub for supplying British troop requirements in India and elsewhere, providing evidence for the ways in which it was incorporated into the empire and, conversely, its contribution to the support and maintenance of the wider British presence in Asia. Dutch and German soldiers garrisoned at the Cape signed up for service in India, troops were acclimatised at the Cape before moving to the subcontinent, and plans were hatched for deploying Indian sepoys in Africa and the Caribbean, using the region as a crucial way station. The expedition against Ile de Bourbon (renamed Ile Napoleon in 1801; present-day Réunion) in 1809 was composed almost entirely of troops from the establishment of Fort St George.[155] And European officers serving in India spent time on furlough in Southern Africa recovering their health. The Royal Navy also provided a medium of connection: there were important links between shore establishments in the region and naval fleets.[156] The naval career of Peter Rainier, on the East Indies station for eleven turbulent years, highlights the ways in which the seas connected people and places across the Indian Ocean world of Britain's naval squadron.[157] For all of these reasons, as the British presence in the region was consolidated and confirmed, the maritime gateway to India became much more closely integrated into the British Asian empire and its principal Indian Ocean concern at the time: India itself.

[154] Wellesley to Curtis, 24 October 1800, *Spencer*, vol. IV, p. 163.
[155] Lord Minto to Robert Dundas, 1 January 1811, *Minto*, p. 248.
[156] John Frederick Day, 'British Admiralty control and naval power in the Indian Ocean, 1793–1815', Ph.D. thesis, University of Exeter, 2012.
[157] Peter A. Ward, *British Naval Power in the East, 1794–1805: The Command of Admiral Peter Rainier* (Woodbridge: Boydell & Brewer, 2013).

Conclusions

Lord Macartney's assessment of the region, as forming 'the master link of connection between the western and eastern world', was a shrewd one. The islands and coastal littorals of the southern Atlantic and Indian oceans were at the centre of Britain's developing empire in the period. Macartney's statement also tells us much about the dynamics of the region. As someone who arrived at the Cape of Good Hope as the first British civilian governor following its acquisition from the Dutch, Macartney's very presence was concrete evidence of the development and extension of British power there. His opinions demonstrate the wider debate about this entire region in contemporary British political, diplomatic and commercial circles. And, crucially, his words also point to the rebalancing and recalibration of the British Empire towards the 'eastern world' that took place over the course of the latter half of the eighteenth century. The chapters that follow set out to trace the role of the South Atlantic, Southern Africa and the south-western Indian Ocean in that process. If this region is a 'key', it is one that unlocks much more than simply the strategic value of its waters. It brings us to the heart of Britain's imperial history, its links with India, and the connections that spanned the Indian and Atlantic oceans.

2 'The key to India': consolidating the gateway to the East

Addressing Parliament on 4 March 1816, Lord Castlereagh reflected on the British approach throughout the long years of the French Wars: 'Our policy has been to secure the Empire against future attack. In order to do this we had acquired what in former days would have been thought romance – the keys of every great military position.'[1] Castlereagh's observations followed the clear instructions issued by the Cabinet three years earlier, as he prepared to negotiate a conclusion to the seemingly interminable wars with France: places of strategic importance must remain British at all costs.[2] In a codicil, members of the Cabinet reflected on 'the colonies and possessions' which the country had 'conquered from her enemies'. They were eager to point out that Britain did not 'desire to retain any of these colonies for their mere commercial value'. In fact, they were perfectly happy to return these if it helped 'to cultivate the arts of peace'. Ostensibly at least, the yardstick for retaining or returning colonial possessions was the extent to which such places 'affect essentially the engagement and security of their own dominion'.[3] In this regard, Malta and the Cape were considered crucial enough for the Cabinet to insist on their retention.[4] As Castlereagh commented to the Prime Minister, Lord Liverpool: 'I consider Malta, the Cape, Mauritius, and Tobago, as *sine qua non*'.[5]

---

[1] House of Commons Debate on Army Estimates, in *The Parliamentary History of England, from the Earliest Period to the Year 1803*, edited by William Cobbett, 36 vols. (London: T. C. Hansard, 1816), vol. 32, p. 1104.

[2] See 'Memorandum of Cabinet', 26 December 1813, in C. K. Webster (ed.), *British Diplomacy, 1813–1815* (London: G. Bell, 1921), p. 124. For the definitive biography of this most important of early- nineteenth-century politicians, see John Bew, *Castlereagh: Enlightenment, War and Tyranny* (London: Quercus, 2011).

[3] 'Memorandum on the Maritime Peace', December 1813, in Webster (ed.), *British Diplomacy*, p. 127. For further details, see Alan Frost, *The Global Reach of Empire: Britain's Maritime Expansion in the Indian and Pacific Oceans, 1764–1815* (Carlton: Miegunyah Press, 2003), pp. 266–7.

[4] Webster (ed.), *British Diplomacy, 1813–1815*, p. xl.

[5] Lord Castlereagh to Lord Liverpool, 19 April 1814 (*ibid.*, p. 178).

Castlereagh's statement could, in truth, have described British policy since at least the Seven Years War. Anticipating Adam Smith by some twenty years, Josiah Tucker, Dean of Gloucester, argued in 1755 against holding colonies at all because of the large financial burdens they imposed and the negligible commercial advantages that formal incorporation bestowed.[6] In 1762, Lord Shelburne linked sea power with prosperity. Large territorial holdings were less important for a sea empire than a network of sailing routes and secure bases: 'Now the possession of territory is but a secondary point and is considered more or less valuable, as it is subservient to the interest of commerce, which is now the great object of ambition.'[7] At the very end of the century, Sir Ralph Abercromby suggested that this sentiment had percolated into the wider population: 'The people of Great Britain in general take little share in the affairs of foreign nations ... [T]hey are little interested in any thing that does not tend to the security and extension of commerce, and the dominion of the sea.'[8] Holding various keys to the Atlantic and the Mediterranean was a cornerstone of British political and military thinking. Contemporaries were acutely aware of the crucial historical link between geography and power. In general, and especially after the loss of thirteen colonies in the Americas, overseas locations were less interesting as colonies per se, and rather more important as strategic positions. Colonial possessions were worth having when they provided raw materials or markets which were not otherwise available, of course, but the best overseas possessions were those locations, small and inexpensive to take and hold, which served as crucial bases for the promotion and protection of commerce and which somebody else had the trouble and expense of administering.[9] At various points during the eighteenth century, places as diverse as Gibraltar, Malta, Bermuda, Halifax, Guadeloupe and Les Saintes were perceived as vital to Britain's national interests and claimed the right to the title of the 'key' to the empire. But given the loss of half its American colonies, the apparent reorientation of the empire towards the East, and the rising importance of Asian trade to Britain in the late eighteenth century, there was now a need to find equivalents for the Asian empire.

[6] Donald Winch, *Classical Political Theory and Colonies* (Cambridge: Harvard University Press, 1965), p. 18.
[7] Quoted in Frost, *Global Reach of Empire*, p. 41.
[8] Sir Ralph Abercromby, 'On the Liberation of South America from the Dominion of Spain' (c.1799), *Londonderry*, vol. VII, p. 269.
[9] N. A. M. Rodger, 'Seapower and Empire: Cause and Effect?', in Bob Moore and Henk Van Nierop (eds.), *Colonial Empires Compared: Britain and the Netherlands, 1750–1850* (Aldershot: Ashgate, 2003), pp. 97–111, pp. 107–9.

This chapter maps the maritime geography of the southern Atlantic and Indian oceans on to British commercial, political and strategic concerns in the late eighteenth and early nineteenth centuries. It considers various places – existing and prospective – that might have helped to secure this gateway to the East and the increasingly important Indian Ocean world beyond. It details the strategic value of individual locations as well as the connections they enabled. This geographical approach introduces the spatial relationship between places regarded by contemporaries as the 'key' to or 'Gibraltar' of Asia, while preserving the unique circumstances and contexts pertaining to each. Ultimately, it shows how these places, and the region as a whole, were conceived of as part of Britain's global maritime empire.

Of course, the locations discussed in this chapter – and their strategic importance to British merchants and military men – were affected by events as well as their geographical location. The chronological period with which this book is concerned witnessed significant upheavals in Britain's relationship with the rest of the world. This chapter is partially concerned, therefore, with the consequences of losing an empire as well as the demands of sustaining and expanding one, as Britain came to terms with the shock of losing thirteen of its American colonies. One of the ways in which this loss might be mitigated was a reorientation of interests and priorities. As one author, in arguing for the establishment of a British colony in Madagascar some years later, put it:

Shall we rest contented with the loss of America and tamely circumscribe ourselves to our present discomforted colonies? And shall we not look forward to other channels of trade when we are assured of a commercial correspondence with the greatest part of the Eastern and North Western World. Surely No![10]

Control of strategic bases and commercial rights in the East were the points around which the peace negotiations at the end of the American War turned.[11] Immediately after the signing of the Treaty of Paris in 1783, the long-term effects of this perceived calamity were still unknown, but questions were already being asked about its impact on Britain's wider imperial portfolio. Not many people were as sanguine as Lord Macartney who believed that the British Empire was 'a great deal stronger' without its American component, which had been 'too heavy for the edifice which it was thought to adorn'.[12] George III, for example,

---

[10] HRO, 38M49/5/61/20, 'Observations on the Island of Madagascar by Colonel Sir George Young' (c.1806–7), p. 8, note.
[11] Frost, *Global Reach of Empire*, p. 117.
[12] Quoted in P. J. Marshall, *The Making and Unmaking of Empires: Britain, Inida, and America c. 1750–1783* (Oxford: Oxford University Press, 2007), p. 362.

was sure that it would 'annihilate the rank in which the British empire stands among the European states'.[13] However, P. J. Marshall has made the convincing case that neither the United States nor Britain suffered as much as contemporaries had predicted.[14] One of the reasons for this was Britain's fast-developing interests half the world away, in the Indian subcontinent.

In March 1780, Sir John Dalrymple suggested that 'England might very well put up with the loss of America, for she would then exchange an empire of dominion which is very difficult to be kept for an empire of trade which keeps itself.'[15] Sir John's brother agreed. William Dalrymple's solution, however, went a step further. It involved the acquisition of critical way stations along the maritime route to Asia: 'We have lost America, and a half way house would secure us India, and Empire to Britain.'[16] Later, a somewhat shadowy figure, Benjamin Stout, made a similar point: 'If by any chance, the West India islands should be lost to [the British], or any natural convulsion of the seasons render them for a certain time unproductive, the British settlements in Africa might supply the deficiency, and their markets [of] rum and sugar be universally supported.'[17] There was a new emphasis on India and defending Britain's growing imperial portfolio in Asia. Protecting the remaining empire did not just mean consolidating commercial opportunities in Asia; it also meant protecting and defending the route there. In this respect, however, Britain was a long way behind other countries. Edward Thompson, in his expedition to South Atlantic waters in 1785 to survey the coasts of Southern Africa, commented on 'the superior advantage the Dutch, Portuguese & French have reaped over us in their Indian Navigation & commerce'. He attributed this squarely to 'their having more convenient ports of refreshment in their passages':

For while we are compelled to Rio de Janeiro and to St Helena where little provision is to be obtained, they enjoy every advantage [of] the Cape of Good

[13] Quoted in P. J. Marshall, *Remaking the British Atlantic: The United States and the British Empire after Independence* (Oxford: Oxford University Press, 2012), p. 119.

[14] *Ibid.*, p. 1.

[15] Sir John Dalrymple to Lord George Germain, 1 March 1780, in *Report on the Manuscripts of Mrs Stopford-Sackville, Historical Manuscripts Commission*, 2 vols. (London: HMSO, 1904), vol. I, p. 159.

[16] NAS, GD51/3/17/2, Diana Dalrymple to William Devaynes, 17 November 1785.

[17] Benjamin Stout, *Narrative of the Loss of the Ship Hercules*, edited by A. Porter (1798; revised edition, Port Elizabeth: Historical Society of Port Elizabeth, 1975), p. 14. For further details, see David Johnson, *Imagining the Cape Colony: History, Literature and the South African Nation* (Edinburgh: Edinburgh University Press, 2012), pp. 91–100.

Hope & the fertile Kingdom of Angola, where the Portuguese & French put in, & by this means the latter have escaped our Cruisers in War.[18]

Twenty years later, the picture was very different.

The approaches to India

Recently, scholars have shown a renewed interest in investigating the motivations behind the rise of British power in India.[19] Much academic ink has been spilled on debating whether India was as important to the British Empire as some would have us believe.[20] Nevertheless, for contemporaries, the route to India was a lifeline for the British Empire in such distressing times. If the views of Abbé Raynal are representative, then Britain could not afford to neglect this part of the world:

No event has been so interesting to mankind in general, and to the inhabitants of Europe in particular, as the discovery of the new world, and the passage to India by the Cape of Good Hope. It gave rise to a revolution in the commerce, and in the power of nations; and in the manners, industry, and government of the world in general.[21]

The commercial revenue produced by a successful navigation of the route was vital to the British economy. By 1780, India had become so much the subject of public attention that one political commentator asserted that 'almost every one' had 'a competent knowledge of the history, manners, and politics of that country'.[22] John Bruce's view, published in 1793, might be taken as representative: 'The importance to the government and revenues of the British possessions in Asia, will readily be admitted, if we consider the extent of the British provinces, the number of the inhabitants, or the actual amount of the revenues.'[23] The tonnage of ships employed by the East India Company that year was 81,000, requiring

---

[18] TNA, CO 267/9, Memorandum of Edward Thompson, 9 March 1785.
[19] See G. J. Bryant, *The Emergence of British Power in India, 1600–1784: A Grand Strategic Interpretation* (Woodbridge: Boydell & Brewer, 2013).
[20] For an excellent introduction to the historiographical debates, see Seema Alavi, 'Introduction', in Seema Alavi (ed.), *The Eighteenth Century in India* (New Delhi: Oxford University Press, 2002), pp. 1–56. See also David Washbrook, 'The Indian Economy and the British Empire', in Douglas M. Peers and Nandini Gooptu (eds.), *India and the British Empire* (Oxford: Oxford University Press, 2012), pp. 44–74.
[21] Quoted in Frost, *Global Reach of Empire*, p. 17.
[22] Anon., *Thoughts on Improving the Government of the British Territorial Possessions in the East Indies* (London: T. Cadell, 1780), pp. 49–50.
[23] John Bruce, *Historical Views of Plans, for the Government of British India and the Regulation of Trade to the East Indies* (London: [s.n.], 1793), pp. 272–3.

the service of 7,000 seamen.[24] Almost the entire amount of saltpetre used in the manufacture of gunpowder came from India.[25] British ministers started to write about India in the same terms that their predecessors used about America. In 1781, with the American War having become global as Britain faced France, Spain and the Netherlands in addition to its obstreperous colonists, Henry Dundas asked whether 'the stores and treasure of this country would be best bestowed there [India], or upon inland skirmishes in the woods of America'. For him, the answer was clear: India was 'our last resource'.[26] In 1787, he urged that 'the possessions in India' should be 'properly considered as they ought to be, as the brightest jewel in the British diadem'.[27] Over a decade later, he remained convinced of India's importance. The capture of the Cape of Good Hope was part of defending that ultimate objective. As he told the colony's governor, Lord Macartney, 'Your Lordship is fully possessed of my sentiments with respect to the importance of that settlement to the permanent and essential interests of this country in India.'[28] Meanwhile, in 1784, Lord Carmarthen had pondered whether 'perhaps the future existence of Great Britain as an independent, at any rate as a respectable power' lay in India.[29] And this was not just the view in Britain, as John Blankett told Lord Spencer, First Lord of the Admiralty, in 1798: 'From having been much abroad I know that foreigners look to the East as the source of our great wealth and power.'[30] The French certainly thought so, if a reported conversation between Lord Malmesbury and Monsieur de la Croix in 1797 is any guide. During the negotiations at Lille that year, Malmesbury is said to have 'strenuously insisted' on the Cape 'being ceded to the crown of England'.[31] De la Croix was implacably opposed. Apparently, the Frenchman 'vehemently exclaimed': 'Your Indian empire alone has enabled you to subsidise all the powers of Europe against us, & your monopoly of the Indian Trade has put you in possession of a fund of inexhaustible wealth.'[32]

Given its political and economic importance, threats to Britain's East India trade constantly sent shivers down the spines of merchants and

[24] Peter Ward, 'Admiral Peter Rainier and the command of the East Indies Station, 1794–1805', Ph.D. thesis, University of Exeter, 2010, p. 9.
[25] C. Northcote Parkinson, *Trade in the Eastern Seas* (Cambridge: Cambridge University Press, 1937), p. 78.
[26] Quoted in Marshall, *Remaking the British Atlantic*, p. 122.
[27] 7 March 1787, *Parliamentary Register* 22 (1787), p. 265, quoted *ibid.*, p. 125.
[28] UWits, A88/b47, Henry Dundas to Lord Macartney, 18 June 1798.
[29] Quoted in Marshall, *Remaking the British Atlantic*, p. 120.
[30] John Blankett to Lord Spencer, 3 July 1798, *Spencer*, vol. IV, p. 176.
[31] Stout, *Hercules*, p. 14.
[32] CRO, D LONS/L13/1/91, 'The Importance of the Cape of Good Hope Considered' (c.1815–16), pp. 45–6.

ministers alike, especially at times of war. Wherever these gateways were located, the crucial criterion for assessment was their relationship with India. An example of the way in which such threats to British possessions in the subcontinent, and the solution to militate against them, were represented can be found further north in the African continent. Egypt offers one of the best-known examples in the period of British troops operating beyond India as they defeated Napoleon's expeditionary force there in an effort to safeguard the subcontinent.[33] But the approaches to India, and Egypt in particular, had been of concern for many years before then. George Baldwin had tried in vain to awaken British commercial interest in the possibilities offered by Egypt.[34] At the request of the newly established Board of Control in London, he prepared a memorial on the resources and strategic situation of Egypt. Baldwin was a merchant and writer with significant experience in Egypt and was keen to point to its pivotal position and trading potential. A version of his memorial, written between 1773 and 1785, remarked that 'the importance of this situation to England [is] in subservience to her commercial and political correspondence with India'.[35] Baldwin's account may have acted as blueprint for others.[36] And in an indication of an increasingly global circulation of news and intelligence, even Macartney, at the Cape, received updates.[37] He was certainly alive to the threat, writing a three-page note on French ambitions towards Egypt.[38]

The importance of Ceylon also weighed heavily in British thinking.[39] It was even more sensitive in terms of its location, as a sort of geographical Achilles heel threatening the security of the Indian subcontinent. And, although he valued the Cape, William Pitt looked upon this island, 'of all the places upon the face of the globe', as 'the one which would add most to the security of our East-Indian possessions, and as placing our dominions in that quarter in a greater degree of safety than

---

[33] For further details, see Piers Mackesy, *The British Victory in Egypt, 1801: The End of Napoleon's Conquest* (Abingdon: Routledge, 1995).

[34] Rosemarie Said Zahlan, 'George Baldwin: Soldier of Fortune?', in Paul Starkey and Janet Starkey (eds.), *Travellers in Egypt* (London: I. B. Tauris, 1998), pp. 24–38.

[35] BL, Add. MS 38346, f. 248 [George Baldwin], 'Speculations on the Situation and Resources of Egypt (1773–1785)'. The memorial was published in 1801 in George Baldwin, *Political Recollections Relative to Egypt* (London: T. Cadell and W. Davies, 1801).

[36] See, for example, UWits, A88/b51, 'Memorandum on the Importance of Egypt to France', 20 April 1798.

[37] UWits, A88/b52, M. Faujas de St Fond to unknown recipient, 11 June 1798; A88/b47, Dundas to Macartney, 18 June 1798.

[38] UWits, A88/497 [Lord Macartney], 'Notes on French Ambitions of Conquering Egypt' [1798].

[39] See Colvin R. de Silva, *Ceylon under British Occupation, 1795–1833*, 2 vols. (Colombo: Colombo Apothecaries' Company, 1953–62), vol. I, pp. 17–20.

they had been in from the first hour that we set foot on the continent of India'.[40] Thomas Maitland, governor of Ceylon from 1805 to 1811, was convinced that the island (and particularly the harbour at Trincomalee) was 'the real key by possession of which alone you can hold the naval superiority of India'.[41] Lord Macartney reiterated these points in correspondence with Dundas, suggesting that both the Cape and Ceylon should be retained: 'If we should be able to keep both, the Indian World may long be our own; if not, our tenure will, I am afraid, be very insecure.'[42] But he was explicit in his opinions on Ceylon and its critical position:

If we give up Ceylon being situated at the extremity of the peninsula of India, it would become an immediate and terrific enemy to us in that quarter as commanding the power of invading from thence both the coasts of Malabar and Coromandel. To a maritime power the excellent harbour of Trincomalee is a jewel of inestimable value and holds the Bay of Bengal at its mercy and affords every facility of overawing and controlling the navigation of the straights of Sunda and Malacca. Our Asiatic commerce and marine will consequently lie open to the depredations of the masters of Ceylon.[43]

But Macartney was writing from the Cape, another linchpin in Britain's maritime empire.[44] And while he was prepared to admit that 'Ceylon should preponderate if put into the scale against the Cape', he cautioned Dundas not to forget that 'the Cape in an enemy's hands may become a powerful instrument for their recovering of Ceylon'.[45] Although the proximity of Egypt and Ceylon to India made them obvious points of concern, the maritime route provided the crucial arterial connection between Europe and the subcontinent, facilitating British trade with Asia and providing vital 'keys' to be defended, protected or acquired.

Contemporaries were eclectic in their use of the term 'the key to India' and, at any one time, there were a number of 'keys' scattered across the southern reaches of the Atlantic and Indian oceans.[46] There was no obvious single gateway to the East. Many places – from Buenos Aires

---

[40] Quoted in William Gordon Perrin (ed.), *The Naval Miscellany: Volume 3* (London: Naval Records Society, 1928), pp. 194–5.

[41] TNA, CO 54/22, Thomas Maitland to William Windham, 20 September 1806, cited in de Silva, *Ceylon under British Occupation*, vol. I, pp. 20–1.

[42] NAS, GD51/1/530/5, Macartney to Dundas, 9 March 1798.

[43] NAS, GD51/1/530/3, Macartney to Dundas, 4 February 1798.

[44] Contemporaries were aware of the historical connections between Ceylon and the southern Indian Ocean, and the Cape in particular. See RH, MSS.Afr.b.4.155; MSS.Afr. b.4.177, 'Letters from W. Huskisson to R. Dundas, wishing to know if his letters on the subject of trade between the Cape and Ceylon are being considered'.

[45] B'hurst, MS.063/6, Macartney to Dundas, 9 March 1798.

[46] For other 'keys' to India, see L. C. F. Turner, 'The Cape of Good Hope and the Anglo-French Conflict, 1797–1806', *Historical Studies. Australia and New Zealand* 9 (1961), pp.

and Rio de Janeiro in South America to Madagascar and the Seychelles in the Indian Ocean – had claims on the title. Three volcanic islets in the South Atlantic offered further potential for protecting trade and defending the entrance to Asian seas: St Helena, which had been in British hands since the 1650s, when the East India Company secured it as a safe port against the Dutch; Tristan da Cunha, a popular haven for American ships, which was eventually annexed in 1816 (ostensibly to prevent France from using it as a base to rescue Napoleon, incarcerated on nearby St Helena); and Ascension (uninhabited until 1815, when Napoleon landed at St Helena, 700 miles to the south-east). Other places – notably the Cape of Good Hope, Mauritius and the Comoro Islands, especially Nzwani (Anjouan) – were regarded as particularly valuable and important.[47] The Cape was, perhaps, one of the places most frequently designated as 'the key to Asia' or the 'Gibraltar of the Indian Ocean'.[48] With its bays, harbours and inlets – together with a potentially rich, fertile and productive hinterland – the Cape was so important to Britain's eastern trade and the securing of communications with India that it was captured twice and eventually retained at the end of the French Wars. Its attractions – fresh water and vegetables, as well as taverns, inns and brothels – drew in over 200 ships from all nations between July 1783 and May 1784, putting it on a par with many European ports at the time.[49] And, even though the present study focuses on locations south of the Equator, places such as Trincomalee, the Andamans, Penang and even the Chagos Archipelago were considered to be positions of strategic importance.[50] For much of the period, as we have seen, the French threat to British India also came via Middle East, as Edward Ingram's magisterial work has underlined, bypassing the southern maritime gateway entirely.[51] But, in the age of sailing ships

368–78, p. 371. For 'keys' to the Indian Ocean more generally, see Herbert Richmond, *The Navy in India, 1763–1783* (London: Ernest Benn, 1931), pp. 122–3.

[47] For more on the place of the Comoros in Britain's Indian Ocean world, see Edward A. Alpers, 'The Islands of Indian Ocean Africa', in Shawkat Toorawa (ed.), *The Western Indian Ocean: Essays on Islands and Islanders* (Port Louis: Hassam Toorawa Trust, 2007), pp. 1–19, p. 6.

[48] Gerald S. Graham, *Great Britain in the Indian Ocean: A Study of Maritime Enterprise, 1810–1850* (Oxford: Clarendon Press, 1967), p. 24. For a discussion of the term 'Gibraltar' in other oceanic contexts, see John Mack, *The Sea: A Cultural History* (London: Reaktion, 2013), p. 38.

[49] James R. Fichter, *So Great a Profitt: How the East Indies Trade Transformed Anglo-American Capitalism* (Cambridge, MA: Harvard University Press, 2010), p. 38.

[50] William A. Spray, 'British Surveys in the Chagos Archipelago and Attempts to form a Settlement at Diego Garcia in the Late Eighteenth Century', *Mariner's Mirror* 56 (1970), pp. 59–76, p. 59.

[51] See the following by Edward Ingram, *The Beginning of the Great Game in Asia, 1828–1834* (Oxford: Clarendon Press, 1979); *Commitment to Empire: Prophecies of the Great Game in Asia, 1797–1800* (Oxford: Clarendon Press, 1981); *In Defence of British India: Great*

and maritime empires, the domination and defence of sea routes played a vital role, as the leaders of the East India Company reminded the secretary of state in 1781: 'No fleet can possibly sail to, or return from, India without touching at some proper place for refreshment, and, in time of war, it must be equally necessary for protection.'[52] It is also worth recalling that these were seen as connected spaces; each individual part of the chain impinged upon the security of the others. As Lord Macartney put it, the Cape was 'as essential to Ceylon as Ceylon is to India'.[53]

By the conclusion of the Revolutionary and Napoleonic Wars, Britain had succeeded in neutralising some of this threat by creating its own connected space in the southern arc of the Atlantic and Indian oceans. By that stage, it had captured, or secured, bases at Ascension, Tristan da Cunha, St Helena, Cape Town and Simonstown in the South Atlantic, in addition to Trincomalee, Mauritius and Bombay in the Indian Ocean.[54] In short, Britain's seaborne prowess rested not only on its commercial fleet, its naval squadrons and their sailors, but on these numerous anchors of empire in prime locations. It is against this backdrop that this chapter assesses the gateway to India formed at the southern ends of the Atlantic Ocean, Indian Ocean and African continent. Even though the area had apparently few commercial or economic benefits to offer, there were other reasons why Britain might 'be willing to undertake an incumbrance of its garrison'.[55] The coastline of Southern Africa, and the surrounding islands and seas, became an arena of European power politics precisely because of its strategic position. It offered 'a vital link in a line of oceanic communication between East and the West', providing essential bases from which to control the commerce of three continents and three oceans.[56] The discussion that follows is concerned with these bases, or 'keys'. They were the agents that unlocked and energised connections; catalysts that changed the nature of this maritime space and Britain's relationship with it.

Britain in the Middle East, 1774–1842 (London: Cass, 1984); *Britain's Persian Connection, 1798–1828: Prelude to the Great Game in Asia* (Oxford: Clarendon Press, 1992).
[52] BL, IOR, H/154, p. 281, Laurence Sulivan and Sir William James to the Earl of Hillsborough, 25 October 1781.
[53] Quoted in CRO, D LONS/L13/1/91, 'Importance of the Cape', p. 33.
[54] Barry Gough, *The Falkland Islands/Malvinas: The Contest for Empire in the South Atlantic* (London: Athlone Press, 1992), p. 51.
[55] Foreign Office to Lord Clancarty, 30 July 1814, *RCC*, vol. X, p. 145.
[56] Mabel V. Jackson Haight, *European Powers and South-East Africa: A Study of International Relations on the South-Eastern Coast of Africa, 1796–1856* (London: Routledge & Kegan Paul, 1967), p. 16.

'Unfrequented parts'

The strong presence of other rivals in the region meant that, initially at least, much British attention focused on finding underdeveloped locations to support their shipping and sustain their Asian trade in the same way as the Cape and Ile de France did for the Dutch and the French respectively. If seas and oceans are not just 'conduits for the movement of ideas' but also spaces of 'imaginative projection' then the southern arc of the Atlantic and Indian oceans offered fertile spaces for such forays.[57] 'Fabulous' geographies have existed as long as Europeans have engaged with this oceanic region.[58] The area south of the Equator was, even in the late eighteenth century, still relatively underexplored. The instructions given to the captain of the *Swallow*, sent by the East India Company to inspect the south-west coast of Africa in 1782 in the hope of finding an alternative harbour to the Cape, made this clear. 'Every part of this unfrequented ocean you sail through', the Company's Secret Committee remarked, 'is so much knowledge gained.'[59] Geographical ambiguities held out the prospect of finding further locations that could answer Britain's maritime and strategic needs in the area. Identifying and developing places to refresh and revictual was absolutely vital and played a large part in defining the British engagement – from both a Crown and Company perspective – with the region. Many of these plans or projects presented to ministers or merchants were based more on an imaginative engagement – an indication of the fantasies that animated European travel and exploration there – than on reality. But advocates of such schemes were quick to point out the long-term value of such speculative endeavours. As John Call, dismissing any moral qualms, reminded Lord Sydney in 1785:

Upon these occasions it has often happened that the first projectors or undertakers have been deemed little better than madmen – or have acted in a character bordering on piracy. Notwithstanding this, it is to such reputed madmen, pirates and projectors that the European nations owe the establishment and trade of the East and West Indies; North and South America; and the western coast of Africa.[60]

[57] Kären Wigen, 'Introduction', in Jerry H. Bentley, Renate Bridenthal and Kären Wigen (eds.), *Seascapes: Maritime Histories, Littoral Cultures, and Transoceanic Exchanges* (Honolulu: University of Hawai'i Press, 2007), pp. 1–18, p. 1.

[58] Roxani Margariti, 'An Ocean of Islands: Islands, Insularity, and Historiography of the Indian Ocean', in Peter N. Miller (ed.), *The Sea: Thalassography and Historiography* (Ann Arbor, MI: University of Michigan Press, 2013), pp. 198–229, p. 200.

[59] TNA, CO 77/25, p. 124, 'Heads of Instructions given by the Secret Committee to the Captain of the Swallow', September 1783.

[60] TNA, HO 42/7, p. 49, Copy of a Paper left with Lord Sydney by Colonel [John] Call [c.1785].

An examination of some of these schemes further illuminates the sorts of attributes and facilities that any way station in the region was expected to fulfil.

One of the places identified as offering a potential British foothold in the gateway to India was the shadowy 'Pepys's island', vaguely located in the South Atlantic. The instructions to Captain John Byron, as he prepared to embark on a circumnavigation of the globe in the aftermath of the Seven Years War, cited the observations of previous seafarers as proof of its existence: 'There is reason to believe that Lands and islands of great extent hitherto unvisited by any European power may be found in the Atlantick Ocean between the Cape of Good Hope and the Magellanick Streight, within latitudes convenient for Navigation.'[61] The instructions proceeded to give Byron detailed directions. One of the possibilities was the prospect that he would discover 'land or islands in your passage from the Cape of Good Hope to Pepys's Island which have not already been discovered or taken notice of by former Navigators'.[62] Ships passing through the South Atlantic, Byron's instructions made clear, should be on the alert for prospective victualling stops in the area. This impulse to facilitate the burgeoning British trade with Asia became even more of an imperative following the War of American Independence.

This geography of possibilities relating to islands in the South Atlantic was set out by Alexander Dalrymple in 1782, as he provided information to the East India Company about the places 'where water and refreshment may be had between England and the Cape'.[63] As early as 1772, he had written to Lord North advocating an expedition to the South Atlantic. In asking for 'a grant of such lands, as are at present unoccupied by any European state, in the ocean south of the equator', Dalrymple demonstrated his firm belief that 'colonies formed in temperate climates' would be hugely beneficial for 'the prosperity of this kingdom'.[64] Dalrymple was hydrographer to the Company (and, from 1795, to the Admiralty as well), but his 1782 memorandum needs to be seen in the wider political context of the time. It came at a time of great upheaval in the balance of the British Empire. The thirteen mainland colonies of North America that had declared independence were on the cusp of

---

[61] Admiralty, Secret Instructions to Byron, 17 June 1764, in Robert E. Gallagher (ed.), *Byron's Journal of his Circumnavigation, 1764–1766* (Cambridge: Hakluyt Society, 1964), p. 3.

[62] *Ibid.*, p. 4.

[63] TNA, CO 77/25, p. 121 [Alexander Dalrymple], 'Memo communicated to the Chairman of the India Company', January 1782.

[64] Alexander Dalrymple to Lord North, 18 July 1772, quoted in Alexander Dalrymple, *A Collection of Voyages chiefly in the Southern Atlantick Ocean* (London: J. Nourse, 1775), pp. 2–3.

achieving it, and the war had also gone global with the Dutch and French in particular keen to capitalise on Britain's American difficulties. Added to this was the East India Company's trade with Asia, and its territorial interests in the Indian subcontinent, which had made a significant impact on British politics and society.[65] In this context, Dalrymple's memorandum might appear negligible. He described what was 'said to be a very large island which has a good harbor on the east side, with plenty of wood and water'. Located about 45 degrees South and 30 or 40 degrees West, this island promised much. The problem for Dalrymple, as well as for those looking for it, was that the only account Dalrymple had 'seen of it is Seinas's quotation of La Roche's voyage of 1675'. The island to which he alluded, 'Ascensão between Trinidada and Brazil', had garnered praise from the Portuguese regarding its plentiful supply of water. The only drawback seemed to be the difficulty of locating it, which, unsurprisingly, led 'some people [to] doubt the existence of the island'.[66] Nevertheless, by virtue of the victualling and navigational possibilities it offered, the island repaid attention:

This island is of the most essential consequence as its difference of latitude beyond the usual track in a passage to India will not exceed ten days sail and is therefore much less out of the way than Brazil, besides being so much further advanced on the voyage, which is a very great advantage.[67]

Dalrymple's would not be the last time that an extension to the British presence in the region was mooted.

In July 1783, Edward Thompson suggested to Lord Keppel that he should explore the south-west coast of Africa between 20 and 30 degrees South 'where there was a fertile country defended North from the Portuguese and south from the Dutch by the high, barren, inaccessible, mountains – & between these extremes there were fine harbours'. That at Cape Voltas would 'answer in point of Harbour, climate and fertile country'. Thompson proposed settling there 'for our Indiamen to call at & refit & come up with [the] SE Trade [wind] in war to avoid the enemy – without returning the beaten road from the Cape, & the necessity of putting into the Rio de Janeiro'. Apparently, Keppel and Portland had 'minutely attended' to Thompson's proposal but thought that 'in so infant a peace it would be dangerous to alarm our new friends by exploring' further. According to Thompson, 'they therefore proposed to postpone it until the succeeding year – when vessels should sail under my [Thompson's] direction'.[68]

---

[65] See Marshall, *Making and Unmaking of Empires*, pp. 1–56.
[66] TNA, CO 77/25, pp. 122, 121 [Dalrymple], 'Memo'.   [67] *Ibid.*, p. 122.
[68] BL, Add. MS 46120, f. 7, Diary entry, 31 July 1783.

Thompson revived the idea two years later, and wrote a wide-ranging discussion of the nation's position in the East which he mentioned to Charles Jenkinson on 20 February 1785. He then wrote up a proposal to settle the area with American Loyalists which he passed to Sydney on 21 March.[69] Yet again, he too was relying on the tales of previous travellers, notably those of Colonel de Prem who had commanded the Dutch garrison at the Cape.[70] If successful, the possibilities for supporting long-distance maritime trade were promising, as Thompson had previously confided to his diary (adding a helpful point of comparison with the French while doing so):

The partial account of those countries gives us a situation between Cape da Sierra and Cape Das Voltas – and the latter I believe from every account I can glean will answer in point of Harbour, climate and fertile country ... For the French have adopted a similar course and have ran [sic] along Africa to the Portuguese ports of St Philip de Banguela and St Paul de Loanda.[71]

Alexander Dalrymple had also suggested reconnoitring somewhere on the south-west coast of Africa.[72] He conceived that:

It would be of the utmost importance for one of the Company's packet vessels to make the course of the Southern Atlantic Ocean, to ascertain whether ships can water at Trinidada, Ascensão ... as well as to examine the islands that Tristan da Cunha & the W. Coast of Africa between the No[rth] extremity of the Dutch districts & the South extremity of the Portuguese territory on the coast of Angola. They should confine their observations to the unfrequented parts.[73]

On 25 May 1785, the Beauchamp Committee met to hear proposals for the establishment of a penal settlement. Two localities were suggested: the bay of Das Voltas and Botany Bay on the New South Wales coast. On the basis of Thompson's submissions, the committee plumped for the African option, which seemed to be the most practicable for the proposed penal settlement, as well as holding the desired strategic advantages. Thompson was chosen to undertake the task, eventually setting off in September 1785 on his mission. He was instructed 'to fix a settlement about Cape Voltas' which 'would answer every purpose to government and be a safe retreat for our East India ships on their return to refresh and to protect them from the enemy as the French have used Portuguese settlements in Angola'. But his mission was predicated on

[69] TNA, CO 267/9, Memorandum, 9 March 1785.
[70] Hugh Popham, *A Damned Cunning Fellow: The Eventful Life of Rear-Admiral Sir Home Popham KCB, KCH, KM, FRS, 1762–1820* (Tywardreath: Old Ferry Press, 1991), p. 18.
[71] BL, Add. MS 46120, f. 7, Diary entry, 31 July 1783.
[72] Frost, *Global Reach of Empire*, pp. 145–6.
[73] TNA, CO 77/25, p. 119 [Dalrymple], 'Memo'.

luck and chance. Nobody really knew whether or not such a place existed: 'These are but hints but may, if attended to, be made highly useful to the nation.'[74] Unfortunately for Thompson, his luck ran out before he could even cross the Equator: he 'caught a fever' at Appollonia on the coast of present-day Ghana and died on 17 January 1786.[75] The *Naval Chronicle* quoted the ship's surgeon's explanation for Thompson's 'distemper', blaming the 'stench' arising from 'a diversity of animals peculiar to Africa, and which the Commodore [Thompson] intended as presents on his return to Britain'.[76] The mission was continued by Lieutenants Thomas Boulden Thompson and Home Riggs Popham, although the penal settlement was never established.[77] Ten years later, in December 1795 with the Cape in British hands, the Royal Navy explored the south-western coast of Africa again. Captain Alexander in HMS *Star* was despatched to investigate the coast and report observations concerning soundings, the availability of shelter, wood, food and water, and 'to warn off all foreign ships from the whale fishery . . . and to use every means of conciliating the natives to our interests'.[78]

At the same time as Thompson's expedition was sailing in Atlantic waters, in the Indian Ocean precisely the kind of maritime exigencies that Dalrymple's and Thompson's schemes had been conceived to facilitate brought another area of the region to the attention of British travellers. On 12 February 1785, the *Pigot* set sail from Madras. Three months later, the homeward-bound Indiaman anchored at the mouth of the Krom River, near the site of the present-day town of Cape St Francis and some 500 miles east of the Cape of Good Hope.[79] Fed by locals for a month, the surviving passengers had the opportunity to survey their surroundings. They were pleasantly surprised, finding the area to be a fertile one with abundant crops:

The country [has] a most luxuriant soil with regular hills and dales containing the most beautiful sheep walks which extend many miles up the country and only want the hand of the ploughman and gardener to produce everything that grows in Europe, or indeed in the world. It . . . abounds with all kinds of cattle and game,

[74] TNA, CO 267/9, Edward Thompson to [Sydney?], 15 February 1785.
[75] Jill Kinahan, 'The Impenetrable Shield: HMS *Nautilus* and the Namib Coast in the Eighteenth Century', *Cimbebasia: Journal of the State Museum, Windhoek* 13 (1990), pp. 23–67, p. 24.
[76] Quoted in Popham, *Damned Cunning Fellow*, pp. 18–19.
[77] Kinahan, 'Impenetrable Shield', p. 24.
[78] TNA, CO 49/1, Blankett to Dundas, 23 December 1795. For further details, see Jill Kinahan, *By Command of Their Lordships: The Exploration of the Namibian Coast by the Royal Navy, 1795–1895* (Windhoek: Namibia Archaeological Trust, 1992), p. 27.
[79] For confirmation of this story, see UWits, A88/9, Lord Macartney's diary entry for 18 October 1785.

the largest and fattest sheep and oxen we ever saw, and in the greatest number besides. Deer, goats and hogs, excellent horses of a small kind and tractable, all kinds of grain, excellent wheat and barley, European and tropical fruits and vegetables, potatoes, cabbages etc. etc. with milk, butter, fowls etc. all equal in their several kinds to the best in Europe. The climate as mild as the south of France, neither experiencing extreme heat or cold and productive of the choicest wines.[80]

Lieutenant Henry Pemberton was one of the travellers, and he decided to share this information with Henry Dundas and other influential people in London. Pemberton observed that 'as the principal connection of Great Britain now centers in the great the extensive and opulent country of India that a port on the South East Coast of Africa would be of the utmost benefit to this nation in general and to the Honourable the East India Company in particular'.[81] And he listed the various reasons that would make 'the possession of a port on this coast' an 'object of national importance'. Ultimately, he asked his readers to reflect on 'the intimate connection of Great Britain, both political and commercial, now with India and that from the Channel to the coasts of Malabar and Coromandel the English don't possess a single port capable of affording shelter and protection or refreshment to their ships'.[82] A port on this coast would be extremely useful for a whole variety of reasons: ships and men could refresh there; a protected harbour would offer shelter; forces stationed there might swiftly attack the Cape of Good Hope or Ile de France; felons could be used to establish the settlement as the indigenous people who inhabited the borderlands would discourage escape.[83]

William Dalrymple was also aboard the *Pigot*, returning home from India because of ill health. He was now a colonel, in the 73rd Regiment, but he had been at the Cape before. On this occasion, he travelled 550 miles 'purposely to acquire military knowledge of the country and the disposition of the inhabitants in case of our going again to war with the Dutch'.[84] While there, he had 'premeditated in his mind in case of war a plan of attack'. His perambulations 'to the eastward of the Cape' allowed him to 'observe the harbours, examine the passes through the mountains, and the rivers which divide the provinces with a military eye, and from speaking the French and the Dutch language become intimately acquainted with many of the inhabitants and know their disposition

[80] BL, IOR, G/9/1, p. 20, Henry Pemberton, 'A Narrative with a Description and Drawing of Croem or Crontz Riviere Bay situate on the South East Coast of Africa' [1785].
[81] *Ibid.*, p. 21.   [82] *Ibid.*, p. 23.
[83] For more on this last aspect, see Emma Christopher, *A Merciless Place: The Fate of Britain's Convicts after the American Revolution* (Oxford: Oxford University Press, 2010), pp. 315–16.
[84] TNA, PRO 30/8/128, p. 76, William Dalrymple to William Pitt, 4 October 1787.

towards England and France'.[85] From the eastern Cape, Dalrymple travelled overland to Cape Town and asked his wife to pass on reports to Henry Dundas, William Pitt, the Prime Minister, and William Devaynes, Chairman of the East India Company. Dalrymple was firmly of the belief that 'a settlement on the Caffre Coast wou'd be of the most important consequences to Britain and the India Company'. Diana Dalrymple subsequently sent memorials to each man which described the climate of the area as wonderfully healthy, with fertile soil, and abundant game and fish. The region 'abounds with cattle, sheep and goats':

The country produces in their spring all European fruits, veg[etables] and wheat and in the summer the fruits of the torrid zone, Indian corn and grapes of which they make exquisite wine. The climate and country is perhaps the paradise of the universe. The looks of the peasantry manifest it as the progeny of the Dutch and German settlers are an even more beautiful race of people than the English.[86]

Importantly, Dalrymple's plan contained a comparative element, considering a prospective British settlement on the south-eastern coast of Africa in relation to the British presence elsewhere in the region. Perhaps unsurprisingly, other places came up short. He pointed, for example, to St Helena's vulnerability:

We should in a few years derive every advantage from a settlement here, that the Dutch have from the Cape; and in time of war and returning home would refresh here; with this additional advantage that the French would not be so likely to capture our ships as they could not know whether they would touch at St Helena or at the settlement I propose.[87]

Dalrymple summarised other potential calling points along this maritime arc to the East Indies: 'in going out [to India] our ships generally touch at the island [of] Johanna in the Mosambique Channel for refreshment'. But, as the climate there was rather unhealthy and ships had to 'run close by this shore, it would be much more to our interest to touch at a port of our own'. The inlet where the *Pigot* found itself offered 'the finest climate I believe in the universe, and where all kinds of refreshments may be had, besides the advantage of dividing the voyage more equally as the run outward bound is too far to Johanna'. He suggested an expedition:

In this plan I clearly foresee the greatest advantage to my country, and to be the founder of this colony is my ambition. We have lost America, and a half way house would secure us India, and Empire to Britain. We are at a loss where to send our

[85] TNA, PRO 30/8/128, p. 78, William Dalrymple memorandum [c.1787].
[86] *Ibid.*, p. 79.
[87] NAS, GD 51/3/17/2, Diana Dalrymple to Devaynes, 17 November 1785.

convicts. To send them to this country would indeed be a paradise to them, and settlers would croud here. It is the finest soil I ever saw, with a divine climate.[88]

In order to facilitate his plan, Dalrymple offered to raise a regiment consisting of 200 Irish soldiers in six months, something he had done in 'the late war'. Dalrymple was firmly of the opinion that acquisition of ports 'would add permanency to our empire in India as 'tis the key to it':

By having several ports, our fleets of Indiamen could refresh there, in their way out to India and on their return home, [they] would in time of war avoid the French cruisers. Whereas by having St Helena as our only port, the French from cruising in the latitude of it in time of war are certain of falling in with the Indiamen homeward bound and who are obliged to refresh there.[89]

William Devaynes seemed to be swayed by Dalrymple's arguments, telling Pitt and Dundas that he thought the idea 'of very material importance' for such a settlement might be of the 'greatest utility to us and prejudice to our enemies'.[90] As such a settlement might 'answer in some respects the purposes of the Cape' and 'serve also as a receptacle for convicts', it was worth considering in more depth. Pitt asked Devaynes to send the plan to Grenville and Howe for their consideration.[91] Although nothing came of it in this instance, British eyes would soon train a much more sustained gaze on Southern Africa with the capture of the Cape in 1795. Even then, however, schemes for prospective settlement in the uncharted east of the colony were under consideration by some during the short first British occupation.

Benjamin Stout was the captain of an American ship, the *Hercules*, which had apparently been shipwrecked on the coast of the Eastern Cape in 1796.[92] He lauded the landscape in familiar terms:

This country, which skirts the Eastern coast, for many hundred miles, and stretches into the interior to a considerable extent, abounds in timber of the best quality; possesses many fine harbours; is blessed with the richest pasturage that feeds innumerable herds of the finest cattle; the lands during the season are carpeted with flowers that perfume the surrounding atmosphere, and their shores are frequented by fish of every quality and description.[93]

[88] *Ibid.*   [89] TNA, PRO 30/8/128, p. 76, William Dalrymple to Pitt, 4 October 1787.
[90] NAS, GD 51/3/17/1, Devaynes [to Dundas], 17 September 1785.
[91] Pitt to William Grenville, 2 October 1785, in *Report on the Manuscripts of J. B. Fortescue, Esq., preserved at Dropmore, Historical Manuscripts Commission*, 10 vols. (London: HMSO, 1892–1927), vol. I, p. 257.
[92] Much controversy surrounds Stout's identity, his loyalties, and even whether or not a ship called the *Hercules* was wrecked off the coast of Africa at this time. Some authorities, notably E. C. Tabler, believed that Stout's book was 'propaganda aimed at ensuring that the British keep the Cape of Good Hope and extend the settled area as a safety and commercial measure'. See E. C. Tabler, 'Loss of the Ship *Hercules*', *Africana Notes and News* 17 (1966), p. 88.
[93] Stout, *Hercules*, p. 12.

And, somewhat fancifully, he enumerated the products, from grapes and tobacco to sugar cane and spices that could be cultivated here. Despite the fact that he was – ostensibly at least – an American advocating an American settlement here to John Adams, Stout made some grand claims for this 'half-way house': he recognised that it could 'ultimately prove of more value to the British Empire, *than all their settlements in the East and West Indies put together*'. And it could 'remain for centuries the most valuable possession of the Crown of England'.[94]

Lady Anne Barnard, who resided at the Cape during the first British occupation, reported Captain William White's account of his visit to Delagoa Bay, in what is southern Mozambique today. White was just the latest in a long line of European travellers and merchants who had eyed this bay with commercial intent. Although the Dutch and the Portuguese held nominal sway in the region, it had long attracted British interest too.[95] In 1683, when the English ship *Johanna* was wrecked near the bay, the survivors discovered that they could procure all their requirements nearby and carry on a lucrative trade with the local Ronga people.[96] Encouraged by this success, as many as five English vessels visited the bay per year during the 1680s.[97] Various sorties to the region were attempted in the first half of the eighteenth century.[98] And, by 1757, British merchants were making regular voyages from India to procure ivory.[99] At any one time, there could be up to twelve British boats gathering and purchasing ivory along the coast.[100] But this trade, and the British involvement in the region, was on a much smaller scale than the one advocated by William White. White, an officer in the 73rd Regiment, published his account in London in 1800.[101] Captain White, Lady Anne recounted, 'thinks that there might be a very good settlement formed here [Delagoa Bay] as there is a fine harbour and the river called English river is broad and navigable for some miles up'. He thought that ships laden with a host of what Europeans would regard as trinkets of little

[94] *Ibid.*, pp. 15, 18 (emphasis in original).
[95] For an overview, see Colin Coetzee, 'Die Stryd om Delagoabaai en die suidooskus, 1600–1800', Ph.D. thesis, University of Stellenbosch, 1954.
[96] See Alexander Hamilton, *A New Account of the East Indies: Giving an Exact and Copious Description of the Situation*, 2 vols. (1727; London: C. Hitch and A. Millar, 1744), vol. I, pp. 5–7.
[97] Alan Kent Smith, 'The struggle for control of southern Mozambique, 1720–1835', Ph. D. thesis, UCLA, 1970, p. 39.
[98] *Ibid.*, pp. 43–4, 58–62.
[99] BL, IOR, P/341/48, pp. 561–2, Bombay Public Consultations, 1781.
[100] Smith, 'Struggle for Control of Southern Mozambique', pp. 162–3.
[101] William White, *Journal of a Voyage performed in the Lion Extra Indiaman, from Madras to Columbo, and Da Lagoa Bay, on the Eastern Coast of Africa* (London: John Stockdale, 1800).

value 'might be victual'd completely for a trifle'.[102] Indeed, a few years later, Thomas Ramsden, master of the *Perseverance*, saw similar potential for 'British subjects of a highly beneficial trade with a country, fertile and abounding in products, which the wants and luxuries of mankind have made to be regarded as great riches ... watered by many rivers, one of which is nearly as broad as the Thames and is navigable for boats several hundred miles into the interior'.[103] In addition to these benefits, William White described the climate as 'healthy' and the country as 'a fine one rising gently from the sea till the distant mountains are lost in the clouds'. The local ruler, 'Capelas', would, according to White:

cheerfully grant a territory for 600 settlers for a cask or two of rum annually, and he [White] is apt to think it would be an excellent place if the war continues with France for our ships cruising off the Mauritius to put in at and refresh themselves, instead of going 230 leagues round to the Cape with the chance of danger and detention from foul winds.[104]

This mention of the war is a reminder of the ever-present clouds of conflict, real or threatened, that hung over every British plan for settlement in the region. 'Should it ever be in contemplation to attack the Ile de France', William White 'supposes this might be a most excellent rendezvous for the fleet'.[105] This gnawing fear of the French, amplified in Lady Anne's accounts by virtue of her presence in Africa, will be discussed further in Chapter 3. But the seas and coastlines of the region also supported a number of long-established settlements and it is with those places, and the British perceptions of their strategic importance in consolidating the gateway to the East, that the remainder of this chapter is concerned.

The Cape of Good Hope

In November 1794, Sir John Dalrymple, one of the minor literati of the Edinburgh circuit, wrote to Henry Dundas in London. The opening shots of the war with Revolutionary France had left Britain in a febrile state and its politicians unnerved by a combination of French military successes in continental Europe and the possibility of domestic unrest.[106]

---

[102] *Journals*, pp. 417–18.
[103] AHU, CU, Moç. CX150/96, 'Transcription of an Account by Thomas Ramsden, Master of the *Perseverance*, given to Francis Warden, of the occurrences in the Bay of Delagoa, 17 May 1816'. Ramsden's list of products included 'ivory, gold, ambergris, cotton, tobacco, sandalwood, gums, hides and skins'.
[104] *Journals*, pp. 418–19.   [105] *Ibid.*, p. 419.
[106] Roger Knight, *Britain against Napoleon: The Organisation of Victory, 1793–1815* (London: Penguin, 2014), pp. 61–2.

As Dalrymple was quick to point out, both the British government and the general public needed something positive to sustain them in this time of trouble. Dalrymple saw himself as the person to provide 'grand ideas', and he had already conceived of a plan to 'bring off the French fleet from Toulon'.[107] But now his attention turned to the Indian Ocean world and the ways in which Britain could gain a strategic and military advantage over their French adversaries there. Dalrymple's plan revolved around the British response to the French triumph in the Netherlands. He advised Dundas:

> The moment when that happens you ought to be prepared to seize the Cape of Good Hope either by a small fleet from England or by an attack from India which last perhaps be best because the run on the trade wind is shortest. The pretence and the just pretence may be that you hold it for Holland against the usurped power of France in Holland.

Dalrymple was returning to, what was for him, an old theme: 'In the last Dutch war I presumed to advise Lord George Germain to attack the Cape of Good Hope.' But, according to Dalrymple, 'others thwarted me saying that the place was very strong'. Now he revisited the idea emboldened with the evidence garnered by his brother, Colonel William Dalrymple.[108] On his way to India, the younger Dalrymple had been instructed by Sir John 'to examine the state of things' and assess whether or not the Cape was as well defended as some people made out. With his 'very sharp eye', the evidence gathered by William was conclusive, or at least conclusive enough for his brother to present his scheme to Dundas: 'He was twice there and said it was quite weak.' For Dalrymple, the benefits of pursuing such a policy were self-evident: 'If we get possession of the Cape, India is safe from attack from Europe, and Bourbon and Mauritius are open to attack from the Cape as well as from India.'[109] Dalrymple's views about the Cape, his plan to capture it and his assessment of its value to Britain's burgeoning Indian Ocean empire were not unique. The Cape of Good Hope, which had been a Dutch possession since 1652, and the adjacent coastline of Southern Africa, came to be regarded as one of the most crucial places along the route to India. Dundas did not need to be convinced: by the time Dalrymple had sent his letter British ministers were preparing to seize the 'frontier fortress of India'.[110]

---

[107] The following account is based on NAS, GD51/1/486, Sir John Dalrymple to Dundas, 30 November [1794].
[108] For more on William Dalrymple, see pp. 53–5 above.
[109] NAS, GD51/1/486, Sir John Dalrymple to Dundas, 30 November [1794].
[110] Turner, 'Cape of Good Hope and the Anglo-French Conflict', p. 369.

The Cape of Good Hope had been part of the East India Company's wider strategic vision as early as 1613, when the directors seriously considered setting up a half-way station to India at Saldanha Bay.[111] And, at the end of the seventeenth century, the 'Company of Scotland trading to Africa and the Indies', best known for its catastrophic schemes to colonise Darien on the isthmus of Panama, pondered the value of a base near the Cape that would serve, like St Helena for the English, as a Scottish entrepôt between East and West.[112] However, the Dutch became the first Europeans to establish a permanent base in Southern Africa, when Jan van Riebeeck set up a small colony in 1652. It was intended to be a victualling station for passing East Indiamen. The Dutch East India Company (Vereenigde Oost-Indische Compagnie, or VOC) had used the Cape since the seventeenth century, and it became a crucial link in their Asian operations. But they never regarded it as commercially viable; according to Captain John Blankett, 'the Dutch never considered the Cape in a commercial view, but merely as a place of refreshment for the carrying on their commerce to India, & on this principle formed all their Colony arrangements'.[113] Horatio Nelson concurred. One of the Royal Navy's most esteemed commanders told the House of Lords that he considered it as 'merely a tavern on the passage, which served to call at, and thence often to delay the voyage'.[114] Even for a commercial concern such as the British East India Company, the potential acquisition of the Cape from the Dutch was, at its most basic, a strategic objective. Most people agreed that the colony would never be economically advantageous.

For nearly two centuries this arrangement worked to everybody's advantage and mutual satisfaction, with the Dutch colony supporting and supplying the East Indiamen of a number of European countries. Jacques-Henri Bernardin de Saint Pierre, a French author and botanist returning from the Ile de France, remarked that the major European powers generally 'maintained a good understanding in these roads, when discord has reigned in every place else throughout the two hemispheres'.[115] Perhaps one of the clearest indications of the nature

[111] Marcus Arkin, 'John Company at the Cape: A History of the Agency under Pringle (1794–1815)', Archives Year Book for South African History 1960 (Pretoria: Government Printer, 1961), pp. 177–344, p. 189.
[112] Philip J. Stern, The Company-State: Corporate Sovereignty and the Early Modern Foundations of the British Empire in India (Oxford: Oxford University Press, 2011), p. 159.
[113] TNA, WO 1/329, p. 44, Blankett to Evan Nepean, 25 January 1795.
[114] House of Lords Debate on the Preliminaries of Peace with France, 3 November 1801, in Parliamentary History, vol. 36, p. 185.
[115] Jacques-Henri Bernardin de Saint Pierre, A Voyage to the Island of Mauritius (or, Isle of France) the Isle of Bourbon, the Cape of Good Hope (London: W. Griffin, 1775), pp. 211–12.

of Britain's strategic interest in the region was its willingness to give up hard-won gains on the Indian subcontinent following the Fourth Anglo-Dutch War (part of the expanded War of American Independence), in exchange for access to the incomparable refreshment, repair and revictualling possibilities offered by the Cape of Good Hope, the fulcrum of the southern oceans' wind and current systems. The colony's bays provided anchorage for most of the year. And, while the docks at Simon's Bay were not extensive enough to permit either careening or rebuilding, they were adequate to the making of other repairs. Cape Town's fortifications were sound, while the climate of the colony was healthy and its agriculture abundant. In return for handing back Negapatam on the south-east coast of India to the Dutch, Britain wanted the guarantee – at least – of free access to Trincomalee and the Cape.[116] British ministers continued to push this agenda throughout the 1780s. At the end of 1787, Constantine John Phipps, Lord Mulgrave, drafted a treaty of 'Defensive Alliance and Mutual Guarantee of Territories and Commerce at the Cape of Good Hope, and in the East Indies' to propose to Holland.[117] Despite the fact that it was never signed, the proposal highlights the importance of the Cape to British strategic thinking in the period. The objective of this document was, Mulgrave observed, to maintain 'the general tranquillity of Europe', but most especially 'that of the European settlements in the East Indies'.[118] The treaty provided for this by uniting the interests of Britain and Holland, and confirming 'their reciprocal security by a treaty of defensive alliance and mutual guarantee for all their possessions at the Cape of Good Hope and in the East Indies'.[119] Specifically in relation to the Cape of Good Hope, and in case of war, Britain was 'to have the use of the Cape exclusively for men of war', and the Dutch were not permitted to help or supply Britain's enemies. Indeed, the treaty even went so far as to allow Britain to establish 'an Hospital for seamen and soldiers' there, as well as a magazine for naval stores.[120] It looked like an ideal solution: Britain avoided the cost of the colony's upkeep but enjoyed all the benefits of access. Everything was set fair. Until, that is, Britain and the Netherlands found themselves on opposing sides of a particularly belligerent European argument.

---

[116] See Frost, *Global Reach of Empire*, pp. 143, 141.
[117] G. S. Misra, *British Foreign Policy and Indian Affairs, 1783–1815* (London: Asia Publishing House, 1963), p. 19.
[118] TNA, PRO 30/8/360, pp. 199–212, p. 199, Lord Mulgrave, 'Sketch of the Heads of a Treaty of Defensive Alliance and Mutual Guarantee of Territories and Commerce at the Cape of Good Hope, and in the East Indies to propose to Holland' [undated].
[119] *Ibid.*, pp. 202.   [120] *Ibid.*, pp. 207–9.

By the end of the eighteenth century, conflict with European rivals forced the British East India Company to reconsider the strategic value of the region to the protection of its trade and to contemplate the possibility of taking it outright. This had already been evident during the Fourth Anglo-Dutch War. In September 1780, on his way to take up his command in India, Sir Edward Hughes submitted plans to Lord Weymouth, the Secretary of State responsible for Indian affairs, for the capture of the Cape, which precipitated the abortive expedition led by Commodore George Johnstone.[121] Henry Rooke, a major in the 100th Regiment of Foot, witnessed this ignominious failure. Rooke was unforgiving in his assessment of what he described ironically as 'our famous expedition, from which so much was expected'. He observed that the attempt 'tamely terminated in the capture of some Dutch Indiamen that we surprised in Saldanha Bay', and he attributed this to the fact that 'we had been expected at the Cape for some time'.[122] Like many contemporaries, Rooke worried about the impact of allowing the Cape to remain in Dutch hands. Because of the frequency with which 'our Indiamen generally touch there for refreshment', the Cape 'would have been a most desirable acquisition to us, and I fear we shall have great reason to regret the failure of this expedition during our war with the Dutch'.[123]

Notwithstanding this failure, another plan was soon mooted. Writing in October 1781, the Chairman and Deputy Chairman of the Company urged Lord Hillsborough to mount a British military assault on the region to secure it against rivals. Laurence Sulivan and Sir William James set out in clear terms the value that they ascribed to it: 'That the power possessing the Cape of Good Hope has the Key to and from the East Indies, appears to us self-evident and unquestionable. Indeed one must consider the Cape of Good Hope as the Gibraltar of India.' For them, the Cape was 'a place of consequence and resource, and of such importance to the preservation and welfare of India'.[124] Henry Pemberton was familiar with the southern coast of Africa from his time at 'Croem Riviere Bay'. But his account also included a sketch map of Table Bay, further highlighting places where 'you may get all sorts of refreshments' as well as giving more detailed technical information about the swells, surf and

---

[121] L. C. F. Turner, 'The Cape of Good Hope and Anglo-French Rivalry, 1778–1796', *Australian Historical Studies* 12 (1966), pp. 166–85, pp. 168–72.
[122] Henry Rooke, *Travels to the Coast of Arabia Felix ... containing a Short Account of an Expedition undertaken against the Cape of Good Hope* (London: R. Blamire, 1783), p. 17. For another account of the raid, see Silas James, *Narrative of a Voyage to Arabia, India etc. containing ... A Description of Saldanha Bay* (London: The Author, 1797).
[123] Rooke, *Travels to the Coast of Arabia Felix*, p. 19.
[124] BL, IOR, H/154, pp. 279–80, Sulivan and James to Hillsborough, 25 October 1781.

depth of the water.[125] And his reflections led him to put things in a broader context:

From its proximity to India it may be concluded that whatever European nation uninterruptedly possesses the Cape of Good Hope and its dependencies together with the many excellent bays and harbours on the most extensive coast, this most fruitful and healthful country, this nursery of men as hardy and as robust as the European, cannot fail in time to become masters of all India.[126]

The same concerns surfaced just over a decade later.

In 1793, Henry Dundas tried to persuade Lord Grenville of the value of fighting a war at sea and on the fringes of empire: 'The preservation of the Cape of Good Hope is an object of so much importance, both to Holland and Great Britain, [that] it is impossible for this country to view with indifference any circumstance that can endanger the safety of that settlement.'[127] These fears were not groundless: an official report issued in Paris in January 1793 recommended that a French force should be sent to secure the Cape, Java and Ceylon.[128] To Dundas, the Cape was the linchpin in a comprehensive strategy to obtain two great objectives of the war: 'termination of the anarchy in France' and 'the safety of Holland'.[129] Although he needed little convincing of its importance, Sir Francis Baring, one of the directors of the East India Company, wrote to Dundas drawing on many of the same arguments used by his predecessors, Sulivan and James, a decade earlier. Even employing similar forms of language, Baring also advocated an attack on the Dutch outpost:

The importance of the Cape is in my opinion comprised under two heads – as a place of refreshment for our ships on their return from India, as St Helena is unequal to the supply, and we should be much distrest for a substitute if the Cape is lost to us. Secondly, whoever is Master of the Cape will be able to protect, or annoy, our ships out and home, serving at the same time as an effectual check upon Mauritius.[130]

He recognised the importance of the Cape as consisting 'more from the detriment which would result to us if it was in the hands of France, than from any advantage we can possibly derive from it as a colony'. Baring reminded Dundas:

It commands the passage to and from India as effectually as Gibraltar doth the Mediterranean; and it serves as a granary for the isles of France; whilst it furnishes

---

[125] BL, IOR, G/9/1, p. 27, Pemberton, 'Narrative'.   [126] *Ibid.*, p. 23.
[127] Dundas to Lord Grenville, 23 April 1793, *RCC*, vol. I, pp. 10–11.
[128] J. Holland Rose, *The Life of William Pitt. Volume 2: William Pitt and the Great War* (London: G. Bell, 1934), p. 250.
[129] Frost, *Global Reach of Empire*, p. 252.
[130] Sir Francis Baring to Dundas, 4 January 1795, *RCC*, vol. I, p. 17.

no produce whatsoever for Europe & the expence of supporting the place must be considerable.[131]

In the same month, one Isaac Byers, from Bideford in Devon, took it upon himself to write to William Pitt to argue for the capture of the Cape. He spoke from personal experience, having 'been at the Cape of Good Hope, Batavia and some other Dutch settlements in India and served several years on the Company's military establishment in India' before 'ill health obliged me to return with my family to my native country'. He regarded the Cape as 'a place affording every refreshment requisite on a long voyage' with 'two fine bays', and which 'would be of especial service to all British ships going to or coming from India'.[132]

Throughout the 1790s, the naval officer John Blankett reported regularly to a number of Cabinet members on the route to the East, and the best way to preserve it.[133] He was much enamoured of the Cape, finding it 'in general very fertile'.[134] Blankett championed the commercial prospects offered by the Cape:

Considered as an entrepôt, the situation of this colony is very favourable to an expansive commerce. America and Africa might be furnished from thence with all the produce of India and China and many parts of Europe and Asia could find a rent and return for many of their productions without being subject to the risque and expence of a longer Navigation.[135]

Yet even he recognised that it was a point of great strategic importance, and needed to be viewed in such a light. It had to be considered on two levels: 'first how it would suit us and then how it would annoy us in other hands'.[136] From a British perspective, and given Napoleon's designs on India, a Dutch state weakened by war at home and dispersed colonial commitments abroad could not be judged as capable of holding it. Ultimately, Blankett's views of the Cape were shaped by the consideration that, as he put it, 'what was a feather in the hands of Holland, will become a sword in the hands of France'.[137] John Bruce, in his 'Sketches of the Political and Commercial History of the Cape of Good Hope', was of the same opinion. According to Bruce, the Cape had the potential to compensate for the loss of the mainland American colonies: 'the situation of the Cape, relative to the West Indies, would, if the country was properly

---

[131] *Ibid.*, p. 22.
[132] TNA, PRO 30/8/118, pp. 208, 206, Isaac Byers to Pitt, 31 January 1795.
[133] See, for example, Blankett's letters to Chatham (TNA, PRO 30/8/365, pp. 215–26) and Hawkesbury (BL, Add. MS 38226, ff. 105–17).
[134] BL, Add. MS 38226, f. 112, Blankett to Lord Hawkesbury, 25 February 1790.
[135] *Ibid.*   [136] TNA, WO 1/329, p. 47, Blankett to Nepean, 25 January 1795.
[137] *Ibid.*, p. 48.

cultivated, enable it to supply our islands with provision of the same kind which they now draw from the United States of America'. And, looking east, Bruce remarked on the colony's strategic importance: 'The Cape, in the hands of the English, would become equally a check upon the French and the Dutch, the only Nations likely to disturb the peace of India.'[138] It was, for Bruce, 'invaluable in the hands of a maritime power, and is really and truly the key to India, for no hostile fleet can pass or repass'.[139] The value of the Cape as a positive boon in British hands – offering sustenance and security to passing British shipping, and simultaneously forestalling the build-up of any French interests in the Indian Ocean – pervaded British opinion about the region. The need to prevent Revolutionary France from acquiring the Cape as a base from which to attack British interests in India eventually forced the point and led to its capture in 1795, when it was taken from the Dutch.[140] Following the signing of the Treaty of Amiens in 1802, it was handed over to the Batavian Republic. But renewed threat from Napoleon's France led to the retaking of the Cape in 1806, and it remained in British hands for over a century. It became part, therefore, of the worldwide web of British imperial possessions and interests that dominated the nineteenth-century world.

After the capture of the Cape in 1795, its stock as a strategic hub remained high. Its value in the early stages of the war was highly regarded in London. Lord Spencer, the First Lord of the Admiralty, congratulated Elphinstone 'on the very valuable acquisition' of the Cape, which, 'if proper use is made of it will prove I am convinced one of the most advantageous we ever made'.[141] Dundas wrote to Spencer reaffirming his conviction: 'My mind is long and invariably made up to the conviction that the Cape of Good Hope is in truth and *literally* so the key to the Indian and China commerce.'[142] Although Spencer was less enthusiastic than his cabinet colleague, he too recognised its value. He wrote to Elphinstone acknowledging that its anchorages were open to the winds

[138] KCL, DT2042, John Bruce, 'Sketches of the Political and Commercial History of the Cape of Good Hope' (1796), pp. 316–17, 350. For more confirmation of Bruce as the author of these 'sketches', see the copy in the Macartney Papers in the Brenthurst Library, Johannesburg, which is inscribed on fly-leaf, 'For the Right Honourable Lord Macartney, by John Bruce, India Office, Whitehall, 17 December 1796'.
[139] B'hurst, MS.060, John Bruce, 'Plans for the Government and Trade of the Cape of Good Hope', p. 245.
[140] BL, IOR, H/738, pp. 1–15, Sir John Malcolm, 'Account of the Cape of Good Hope in 1795'. See also Maurice Boucher and Nigel Penn (eds.), *Britain at the Cape, 1795 to 1803* (Johannesburg: Brenthurst Press, 1992); Hermann Giliomee, *Die Kaap Tydens die Eerste Britse Bewind, 1795–1803* (Cape Town: HAUM, 1975).
[141] BL, Add. MS. 75856, f. 275, Spencer to George Keith Elphinstone, 29 December 1795.
[142] Dundas to Spencer, 5 November 1797, *Spencer*, vol. II, p. 215.

and there was nowhere to repair stricken vessels, but remarking that it was the only convenient port between Brazil and the East Indies. And, moreover, it was absolutely crucial in the war against France:

> The Cape is a situation of so much importance that a very respectable naval force should always make its Head Quarters, and as the French have sent some strong frigates to the Mauritius, we have also sent out some of our best frigates for their annoyance, and the protection of our trade.[143]

It was able to provide all kinds of food and water and act as a hospital for the recuperation of sickness, especially scurvy, on the long journey eastwards.[144] John Malcolm assessed the value of the colony:

> The Cape, while we retain such a communication as we have at present with India, must be of great value to us for two reasons. In the first place, it furnishes in profusion every refreshment for our ships and in the second place we might suffer severely from its situation were it in the hands of a powerfull enemy.[145]

As the first British governor on the ground, Lord Macartney was in a good position to provide a rounded assessment. He received a copy of Bruce's 'Sketches' in December 1796. But he annotated it with his own first-hand impressions of the colony and, when he returned to Europe, he left an eight-page commentary on the 'Sketches' for his successor.[146] Macartney remained unconvinced by the economic or commercial prospects of the Cape, but 'its immediate political, naval and military advantages are so striking, and of such splendor, that every other consideration is for the moment almost extinguished in the blaze'.[147] Macartney also wrote a 'few lines' to William Richardson at East India House about the Cape of Good Hope, 'which from its necessary connection with our Indian Empire must be an interesting object to you'. While Macartney posed a somewhat inscrutable rhetorical question – 'It is either a possession of importance to Great Britain or it is not' – the earl's answer was crystal clear. If Britain could 'contrive at a peace to keep this place ... the whole Indian World is our own'. 'If not', Macartney reasoned, 'I think our tenure to be very insecure.'[148] For Macartney, the possession of the Cape was 'of the first importance to the security of India'.[149] From 'its position on the globe', the colony had the potential to contribute 'greatly to the security of our

---

[143] BL, Add. MS 75856, f. 287, Spencer to Elphinstone, 8 August 1796.
[144] Not everyone agreed with this assessment. For examples of dissenting voices, notably the leading military officers (the 'scarlet and blew coats'), see Lady Anne Barnard to Dundas, 10 July 1797, *Letters*, p. 41.
[145] BL, IOR, H/738, p. 14, Malcolm, 'Account of the Cape'.
[146] Johnson, *Imagining the Cape Colony*, p. 80.
[147] TNA, WO 1/329, p. 17, Macartney to Dundas, 10 July 1797.
[148] RH, GB 0162 MSS.Afr.s.1,2, Macartney to William Richardson, 28 February 1798.
[149] NAS, GD51/1/530/2, Macartney to Dundas, 15 December 1797.

territories in Southern India'.[150] Macartney's views were shaped by his experience in the colony and by the views of others. In May 1797, he received a memorandum from 'Sir J. C.' (presumably Sir James Craig), which discussed the articles furnished by the Cape for 'subsistence and for trade'. Concluding his remarks, however, Craig suggested that, although cattle, corn, wool and ivory exports could become valuable in the future, the Cape was principally important for its strategic position and not for trade.[151]

On his way to take up his post as governor general in India, Richard Wellesley, Earl of Mornington, wrote to Henry Dundas from the Castle of Good Hope. He too expressed doubts about the long-term economic viability of the Cape. Southern Africa was, on the contrary, more to be valued as a strategic link in the chain of Britain's Indian Ocean world. He may have doubted its commercial and economic qualifications, but he admitted that he 'had not estimated so highly its value with reference to the defence of our trade to the east, and of our territories in India'.[152] It was dangerous to let the French harbour ambitions of conquering it. Wellesley advised Dundas and his colleagues in the Cabinet to 'look for its value in the positive advantages it would afford to the enemy or a military and naval station for offensive purposes against you'. It was also to be feared as a potential naval station because 'an enemy's squadron stationed at the Cape could not fail to intercept the greater part of our trade to and from the East'.[153] The logical corollary of these opinions was to strengthen Britain's own military capacity in the region, and to draw the Cape into the tactical, as well as the strategic, thinking of those charged with defending the Indian subcontinent. From Wellesley's perspective, therefore, it seemed to be much more efficient and economical in the long run to pay for maintaining an establishment at the Cape rather than having to send out fully armed fleets to dissuade marauding enemies. He asked the rhetorical question as to which would be the 'heavier expense':

to retain the Cape keeping up a large naval and military establishment here, and using it as an outpost to your Indian empire, or to leave the Cape in the hands of the enemy, and by doing so incur the necessity of increasing to a vast amount the protecting naval force requisite for the defence of your Indian and China trade?[154]

And, fresh from victory over Tipu Sultan at Seringapatam and recently raised in the peerage to Marquis Wellesley, he reiterated the connection:

---

[150] NAS, GD51/1/530/1, Macartney to Dundas, 24 October 1797.

[151] UWits, A88/67 [James Craig] to Macartney, 'Memorandum on the Productions of the Cape', 18 May 1797.

[152] Richard Wellesley to Dundas, 28 February 1798, *Two Views*, p. 41.

[153] *Ibid.*, pp. 41, 42.   [154] *Ibid.*, p. 42.

'The importance of the Cape in its relation to India increases every hour; and the connection between the settlements becomes more intimate in every view of our military, political, and commercial, interests.'[155] 'The great utility of the Cape of Good Hope', in Wellesley's eyes, was its ability 'to serve as an outpost to our Indian Empire'.[156]

Travellers were still enamoured of the agricultural and settlement prospects offered by the Cape, however. Richard Renshaw, an officer in the Royal Artillery, sailed from Spithead on the *Crescent* on 28 February 1796. On his way to Egypt, he called at the Cape and was impressed by the 'temperate climate', 'fertile soil', and 'mild and peaceful race of natives'.[157] John Barrow found it 'favourable for carrying on a speedy intercourse with every part of the civilized world', and admired 'its intrinsic value, as capable of supplying many articles of general consumption to the mother-country' and as 'a port solely for the numerous and valuable fleets of the East-India Company to refresh at'.[158] And Benjamin Stout – perhaps stretching the bounds of credibility somewhat – ventured that even if Britain gave up all its other conquests at the end of the war but 'preserves the Cape of Good Hope and its dependencies, she will ultimately be the gainer by the war'.[159] Robert Percival, a captain in the 18th Irish Regiment and one of the first British officers to enter Cape Town after its surrender in September 1795, remarked that the situation of the Cape of Good Hope, 'placed as it is directly in the middle between the two great divisions of the British empire, forces itself upon the attention of Great Britain, as a possession which would not only contribute to her prosperity, but which seems almost essential to her safety'. In Percival's view, 'for the purpose of defending our own foreign possessions, or keeping our enemies in check, no station can indeed be found comparable to the Cape of Good Hope'. It offered the means to defend Indian territories, keep European enemies in check, move troops quickly and, generally, to counteract 'every attempt which might be prejudicial to our interests'.[160] Like others, Percival expressed fears about the

[155] NAS, GD51/3/2/55, Wellesley to Dundas, 7 October 1800.
[156] Wellesley to Sir George Yonge, 24 October 1800, in Robert Montgomery Martin (ed.), *The Despatches, Minutes & Correspondence of the Marquess Wellesley during his Administration in India*, 5 vols. (London: W. H. Allen, 1836–37), vol. II, p. 405.
[157] Richard Renshaw, *Voyage to the Cape of Good Hope and up the Red Sea* (Manchester: J. Watts, 1804), pp. 14–15.
[158] John Barrow, *An Account of Travels into the Interior of Southern Africa, in the Years 1797 and 1798*, 2 vols. (London: T. Cadell and W. Davies, 1801–4), vol. I, pp. 1–2.
[159] Stout, *Hercules*, pp. 18–19.
[160] Robert Percival, *An Account of the Cape of Good Hope* (London: C. & R. Baldwin, 1804), pp. 329–30.

possibilities and potential offered to enemies by the geographical situation of the Cape. He was convinced that:

The Cape in the hands of the tributary republic of Holland, can only be considered as a French colony; and when we consider that Bonaparte looks upon our Indian territories as the great resource of our national power, we cannot suppose that he will long neglect to avail himself of the advantages which the local situation of the Cape presents for our annoyance.[161]

And Percival worried that the forces which any prospective enemy 'might dispatch from this station against our East-India settlements, would be far more dangerous than the same, or a much greater number, sent out direct from Europe':

As the climate of the Cape seems in a particular manner fitted not only for recruiting the health of the soldier, but also for preparing him to endure the heats of India, our enemy's troops would on their arrival be enabled to cope with our forces on equal terms, and even with the advantages of unbroken health and spirits on their side. We may be rest assured that the enemy who could undertake the romantic scheme of penetrating by Egypt and the Red Sea to our eastern empire will not overlook the easier and far more sure means, of effecting his purpose which are presented to him by the Cape of Good Hope.[162]

He lamented, with 'the strongest emotions of regret', the danger of the French being 'possessed of a station which affords them the means of undermining the pillars of our commercial grandeur'.[163]

Views such as these were expressed regularly throughout the early years of British rule at the Cape. Even those who remained unconvinced about its value as a colony recognised its strategic importance. Sir Roger Curtis wrote a long letter to Lord Spencer at the Admiralty in January 1800, ranging widely over the arguments for retaining or returning the colony. He remarked on the impracticality and unsuitability of using Saldanha Bay, Table Bay and Simon's Bay for shipping, the inclement weather and sailing conditions, and the lack of cultivated land as well as the 'depredations from the Boshesman, Hottentots and the Caffres'.[164] But, crucially, Curtis recognised that there might be other considerations to be borne in mind:

This colony, merely as a colony, can never be of any advantage to Great Britain. What advantage the Cape may be as a port, or what mischief it may be to Great Britain if in the hands of another nation, are questions of a nature very distinct from colonial considerations.[165]

---

[161] *Ibid.*, p. 329.   [162] *Ibid.*, pp. 329–30.   [163] *Ibid.*, p. 338.
[164] Roger Curtis to Spencer, 12 January 1800, *Spencer*, vol. IV, pp. 208–10.
[165] *Ibid.*, p. 207.

The second British governor of the colony, Sir George Yonge, described it in terms that would be recycled many times over the years, both by himself and others: 'The value and importance of this Colony encreases every Hour, and well deserves Support and Protection.'[166] Although Yonge claimed to recognise that 'Of the Importance of this Colony I need say nothing to you', he still bombarded Henry Dundas with the same message: the importance of the Cape 'grows in its every hour. It is and will become the centre of commerce with India, America, and Europe.' Yonge was keen to point out that it was not just his opinion. He cited the example of the captain of an American frigate 'sent to protect the American commerce in India which has been much harrass'd by French Privateers fitted out at the Mauritius'. The officer 'confess'd' that American commerce with Asia depended on 'the Assistance of the Cape, which He Called the Key of India'.[167] Dundas received another 'reminder' in November:

The situation of the Cape makes it the Gibraltar of this part of the world, and it is so acknowledged by France, Holland, America, & by the East India Company, by the unanimous concurrent voice of all these It is admitted & confessed, that an active power possessed of the Cape will command all communication between the Eastern & Western World.[168]

And in January 1801, Yonge reiterated: 'This Place is the great out post of India, & it will be desireable always to consider it as the Depot, or Point of Departure from whence any measures, either of offence or defence, may be forwarded, as the best use which can be made of it, and indeed which our enemies would no doubt adopt were it once more in their Power.'[169] Later in the same month, Yonge wrote to India: 'This colony ... by its situation is capable of being the great outwork and bulwark of India and as holding the Key of the East'.[170] And Lady Anne Barnard, wife of the resident colonial secretary in Cape Town, also mused on the Cape's ultimate fate at the end of the war. She and her husband, Andrew, hoped it would be possible to keep the Cape because 'barren and ill-cultivated as it now is', it struck the couple as having 'great powers in itself to become one of the finest countrys in the world'.[171] And Lord Macartney wrote to Henry Dundas from Curzon Street in London about the prospect of returning the Cape at a prospective peace: 'I should indeed be a poor geographer and a poorer statesman were I to

[166] Yonge to Dundas, 12 January 1800, *RCC*, vol. III, p. 25.
[167] TNA, WO 1/332, p. 184, Yonge to Dundas, 29 March 1800.
[168] Yonge to Dundas, 15 November 1800, *RCC*, vol. III, p. 358.
[169] Yonge to Dundas, 12 January 1801, *RCC*, vol. III, p. 406.
[170] BL, Add. MS 13785, f. 47, Yonge to Wellesley, 24 January 1801.
[171] Lady Anne Barnard to Dundas, 29 November 1797, *Letters*, p. 96.

advise our parting with it, but in the last extremity.' Whatever its commercial potentiality, the paramount consideration ought to be its situation as 'a great military station and the master key of India'.[172]

Not everyone was convinced, however. Crucially, in a debate on the preliminary articles of a peace treaty, Lord Hobart, Secretary of State for War and the Colonies, remarked to the House of Lords that the Cape had already cost one million pounds and that it was 'a peculiarly expensive, insecure and extremely inconvenient port of refreshment'.[173] Notwithstanding views to the contrary, as the Secretary of State, Hobart's opinions clearly carried weight and the colony was duly given up. Ultimately, the transfer of the colony to the Batavian Republic under the Treaty of Amiens proved to be short-lived. But news of the peace, and its consequences, struck Cape Town like a 'thunderbolt'. Lady Anne Barnard reported that, among the small British community there, 'people think it a bad peace ... General [Francis] Dundas calls it a shameful peace'.[174] Percival fulminated against the return of the colony. It was, he maintained, 'a matter absolutely required by political prudence, that we should lose no time in regaining this colony':

During a war the safety of our East-India trade can no otherwise be secured; and equally in peace and war, the Cape may be made use of for such preparations as may afterwards be employed to wrest from us our most valuable possessions.[175]

John Barrow, acolyte of Lord Macartney and future Second Secretary of the Admiralty, shared the view of many that retention of the Cape would give Britain a valuable base from which to protect its eastern trade and security.[176] He adduced the additional advantage of encouraging British commerce with South America too, for it was conveniently situated as a base for an extensive trade which might be opened with the coast of Brazil and the ports of South America.[177] Barrow's published account of the colony, based on his experiences there during the first British occupation, acted as a clarion call for those who esteemed it.

In December 1804, Henry Phipps, Lord Mulgrave, expressed the view that in French hands it would endanger India.[178] This view was

---

[172] NAS, GD51/1/530/12, Macartney to Dundas, 25 April 1801.

[173] House of Lords Debate on the Preliminaries of Peace with France, 3 November 1801, in *Parliamentary History*, vol. 36, p. 190. For more on this, see Turner, 'Cape of Good Hope and the Anglo-French Conflict'.

[174] Lady Anne Barnard to Wellesley, 12–15 December 1801, *Letters*, p. 277.

[175] Percival, *Account*, pp. 330–1.

[176] For more on Barrow, see Christopher Lloyd, *Mr Barrow of the Admiralty: A Life of Sir John Barrow, 1764–1848* (London: Collins, 1970).

[177] Barrow, *Account of Travels*, vol. II, p. 305.

[178] Henry was the brother of Constantine John Phipps. Henry succeeded his brother as the third Baron Mulgrave in 1792.

exacerbated when the Toulon and Cadiz squadrons united in 1805. Rumours abounded in February and April 1805 that Admiral Villeneuve was heading for India via the Cape.[179] While Mulgrave expressed the usual doubts about the economic viability of the region to William Pitt in 1804, he acknowledged other reasons for its retention. He considered the Cape to be 'merely offensive in the hands of [the French] and merely defensive in the hands of [Britain], attended with expence, or at least producing no profit'.[180] Even Britain's greatest adversary of the day recognised the value of the Cape for British strategy. In May 1805, Napoleon told the Grand Pensionary of Holland, Schimmelpennick, that Villeneuve's combined fleet was heading for India: 'Of all the enterprises which England is able to undertake we see only one which is rational, it is the conquest of the Cape of Good Hope.'[181] The short Dutch interregnum and the colony's speedy reconquest by Sir David Baird and his men in 1806 perhaps provides the clearest indication of the widespread acceptance of these views about the importance of the Cape.[182]

Most politicians and strategists agreed that the crucial point in securing and retaining the Cape was its relative proximity to India, and Britain's commercial and political interests there. By the time the Cape Colony was acquired for a second time, in 1806, economic factors were decidedly and obviously secondary to the strategic location astride the route to India.[183] On both occasions when British troops had taken the Cape then, their actions had been born of a fear that, in John Blankett's evocative phrase, 'what had been a mere feather in the hands of Holland, will become a sword in the hands of France'.[184]

The view of the Cape as a strategic outpost of India, and its value as fulfilling a number of functions, became a political and military orthodoxy. In 1805, Lord Castlereagh remarked to Lord Cornwallis, Wellesley's successor as governor general in India, that:

[179] Christopher D. Hall, *British Strategy in the Napoleonic War, 1803–15* (Manchester: Manchester University Press, 1992), p. 125.

[180] Quoted in Alan J. Guy, 'British Strategy and the Cape of Good Hope in the Era of the French Revolutionary and Napoleonic Wars', in Peter B. Boyden, Alan J. Guy and Marion Harding (eds.), *'Ashes and Blood': The British Army in South Africa, 1795–1914* (London: National Army Museum, 1999), pp. 32–43, p. 33. As Guy points out, although the term was not current until the 1860s, the idea of 'imperial defence' was the principal motivation for taking the Cape.

[181] Quoted in Turner, 'Cape of Good Hope and the Anglo-French Conflict', p. 374.

[182] UWits, A886f, George Hardinge to Home Popham, 26 October 1804.

[183] Ronald Hyam, 'British Imperial Expansion in the Late Eighteenth Century', *Historical Journal* 10 (1967), pp. 113–24.

[184] TNA, WO 1/329, p. 48, Blankett to Nepean, 25 January 1795.

The true value of the Cape to Great Britain is its being considered and treated at all times as an outpost subservient to the protection and security of our Indian possessions. When in our hands it must afford considerable accommodation and facilities to our intercourse with those possessions, but its occupation is perhaps even more material as depriving the enemy of the best intermediary possession between Britain and India, for assembling a large European armament for service in the East Indies.[185]

This sentiment, which had developed well before the first British acquisition of the Cape, prevailed into the early years of the second British occupation. For Sir John Cradock, who succeeded Lord Caledon as governor, the importance of the region was obvious to 'every person who reflects upon history or the geographical position of the world'.[186] When called upon to decide whether to send reinforcements to help quell a supposed mutiny in the subcontinent, Lord Caledon considered that his first duty as governor of the Cape Colony was to safeguard India:

If the point under discussion turns upon the comparative object of securing one possession at the risque of losing the other, I believe I may state it with some confidence as the opinion of one of His Majesty's principal ministers, that the true value of this Colony is its being considered at all times as an outpost subservient to the security and protection of our E. I. Possessions.[187]

And one of Caledon's successors, Lord Charles Somerset, agreed that 'the great importance of this place to Great Britain consist[s] chiefly in its being the outwork of India'.[188] Like most of the other commentators and officials discussed above, these men saw the Cape's situation as being, to a large degree, determined by its relationship with the Indian possessions and interests that Britain had been steadily building up during the eighteenth century. The Cape of Good Hope was understood as forming part of a strategic Indian Ocean world. Even Thomas Brooke, a great advocate of the claims of St Helena, recognised 'the superior internal resources' of the Cape, 'its extent, and, above all, its position, so critically adapted for the annoyance or protection of our Eastern dominions, render it an object of

---

[185] Castlereagh to Lord Cornwallis, 10 September 1805, quoted in Gerald S. Graham, *The Politics of Naval Supremacy* (Cambridge: Cambridge University Press, 1965), p. 40. Technically, Cornwallis was also Wellesley's predecessor, as he had served as governor general from 1786 to 1793. It is unlikely that Cornwallis ever saw these words from Castlereagh as he died in India on 5 October 1805.

[186] Sir John Cradock's response to an address by merchants of the Cape Colony on his departure, 30 April 1814, *RCC*, vol. X, p. 104.

[187] BL, IOR, G/9/10, p. 138, Lord Caledon to Henry Grey, 15 October 1809.

[188] BL, IOR, G/9/4, p. 112, Lord Charles Somerset to William Fullerton-Elphinstone, 19 June 1815.

supreme importance'.[189] In proposing greater imperial involvement at the Cape, George Flower, from Marden in Hertfordshire, recounted the geographical advantage offered by the colony 'midway between the Mother Country, her large possessions in the East, her distant settlement of New Holland, and the empire of China'. In such a situation, at 'the centre of the world', the Cape presented 'an advantageous situation for commerce with the two Americas'.[190] As the nineteenth century progressed, more people would express the sentiments of the anonymous author of a pamphlet composed around 1815, who described the colony, 'even in its infancy', as being 'peculiarly calculated to answer some of the extraordinary circumstances of the present moment'.[191]

The South Atlantic

As an 'intermediate port between Europe and the East', and perhaps because of its geographical position at the tip of a major landmass, the Cape was often held up as 'exclusively worthy of the national attention'.[192] But this was not a view held by Thomas Brooke, Government Secretary on St Helena (and no relation of the governor, Robert Brooke), or others who pushed the claims of the island and other locations in the South Atlantic.[193] For them, there were other, alternative, keys to Britain's Asian empire. Often these were island outposts, located in the harsh waters of the South Atlantic but all the more valuable because of this. As we have seen, British exploration in the South Atlantic after the Seven Years War had focused on finding uninhabited islands.[194] These places, by potentially answering the provisioning needs of British ships and offering security to maritime trade, were equally as valuable as somewhere like the Cape. Thomas Brooke compared St Helena favourably with the Cape: 'The water there [St Helena] is as pure and as wholesome as at the Cape, and can be procured with equal facility and equal expedition.'[195] In fact, 'merely as ports of refreshment and of rendezvous for East India convoys, the balance is in favour of St Helena'. And Brooke hoped the island would always be regarded 'as an important and essential part of the British Empire'.[196]

---

[189] Thomas H. Brooke, *A History of the Island of St Helena: From Its Discovery by the Portuguese to the Year 1823* (London: Kingsbury, Parbury, and Allen, 1824), p. 426.
[190] George Flower to Earl Bathurst, 20 September 1815, *RCC*, vol. X, p. 349.
[191] CRO, D LONS/L13/1/91, 'Importance of the Cape', p. 3.
[192] Brooke, *St Helena*, p. 426.
[193] See Alexander H. Schulenburg, 'Transient observations: the textualizing of St Helena through five hundred years of colonial discourse', Ph.D. thesis, University of St Andrews, 1999, p. 80.
[194] See pp. 49–50 above. [195] Brooke, *St Helena*, p. 427. [196] *Ibid.*, p. 428.

Of all the territories considered in this book, St Helena was part of Britain's Asian empire since the earliest days of the East India Company's trading ventures.[197] Despite its remote location, English interest was represented as early as the late 1650s, in the form of a charter to govern the island from Oliver Cromwell in 1657 and the decision by the East India Company to fortify and colonise it the following year. On 15 December 1658, forty men left England to take St Helena and begin a plantation there.[198] The Company's interest in the island was confirmed at the Restoration in 1660 when it received a royal charter. By the 1680s, it was regularly referred to as 'The Company's Island'.[199]

Although it was referred to as 'the most lonely island in the universe' in 1786, descriptions of the delightful, commodious and fertile landscape of the island abounded.[200] St Helena was 'an earthly paradise', 'miraculously discovered for the refreshing and service' of ships. In his *Voyage to the East Indies*, the Dutch traveller Jan Huyghen van Linschoten called it a 'boye [buoy] placed in the middle of the Spanish seas'. While, in 1644, Richard Boothby called the island 'healthful, fruitful and commodious'. It 'was a place for trading with all nations at their return out of India' and, apparently, it could be defended easily too.[201] Paradisiacal descriptions of the island continued into the following century. Major Rennet penned a letter to Lord Macartney, long before the earl had taken up his position at the Cape, enclosing his 'account of the island of St Helena in 1779', in which Rennet described its geographical situation, vegetation, population and society. For Rennet, the interior of this 'most singular island rising in the middle of the sea' was 'beautifully varied' with 'very fine verdure'.[202] Robert Brooke, St Helena's governor for the last decade of the eighteenth century, composed an account of his bailiwick in 1792. In this account, Brooke went to great lengths to convey the mildness of the climate and the prospects of the island. It was 'situated in the midst of the trade winds'; combined with the 'lofty' hills and 'wooded' centre, 'the island is

---

[197] See Philip Gosse, *St Helena, 1502–1938* (London: Cassell, 1938); Philip J. Stern, 'Politics and Ideology in the Early East India Company-State: The Case of St. Helena, 1673–1696', *Journal of Imperial and Commonwealth History* 35 (2007), pp. 1–23.

[198] Stephen Royle, *The Company's Island: St Helena, Company Colonies and the Colonial Endeavour* (London: I. B. Tauris, 2007), pp. 17–18.

[199] See, for example, BL, IOR, E/3/90, pp. 89–98, 1 August 1683.

[200] See *Daily Universal Register*, 16 November 1786, quoted in James H. Thomas, 'The Isle of Wight and the East India Company, 1700–1840: Some Connections Considered', *Local Historian* 30 (2000), pp. 4–22, p. 20, n. 1.

[201] Quoted in Royle, *Company's Island*, pp. 23, 17.

[202] UWits, A88/10, 'Account of the Island of St. Helena in 1779, by Major Rennet', 11 November 1785.

generally peculiarly blessed with refreshing showers'.[203] For another traveller, 'health and long life are the necessary consequences' of the clement climate.[204] Helpfully, the island also offered secure anchorage: along the whole leeward coast 'ships may anchor under 23 fathom water in perfect security in all seasons of the year'.[205] Brooke was clear:

The island has been esteemed valuable merely on account of its situation, being safe and commodious at all seasons for ships to touch at returning from India, that its waters are excellent, and that those afflicted with the scurvy recover more rapidly on its shores than on any other perhaps in the world.[206]

The fruitful possibilities of the island were just one of the reasons cited for retaining it. David Smallman asserted that the Company held on to the island even when it provided no profit to shareholders because of 'a strategic importance that could not be evaluated in a simple profit and loss ledger'.[207] Francis Rogers, a Company merchant, described how the island could become a 'general rendezvous for our English shipping homeward bound from India, both for water and refreshments, and convoy in wartime'.[208] And Jacob Bosanquet, one of the Company directors, regarded the island as 'the principal link of that chain which connects this country with her Indian possessions and of undoubted great importance'.[209] St Helena's position at the crossroads of Britain's imperial interests was affirmed by residents of the island in their correspondence with James Anderson, a botanist in Madras:

We think the situation of this island is peculiarly well adapted to render it an intermediate nursery for the preservation of such plants as may not have strength to endure the whole course of a voyage to Europe or to the Eastern world.[210]

William Innes Pocock, a naval officer and amateur artist of some distinction, made three voyages to the Cape of Good Hope, St Helena and China in the *St Albans* between 1807 and 1810. In the last of these, the convoy was so damaged in a storm off the Cape that it was forced to stay at

[203] BL, IOR, G/32/165, p. 1, Robert Brooke, 'Account of St Helena with Various Observations Annexed' [1792].

[204] William Innes Pocock, *Five Views of the Island of St Helena from Drawings taken on the Spot* (London: S. and J. Fuller, 1815), p. 7.

[205] BL, IOR, G/32/165, p. 2, Brooke, 'Account of St Helena'.   [206] *Ibid.*, p. 4.

[207] Royle, *Company's Island*, p. 128.   [208] *Ibid.*, p. 128.

[209] BL, IOR, H/88, p. 392, Dissent of Jacob Bosanquet to the plan proposed by Thomas Grenville, 15 October 1806.

[210] Robert Brooke, David Kay, Rev Mr Wilson (Treasurer), N. Bazett, Wm Wrangham to James Anderson, dated St Helena, 14 June 1788, in James Anderson, *Correspondence for the Introduction of Cochineal Insects from America, the Varnish and Tallow Trees from China, the Discovery and Culture of White Lac, the Culture of Red Lac. And also for the Introduction, Culture and Establishment of Mulberry Trees and Silk Worms . . . .* (Madras: Joseph Martin, 1791), pp. 4–5.

St Helena to refit. While there, Pocock made several sketches of the island, which, with an account of its history, he published as *Five Views of the Island of St Helena* in 1815, presumably hoping to capitalise on the fame acquired by the island in the wake of Napoleon's exile there.[211] The island was the ultimate example of the chains of maritime connectivity that forged this oceanic world: 'Whatever the Island enjoys beyond air, water, and water cresses, has been brought from elsewhere; and for it, is indebted to human industry and ingenuity.'[212] Despite its promising climate, Pocock was quite negative about St Helena's prospects ('Nothing is obtained but by great exertion from this ungrateful soil').[213] But the island was of vital strategic importance, nevertheless. This was particularly so when other, rival empires had interests in the region:

While a rival and hostile company was in possession of the Cape of Good Hope, it was absolutely necessary that St. Helena should be kept in a state of defence, capable of repelling any attack that a foreign power could make upon it.[214]

And the consequences of its falling into enemy hands were even more unthinkable:

If left totally unoccupied, it would afford a point from whence an active squadron might intercept nearly all the trade from India. No half measure will do; it must be fortified and garrisoned to rely on itself, or be left to a squadron stationed there.[215]

Some years later, when Alexander Walker, the island's governor, established an Agricultural and Horticultural Society at a Public Meeting on 3 July 1823, his public address reiterated the theme and reaffirmed the island's valuable position for Indian trade. It was, he said, 'devoted to the relief and encouragement of mariners: she is the main link that connects the commerce of India with that of Europe'.[216] And, despite his bleak assessment of its situation, the anonymous author of an extensive description of the island published in 1805 recognised the advantages offered by St Helena:

The possession of this unpromising spot, which nature had removed so far from strife and contention, has been disputed by the nations of Europe, because it abounds with excellent water; affords a convenient place of refreshment to fleets, and may, in time of war, be converted into a military station of great strength and importance.[217]

[211] J. K. Laughton, 'Pocock, William Innes (1783–1836)', rev. Andrew Lambert, *Oxford Dictionary of National Biography*, Oxford University Press, 2004 (www.oxforddnb.com /view/article/22429, accessed 11 June 2014).
[212] Pocock, *Five Views*, p. 7.   [213] *Ibid.*, p. 6.   [214] *Ibid.*, p. 11.   [215] *Ibid.*
[216] Brooke, *St Helena*, p. 413.
[217] Anon., *A Description of the Island of St Helena* (London: R. Phillips, 1805), p. 6.

The climate was apparently so salubrious that sick men and unseasoned troops could recuperate and acclimatise quickly. And, while its 'rude and naked aspect' seemed to promise little, there were 'few places, indeed, which unite so many advantages as this volcanic rock':

Its full value and importance, as a convenient station for the shipping of the company, will be yet more apparent, when we consider how few places there are (if any besides this) in the route to India, or the Oriental seas, where vessels can, at all seasons, touch with safety, as they do here.[218]

Nineteenth-century historiography continued this tradition, locating St Helena at the crossroads of empire. In his historical and topographical description of the island published in 1875, John Melliss, suggested that it was 'really a fortification, and, as the key to the whole of the South Atlantic, is one of England's greatest fortresses, and as such ought to be under the control of either the Admiralty or the War Department'.[219] For Edward Wheeler Bird, writing under the pseudonym 'PhiloIsrael', the role of St Helena was to be 'one of England's greatest fortresses'.[220]

Setting aside the long-time British presence in St Helena, control of the rest of the South Atlantic area was only secured by the second capture of the Cape in 1806.[221] Interest in the region had always existed, of course. Throughout the eighteenth century, British travellers had been promoting its importance. For many, it was a gateway not to the Indian but to the Pacific Ocean. Admiral Anson, reflecting on his circumnavigation in the 1740s, urged the colonisation of the Falkland Islands as a way of creating a station on the route around South America, which would 'open to us facilities of passing into the Pacifick Ocean'. This would have the effect of rendering 'all that southern navigation infinitely securer than at present'.[222] Immediately upon receiving the report and charts which John Bryon sent home on the *Florida* storeship on 22 June 1766, Lord Egmont prepared a report for the Cabinet in which he cautioned that the business was of 'very great moment & of the most secret nature'.[223] In this

---

[218] *Ibid.*, pp. 118–19.
[219] John C. Melliss, *St. Helena: A Physical, Historical, and Topographical Description of the Island* (London: Reeve, 1875), p. 44.
[220] Philo-Israel [Edward Wheeler Bird], *The Geography of the Gates* (London: Robert Banks, 1880), p. 103. For further discussion, see Schulenburg, 'Transient Observations', pp. 175–6.
[221] Rudy Bauss, 'Rio de Janeiro: Strategic Base for Global Designs of the British Royal Navy, 1777–1815', in Craig L. Symonds *et al.* (eds.), *New Aspects of Naval History* (Annapolis, MD: Naval Institute Press, 1981), pp. 75–89, p. 85.
[222] Richard Walter, *A Voyage Round the World, in the Years MDCCXL, I, II, III, IV* (London: Richard Walter, 1748), p. 92.
[223] Lord Egmont to Duke of Grafton, 20 July 1765, in Gallagher (ed.), *Byron's Journal*, p. 160.

document, Egmont argued that 'Falkland's island' was 'undoubtedly the Key to the whole Pacifick Ocean'.[224] But the South Atlantic was not only a useful gateway to the South Pacific. Control of its waters, as well as the acquisition of significant locations there, could also help to protect, defend and secure British maritime routes to Asia.

The tiny, windswept island of Tristan da Cunha in the South Atlantic is an example of the flexible nature of the empire and British claims in the region. As early as 1684, John Gayer, commander of the *Society*, was given a report from the previous year's voyage and ordered to sail there on his outbound journey to India. Gayer was instructed to survey the island, judge its harbours and potential for provisioning ships, and catalogue the flora and fauna. He was also to leave three pigs and a letter in a bottle to mark a claim to any island he considered inhabitable.[225] The 'peculiar situation of the little spot', as Lord Charles Somerset later termed it, made Tristan of interest to planners and politicians looking to secure the route to the East throughout the period.[226] The island covers 30 square miles, most occupied by a 6,000-foot-high volcano. A small plain to the north-west, two square miles in size, provides the only flat land. It is within the latitudes of the 'roaring forties', the westerly winds that carry ships around Africa to Asia.[227] It is also remote: the nearest mainland, at the Cape of Good Hope, is 1,700 miles away.[228] On first glance, then, the island's prospects as a crucial way station for the British Asian empire were not promising. But in a memorandum to the Chairman of the East India Company, Alexander Dalrymple summed up Tristan's attributes admirably: here 'ships may get water but it lies in a tempestuous climate; the road however is very good as it is a straight coast'.[229]

Thirty years later, Jonathan Lambert, an American who had decided to found a settlement on the island, brimmed with enthusiasm for its prospects. When he was questioned by a Royal Navy officer, Lambert spoke of the abundance of goats and hogs to be found in the interior, the 'most delicious flavor' of the fish, caught from rocks with nothing more than a 'common wicker basket', and seemed confident of the inevitable progress of the colony.[230] The *St Helena Monthly Register* for September 1811

---

[224] *Ibid.*, pp. 160–1.   [225] Stern, *Company-State*, p. 73.
[226] Somerset to Bathurst, 8 June 1815, *RCC*, vol. X, p. 306.
[227] Benjamin F. Seaver to Robert Stopford, 2 March 1811, *RCC*, vol. VIII, pp. 7–9.
[228] For further details, see James Fichter, 'The British Empire and the American Atlantic on Tristan da Cunha, 1811–16', *Journal of Imperial and Commonwealth History* 36 (2008), pp. 567–89, p. 569.
[229] TNA, CO 77/25, p. 121 [Dalrymple], 'Memo'.
[230] TNA, ADM 1/20, 'A Report concerning the Islands of Tristan d'Acunha and Gough, as represented by Captain Heywood of His Majesty's Ship Nereus', enclosure in M. De

carried a description of the island, 'given by Benjamin F. Seaver', which argued for its advantages to shipping:

Any vessel may be watered (the weather being any ways moderate) in twelve hours; procuring at the same time sufficient quantity of fire wood ... The anchoring ground is in all respects far preferable to the Road of Funchal, in the Isle of Madeira, from the circumstance of its being a straight shore ... the land fit to be cultivated on the large island ... capable of producing corn, cotton, tobacco, hemp, and the grape vine.[231]

Even John Pringle, the East India Company's solid and steady agent at Cape Town remarked, in response to this report by 'Captain Seaver of the Colonial Brig *Charles*' about the charms of the isolated island, that the situation of Tristan appeared 'well calculated for outward bound ships watering and refreshing without dangerous delay'. Indeed, 'the whole narrative is interesting and may be worth the attention of the Honorable Court'.[232] In 1815, Peter Gordon, commander of the country ship, *Bengal Merchant*, was of the opinion that its situation 'in the direct route from Europe and the United States to India, China and New Holland, together with its relative distance from those places' made Tristan 'a very convenient place for vessels which are only in want of water and such other articles as the islands supply, to touch at'.[233] The benefits of reinforcing the small number of inhabitants, already well disposed to British protection, with some ewes and rams as well as a few plants and seeds, and 'if not too great a favour a head or two of black cattle', would be 'more national than individual' according to Gordon.[234]

Captain Warren of HMS *President*, who was ordered to Tristan to assess the island's naval importance, was also positive about its value. Of course, as a naval man, Warren was acutely aware of the island's benefits for shipping but also of the danger of allowing it to fall into the wrong hands. According to Pringle, Warren was 'decidedly of the opinion that this island from its situation, half way to India & capability [*sic*] ought to be taken possession of before any other nation seizes it'. Vessels not wishing to touch at the Cape – American or perhaps French – 'would be sure of obta[ining] excellent water in abundance and without any difficulty or delay – vegetables also would soon be plentiful and fruit with

Courcey to Admiralty, 5 August 1811. See Fichter, 'British Empire and the American Atlantic on Tristan da Cunha', p. 568.

231 *St Helena Monthly Register*, September 1811, pp. 13–14.
232 BL, IOR, G/9/7, p. 160, John Pringle to William Ramsay, 5 March 1811. Pringle's caveat was that the East India Company already used St Helena and the Cape for such tasks.
233 Peter Gordon to Henry Alexander, 27 May 1815, *RCC*, vol. X, p. 304.
234 *Ibid.*, p. 305.

variety of other refreshments in a short time'. Pringle reported that
Warren found several small plains 'very fit for cultivation' on the island,
all quite small, 'divided from each other by perpendicular Cliffs and only
accessible by Boats'.[235] With a limited commitment – Warren advised
that a Martello Tower 'capable of containing twenty or thirty men ...
would be sufficient to cultivate the land and defend themselves ... against
any depredations' – the island could provide an excellent staging post on
the way to and from India.[236] In 1813, Admiral Sir Charles Tyler ordered
HMS *Semiramis* 'to proceed to the island of Tristan da Acunha and
examine its anchorage and endeavour to ascertain if ships can obtain
without risk supplies of water'.[237] Earl Bathurst eventually authorised
the taking of Tristan in September 1815, as long as this was performed
'consistent with the strictest economy', and yet another part of Britain's
Indian Ocean jigsaw fell into place.[238]

Even locations on the mainland of South America were perceived as
potentially important places for the protection and promotion of Britain's
economic and political interest in the Indian subcontinent. In the middle
of the eighteenth century, Henry Hutchinson advocated drawing South
America into Britain's Indian Ocean orbit:

We might hereafter if necessary, from this colony carry on a trade to China, & the
East Indies, without carrying any bullion out of Great Britain, in this manner the
China and India trade under proper regulation might turn out more beneficial to
the nation.[239]

Rio de Janeiro was used as a naval base from 1777, becoming a focal point
of British naval and commercial interests. It provided a 'stepping stone'
for British interests, not just in Spanish America but also with Asia and
the South Pacific. It offered abundant stores, a well-protected harbour,
and a strategic location, making it 'the major logistical link between Great
Britain and her expanding empire'.[240] And Home Popham evoked the
ever-present spectre of the French in arguing for its defence. The city's
'particular situation' meant that it presented 'the most probable point for

---

[235] BL, IOR, G/9/7, p. 210, John Pringle to William Ramsay, 11 March 1811.
[236] *Ibid.*, p. 211.   [237] UWits, A124, Sir Charles Tyler, Journal, 13 February 1813.
[238] Bathurst to Somerset, 19 September 1815, *RCC*, vol. X, p. 346. For a detailed discussion of the British interaction with the island immediately subsequent to this capture,
specifically through the activities of the Royal Navy there, see Stephen A. Royle,
'Perilous Shipwreck, Misery and Unhappiness: The British Military at Tristan da
Cunha, 1816–1817', *Journal of Historical Geography* 29 (2003), pp. 516–34.
[239] BL, Add. MS 47014C, f. 122, Henry Hutchinson, 'Colony in South America of
Importance' [1760s].
[240] Bauss, 'Rio de Janeiro', pp. 75, 76.

the enemy, I mean France, not only to take possession of, but to furnish supplies to counteract all our operations'.[241]

   In general, British ministers tried to avoid being drawn into the particularly febrile maelstrom of Latin American politics, if at all possible. They received lots of plans for the conquest of South America but all forays had been resisted.[242] But the Revolutionary and Napoleonic Wars highlighted, as never before, the importance of the region to Britain's wider, especially Asian, interests. In January 1797, the British presence at the Cape encouraged the Lords Commissioners of the Admiralty to consider using 'a detachment of troops and a squadron of ships from the Cape of Good Hope' to launch an attack 'on some part of the Spanish possessions on the South West coast of America as soon as the necessary arrangements can be made for that purpose'.[243] Meanwhile, Henry Dundas, in a 'most secret' letter, warned the governor, Lord Macartney, of plans to send an attacking force from the Cape under General Craig to the south-west coast of Spanish America. Such was the apparent necessity of the assault that Dundas cautioned Macartney that the operations must be expedited at the Cape and the expedition must go ahead even if all the relieving divisions did not arrive in Southern Africa.[244] In the end, the expedition was cancelled.[245] But the fact that the Cape was being factored into the military and tactical operations highlights two points: first, the prospective place of South America in securing Britain's Indian Ocean world and, second, the logistical role that the Cape was perceived as playing in Britain's global empire.[246] As the first British civilian governor of the Cape, Macartney was acutely aware of the intersections and overlaps that drew the entire region into Britain's imperial interest. In considering the possible tactics to be employed by a French expedition sent to attack India, he concluded: 'The River of Plate (or possibly if circumstances admit of it, Rio de Janeiro) will be their place of rendezvous, from whence they could proceed directly to Mangalore or Ceylon without touching at the Isle of France.'[247]

   British fear of attacks launched from South America on its trade to Asia was, ostensibly, one of the reasons that encouraged military

[241] TNA, PRO 30/8/345, p. 83, Popham to Charles Yorke, 26 November 1803.
[242] See Hall, British Strategy in the Napoleonic War, p. 145. For further details, see John Lynch, 'British Policy and Spanish America, 1783–1808', Journal of Latin American Studies 1 (1969), pp. 1–30, pp. 15–18; BL, Add. MS 37847, f. 255; BL, Add. MS 37884, ff. 15–17.
[243] TNA, ADM 2/1352, p. 11, Admiralty to Thomas Pringle, 26 January 1797.
[244] UWits, A88/47, Dundas to Macartney, 21 January 1797.
[245] UWits, A88/56, Dundas to Macartney, 4 March 1797.
[246] These points are discussed in greater detail in Chapters 3 and 5 respectively.
[247] NMM, CHN/8/5, Macartney to Sir Hugh Christian, 27 April 1798.

commanders and governors on the ground to acquiesce in Sir Home Popham's ill-judged assault on Buenos Aires in 1806.[248] It was a scheme that had occupied Popham for some time. In 1803, he reminded Charles Yorke at the Home Office that 'the continent of South America' was 'a topick that has occupied the attention of the ablest statesmen for a series of years' because the advantages which Britain would derive from a successful assault on key targets would be 'incalculable'.[249] Popham proceeded to cite a series of facts and figures to support his assertions. And in doing so, the role of India, and Britain's Asian trade, played its part:

It must be evident to every person who possesses a knowledge of the geographical situation of that Great Continent; its population and resources, that any permanent influence of Great Britain ... must offer the greatest commercial advantages, not only to this country but to our possessions in India.[250]

Popham's success in escorting the expedition that took the Cape of Good Hope in 1806 encouraged him to revive and promote a similar plan for taking Buenos Aires. The area around the River Plate, in the southern cone of South America, was regarded (or represented) by Popham as a potential springboard for an attack on Asian trade. At least this was one of the reasons that persuaded the military commander at the Cape, Major-General Sir David Baird, to assign him a small group of soldiers. Popham set off to conquer Buenos Aires in April 1806. On his way from the Cape, he made the same case to the governor of St Helena. He told Robert Patten that capturing Buenos Aires would be 'an additional safeguard to the trade of the Honourable East India Company', and persuaded him to assist by committing more than one thousand troops to the operation.[251] The expedition proved, however, to be the catalyst for a catalogue of military disasters for Britain in the region.[252] Andrew Blayney, a senior army officer who served in South America in 1807, was forthright in his description of 'our defeat and disgrace at Buenos Aires'.[253] But if South America proved to be an awkward place in which to gain a foothold, there were even greater obstacles in the south-western corner of the Indian Ocean.

---

[248] See C. F. Mullett (ed.), 'British Schemes and Spanish America in 1806', *Hispanic American Historical Review* 27 (1947), pp. 269–78.

[249] TNA, PRO 30/8/345, pp. 80–1, Popham to Yorke, 26 November 1803.

[250] *Ibid.*, p. 82.

[251] TNA, ADM 1/58, pp. 248–9, Popham to Robert Patten, 13 April 1806.

[252] See Ian Fletcher, *The Waters of Oblivion: The British Invasion of the Rio de la Plata, 1806–1807* (Tunbridge Wells: Spellmount, 1991).

[253] US, WP1/175/9, Lord Blayney to Sir Arthur Wellesley, 24 August 1807.

The south-western Indian Ocean

In response to yet another plan to attack Spanish settlements in South America, Sir Hugh Christian, commander-in-chief of the Royal Navy squadron at the Cape, gave his opinion about where he thought British priorities ought to lie. His assessment was blunt and to the point: 'The Mauritius is surely a much greater object.'[254] In this calculation, Christian's mirrored that of Macartney. As the two men corresponded in late April and early May 1798, Britain already controlled large swathes of the oceanic arc leading to the lucrative markets of Asia. St Helena and, more recently, the Cape were British possessions; local political instability, allied with Britain's powerful naval resources, ensured that South America and islands elsewhere in the South Atlantic were also well within the British sphere of influence. But the south-western gateway to the Indian Ocean – with Mauritius (otherwise known as the Ile de France) at its heart – had an additional complication, and one which was altogether more dangerous for British shipping activities and political ambitions. Unlike the South Atlantic or Southern Africa, the biggest threat to Britain's Indian interests – France – was already well established here.

French views on the importance of the islands of the region are perhaps best summed up in a letter written by the governor general of the Ile de France, Charles Decaen, to Napoleon in 1803. In it, Decaen remarked on the 'happy situation' of the island and the fact that 'de son point, on embrasse le monde'.[255] His opinions echoed many others. Jacques-Henri Bernardin de Saint Pierre, perhaps most famous as the author of *Paul et Virginie* (1788), travelled to the Ile de France in the late 1760s. Although he was less convinced than Decaen, Bernardin de Saint Pierre remarked on the general impression of the island: 'The Isle of France is looked upon, as a fortress which assures to us our possessions in India.'[256] Jacob Haafner, who served with the Dutch East India Company in India, called at the island in December 1768. He confirmed its importance to the French. It was 'a not unimportant benefit to have a safe harbour in the Indian Sea in which their ships can seek shelter in the adverse monsoon, and to possess a depot for troops, ammunition and other necessities. Here, within a month to three to four at most, they can send and receive news and orders to and from Pondicherry.' He cited the Ile de France as

---

[254] NMM, CHN/3/2, Christian to Macartney, 2 May 1798.
[255] Quoted in Huguette Ly-Tio-Fane Pineo, *In the Grips of the Eagle: Matthew Flinders at Ile de France, 1803–1810* (Moka, Mauritius: Mahatma Gandhi Institute, 1988), p. 55.
[256] Bernardin de Saint Pierre, *Voyage to the Island of Mauritius*, p. 173. His reservations rested on the island's isolation from India ('fifteen hundred leagues from Pondicherry') and the fact that 'neither pitch, tar, cordage, or mast timber are found here; nor is the wood of a proper sort for any other branch of building' (p. 174).

being of 'vital importance' because, without it, the French 'would long ago have already succumbed to their treacherous competitors, the English, and would have had to abandon their possessions in India'.[257] These views were corroborated by a British soldier reconnoitring them as 'these citadels of French power in the East'.[258]

Lord Sandwich remarked as early as 1779 that the defences of the Ile de France 'probably are too strong to be attempted without great uncertainty'.[259] Two decades later, Sir George Yonge followed this long-standing orthodoxy. He understood that 'their works [are] strong, their artillery good and well [armed.] I don't suppose it would be possible to succeed without an armament of 10,000 men and a strong naval force for their support'.[260] Sir Roger Curtis was similarly pessimistic about British chances of capturing the island: 'I am led to believe that this island is next to being impregnable.'[261] While the naval surgeon-cum-naturalist Charles Telfair observed that 'the capture of the Isle of France must be an object of no common accomplishment: the task is not to be executed by a feeble hand'.[262]

This air of menace meant that this particular part of the region – equally as important on the route to and from India as the South Atlantic or South Africa – presented a different character to those concerned with preserving Britain's access to that maritime seaway. There were, of course, some potentially positive advantages to be derived. Martin Bickham, an American supercargo owner who arrived on the Ile de France in 1798, remarked that 'the situation of this island is so convenient for trade, and its port so commodious that there will be doubtless a great deal of good business done here. It can be looked upon in a manner, as the store house of the eastern world.'[263] And, when the British eventually conquered the island, Robert Farquhar was positive about the island's climate, soil and maritime capabilities:

It is almost superfluous to note that Port Louis in this island affords facilities which are scarcely enjoyed in any other port throughout the world, for the

[257] 'Jacob Haafner's description of Mauritius', in Toorawa (ed.), *Western Indian Ocean*, pp. 77–86, p. 77.
[258] NUL, Mi 2F 18, Henry Keating to Nesbit Willoughby, 27 December 1810.
[259] NMM, SAN F/22/52, Lord Sandwich, 'Thoughts upon an Expedition to the S. Seas', November 1779.
[260] BL, Add. MS 13785, f. 23, Yonge to Wellesley, 7 February 1800.
[261] Curtis to Spencer, 28 November 1800, *Spencer*, vol. IV, p. 241.
[262] [Charles Telfair], *Account of the Conquest of the Island of Bourbon ... By an Officer of the Expedition* (London: T. Egerton, 1811), p. 34.
[263] Martin Bickham to Stephen Girard, c.1802, in John Bach McMaster, *The Life and Times of Stephen Girard, Mariner and Merchant*, 2 vols. (Philadelphia: J. B. Lippincott, 1918), vol. I, p. 417.

immediate supply of ships which may touch here on their way to and from England in order to fill their water and take in provisions.[264]

But these advantages were, for the British at least, heavily outweighed by the negatives. As 'the only French possessions east of the Cape', the Ile de France and its satellites furnished 'the only means our arch-enemy can command for annoying us in this quarter of the world'.[265] In this case, positive advantages – economic, political or strategic – were less important than the French presence and its potential to inflict severe damage on British trading connections. In one of his first letters from India following his arrival there as governor general, Lord Minto described the damage that the Ile de France could wreak on Company shipping:

The Mauritius affords a secure port for equipping and refitting ships of war and other cruisers against our trade, and a place of refuge and safety for them and their prizes. Every project of the enemy which requires a naval and military force, will find facilities in the possession of the Mauritius. Troops, stores, and shipping may be almost imperceptibly assembled there, separately and in detail, which could not without extreme hazard of failure, be dispatched in a body from France.[266]

It was perhaps for this reason that, once the Cape was under British control, this region of the Indian Ocean became 'every day more and more an object of attention'.[267] In July 1800, Lady Anne Barnard wondered 'if our Ministry will prosecute the plan of taking the Mauritius or of negociating [sic] with them in the manner Mr B[arnard] proposed to Mr D[undas]'.[268] It certainly continued to energise debate and to elicit comment through the Revolutionary and Napoleonic period, leading to its eventual capture just over ten years later.[269] Assessing the situation in 1810, the newly installed British governor of Mauritius, Robert Farquhar, reiterated that the island was 'the true key of India, being as admirably situated for affording effectual protection to our Commerce as it is for annoying the Enemy'.[270] Meanwhile in India, Minto regarded the taking of Mauritius as one of the most important services 'that could be rendered to the East India Company and the nation in the east'.[271]

264 BL, IOR, H/701, p. 165, Robert Farquhar to Lord Minto, 5 February 1811.
265 Lord Minto to Lady Minto, 26 March 1810, *Minto*, p. 243.
266 Minto to Chairman of the East India Company [n.d.], *Minto*, p. 241.
267 NMM, CHN/8/6, Macartney to Christian, 27 April 1798.
268 7 July 1800, *Diaries*, vol. II, p. 186.
269 See pp. 96–9, 219–22 below. For more on the capture of the island, see TNA, ADM 1/64, Stopford to Admiralty, 26 October 1811. See also NUL, Mi 2F 839/12, p. 12, 'Account of the Career of Sir Nesbit Willoughby, 1790–1832' [c.1832].
270 Farquhar to Lord Liverpool, 30 August 1810, *RCC*, vol. VII, p. 365.
271 Minto to Robert Dundas, 25 January 1811, *Minto*, p. 248.

Since the beginnings of European long-distance trade with Asia, this corner of the Indian Ocean had offered an interconnected network of locations.[272] On his way to Goa in the early seventeenth century, for example, the Frenchman François Pyrard observed that 'Moçambique' was a place of great importance to the King of Spain. The south-eastern coast of Africa served as 'a fortress and a haven well adapted for a refuge to ships on the outward voyage from Portugal to Goa to shelter, after they passed the Cape of Good Hope'. Most importantly, from Pyrard's perspective, was the fact that it served as 'a sentinel or a bulwark at the entering in of the Indies, or a kind of hostelry for the refreshing of the Portuguese'.[273] By the eighteenth century, the Iles de France and Bourbon had become the focal point of the region's localised system of exchange. Many of Mauritius's supplies came from nearby islands. A great deal of rice, and the majority of the cattle, were obtained from Madagascar.[274] Bernardin de Saint Pierre believed that it was 'indispensably necessary' to the colony's survival.[275] Most of the corn consumed by islanders – a mixture of French settlers and their African slaves – and some of the cattle, came from the neighbouring island of Bourbon. Sir Roger Curtis thought that, as a result, any power who wished 'to keep Isle France' required 'possession of Isle Bourbon'.[276] Like its larger sister, Bourbon was 'an object of apprehension to the government of India, and a perpetual drain upon its commerce' until its capture in 1809.[277] John Kelso, captured by the French and detained at the Ile de France, observed that the French islands were 'of no immaterial consequence to Great Britain and the Honourable Company':

For the total expulsion of such an enemy as the French nation from the vicinity of the most valuable territory in the world, which the possession of the islands of Bourbon and Isle of France would have the effect to produce, I should imagine, would be no unimportant consideration to them.[278]

When it eventually fell to British arms, it simply confirmed the importance of Mauritius, as Robert Farquhar suggested: 'The short period that

---

[272] See Rosabelle Boswell, 'Islands in the (Global) Stream: The Case of Mauritius and Seychelles', in Pamila Gupta, Isabel Hofmeyr and Michael Pearson (eds.), *Eyes Across the Water: Navigating the Indian Ocean* (Pretoria: UNISA Press, 2010), pp. 286–303.

[273] François Pyrard, *The Voyage of François Pyrard of Laval to the East Indies, the Maldives, the Moluccas and Brazil*, edited by Albert Gray, 2 vols. (London: Hakluyt Society, 1890), vol. II, p. 224.

[274] B'hurst, MS.053, p. 37, 'Account of the Island of St Mary's' (October 1800).

[275] Bernardin de Saint Pierre, *Voyage to the Island of Mauritius*, p. 176.

[276] Curtis to Spencer, 28 November 1800, *Spencer*, vol. IV, p. 241.

[277] [Telfair], *Account of the Conquest of the Island of Bourbon*, p. 2.

[278] John Kelso to David Cathcart, 20 March 1808, *Londonderry*, vol. VIII, pp. 173–4.

we have been already in the occupation of this Island teaches us (without adverting to the millions previously lost by the Hon'ble Company and private merchants) the extreme importance of the conquest of the Isle of France.'[279] Charles Telfair, whose family's financial plight had forced him to join the Royal Navy in 1797 at the age of nineteen, served at the capture of Bourbon.[280] After the surrender of the island, he published an anonymous account of its capture with a valuable index on the state of its agriculture and commerce. Telfair was in no doubt as to Bourbon's value as an addition to Britain's interests east of the Cape, and as a further buttress to the edifice of the country's Asian empire:

An island so peculiarly favoured by nature, blest with the happiest climate, enriched with the choicest productions of a luxuriant soil, placed in the centre of the commerce of India, uniting in itself every advantage which nature can bestow, or industry procure, with a numerous and well-disposed population, is an acquisition of no common value at any period; but in the present state of the war, it acquires a new and extraordinary estimation; and it may be affirmed that, since the conquest of Seringapatam, no acquisition has been made to the eastward of the Cape of Good Hope of equal importance for the preservation of our Indian empire.[281]

The accomplishment of Henry Keating's plans for taking Bourbon 'not only added to the lustre and glory of the British arms', but also secured, 'on the most permanent foundations, the dominion of England against the hostile attempts of France, and to destroy the last remnant of her influence in India'.[282] Ultimately, however, for Telfair, the capture of Bourbon was only a stepping stone to a much greater objective: 'We now want but one link of that chain [i.e. Mauritius], and by its acquisition we shall convert into the most powerful source of security, an instrument we have, by experience, found incomparably adapted to the purposes of annoyance and destruction.'[283]

Similarly, Madagascar had long maintained important commercial and social ties with the French-controlled Mascarenes.[284] In March 1807, Decaen had further strengthened this relationship by employing a commercial agent, Sylvain Roux, and empowering him to deal directly

[279] Farquhar to Liverpool, 30 August 1810, *RCC*, vol. VII, p. 365.
[280] See Marc Serge Rivière, 'From Belfast to Mauritius: Charles Telfair (1778–1833), Naturalist and a Product of the Irish Enlightenment', *Eighteenth-Century Ireland* 21 (2006), pp. 125–44.
[281] [Telfair], *Account of the Conquest of the Island of Bourbon*, pp. 2–3.   [282] *Ibid.*, p. 4.
[283] *Ibid.*, p. 36.
[284] See Auguste Toussaint, *La Route des Îles, contribution à l'histoire maritime des Mascareignes* (Paris: SEVPEN, 1967), pp. 132–3. For useful accounts of the island from a British perspective, see B'hurst, MS.053, pp. 36–8, 'Account of the Island of St Mary's' (October 1800); MS.053, pp. 71–2, 'St Mary's Island, Madagascar' (1800).

with the Malagasy princes. Roux laid the foundations of French settlement at Tamatave and organised a regular supply of rice and cattle to the Ile de France.[285] As a result, Robert Farquhar could assert that it was 'a country on which this island [Mauritius] depends for its subsistence'.[286] John Kelso remarked that the 'mercantile interest' of the two French islands in the area maintained 'constant communications with the fruitful island of Madagascar, by which they profit considerably'.[287] As well as supplying provisions and plantation workers to the Mascarenes, Madagascar was so closely 'linked to that of the coast of Africa that we believe it impossible to separate them'.[288]

Madagascar's strategic position and economic connections meant that it had the potential to cause untold damage to Britain's trade in the East. James Prior was amazed that it had 'not been more firmly grasped and held by France, who, by means of its energies, judiciously directed, might have rendered many of our advantages in India nugatory'.[289] Benjamin Stout was similarly impressed by 'one of the largest and finest islands in the world'. He was astonished that 'no European power hath as yet made a permanent settlement on the coast of this prolific country'.[290] A document in the Hampshire Record Office gives 'a rough outline of the many advantages that may result to this nation from a settlement formed on the west coast of the island'. After a brief geographical orientation, the author lists its many 'natural productions'. But the island also presented dangers. 'Nothing can be more obvious than the advantages' other European powers would derive from establishing settlements on the islands 'as, from its natural productions, they might not only construct ships but fit them out also in a more complete manner than we can in any part of India'.[291] Robert Farquhar was certainly alive to the importance of Madagascar, 'this fruitful and abundant island'.[292] So important was the French settlement founded by Roux on the eastern coast for the survival

---

[285] Pineo, *Grips of the Eagle*, p. 122.

[286] Farquhar to Bathurst, 18 November 1817, quoted in William Ellis, *History of Madagascar*, 2 vols. (London: Fisher, 1838), vol. II, p. 193. See also R. E. P. Wastell, 'British imperial policy in relation to Madagascar, 1810–1896', Ph.D. thesis, University of London, 1944.

[287] Kelso to Cathcart, 20 March 1808, *Londonderry*, vol. VII, p. 166.

[288] BL, Add. MS 18126, Morice, 'Mémoire sure la côte oriental d'Afrique' (Isle de France, 15 June 1777, ed. de Cossigny, 1790). See Gwyn Campbell, *An Economic History of Imperial Madagascar, 1750–1895: The Rise and Fall of an Island Empire* (Cambridge: Cambridge University Press, 2005), p. 6.

[289] James Prior, *Voyage along the Eastern Coast of Africa ... in the Nisus Frigate* (London: Richard Phillips, 1819), p. 60.

[290] Stout, *Hercules*, p. 18.

[291] HRO, 38M49/5/61/20, 'Observations on the Island of Madagascar', pp. 1–2, 4.

[292] BL, IOR, H/701, p. 457, Farquhar to Secret Committee, 2 April 1811. See also NLS, Minto Papers, MS 11683, Farquhar to Minto, 4 January 1811.

of the Mascarenes that its capture was ordered just after the surrender of Ile de France in 1810. A naval detachment under Philip Beaver was ordered to 'summons their surrender and in case of resistance forcibly take possession bringing away or destroying any depot of stores, ammunition or provisions you shall find; destroying any fortifications that may have been erected and bringing away any Europeans forming the garrison'.[293] When British troops seized former French trading stations on the east coast of the island in 1810–11, Farquhar declared Madagascar to be under British sovereignty.[294] He installed British agents and commissioned research to facilitate the establishment of a British settlement.[295] Farquhar was also keen on 'opening a friendly communication if possible with the Portuguese settlers in the straits of Madagascar and on the coast of Africa'. And even the Seychelles were recognised as 'another important post amongst the dependencies of this island [Mauritius] to which it will become necessary as soon as we have leisure to send an English agent'.[296]

But the Iles de France and Bourbon were always uppermost in ministers' minds, as well as those charged with protecting British trade and positions in the area. Captain Lockhart Russell, who was sent by the Bengal Presidency in the early 1770s to assess the islands, ventured 'to pronounce that so long as the present possessions in India are of consideration to the British nation, so long the island of Mauritius will be an object well worthy the attention of an early attack upon a rupture between France and England'.[297] The closeness of the French islands to the Cape even made Curtis anxious for Britain's position there:

The contiguity of the island to this colony, by which in time of war in open hostility, or in time of peace by secretly fomenting discord and giving aid to the discontented subjects, and by exciting the Caffres to war and affording them assistance, greatly disturb the tranquillity of the colony, impede its prosperity, and give to its Government and its inhabitants frequent trouble and continued apprehension.[298]

The increasing importance of the Ile de France and the other Mascarene Islands – Bourbon and Rodrigues – to European (specifically French) maritime trade with Asia had coincided with the appointment of Bertrand-François Mahé de Labourdonnais as governor there. Upon

[293] TNA, ADM 1/63, Albemarle Bertie to Philip Beaver, 13 December 1810.
[294] BL, IOR, H/701, p. 165, Farquhar to Minto, 5 February 1811.
[295] Campbell, *Imperial Madagascar*, p. 61.
[296] BL, IOR, H/701, p. 165, Farquhar to Minto, 5 February 1811.
[297] BL, IOR, H/106, p. 228, 'Report of Capt. Lockhart Russell to the Court of Directors of the East India Company', 24 July 1772.
[298] Curtis to Spencer, 28 November 1800, *Spencer*, vol. IV, pp. 240–1.

assuming his post in 1735, he embarked on a scheme to construct 'docks at which the ships might in their way to India careen or refit as well as at Port L'Orient, and be provided with everything necessary'.[299] In 1781, François Barbé-Marbois, secretary of the French legation to the United States, opined that the Ile de France was 'not an entrepôt for merchandise'.[300] With its defensive capabilities, however, it was still a crucial way station for French shipping: it had significant capacity to destroy British trade, and it had already withstood multiple invasion threats. Sir George Yonge spoke for many in asserting that 'the only annoyance at present to the Cape and indeed to India, is the Mauritius'.[301] It was not without reason, therefore, that the island had acquired the sobriquet 'The Gibraltar of the East'.[302]

From a British perspective, one of the most wide-ranging and considered views of the islands' strategic situation is preserved in a letter sent to the Chairman of the East India Company by an unnamed person employed by the Company 'to obtain such intelligence as could be procured from French officers on parole at Corke, Bandon and Kinsale'. The report has very little to say about the positive advantages that might accrue from possession of this station. In contrast, the intelligence focuses almost entirely on confirming and corroborating reports of hostile French intentions towards British possessions in India. According to the French officers interviewed by this correspondent: 'the Isle of Mauritius is viewed by their ministry in the same light ours do Gibraltar; as this is the Key of the Mediterranean, the French consider Mauritius as the Key of the Indian Ocean, and are, in consequence, determined to render it impregnable'.[303] In order to preserve this foothold in the Asian world, the island's population was provided with 'all things requisite for war'.[304] The French also sent a steady stream of 'workmen and artificers' from Europe. Their role was clear: 'The fortifications of this island are continually improving and increasing. Wherever any sort of landing appears in the least degree practicable, batteries have been constructed, and strong defences formed.'[305]

---

[299] NMM, P/16/12, pp. 214–15, Thomas Pennant, 'Outlines of the Globe'.
[300] Fichter, So Great a Profitt, p. 159.
[301] TNA, WO 1/332, p. 184, Yonge to Dundas, 29 March 1800.
[302] C. Northcote Parkinson, War in the Eastern Seas, 1793–1815 (London: Allen & Unwin, 1954), p. 15.
[303] BL, IOR, H/153, p. 403, 'Extract from a letter to Chairman of the East India Company by a person employed by the Chairman to obtain such intelligence as could be procured from French officers on parole at Corke, Bandon and Kinsale, sent by the Chairman and the Vice-Chairman to Sir Stanier Porter for the attention of the Earl of Hillsborough', 9 August 1781.
[304] Ibid., p. 407.   [305] Ibid., p. 404.

The island's military capabilities were equally as strong as its physical fortifications. Officers of the garrison had served in India, the sailors on the station were also used to 'hot climates', and their ships were 'in excellent condition, completely sound in all requisites and every one of them manned far above its usual complement'.[306] Meanwhile, every male was enrolled in 'a very formidable militia', while the French government at home adopted a policy of 'encouraging chiefly disbanded soldiers to go over and settle in the Mauritius ... by which means they become a deposit and a seminary of recruits for their forces in India, and for the troops daily arriving from Europe. This militia consists of more than four thousand.'[307] Taken together, during the last six years 'no labour nor expense have been spared to render the Mauritius of every possible utility to the designs of France against England'.[308]

Britain had always found Mauritius much less a key in its hand than a thorn in its side, and this situation continued as the eighteenth century drew to a close. William Pitt, the Prime Minister, spelled out the central problem presented by Mauritius to British Asian interests in unequivocal terms: 'As long as the French hold the Île de France, the British will never be masters of India.'[309] The doleful impact of Mauritius on the balance sheet of British imperial strategy and economic activity placed it high on the political agenda during the Revolutionary and Napoleonic Wars. The island offered two particularly poisonous barbs, making it the scourge of Britain's Asian trade: its ability to sustain a large fleet of privateers, and its potential to act as a springboard from which to launch more audacious and potentially disastrous assaults on Britain's interests in India.

The devastating impact that privateers wrought on British shipping passing through the region was a constant problem throughout the eighteenth century. It was certainly something that was much commented upon at the time by concerned British merchants and nervous ships' captains. Mahé de Labourdonnais's naval building programme and his scheme 'to cruise in the Indian seas, a plan he executed after[wards] to almost the subversion of the English empire in those distant parts' became a *cause célèbre*.[310] Given the difficulty of sending regular forces to the island, privateering activity played a critical part in carrying out French designs. Although the Royal Navy's presence at the Cape eliminated the dangers posed by 'their ships of war', problems remained: 'the inhabitants

[306] *Ibid.*, p. 407.   [307] *Ibid.*, p. 404.   [308] *Ibid.*, p. 408.
[309] Quoted in John Addison and K. Hazareesingh, *A New History of Mauritius* (London: Macmillan, 1984), p. 43.
[310] NMM, P/16/12, pp. 213–14, Pennant, 'Outlines'.

vest their property in privateers, and live by the success of their cruises'.[311]

Privateers inflicted heavy losses on British commerce during the Revolutionary period.[312] During the first sixteen years of the Revolutionary War, British merchant losses were staggering. The economic devastation caused by these privateers is difficult to calculate. One contemporary estimated the value of shipping captured between 1793 and mid-1804 at £2.5 million.[313] More recent scholarship has suggested that French privateer attacks on British commerce cost £4 million in the first seven years of the war.[314] Looking back in 1810, Lord Minto described how, 'from the Isle of France all the cruisers have been sent out against our trade; against which a very large squadron have done little to protect us. The losses of the Company, as well as of the general trade, have been enormous.'[315] Across the entire period, between 1793 and 1810, Mauritian privateers and French naval squadrons operating from the island captured more than five hundred British and allied prizes, estimated to be worth at least eighty million gold francs.[316] The Ile de France was described as a 'spectre' which haunted British sailors and statesmen alike. It was, as Mabel Haight put it, 'the one black spot in the clear blue of the Indian Ocean'.[317] On her way to India in 1798, where her husband was to be installed as governor of Madras, Henrietta Clive conveyed the anxiety that troubled many British travellers as they prepared to enter the Indian Ocean. The *Dover Castle*, the ship in which she was sailing, called at the Cape of Good Hope. Thinking that 'we might meet with some French vessels from the Isle de France':

It was proper to enquire about them that my history might not be improved by being taken prisoner and my valour, I confess, would not have been great upon

---

[311] TNA, WO 1/332, p. 184, Yonge to Dundas, 29 March 1800.

[312] A number of historians have warned of misinterpreting the statistics in relation to the value of the Mascarenes as a collective gateway to India. Nevertheless, if the economic data are ambiguous, the representational and rhetorical power of these islands was considerable for contemporaries. See Fichter, *So Great a Profitt*, p. 159.

[313] William Milburn, *Oriental Commerce, Containing a Geographical Description of the Principal Places in the East Indies, China and Japan, with their Produce, Manufactures and Trade*, 2 vols. (London: Parry, Black and Co., 1813), vol. II, p. 566, citing 'a gentleman at Madras'.

[314] Hall, *British Strategy in the Napoleonic War*, p. 187. See also A. G. Field, 'The expedition to Mauritius and the establishment of British control', MA thesis, University of London, 1931.

[315] NLS, Minto Papers, MS 11065, Lord Minto to Lady Minto, 26 March 1810.

[316] Richard B. Allen, *Slaves, Freedmen, and Indentured Laborers in Colonial Mauritius* (Cambridge: Cambridge University Press, 1999), pp. 12, 20.

[317] Haight, *European Powers and South-East Africa*, p. 111.

such an occasion. I have thought with some little horror of a retreat into the hold when I heard of a strange sail being in sight.[318]

Things appeared no better to those with professional expertise. In 1795, John Blankett of the Royal Navy wrote to his colleague Evan Nepean, alluding to the potential problems that the island could cause. Although it was 'now kept quiet for want of means to fit out their cruisers' any alliance with the Dutch could prove to be disastrous as, 'aided by the assistance of the Cape', Mauritius 'will become a nest of pirates, secure and unattackable amongst their own rocks'.[319] This pessimistic prognosis came to fruition, as Admiral Elphinstone remarked:

The Mauritius is the only place in these parts in the possession of the French, its present utility to them is therefore considerable, and affords every refuge and shelter to their Cruizers in these Seas, by which the British Commerce is greatly annoyed; upon these grounds the subduction of it becomes an important value to His Majesty's Service.[320]

Even as the British presence elsewhere in the region was consolidated, Lord Macartney lamented the French privateers' ability to evade naval blockades. Macartney was the first British governor to be based in relatively close proximity to the island and with a naval squadron at his disposal. He ordered Captain Losack to cruise around the island in an effort to capture the French corsairs operating there.[321] As Macartney and his successors discovered, however, the French continued to prey on Portuguese and British shipping, so much so that the Portuguese governor had to apply to the Cape for assistance.[322] Andrew Barnard was painfully aware of the way in which 'for some time past the trade of India has suffered very considerably from the number of cruisers sent out from the Mauritius and I am told that more privateers are fitting out there'.[323] In early 1800, Sir Roger Curtis, naval commander-in-chief, pleaded for more forces which were 'necessary to watch the motions of the Enemy at Mauritius, as well to be a check upon the Privateers there fitted out for the annoyance of the Indian Trade'.[324] As it was 'greatly annoyed by the privateers which are fitted out from the island', more frequent patrols or, if possible, the capture of the island 'would render the

[318] Henrietta Clive to Lady Douglas, 7 June 1798, in Nancy K. Shields (ed.), *Birds of Passage: Henrietta Clive's Travels in South India, 1798–1801* (London: Eland, 2009), p. 52.
[319] TNA, WO 1/329, p. 48, Blankett to Nepean, 25 January 1795.
[320] TNA, ADM 1/55, Elphinstone to Admiralty, 30 July 1796.
[321] NMM, CHN/8/6, Macartney to Christian, 27 April 1798.
[322] AHU, CU, Moç., CX83/11, Menezes da Costa to Francis Dundas, 8 July 1799.
[323] RH, GB 0162 MSS.Afr.s.1,2, Andrew Barnard to Dundas, 20 October 1799.
[324] Curtis to Nepean, 4 January 1800, *RCC*, vol. III, p. 14.

trade of every description in India more secure'.[325] Sir George Yonge similarly wondered:

Whether it is adviseable to attempt the reduction of this nest of pirates, is more than I can pretend to judge. This I know, its reduction would be a great security to this Colony, and indeed to all the Indian commerce.[326]

Richard Wellesley wrote to Dundas later in the year that 'the Isle of France covers our coasts with privateers, and infests every track of the trade of India'.[327] He urged retributive action against the Mascarenes, 'those prolific sources of intrigue in peace, and of piracy and buccaneering in war'.[328] Peter Rainier lamented the deficiencies of the squadron whose 'service has hitherto . . . answered very little purpose'.[329] And one did not need to be in the loftier positions of civilian or naval command to recognise the threat. Matthew Godwin, a lieutenant in the *Tremendous* on the Cape station, believed that French ships 'in these seas' were doing 'a vast deal of mischief to our Trade in India'.[330]

And the attacks continued unabated. The Royal Navy blockade was still ineffective in 1804 when Matthew Flinders reported the ease with which the French evaded it.[331] In 1805, Vice-Admiral Pellew referred to the commercial risk they posed, and an unsigned memorandum in Dundas's papers depicts the islands as a base for attacking India and as a source of privateering.[332] Matthew Flinders, who had been detained on the island by a suspicious governor on his way back from charting Australia, recounted the clash between the *Warren Hastings* and *La Piémontaise* in July 1806. The encounter had resulted in the deaths of a dozen men and the capture of the British East Indiaman's cargo. When the French ship returned to port in December 1806, Flinders reported: 'This ship has taken, or done injury to the English commerce, to the amount of a million and half of dollars, within the last eight months!'[333] In 1809, Captain Nesbit Willoughby, who would go on to play an important part in the eventual capture of the islands, reported on the French fleet returning to port with their prizes: two large East Indiamen, the

[325] Curtis to Spencer, 28 November 1800, *Spencer*, vol. IV, pp. 240–1.
[326] TNA, WO 1/332, p. 184, Yonge to Dundas, 29 March 1800.
[327] NAS, GD51/3/2/55, Wellesley to Dundas, 7 October 1800.
[328] Quoted in P. E. Roberts, *India under Wellesley* (London: G. Bell and Sons, 1929), p. 147.
[329] BL, Add. MS 75834, Peter Rainier to Spencer, 10 December 1799.
[330] DRO, 152M/C1800/ON11, Matthew Godwin to unnamed recipient, 10 February 1800.
[331] Marina Carter, *Companions of Misfortune: Flinders and Friends at the Isle of France, 1803–1810* (London: Pink Pigeon Press, 2003), p. 116.
[332] NAS, GD 51/2/274, Unsigned memorandum [November 1804]. See also Hall, *British Strategy in the Napoleonic War*, p. 186.
[333] Quoted in Carter, *Companions of Misfortune*, p. 116.

Ceylon and the *Windham*.[334] These were just two examples of a wider malaise affecting British shipping. Between 1803 and 1809, French privateers sank some 15,000 tons of East India Company shipping in the Indian Ocean.[335] The merchants and shipowners of Calcutta were aghast at the depredations in 1808. Underwriters had to pay out £290,000 in claims in a two-month period for losses due to French attacks.[336] In ten months of 1810, a contemporary estimated 'the insurance offices of Bengal were losers of three million sterling by captures'.[337] They were so appalled that they petitioned the Lords Commissioners of the Admiralty to request an explanation as to why 'the trade in the Bay of Bengal has been left so much exposed to the depredations of the enemy' by the naval squadron based there.[338] And in 1809, the capture of two British merchant ships, the *Streatham* and the *Europe*, caused the merchants of Calcutta to petition the government in London again. For 'the protection of commerce', they recommended 'enlarging, if possible, the scope of the convoys' travelling back to Europe. The precautionary measures were necessary because, according to the merchants, 'as long as the islands of Mauritius and Bourbon remain in possession of the Enemy, effectual protection of our ships cannot be afforded'.[339]

As we have seen, then, the danger of French ships using Mauritius to prey on British shipping in the southern Indian Ocean was an ever-present one. But the island had an even more diabolical potential: as a springboard for a more serious French assault on British interests in the Indian subcontinent. Mahé de Labourdonnais had shown the potential of the Ile de France by converting the island into a base for operations against the British in India during the War of the Austrian Succession, compelling the surrender of Madras in 1746 with a small squadron equipped there.[340] In June 1785, Daniel Hailes passed on a spy's report that a 64-gun ship *armé en flûte* had sailed for Bourbon with naval stores and 300 troops.[341] News of French

[334] NUL, Mi 2F 10, Willoughby to Samuel Pym, 23 August 1810.
[335] C. H. Philips, *The East India Company, 1784–1834* (Manchester: Manchester University Press, 1940), p. 155.
[336] Hall, *British Strategy in the Napoleonic War*, p. 95.
[337] 'Southern-Ocean: Mauritius', *Naval Chronicle* 29 (1813), p. 130.
[338] TNA, ADM 2/1366, p. 166, William Wellesley-Pole to Edward Pellew, 6 September 1808.
[339] BL, IOR, O/6/4/245–57, p. 254, 'Abstract of Correspondence between the Governor of Bengal and Rear Admiral Drury and the Officers of His Majesty's Navy respecting Convoys', Merchants' and Agents' Petitions', 19 October 1809. See Stephen Taylor, *Storm and Conquest: The Battle for the Indian Ocean, 1808–10* (London: Faber & Faber, 2007), p. 219.
[340] Toussaint, *Route des Iles*, p. 94.
[341] BL, Egerton MS 3499, p. 116, Daniel Hailes to Lord Carmarthen, 2 June 1785.

troops massing on the islands was always worrying. The French establishment on the Ile de France had been of concern to the Dutch when they were in charge at the Cape. William Eliot, Secretary of the Embassy and Acting Minister Plenipotentiary at The Hague, informed Lord Grenville that the government of the United Provinces had received intelligence from the Cape dating from the middle of January 1794, which 'speak of a considerable force being collected by the French at the Isle of Bourbon, and at the Mauritius capable of inspiring them with some uneasiness'. Such concerns were exacerbated by another account of a fleet of six French ships of the line which the Dutch supposed 'to have sailed some months since with an intent of making an attack on the Cape'.[342] Of course, British suspicions centred on the French intentions towards India. Lieutenant George Gordon of the Bombay Army wrote surreptitiously from the island to the Bombay Presidency in 1796, warning of the high state of efficiency of the French naval squadron there and its plans to take troops and cannon to the Indian mainland.[343] Four years later, Richard Wellesley asked Sir Roger Curtis to keep a squadron cruising off the Mascarenes in order to intercept any French forces destined for India.[344] He pointed to the 'piratical power' of the French island, which he said was 'absolutely essential' to eliminate.[345]

For those concerned with safeguarding the route to the East, the obvious solution was to acquire Mauritius and establish a more secure footing in the south-west corner of the Indian Ocean.[346] The East India Company, acutely aware of the importance of the island, had advocated this as early as 1747, when the Company's Secret Committee suggested the launching of an expedition under Admiral Edward Boscawen of the Royal Navy.[347] In 1793, the government in London finally resolved to launch an attack on Mauritius and Bourbon. It communicated directly to the Board of Commissioners for the Affairs of India. On this occasion, the military position in India was too uncertain to admit of launching the expedition. The governor general, Sir John Shore, thought it was neither advisable nor practicable. By 1795, the French had reinforced the islands, making an assault impossible.[348] The capture of the Cape, and the

---

[342] William Eliot to Lord Grenville, 16 April 1794, *RCC*, vol. I, pp. 16–17.

[343] Quoted in Ward, 'Admiral Peter Rainier', p. 82.

[344] Wellesley to Curtis, 24 October 1800, *Spencer*, vol. IV, p. 159.

[345] Martin (ed.), *Despatches, Minutes and Correspondence of the Marquess Wellesley*, vol. II, pp. 307, 754.

[346] Britain's arch-nemesis in the period, Napoleon Bonaparte, declared himself puzzled by Britain's oversight in not capturing Mauritius: 'I have never been able to understand why they didn't take it. It's sheer idiocy on their part.' See Taylor, *Storm and Conquest*, pp. 196–7.

[347] H. C. M. Austen, *Sea Fights and Corsairs of the Indian Ocean: Being the Naval History of Mauritius from 1715 to 1810* (Port Louis: R. W. Brooks, 1935), pp. 21–2.

[348] Misra, *British Foreign Policy and Indian Affairs*, pp. 28–9.

consequent British foothold in the region, changed the situation. In July 1796, Admiral George Keith Elphinstone, having recently taken the Cape, thought that troops there might be employed better at Mauritius because 'the Isles of Mauritius offer themselves as most conveniently situated for our operations'.[349] Although the plan was eventually abandoned, Elphinstone made preparations to attack from South Africa in 1796.[350] Arthur Wellesley identified the same solution in 1797: 'Mauritius ought to be taken. As long as the French have an establishment there, Great Britain cannot call herself safe in India.'[351] His brother, Richard Wellesley, deemed 'the reduction of the Mauritius' to be 'an object of the utmost importance to the security of India and I know nothing that would tend so much to lessen the influence of France in this quarter'.[352] While in 1799, Admiral Peter Rainier wrote to Lord Spencer asking if either he or Sir Roger Curtis at the Cape could be given sufficient ships to enforce a permanent blockade of the French island.[353]

Ultimately Mauritius was undone by its very connectivity and the contiguous nature of the oceanic space in which it was located. Towards the end of 1808, the Secret Committee directed the Bombay government to adopt measures for the occupation of the island of Rodrigues with the ultimate object of enabling British ships from the Cape to maintain an unbroken blockade of the French islands in the region.[354] Lord Minto decided to take advantage of the situation.[355] The eventual capture of the tiny island of Rodrigues, four hundred miles east of Mauritius, demonstrates the interconnected nature of the region's geopolitical position. It was occupied in 1809 by a detachment of troops from Bombay, including both European soldiers and Indian sepoys, under the command of Lieutenant-Colonel Keating. This enterprise was, according to Lord Minto, 'conducted and executed in a very masterly manner, and with entire success'. And, with a modest reinforcement of about 2,000 men from the subcontinent, together with the forces already at Rodrigues, Rowley and Keating were confident of conquering the island of Bourbon. This, they considered, was 'an important step towards the reduction of the Isle of France', which eventually surrendered to British arms in

[349] TNA, ADM 1/55, Elphinstone to Admiralty, 30 July 1796.
[350] James Craig to Dundas, 30 July 1796, *RCC*, vol. I, p. 415; Craig to Dundas, 3 August 1796, *RCC*, vol. I, p. 424.
[351] Quoted in Parkinson, *War in the Eastern Seas*, p. 159.
[352] BL, Add. MS 13456, ff. 59–60, Wellesley to Dundas, 28 February 1798. For Wellesley's abortive raid, see NAS, GD51/3/2/55, Wellesley to Dundas, 7 October 1800; Roberts, *India under Wellesley*, pp. 147–8; Ward, 'Admiral Peter Rainier', pp. 147–53.
[353] BL, Add. MS 75834, Rainier to Spencer, 10 December 1799.
[354] Misra, *British Foreign Policy and Indian Affairs*, pp. 84–5.
[355] NLS, Minto Papers, MS 11622, pp. 27–44, Minto to Secret Committee, 30 April 1810.

December 1810.[356] In January 1811, the *St Helena Monthly Register* summed up the situation:

The value of the Mauritius to the French Government, arises from these political reasons which induce it to wish to preserve an establishment in the Indian seas. Had not this island been possessed by the French, they would have lost every check whatever on the prosperity of the commerce of British India ... The expence of a force necessary to capture the Mauritius is great, very great, and the returns from the island are totally inadequate to the costs; yet vessels fitted out, or rather repaired and furnished at this island as ships of war have done great damage among our Indian shipping. The number, at present sailing under the British flag, form an irresistible temptation to French cupidity ... That island thereby became a nest of pirates, and the fate which belongs to such a station is now, by the bravery of our Army and Navy, decided.[357]

The relief was equally palpable in India, where one of Matthew Flinders's contacts reported the rejoicing among the merchants of India about the fact that the 'nest of privateers' had finally been extinguished: 'it is incredible the satisfaction which the capture of that island has diffused all over India'.[358] And, back in Britain, one speaker told the House of Commons in February 1813 that 'the reduction of the Isle of France' would prove to be 'the most important of all our colonial conquests since the commencement of the War'.[359]

This was all in the future, however, when Sir George Yonge wrote to Marquis Wellesley in January 1801. Then Wellesley's schemes for Mauritius were still current. With regard to the 'the Isle de France', Yonge hoped that it was 'more at the mercy of India than India at hers'.[360] The truth was more complicated. As we have seen, throughout the eighteenth century, the defence of British interests in India was directly tied to the gateways to the Indian Ocean in the southern hemisphere. Given its importance, it is perhaps unsurprising that relief at the news of the capture of Mauritius was reflected in the instructions to fire the guns at the Tower of London in celebration.[361] As the French Wars neared their conclusion, the island was still considered as absolutely 'necessary to protect Indian commerce'.[362] Mauritius was one of the key locations for testing and securing British power in the region. Not until the events of 1810 did Mauritius eventually became one of the stars

---

[356] NLS, Minto Papers, MS 11065, Lord Minto to Lady Minto, 26 March 1810.
[357] *St Helena Monthly Register*, January 1811, pp. 32–3.
[358] Quoted in Carter, *Companions of Misfortune*, p. 133.
[359] NUL, Mi 2F 839/12, p. 12, 'Account of the Career of Sir Nesbit Willoughby'.
[360] BL, Add. MS 13785, ff. 41–2, Yonge to Wellesley, 24 January 1801.
[361] Hall, *British Strategy in the Napoleonic War*, p. 190.
[362] See 'Memorandum of Cabinet', 26 December 1813, in Webster (ed.) *British Diplomacy*, p. 124.

of Britain's Indian Ocean world rather than the rock on which its eastern ambitions perished.

Conclusion

This chapter has explored the British representation of the southern reaches of the Atlantic and Indian oceans, the claims of various places to the title of 'key' to the East, and their individual (and collective) political and strategic value. In a variety of instances, institutions and individuals – from the government and the Royal Navy to the East India Company, and from sailors, merchants and travellers to politicians and policymakers – used words such as 'key', 'gateway', 'Gibraltar' and 'half-way house' to describe the places at the entrance to the Indian Ocean. These locations provided access, defended routes and facilitated connections. And, by the end of the Revolutionary and Napoleonic Wars, most of them were in British possession. But this accounts for only part of the story. The British interest in the region cannot be understood without considering rival European empires or issues of rising settler identity, both of which influenced the tone and extent of British activity in the region. It is to this theme that the following chapter turns.

'A sword in the hands': European rivals,
      imperial designs, colonial problems

Commercial and strategic interest in the southern reaches of the Atlantic
and Indian oceans was not confined to Britain. The region's position at
the crossroads of maritime trading routes, spanning several oceans and
continents, situated it at the heart of a rapidly globalising world. Indeed,
the long-distance European East India trade with Asia, to which this
region offered the principal maritime gateway, was partially responsible
for this. Unsurprisingly, then, it attracted European powers aplenty.
Robert Brooke, governor of St Helena, reported in 1792 that 'the
French have lately given great encouragement to the Americans to settle
in [Ile de] France and carry on the Southern Whale Fishery. The Dutch
are also busy at the Cape informing plans to circumvent us in the trade'.[1]
Competing interests were reflected most noticeably on the seas, which
conveyed the ships of different European countries and competing char-
tered companies to and from the Indian Ocean. After capturing the Cape,
George Keith Elphinstone observed:

The seas are infested with Americans, Danes, Genoese, Tuscans, etc., or in other
terms smuggling ships, mostly belonging to Britain and Bengal, entrenched with
oaths and infamy, who trade to the French islands [Ile de France and Bourbon]
and all the ports in India, changing their flags as it is most convenient to them.[2]

Colonel George Young was surprised that 'the Russians, Americans,
French, and Dutch have not as yet settled on the North West coast of
this fruitful island' of Madagascar.[3] Just as there were significant connections and overlaps between the southern oceans and other areas of British
interest around the world, principally India, so *within* the region a variety
of European empires contended for control of a series of strategic

[1] BL, IOR, G/32/165, p. 29, Robert Brooke, 'Account of St Helena with Various
Observations Annexed' [1792].
[2] Quoted in J. Holland Rose, *The Life of William Pitt. Volume 2: William Pitt and the Great
War* (London: G. Bell, 1934), p. 253.
[3] HRO, 38M49/5/61/20, 'Observations on the Island of Madagascar by Colonel Sir George
Young' (*c*.1806–7), p. 4.

locations and dominance of trading routes. As a result, the history of the
expanding and developing British presence in the southern Atlantic and
Indian oceans cannot be written in isolation or without reference to other
competing interests.

Of course, one of the ways in which Britain could keep rivals away from
its Asian commercial interests was to prevent them from getting anywhere
near its Indian territories in the first place. As impractical as it sounds,
Henry Dundas gave the matter some light consideration when he suggested that the East India Company might 'establish warehouses at the
Cape and to permit sales of their goods to take place there'. Dundas
elaborated on the wisdom of such a course of action 'both with a view
to their own commercial interest and with a view to the general and
permanent interests of the empire'. Building up a Company presence in
Southern Africa:

would in all probability reduce all other nations to withdraw themselves from the
trade direct to India and China and induce them to provide themselves with the
articles of those countries from the warehouse at the Cape. They would thereby
save themselves half the expense of their voyages, and Great Britain would
gradually but ultimately be relieved from the danger which necessarily attends
its dominions in India from being exposed to the intercourse and intrigues of other
European powers trading there.[4]

That this was not as far-fetched as it appears is corroborated by William
Innes Pocock's account of the means by which American traders used the
island of St Helena to facilitate their business. They 'bring provisions
which are always saleable, and procure in return the produce of the East at
this place, rather than make the longer and more precarious voyages to
India and China'.[5]

Ultimately, however, British interest and activities in the region need to
be seen in the context of other European empires.[6] At the outset of the
period under discussion here, Britain's rivals had a more established
presence across the region. The Spanish in South America, the Dutch
at the Cape, the French in the south-western Indian Ocean, and the
Portuguese in South-East and South-West Africa eclipsed the tiny (and
sometimes disputed) British presence on a few volcanic islands in the

[4] KCL, DT2042 [Henry Dundas], 'Suggestions respecting the Cape of Good Hope'
[c.1796], unpaginated.
[5] William Innes Pocock, *Five Views of the Island of St Helena from Drawings Taken on the Spot*
(London: S. and J. Fuller, 1815), p. 8.
[6] For an analogous approach which explores rival European attempts to gain access to the
Pacific Ocean and the Asian trade through control of western North America, see Paul
W. Mapp, *The Elusive West and the Contest for Empire, 1713–1763* (Chapel Hill, NC:
University of North Carolina Press, 2011).

South Atlantic. By focusing on the region in the context of its various European claimants, as well as its increasingly vociferous settler communities, this chapter sheds light on its place in the fierce intra-European rivalries that affected the wider world in the late eighteenth century. The extra-European context of the conflict between Britain and France in particular, and its playing out in the southern hemisphere, offers insights into how these rivalries affected the wider global geopolitical balance.

This chapter explores the ways in which British fears about their position in the region played out in practice, demonstrating how the priorities and enmities of European powers mapped on to the situation in the southern seas and their adjacent landmasses. The fears and alarms that transfixed politicians in Europe, as well as broader geopolitical threats and rivalries, were refracted by distance and local context for people serving these empires beyond Europe. The discussion begins by tracing the complex British attitude towards the French presence in the south-western Indian Ocean and the fear of an expansion of that presence through the capture of the Cape. It also examines the impact of the French Revolution on the debates in Britain, and in the region itself, about the situation in the South Atlantic and Southern Africa. Building on this, the dangers posed by other rivals are investigated. The United States, a country born of a dangerous revolutionary movement, was feared mainly on the grounds of its commercial ambitions and expertise. Meanwhile, however, a more serious threat to European metropolitan hegemony was thrown up by the outbreak of various settler rebellions. Questioning the basis of European imperial power, these presented opportunities and dangers to British officials and statesmen in equal measure. In total, the chapter provides a comparative and contextual lens through which to view British engagement in this gateway to the Indian Ocean.

This was an era of shifting political tectonics, the ramifications of which were felt in the southern Atlantic and Indian oceans. Three major revolutions – in North America, France and Saint Domingue – sent shock waves through the Atlantic world. More broadly, it was a period of political friction and collision: between empires and their subjects, between empires and their rivals, and between empires and their enemies. Social structures were convulsed by a series of political earthquakes that recalibrated, among other things, the nature and extent of the British Empire. But, as scholars have shown, the so-called 'age of revolution' was not confined to the North Atlantic.[7] Across the Southern Atlantic world,

---

[7] C. A. Bayly, *The Birth of the Modern World, 1780–1914* (Oxford: Blackwell, 2004), pp. 88–92.

from Peru and Chile on the west coast of South America to the eastern frontier of the Cape Colony, relationships between colonial settlers and the European polities to which they owed notional allegiance became increasingly unstable and contingent. Suddenly the possibility of greater autonomy, even independence, became an option for communities as diverse as the Spanish colonists in South America, Dutch settlers in Southern Africa, and even a small band of Americans on the tiny islet of Tristan da Cunha. The history of the British Empire in this region is not just about the rise of that empire, then, but also about the threat posed by, as well as the potential decline of, other European empires. And it is about the active role played by Britain in undermining other empires, such as the Spanish, as well as the embryonic proto-nationalist movements that abjured European control entirely and presented a new threat to the security of Britain's Indian Ocean world.

In order to explore these themes, this chapter engages with the wider context of the British presence in the region. The discussion focuses on the threat posed to Britain, its colonial outposts and the safety of the maritime route to India from a range of rivals. Conversely, it also illustrates the British potential to destroy and take advantage of the desuetude of other empires. The rhetoric of imperial consolidation, supported by military and diplomatic action, was consistently deployed in the second half of the eighteenth century to prevent the French from establishing rival interests. The logic behind this approach was simple. Lord Caledon, governor of the Cape Colony in the first decade of the nineteenth century, put it succinctly: 'whatever measure deprives India of succour cannot be otherwise than essentially detrimental to the greatest state possessed by Great Britain'.[8] In most British minds, French threats to take the Cape or St Helena, or to use the Ile de France to launch an assault on the subcontinent, qualified as a clear and present danger to Britain's commercial interests in India and, more generally, its place in the wider Asian world. Conversely, if Britain could reinforce its presence in the southern oceans at the expense of its rivals, then the security of the Indian empire would be considerably enhanced. Politicians, merchants and military men actively worked to bring about the destruction of outposts controlled by competing European empires. Britain was not just building up its own empire at this time, it was also wrecking, confusing and confounding other empires. A more extensive British presence in the region, for example, could wreak havoc on a tottering Spanish Empire in South America, potentially gaining valuable commercial footholds in the process. It held out the prospect of asserting dominance over the waning Dutch Empire

---

[8] Lord Caledon to Albemarle Bertie, 19 October 1809, *RCC*, vol. VII, p. 205.

and exacting a modicum of revenge for the perceived treachery of the Netherlands by their support of the American rebels.[9] It would, in the words of Henry Pemberton, allow Britain to 'play the back game of American Independence'.[10] And it presented the possibility of usurping Portuguese interests around the southern shores of the African continent.

If Britain's physical presence in the region was minimal until the late eighteenth century, fear about its intentions had been rife among its European rivals for decades. In urging the Dutch to join them, for example, the French alluded to Britain's steady accumulation of territories in Asia and warned their continental neighbours of British imperial ambitions in respect of 'your most important establishments, the Cape of Good Hope, the island of Ceylon, and all your commerce with the Indies'. 'Do you believe', the proclamation continued, 'that the English, insatiable for power and lucre, would never take these important places from you, which would assure them of their Indian Empire?'.[11] (These warnings were, of course, borne out only two years later.) In December 1798, Lord Spencer dreamed of the benefits that would result from a British conquest of the Ile de France: 'The loss of that possession would certainly be a great inconvenience to France, and complete the obstruction which has been so happily thrown in the way of her Eastern plans.'[12] And the advantages were not just strategic. There could be significant collateral benefits, in the form of economic and commercial gains, to be had from eliminating a rival. In proposing his mad-cap and ultimately disastrous plan to capture Buenos Aires, Home Popham remarked on the advantages that South America presented.[13] Writing from St Helena to William Marsden, Secretary of the Admiralty, Popham argued that this port on the River Plate was 'the best commercial station in South America'.[14] Even more noteworthy, from Popham's perspective, was the destruction that a successful expedition could visit on Britain's rivals and the domestic approval that would inevitably follow. In an unerring display of

[9] See also Nicholas Tarling, *Anglo-Dutch Rivalry in the Malay World, 1780–1824* (Cambridge: Cambridge University Press, 1962).
[10] BL, IOR, G/9/1, p. 25, Henry Pemberton, 'A Narrative with a Description and Drawing of Croem or Crontz Riviere Bay situate on the South East Coast of Africa' [1785].
[11] 'Extract from a Proclamation of General Dumoriez to the Batavians', February 1793, *RCC*, vol. I, p. 3 (my translation). For a Dutch perspective on the capture of the Cape in 1795, see UWits, A51, 'Historie van de Kaap zeer Krachtig 1795' in which the anonymous poet compares the British to a 'wolf ... in the kraal'.
[12] Lord Spencer to Hugh Christian, 23 December 1798, *Spencer*, vol. IV, p. 189.
[13] For more on the expedition, see Ian Fletcher, *The Waters of Oblivion: The British Invasion of the Rio de la Plata, 1806–1807* (Tunbridge Wells: Spellmount, 1991).
[14] Home Popham to William Marsden, 30 April 1806, in Theodore Hood, *The Life of General the Right Honourable Sir David Baird, Bart.*, 2 vols. (London: Richard Bentley, 1832), vol. II, p. 144.

Schadenfreude, Popham urged that Charles Yorke, Home Secretary in the Addington administration: 'Properly appreciate the ruin which it promises to entail on a great European maritime power; calculate on the universal popularity such an expedition is likely to be attended with.'[15] And, in 1819, James Prior pointed out how worried the Portuguese were about British influence stretching up the east coast of Africa. 'An Englishman', he opined 'is always an object of dread to the Portuguese on this coast, his ideas being supposed to be filled with plans, and his actions pregnant with designs against their commerce.'[16] Given that serious consideration had been given to the conquest of their settlements in East Africa in 1807, the Portuguese anxiety was perhaps justified.[17]

Conversely, the threat to British interests in the region came from three distinct sources. First, there were the indigenous groups, who posed danger to both European imperial and settler colonial ideas of influence and control. William Dalrymple's plan to settle the coast of Southern Africa was subject to the jealousies of the Dutch settlers at the nearby Cape: 'What I write must be kept secret as the Dutch would make every exertion to seize the country if they had the least ideas of our intentions of settling in this neighbourhood.'[18] Some years later, when Britain had captured the Cape from the Dutch, the naval commander feared further rebellion in the district of Graaff-Reinet, already a tinderbox of settler discontent, citing the rumour that the local Afrikaners were 'ready at all times to invite the Caffre to assist them in opposition to the Government'.[19] He was especially worried by the unholy alliance of imperial rivals, colonial malcontents and indigenous marauders coming together at the eastern extremity of the Cape Colony.[20] Although there were 'very few regular troops at Isle France', if the French were 'to send to

---

[15] TNA, PRO 30/8/345, p. 86, Popham to Charles Yorke, 26 November 1803.

[16] James Prior, *Voyage along the Eastern Coast of Africa ... in the Nisus Frigate* (London: Richard Phillips, 1819), p. 26.

[17] See Mabel V. Jackson Haight, *European Powers and South-East Africa: A Study of International Relations on the South-Eastern Coast of Africa, 1796–1856* (London: Routledge & Kegan Paul, 1967), pp. 151–2.

[18] NAS, GD 51/3/17/2, Diana Dalrymple to William Devaynes, 17 November 1785.

[19] Roger Curtis to Spencer, 10 October 1800, in *Spencer*, vol. IV, p. 234. For more on Graaff-Reinet, see Kenneth Wyndham Smith, *From Frontier to Midlands: A History of the Graaff-Reinet District, 1786–1910* (Grahamstown: Institute of Social and Economic Research, Rhodes University, 1976).

[20] This frontier went on to become one of the most fractious intermediate zones of tension and conflict between the rapidly expanding British Empire (or rather spheres of British influence) and other polities that characterised the nineteenth century. Nine wars were waged here between 1779 and 1879. See Richard Price, *Making Empire: Colonial Encounters and the Creation of Imperial Rule in Nineteenth-Century Africa* (Cambridge: Cambridge University Press, 2008), p. 2 and throughout.

the Caffres even a very few men with an extra supply of arms and ammunition, it would enable these savages, when joined by the disaffected persons belonging to that very distant part of the colony, the district of Graaf Reinet, to cause very serious mischief to the Cape and the neighbourhood thereof'.[21] And there were other indigenous groups, such as those Malagasy kingdoms highlighted by Gwyn Campbell, with grand ambitions too. Governments in Europe, and their military forces in the field, had to contend not only with each other but also with 'the dynamics of indigenous imperial interests'.[22]

Second, there was the danger posed by rival European empires, notably the French and their allies. But even the newly independent Americans were beginning to present a serious risk to Britain's commercial operations. In applying for access to trade on the east coast of Africa, for example, the private merchant William Jacob remarked ominously that 'the truth is that in the years 1804 and 1805 no less than twelve vessels under American colour were at some of the ports'.[23] Finally, disgruntled and truculent colonists across the region became increasingly difficult to control and placate by distant European empires. There was certainly discontent at the Cape. A voyage of inspection made between 1789 and 1793 by two ships, the *Zephir* and *Havik*, in the service of the VOC to enquire into the state of defences in the Dutch East Indies and the Cape of Good Hope, found much discontent brewing in Southern Africa under the governorship of Cornelis Jacob van de Graaff.[24] Shortly afterwards, rebellion broke out in the district of Graaff-Reinet (ironically named after Governor van de Graaff and his wife, whose maiden name was 'Reinet').[25] Rumours abounded about 'the state of the Spanish possessions' in Latin America, which were apparently simmering on the brink of open rebellion. Robert Brooke concocted a plan for invading the Spanish colonies on the basis of just such speculation:

A most fatal blow against Spain might be struck in this quarter for by the intelligence I have received from whalers I understand Buenos Ayres and the forts on the

---

[21] Curtis to Spencer, 10 October 1800, *Spencer*, vol. IV, pp. 232–3.

[22] Gwyn Campbell, 'Imperial Rivalry in the Western Indian Ocean and Schemes to Colonise Madagascar (1769–1826)', in Laurence Marfaing and Brigitte Reinwald (eds.), *Afrikanische Beziehungen: Netzwerke und Räume* (Hamburg: LIT Verlag, 2001), pp. 111–30, p. 111.

[23] BL, IOR, H/494, p. 511, 'On an Intended Trade to Abyssinia and the Eastern Part of Africa', William Jacob [to George Rose?], 8 December 1807.

[24] UWits, A81, J. F. L. Greevestein, 'Journal of the Voyage of the *Zephir* and *Havik*', 1789–93.

[25] See UWits, A139, W. S. Van Ryneveld, 'Criminal Claim and Conclusion made and demanded by the Fiscal versus Marthinus Prinsloo and his Accomplices', 29 August 1800.

River Plate might be surprised and taken, the Spaniards being represented as careless, negligent and lazy, of course unprepared for a vigorous defence.[26]

Historians have become increasingly sensitive to perceived calls from colonial settlers for colonial independence from their European masters. Some scholars have suggested that the development of ideas about a distinctive 'colonial' identity among European settlers was 'decisively informed by the models of nationhood generated in the Americas and France'.[27] In contrast, others see such examples not as 'national revolts, but assertions of creole authority'.[28] It is difficult to conclude whether such defiance stemmed from a rejection of imperial authority on the part of the people at the imperial periphery. Ultimately, however, examples such as the expulsion of the *landdrost* from Graaff-Reinet, or the rejection by the population of the Ile de France of the commissioners to enforce the revolutionary ban on slavery, illustrate the fluid nature of loyalties in the region at this time, and the ways in which allegiances were being redefined in the context of wider, global political developments.

Rival threats: France

A central theme of this book is the potential danger posed to Britain by a French presence in the south Atlantic and Indian oceans, and the ways in which it might be neutralised and eliminated. The positive benefits offered by a strategic foothold in the southern oceanic arc were accompanied by a gnawing fear of France, and the damage that an equivalent French presence could wreak on British trade and shipping. East India Company commerce was disrupted as French privateers captured Company ships, while British settlements in India and the southern hemisphere were threatened with attack. And the potential advantages to France from their Indian Ocean islands – namely platforms from which to launch military assaults – meant that the danger to British India was greater than the sum of French possessions in India, a peril that had been emphasised by the Secret Committee as early as 1762.[29] All of this contributed to the long-held fear in Britain about the 'dangers to our Indian Empire' represented by France.[30]

[26] B'hurst, MS.062/12, Robert Brooke to Lord Macartney, 28 October 1796.
[27] David Johnson, *Imagining the Cape Colony: History, Literature, and the South African Nation* (Edinburgh: Edinburgh University Press, 2012), p. 2.
[28] James R. Fichter, *So Great a Profitt: How the East Indies Trade Transformed Anglo-American Capitalism* (Cambridge, MA: Harvard University Press, 2010), p. 169.
[29] See G. S. Misra, *British Foreign Policy and Indian Affairs, 1783–1815* (London: Asia Publishing House, 1963), p. 3.
[30] Lord Grenville to Lord Minto, 24 May 1808, *Minto*, p. 103

The danger posed by France was long-standing and symptomatic of the wider political and military conflict between the two powers. As early as 1671, before the conflict escalated into a global struggle in the eighteenth century, St Helena was threatened by the French. The English government received a report from 'one Baron' who provided intelligence on a scheme 'to propose to the King of France, whether he would incline to be master of the English island of St Helena, and if so it should be put into his hands'.[31] The early eighteenth century foreshadowed the kinds of problems that the French would cause to Britain's growing Asian concerns later in the century. During the War of the Austrian Succession, for example, the French Mascarene fleet harassed British shipping, annexed the Seychelles in 1743, and routed Admiral Edward Peyton's British squadron in 1746 before relieving the siege of Pondicherry and capturing Madras in India.[32]

The success of these ventures illustrates the French ambition to develop their own Indian Ocean 'world' to rival those of the Portuguese, Dutch and British.[33] They began exploring the islands of the Chagos Archipelago in the 1740s, seeing these as 'stepping stones to the East'.[34] This objective gained increasing ground in the second half of the eighteenth century, and French interests expanded. In 1770, Philip Pittman, sub-director of engineers and captain at Fort St George informed East India Company representatives at Bombay that 'the French have taken possession [and] lately established and garrisoned posts on Seychelles and Praslin'. The ramifications for the British position were unclear to Pittman, but he still saw fit to note that 'you are the most capable judges and can best decide what political end, such an acquisition can answer to the French or if it can affect the security of our settlements'.[35] The rise of a plantation economy on the French Mascarene isles of France and Bourbon raised metropolitan awareness of the possibilities of the region. They had advantages of climate, fertile soil and a maritime hinterland with much economic potential.[36]

[31] Quoted in Alexander H. Schulenburg, 'Transient observations: the textualizing of St Helena through five hundred years of colonial discourse', Ph.D. thesis, University of St Andrews, 1999, pp. 162–3.

[32] See Richard Harding, *The Emergence of Britain's Global Naval Supremacy: The War of 1739–1748* (Woodbridge: Boydell, 2013), pp. 316–22.

[33] For a contemporary assessment of this, see B'hurst, MS.053, 'Account of the French Possessions in the Indian Ocean' (1800), pp. 26–9.

[34] Auguste Toussaint, *History of the Indian Ocean*, trans. June Guicharnaud (London: Routledge & Kegan Paul, 1966), p. 4.

[35] BL, IOR, H/105, p. 383, Philip Pittman to Thomas Hodges and Council at Bombay, dated Anjengo, 8 December 1770.

[36] See, for example, John Kelso's discussion of the islands' possibilities in John Kelso to David Cathcart, 20 March 1808, *Londonderry*, vol. VIII, pp. 164–7.

In particular, the strategic value of the Ile de France came increasingly to be recognised. And French reverses in India during the Seven Years War, and their almost total exclusion from the subcontinent afterwards, only intensified this interest in acquiring and maintaining island bases in the Indian Ocean. The Duc de Choiseul, the French Minister for Foreign Affairs, viewed them as a substitute for his country's lost Indian possessions.[37] But this was by no means the limit of their usefulness. In 1770, the Duc, nearing the end of his second term in office, poured 10,000 of the best French troops into the Ile de France with a view to attacking the British settlements in India.[38] Whatever their ultimate purpose, the fortification of these islands required a significant investment in troops and provisions in the second half of the eighteenth century, which only served to heighten British anxiety. Major Thomas Fitzgerald, a member of 'the Military Establishment at Fort St George', Madras, reported that:

The Governor of Mauritius had sent four or five ships to the Cape for provisions, 300,000 weight of bread, 4000 sheep, great quantities of salt beef and pork. 2000 puncheons of wine had already been sent there. The French commissary at the Cape, by name Du Bois, was also providing a great quantity of wheat, barley, and many other kinds of provisions to be sent to the islands.[39]

As this suggests, the help of the Dutch colony in Southern Africa was crucial. The French depended on procuring live cattle and other provisions from the Cape. They also purchased 'great quantities of muslins and cloth both from the English and Danish ships' that called there, which their agent, Monsieur Pacheron, paid for with 'coffee from Bourbon'. 'Without such a supply', one anonymous British report claimed, 'it would be impossible for the French to maintain such a body of troops in the islands'.[40]

But the French were also looking further afield for their supplies, with the potential for expanding their presence in the process. In 1769, Anthony Chamier reported that 'they are now making some fortifications at the island [of] St Mary, off Madagascar; and there are some skilful ingineers [sic] at the Isle of France, who have the charge of these works'.[41] Further information came to light a few days later:

[37] Campbell, 'Imperial Rivalry', p. 116.
[38] Misra, *British Foreign Policy and Indian Affairs*, p. 89.
[39] BL, IOR, H/105, p. 358, Intelligence obtained by Major Thomas Fitzgerald at the Cape of Good Hope, May 1771.
[40] BL, IOR, H/107, p. 38, Intelligence from the Cape concerning French provisioning, extract of letter from George Patterson, Cape of Good Hope, 8 July 1772.
[41] BL, IOR, H/100, pp. 81–2, Extract of a letter from Anthony Chamier to the Chairman and Deputy Chairman of the East India Company, 23 March 1769 [enclosure in BL,

Besides the fortifications making at the island [of] St Mary, the French have made [one] settlement on the island [of] Madagascar. Mr Roos ... formerly a German officer, has carried there 600 men, German & French, and with them has disciplined upwards of 1500 Madagascareens. He is daily increasing the number, and they hope from thence to draw considerable strength.[42]

By 1775, one writer, a 'Mr Petree' [i.e. Petrie], informed the Bengal Council of the East India Company that 'the plan for settling at Madagascar is I am informed a favourite one of the present ministry and they have accordingly sent out a considerable reinforcement to their settlement there this season'.[43] Writing to the Earl of Rochford, then Secretary of State for the Southern Department, Petrie elaborated that France's 'principal colony on Madagascar is at Rio or Bay D'Antogil, on the north east side of the island, where Sobiousky, the Polish officer who made his escape from Kamshatcha to Macao commands'.[44] Even more ambitiously, in 1777, a certain Morice, a former French Compagnie surgeon turned slave supplier to the Mascarenes, proposed the formation of a formal French empire in the western Indian Ocean. Morice's schemes were nothing if not grand: this empire would stretch from Surat, on the west coast of India, to Mozambique, off the south-east coast of Africa.[45] Looking back in the early years of the following century, George Young speculated that 'had the plan of the French Ministry about the year 1770 for a subjugation of the whole island of Madagascar by Boniowski been as well executed as designed, our present power and consequence in the East Indies must certainly have been in their hands'.[46] In arguing for the island's acquisition by British forces, Young conjured up another nightmare scenario: 'a connected chain of ports in the hands of the enemy, who might at all times interrupt our outward and homeward bound shipping to the Indian Ocean'.[47]

The threat posed by the French was not just confined to the building up of their own establishments in the region. The use of their Indian Ocean islands to attack Britain's Asian interests was made abundantly clear in a letter from Thomas Smallwood, 'late second mate of the Ship

IOR, H/100, p. 79, East India Company to Robert Wood, for presentation to Lord Weymouth, 29 March 1769].
[42] Ibid., pp. 87–8.
[43] BL, IOR, H/124, p. 519, Extract of a letter from Mr Petree, 20 October 1775, enclosed in Sir Edward Hughes to Bengal Council, 7 February 1776.
[44] BL, IOR, H/120, p. 152, Mr Petrie to Lord Rochford, 26 October 1775.
[45] Campbell, 'Imperial Rivalry', p. 117.
[46] HRO, 38M49/5/61/20, 'Observations on the Island of Madagascar', p. 5.
[47] Ibid., p. 7. This scenario was repeated later in the century when Lord Macartney reported that there was 'an agent of the Isle of France, one La Vergne, who has deep concerns at Mozambique'. See B'hurst, MS.063/6, Macartney to Henry Dundas, 9 March 1798.

Grantham', to Samuel Braund, the ship's owner. Dated at Copenhagen, it brought 'disagreeable news of the loss of the Grantham'. The ship was taken on 4 January 1759 in sight of the Cape of Good Hope by two French ships of war. They brought the *Grantham* into the Cape where Smallwood discovered even more evidence of a French military build-up in the region: 'We found riding 4 ships of the line and 5 frigates, with several transports of the same nation, all come from the French islands to purchase provisions for the fleet.' The next stage was even more ominous as, according to Smallwood, this detachment was 'to join a strong fleet and sail from thence to the coast of Choromandel to attack Admiral Pocock. They are, I am very certain, able to send 13 sail of the line all stout ships and well manned tho they have many more which must lay by for the want of men.'[48] The capture of British ships sailing into the waters of the southern Indian Ocean by marauding French vessels was a recurring theme. The same thing occurred a few decades later when Edward Parry and Daniel Barwell reported the capture of the *Osterley*, reputedly worth £300,000, off the Cape on 21 February 1779.[49] And the depredations of French privateers reached a climax during the Revolutionary and Napoleonic Wars at the end of the century.[50]

But it was the reinforcement of the garrison at the Ile de France which, ostensibly at least, presented the biggest threat to British India. In late 1768, reports were received that the French were gathering thirty companies of one hundred soldiers each, where they were ideally placed to interfere on either Indian coast.[51] Further information arrived in March 1769, from Anthony Chamier in Paris.[52] This intelligence was confirmed by reports from Bengal, dated September 1768, telling of 4,000 French soldiers at the Ile de France with reinforcements expected imminently: 'It requires no depth of judgement to foresee that the

---

[48] BL, IOR, H/95, p. 153, Extract of letter from Thomas Smallwood to Samuel Braund, 26 May 1759.

[49] For a full account, see BL, IOR, H/143, pp. 185–91, Edward Parry and Daniel Barwell to East India Company, 17 March 1779. On the valuation, see Herbert Richmond, *The Navy in India, 1763–1783* (London: Ernest Benn, 1931), p. 125.

[50] See John McAleer, '"In Trade as in Warfare": Conflict and Conquest in the Indian Ocean, 1600–1815', in H. V. Bowen, John McAleer and Robert J. Blyth, *Monsoon Traders: The Maritime World of the East India Company* (London: Scala, 2011), pp. 126–57.

[51] BL, IOR, H/99, p. 189, Peter Mitchell to Lord Weymouth, 12 November 1768.

[52] See BL, IOR, H/100, pp. 81–2, Extract of a letter from Anthony Chamier to the Chairman and Deputy Chairman of the East India Company, 23 March 1769 [enclosure in BL, IOR, H/100, p. 79, East India Company to Robert Wood, for presentation to Lord Weymouth, 29 March 1769]. For further information on this episode, see Nicholas Tracy, 'Parry of a Threat to India, 1768–1774', *Mariner's Mirror* 59 (1973), pp. 35–48.

assembling such a number of forces at the French islands can bode no good to your settlements in India.'[53]

The number of French troops massing at islands in the region also concerned Charles Purvis, master of the *Valentine*. He called at the Cape in 1770, and remarked: 'I should conceive by the number of French on shore, and the vast crouds on board their ships that their number exceeds the enclosed intelligence.'[54] Harry Verelst, sometime Governor of Bengal, was also aware of the steady increase of French forces in the area. Verelst commented on what he perceived to be 'the notions of the French', giving extensive details on the numbers and regiments destined for the Ile de France.[55] Worryingly for the British, not only were they outnumbered by the French but the latter's troops also seemed much superior to their British rivals. One correspondent told the Secretary of State that 'such of the troops as I saw at Mauritius were able-bodied, well accoutred and appeared infinitely better in every respect under arms than our soldiers in the East Indies'.[56] And the French did not neglect military hardware either. 'Mortar batteries' were being constructed on the island, with a further 'fifteen millions of livres . . . applied to the fortifying of Port Louis', the capital. According to Mr Petrie, this proved 'that the present ministry are bent upon prosecuting the scheme of forming settlements upon Madagascar and of regaining their national consequence in India'.[57] All of this came on the eve of the outbreak of war in the American colonies. Even if, by 1773, the French had apparently 'laid aside all the designs they had formed against India', Britain's conflict with its colonists in America would present new opportunities.[58]

During the War of American Independence, there were further signs that France planned to disrupt British commercial interests and imperial ambitions in Asia. Fighting alone on a number of fronts, the British strategy in the eastern hemisphere was 'to ensure that France did not become the successor in the Indian Ocean to the decaying power of Holland'.[59] As one might expect at a period of heightened tension, there was a constant stream of rumours and reports about proposed French attacks on India.[60] And these were not just pipe dreams.

[53] BL, IOR, H/100, p. 209, President and Select Committee, Fort William, to Court of Directors, 13 September 1768.
[54] BL, IOR, H/102, p. 471, Extract of a letter from Capt. Charles Purvis of the Ship *Valentine*, 23 March 1770.
[55] BL, IOR, H/102, p. 481, Extract of a letter from Harry Verelst to Mr Cartier, April 1770.
[56] BL, IOR, H/120, p. 149, Petrie to Rochford, 26 October 1775.   [57] *Ibid.*, pp. 151–2.
[58] TNA, ADM 1/163, p. 243, Samuel Appleby to Robert Harland, 31 December 1772.
[59] Piers Mackesy, *The War for America, 1775–1783* (London: Longman, 1964), p. 380.
[60] Misra, *British Foreign Policy and Indian Affairs*, p. 1. For a selection of these schemes, see Frost, *Global Reach of Empire*, pp. 93ff., 124–6.

In 1781, the Chairman of the East India Company received a letter in which an unnamed source offered intelligence garnered from French prisoners of war in Cork. As the anonymous correspondent warned, 'it is manifest that a firm and settled determination is formed by the French ministry at any cost and trouble to expel the English from their possessions in India'.[61] The report confirmed French designs on the region, and the steps being taken to fortify their existing locations. Fear of rival power was not just a British malaise, however, as this report demonstrated. Its author pointed out that French activity with regard to Rodrigues, which the French had failed to settle a number of times in the eighteenth century, was founded on an anxiety about British intentions:

They seem, however, apprehensive that the English may entertain a similar design on that or some other of the islands in those seas. In consequence of this apprehension, they are continually dispatching their Mouches [small and swift sailing vessels] on every side, in order to discover whether any such project is in agitation, or taking place any where.[62]

Nevertheless, the French Indian Ocean islands were the source of persistent problems for Britain. In 1781, Mauritius supplied recruits to fight the British in India, and from 1780 to 1783, the island provisioned over one hundred French warships sailing to India.[63] Such was the danger from Mauritius that, as we have seen, it was one of the chief reasons for the British interest in acquiring a more stable and permanent presence at the Cape of Good Hope.[64] On his way to India in 1779, Sir Edward Hughes informed Lord Weymouth, Rochford's successor as Secretary of State with responsibility for Indian affairs, that the French 'must depend chiefly on the Cape for the future support of Mauritius'. Hughes suggested that 'a squadron should be stationed at False Bay between May and August, to interrupt the supplies passing from the Cape to the Islands'.[65] On 5 September, Hughes submitted formal plans to Weymouth for the capture of the Cape.[66] And Hughes was not alone in thinking that the region merited serious consideration. In a memorandum of December 1779, John Dalrymple exemplified the idea that attack was the best form of defence. Dalrymple was not fussy: the capture of the Cape or Buenos

---

[61] BL, IOR, H/153, p. 432, 'Extract from a letter to the Chairman of the East India Company by a person employed by the Chairman to obtain such intelligence as could be procured from French officers on parole at Corke, Bandon and Kinsale, sent by the Chairman and Vice-Chairman to Sir Stainer Porter for the attention of the Earl of Hillsborough', 9 August 1781.

[62] Ibid., p. 431.   [63] Campbell, 'Imperial Rivalry', p. 112.   [64] See pp. 64–73 above.

[65] Sir Edward Hughes to Lord Weymouth, 14 August 1779, in Richmond, Navy in India, p. 124.

[66] L. C. F. Turner, 'The Cape of Good Hope and Anglo-French Rivalry, 1778–1796', Australian Historical Studies 12 (1966), pp. 166–85, p. 168.

Aires or Mauritius would be 'equally advantageous to this country and detrimental to our enemies'.[67]

Underlying this position were, of course, commercial considerations. And French assaults on British positions at this gateway to the lucrative Indian Ocean were not just confined east of the Cape. During the Seven Years War, both the Comte d'Estaing and Froger de l'Éguille proposed the capture of St Helena.[68] An enclosure in a letter from a Mr Benson in 1781, and preserved among the papers of Richard Lewin, described the effect of St Helena falling into the hands of the French.[69] This enclosure was written by Yves-Joseph de Kerguelen-Trémarec, a French explorer who gave his name to the French possessions in the Antarctic. In this document, which was seized from the French ship *Libre Navigator*, Kerguelen is less interested in scientific exploration and rather more concerned with gaining a commercial and strategic upper hand on the British. Adopting a well-known argument, Kerguelen was persuaded that 'the only and best method to wage war with England is to attack its commerce'.[70] He was convinced that the most propitious way to do this was to follow the plan for the 'attack and conquest of the island of St Helena' appended to his comments.[71] He reckoned that 'the capture of the island together with what merchandise would be found deposited there would produce 20 million of livres, the capture of 20 vessels at 3 million each would produce 60 million which would make the immense sum of 80 millions'.[72] But there were yet more compelling reasons for taking St Helena – the impact on the Asian empires of both Britain and France. A successful assault on the island would benefit the French at the same time as denuding the British Empire and harming the latter's long-distance maritime trade with Asia:

Besides one should consider the great advantage of having an excellent retreat for our ships returning from the Isle of France and Bourbon, from the Indies and from China, and also that this island so useful to the English who have no other place to touch at between China and England would in peaceable times be an equilibrium or a restitution for Pondicherry and our establishment in Bengal and on the coast of Malabar.[73]

Building up one's own empire and doing damage to one's rivals were, it seemed, two sides of the one coin.

[67] NMM, SAN F/22/97, Memorandum [of John Dalrymple] [December 1779].
[68] Richmond, *Navy in India*, p. 125.
[69] For more on Lewin, see Thomas Herbert Lewin (ed.), *The Lewin Letters: A Selection from the Correspondence and Diaries of an English Family, 1756–1884*, 2 vols. (London: Archibald Constable & Co., 1909), vol. I, pp. 2, 21–2.
[70] BL, IOR, H/153, p. 581, 'Enclosure in Mr Benson's Letter of 3 August 1781', p. 581.
[71] *Ibid.*, pp. 582–5.   [72] *Ibid.*, pp. 583–4.   [73] *Ibid.*, p. 584.

The conclusion of hostilities with the Americans and their allies, and the consequent granting of American independence, were two of the factors that helped to reorient the British Empire towards the East. It did not stop French designs on India, however. In 1785, Britain's new ambassador to The Hague, Sir James Harris, warned: 'Our wealth and power in India is their great and constant object of jealousy; and they never will miss an opportunity of attempting to wrest it out of our hands.'[74] In writing about Egypt in the 1780s, George Baldwin commented that 'the power of annoying England has been ever a predominant argument with France for the adoption of any design'.[75] The worry was that 'France in possession of Egypt would possess the master key to all the trading nations of the earth'. Baldwin presented a bleak picture:

Enlightened as the times are in the general arts of navigation and commerce, she might make it the emporium of the world. She might make it the awe of the eastern world by the facility she would command of transporting her forces thither by surprize in any number and at any time – and England would hold her possessions in India at the mercy of France.[76]

But Baldwin was not quite the voice in the wilderness that he presented himself as – others also recognised the danger. Later in the century, Sir Ralph Abercromby concurred that 'to allow [Egypt] to remain in [French] possession would threaten the security of our dominions in the East'.[77] The only solution to counteract such machinations, according to Baldwin, was the capture of Egypt by Britain. In many ways, his reasoning closely paralleled those who advocated a similar policy towards the Cape, Mauritius, or the River Plate in South America, any of which could be substituted in place of 'Egypt' in Abercromby's justification for military intervention:

Very little need now be added to prove the communication with India by Egypt to be a necessary link in the chain of our connection with India. A view of its value and importance to France will give us the best impression we can receive of its utility to England. By taking the reverse of the medal to ourselves [sic] I foresee that it is a topick susceptible of infinite speculation.[78]

The need to prevent France occupying strategic locations on the route to India, particularly those around Southern Africa, became even more

---

[74] Sir James Harris to Lord Carmarthen, 4 March 1785, quoted in Frost, *Global Reach of Empire*, p. 124.

[75] BL, Add. MS 38346, f. 253 [George Baldwin], 'Speculations on the Situation and Resources of Egypt (1773–1785)'.

[76] *Ibid.*, ff. 256–7.

[77] Sir Ralph Abercromby, 'On the Liberation of South America from the Dominion of Spain' (*c.*1799), *Londonderry*, vol. VII, p. 269.

[78] BL, Add. MS 38346, f. 249 [Baldwin], 'Speculations'.

pressing as the century neared its end. In 1785, Henry Pemberton suggested that a port on the south-eastern coast of Africa would, 'in case of a war with France', be 'an immediate check upon their islands of Mauritius and Bourbon by cutting off their supplies from the Cape and by starving those islands'. It would also 'annihilate their scheme of making them a depository for European troops till wanted in India'.[79] In 1787, the Prime Minister, William Pitt, recognised the global nature of geopolitics as he mused on developments in Europe to Lord Cornwallis, governor general in Bengal. Any diminution in the power of the Dutch Republic would be dangerous as it 'could hardly fail to render the Republic so dependent on France as to gain that court the absolute disposal of its forces and resources'. The consequence of this 'maritime strength' would spell trouble for Cornwallis in India: 'From its local position and particularly from that of its dependencies in India, I need not point out to Your Lordship how much this country would have to apprehend from such an event.'[80] Pitt concluded that the measure best calculated to deal with such a threat would be the proactive acquisition of Dutch possessions in the Indian Ocean. As 'the first struggle will naturally be for foreign dependencies', Britain would 'certainly be justified in taking possession of those posts on behalf of the majority of the states & to secure them against France'. Principal among these 'dependencies' was the Cape, which ought to be taken sooner rather than later in any prospective conflict: 'If at the outset of a war we could get possession of the Cape & Trinquemalé, it would go farther than anything else to decide the fate of the contest.'[81] Interestingly, the feeling was mutual as the importance attached to the region ('this half way station between Europe and India') by the French government may be understood by the discussions that took place 'between Lord Malmesbury and Monsieur de la Croix' in which 'the latter persisted that the Cape of Good Hope was of infinitely greater importance to England than the Netherlands were to France':

'If', says he 'you are masters of the Cape and Trincomalee we shall hold all our settlements in India, and the Isles of France and Bourbon entirely at the tenure of your will and pleasure they will be ours only as long as you chose we should

---

[79] BL, IOR, G/9/1, p. 25, Pemberton, 'Narrative'.

[80] TNA, PRO 30/8/102, pp. 83–4, William Pitt to Lord Cornwallis, 2 August 1787. Pitt's remarks would seem to confirm that by this stage the Cape had become, in the words of L. C. F. Turner, a 'cardinal factor' in British policy. See Turner, 'Cape of Good Hope and Anglo-French Rivalry', p. 179. For further commentary on the document, see Harlow, *Second British Empire*, vol. II, pp. 383–4.

[81] TNA, PRO 30/8/102, p. 87, Pitt to Cornwallis, 2 August 1787.

retain them, you will be sole masters in India and we shall be entirely dependent on you'.[82]

This sense of trepidation about what France might do in the Indian Ocean heightened as the clouds of war began to gather following the French Revolution. Vice-Admiral Sir Charles Middleton, soon to become a member of the Board of Admiralty, described his own view of the French counter strategy in the event of war, prophesising a major impact on Britain's Indian possessions and trade. He feared that French 'flying squadrons in the East Indies' would soon be 'strong enough to intercept our China and India ships'. In fact, such ships had long been a thorn in the side of British commercial shipping coming from Asia. But Middleton was also anxious about potential assaults on St Helena and the Cape.[83] The old fear of France gaining the upper hand over the Dutch, and their Asian colonies, resurfaced with alarming alacrity when France declared war on the Dutch Republic on 1 February 1793. With French armies bearing down on the Netherlands at the end of 1794, Sir John Dalrymple wrote to Henry Dundas: 'In a month or two the French must have taken Holland to themselves, or which is the same thing they must have thrown the government of it into the hands of the populace to be instruments to France; either of which events will be equally fatal to Holland and England.'[84] Despite the fact that Britain had secured the Cape by the time he wrote, Evan Nepean, at the Admiralty, warned Thomas Pringle to be aware of possible attacks by the French on East India Company shipping in the southern reaches of the two oceans.[85]

The Revolutionary War with France only reinforced the need to control overseas locations. In March 1796, Henry Dundas thought that the 'Eastern World is their only rational object'.[86] John Bruce was fearful of the French obtaining possession of the Cape, 'that outwork of India and China' as it would allow them to 'command the key to Asia' and, ultimately, to 'send an irresistible force to realise the project of Dupleix of adding our India to the French Empire'.[87] The prospect of the French establishing a line of naval stations from the Cape of Good Hope to

[82] CRO, D LONS/L13/1/91, 'Importance of the Cape of Good Hope Considered' (c.1815–16), pp. 44–5.
[83] NMM, MID/10/2/8, Sir Charles Middleton, draft memorandum [October 1793].
[84] NAS, GD51/1/486, Sir John Dalrymple to Dundas, 30 November [1794].
[85] UWits, A88/48, Evan Nepean to Thomas Pringle, 23 January 1797.
[86] Dundas to Spencer, 24 March 1796, Spencer, vol. I, p. 240.
[87] B'hurst, MS.060, John Bruce, 'Plans for the Government and Trade of the Cape of Good Hope', p. 244. Joseph-François, Marquis Dupleix, was appointed governor general of the French establishments in India in 1742. Over the course of a decade in power, and by forging military and political alliances with local rulers, Dupleix aimed to advance French interests on the subcontinent at the expense of the British.

Ceylon to achieve this 'rational object' struck horror into the hearts of British statesmen, officials and military men throughout the war. There was little doubt that, if they succeeded, such a platform offered 'the means of infallibly crushing the British power in the East'. This maritime counterweight to British power would have baleful effects: 'The colossus of our Indian empire must have staggered before now, under the accumulated blows which could thence have been aimed at our commerce, if we may judge by the incalculable mischief which has been effected by the French in this island [Ile de Bourbon], the most enterprising of their colonies.'[88] Without a secure base (or several, in fact) in the region, British shipping would be prey to French assaults and 'it will be absolutely necessary in time of war to have a strong naval force at St Helena to cruise between that island and the Cape for otherwise a few frigates from the latter by taking a proper station might easily intercept all our homeward bound trade from India and China that commonly touch at St Helena'.[89] In 1795, and in response to French interference in the Netherlands, Isaac Byers wrote to William Pitt in Downing Street to outline his ambitious plans for reducing the Cape of Good Hope, Batavia, Ceylon, Malacca, Amboyna and Macassar: 'By this means, Sir, ... I trust that the whole Dutch naval power in the East would receive so great a check that it would require years to recover.'[90] This 'check' would also, of course, prevent these Dutch possessions falling into French hands. This wide-ranging strategic decision was rationalised by ministers such as Henry Dundas, who set out his views on the importance of the extra-European theatre clearly and succinctly:

Great Britain can at no time propose to maintain an extensive and complicated war, but by destroying the colonial resources of our enemies and adding proportionately to our commercial resources, which are, and must ever be, the sole basis of our maritime strength.[91]

Fears about the danger to Britain's Asian trade were rampant, and only partially assuaged by the capture of the Cape in 1795. Lord Spencer wrote to Elphinstone in Southern Africa that it was 'not unlikely that the enemy may before long be turning their thoughts a little more seriously towards an attack in that quarter, and I hope that the force you will have by the

---

[88] [Charles Telfair], *Account of the Conquest of the Island of Bourbon ... By an Officer of the Expedition* (London: T. Egerton, 1811), pp. 35–6.

[89] RH, GB 0162 MSS.Afr.s.1,2, Macartney to William Richardson, 28 February 1798.

[90] TNA, PRO 30/8/118, pp. 206–8, Isaac Byers to Pitt, 31 January 1795. See Misra, *British Foreign Policy and Indian Affairs*, p. 29.

[91] Quoted in P. J. Marshall, *Remaking the British Atlantic: The United States and the British Empire after Independence* (Oxford: Oxford University Press, 2012), p. 120.

time this letter reaches you will enable you to give them a good reception'.[92]

By the turn of the century, and despite the conquest of the Cape, the danger posed by the French was even more pervasive. Richard Wellesley in Bengal told Vice-Admiral Sir Roger Curtis that the only course of action to prevent an attack on India was to set up a blockade around Mauritius: 'It appears highly probable ... that France may endeavour at an early season to throw a strong reinforcement into the Isle of France ... its success would certainly aggravate, in a great degree, the danger of our Indian Empire.'[93] John Kelso, who was captured by the French on his way to Malaya and held captive on the Ile de France, reflected a common fear about Napoleon's designs on India that persisted in the early years of the nineteenth century. Kelso warned that having been 'already completely frustrated in his attempt to visit our immense territory in India by land', Napoleon:

certainly has not lost sight of an expedition by sea, through the medium of the Island of Bourbon and Isle of France; and of this I have good reason to believe General Decaen (governor of both islands) has been apprized. If you reflect on this plan of getting a footing in India, you must immediately see that it would be the wisest and the most likely to be attended with success of any scheme he could possibly form.[94]

The naval commander on station at the Cape, Albemarle Bertie, warned of 'Buonapart's views of connecting the Mauritius, all the islands forming the archipelago of the Seychelles, Zanzibar, Pemba, Madagascar, and the Eastern Coast of Africa into an establishment in those seas, to which Persia was to be joined'.[95] And the fear of the French exercised commentators right up until the end of the war (and beyond). Patrick Colquhoun cautioned readers that 'the immense possessions in India, under the British Government, render the Cape of Good Hope dangerous in the hands of an enemy'.[96]

On the ground, in the South Atlantic itself, similar apprehensions circulated. In 1772, long before the outbreak of revolution or the British capture of the Cape, the East India Company received intelligence, via George Patterson, that an unnamed correspondent (presumably

---

[92] BL, Add. MS 75856, f. 287, Spencer to George Keith Elphinstone, 8 August 1796.
[93] Richard Wellesley to Curtis, 24 October 1800, in Robert Montgomery Martin (ed.), *The Despatches, Minutes & Correspondence of the Marquess Wellesley During his Administration in India*, 5 vols. (London: W. H. Allen, 1836–7), vol. II, p. 408
[94] Kelso to Cathcart, 20 March 1808, *Londonderry*, vol. VIII, pp. 172–3.
[95] UWits, A162f, Bertie to Lord Melville, 13 June 1811.
[96] Patrick Colquhoun, *A Treatise on the Wealth, Power and Resources of the British Empire in Every Quarter of the World* (London: Joseph Mawman, 1815), p. 390.

a high-ranking Dutch colonial official) 'has his own Fears that the French have some intentions of making themselves masters of the Cape, as such a place would be very commodious to insure success to their schemes upon India'.[97] These fears proved to be prophetic. The particularly febrile situation in Southern Africa in the last years of the century made it a source of continued unease. Robert Brooke, on St Helena, worried that French support for the 'Democratic Party' at the Cape would be disastrous for wider British interests. Indeed, it would almost certainly precipitate 'the loss of the place' and, as a result, must 'prove most essentially detrimental to our dearest interests in the East'.[98] Even the following year, with Britain now in possession of the Cape, the potential threat was real. Officials at the War Office were 'perfectly satisfied' with Major-General Alured Clarke's decision to leave the whole of the British force there, rather than proceeding directly to India as had been initially intended. It was vital to protect it: 'The defence of this possession should be carefully secured, as it is likely from its great importance that the enemy will (if practicable) make some attempt to recover it.'[99] And, from the outset of his governorship, Lord Macartney perceived a real threat to Britain's wider 'Indian world' from French machinations: 'In the hands of a powerful enemy, [the Cape] might enable him to shake to the foundation, perhaps overturn and destroy the whole fabrick of our oriental opulence and dominion.'[100] Speaking 'the language of truth and experience, and not in the jargon of pretended Cosmopolites', Macartney was convinced that the French 'are and ever must be our natural enemies'. His forensic analysis of this as it related to the southern oceanic arc is worth quoting as it gives an insight into the sorts of considerations and calculations that those in London and on the Atlantic periphery made:

[The French] can only wish to have the Cape either in their own hands, or in those of a weak power, that they may use it as an instrument towards our destruction, as a channel for pouring through it an irresistible deluge upon our Indian possessions to the southward of the [River] Guadavery. Of this I am so perfectly convinced that, if it shall be found impracticable for us to retain the sovereignty of the Cape, and the French are to become the masters of it either *per se facit per alium* [sic] then we must totally alter our present system and adopt such measures as will shut them out of India entirely, and render the possession of the Cape and of the Isles of France and Bourbon of as little use to them as possible.[101]

[97] BL, IOR, H/107, p. 39, Intelligence from the Cape concerning French provisioning, extract of letter from George Patterson, Cape of Good Hope, 8 July 1772.
[98] RH, GB 0162 MSS.Afr.s.1,2, Brooke to Macartney, 9–17 June 1795.
[99] War Office to Alured Clarke, 16 January 1796, *RCC*, vol. I, p. 311.
[100] TNA, WO 1/329, p. 17, Macartney to Dundas, 10 July 1797.
[101] NAS, GD51/1/530/1, Macartney to Dundas, 24 October 1797.

And he continued to warn of the dangers posed by French designs on Asia or, more precisely, Britain's trade with the subcontinent should the Cape be returned to the Dutch. This 'would be the same thing as delivering it into the hands of the French', because 'it will enable the latter to train and season bodies of troops here sufficient at a favourable opportunity to pour into the southern peninsula of India and I fear to achieve the conquest of it'.[102] Macartney believed that the weakness of the Dutch state reduced it to a satellite of France. Or, as he described it, 'little more than a stalking horse to France, a masked battery to open upon us by that Power whenever prompted by resentment or ambition'. In that scenario, 'the restitution of the Cape and Ceylon to their former possessors would be little short of an actual delivery of them into the hands of the French'.[103]

In spite of control in Southern Africa on behalf of the House of Orange, anxiety about the British position was pervasive. Samuel Hudson, who had travelled to South Africa in the British retinue, felt that:

Our situation at the Cape is truly deplorable, not a man of war to protect us, our military force inadequate to the service required and our internal enemies here will not fail making these circumstances known so that we have every reason to apprehend consequences the most fatal to the real interest of the colony.[104]

Andrew Barnard, writing to Henry Dundas, saw no diminution in the threat of the French. He informed the Secretary of State that a French frigate, the *Prudente*, had been taken by the *Dædalus* off the eastern-most coast of the colony. The French vessel was carrying 'a vast number of Volunteers on board from the Mauritius'. Similarly, a brig taken by a whaler in Delagoa Bay had a large quantity of gunpowder and ammunition on board.[105] It was obvious that the French ships had 'intended giving assistance to the disaffected at Graaf Reinet'.[106] The danger from France did not even require troops on the ground, however. Many people in that region, Barnard concluded, were disgruntled and rebellious, 'having imbibed the cursed French principles of liberty and equality'.[107] Lady Anne Barnard wrote to Macartney about the fact that 'the French took the opportunity of looking in to see what use they could make of the

[102] RH, GB 0162 MSS.Afr.s.1,2, Macartney to Richardson, 28 February 1798.
[103] NAS, GD51/1/530/3, Macartney to Dundas, 4 February 1798.
[104] National Library of South Africa Cape Town, MSB 252, Samuel Hudson Diary, 24 September 1799, quoted in Kirsten McKenzie, *The Making of an English Slave-owner: Samuel Eusebius Hudson at the Cape of Good Hope, 1796–1807* (Rondebosch: University of Cape Town Press, 1993), p. 37.
[105] Andrew Barnard to Dundas, 21 September 1799, *RCC*, vol. II, p. 493.
[106] RH, GB 0162 MSS.Afr.s.1,2, Barnard to Dundas, 20 October 1799.
[107] Barnard to Dundas, 21 September 1799, *RCC*, vol. II, p. 493.

disturbance'.[108] Around the same time, in September 1799, another French vessel, the *Preneuse*, was chased off by the sloop *Rattlesnake* after an action in Algoa Bay.[109] And, although by late 1800 all seemed to be quiet on the eastern frontier of the colony, the threat was ever-present and required very little provocation:

I fancy the smallest spark of fire being thrown there would set everything in a flame. These considerations make me regret that I have it not always in my power to keep a squadron before Mauritius, not only to restrain the privateering carried on from thence, so highly detrimental to the trade in India, but to prevent, as much as possible, the enemy from fomenting disturbances towards our eastern frontier.[110]

For Barnard the lesson was clear: the eastern seaboard of Southern Africa was a soft target for the French. Places like Algoa Bay could accommodate a large number of ships and 'any number of men might be landed there without our knowing a syllable of the matter until we found an enemy established in our country, and our supplies of cattle, &c., cut off'.[111] Sir Roger Curtis concurred. Since 'the disturbances which took place upon the eastern coasts of this colony', it was also necessary 'to have an eye to that part of the Settlement, for it has appeared the knowledge of the discontents drew the attentions of the French, in the hope they reasonably entertained of being able to foment the same'.[112] And the deployment of only a few extra French troops from their base in the southern Indian Ocean could, in Curtis's view, 'cause very serious mischief to the Cape and the neighbourhood thereof'.[113] Macartney's successor as governor, Sir George Yonge, was of the opinion that India would never be safe, 'either in Peace or War, if France had the Cape, any more than if she remains possessed of Egypt'.[114]

Fear of the French never subsided. The potential return of the Cape to the Netherlands at the Peace of Amiens in 1802 elicited uproar among those who saw the region as a crucial bulwark of the British Asian empire. As we have seen, Lord Grenville considered that, 'by ceding the Cape to Holland, we had in point of fact, ceded it to the power of France'.[115] Lord

---

[108] Lady Anne Barnard to Macartney, 9 January 1800, in Dorothea Fairbridge (ed.), *Lady Anne Barnard at the Cape of Good Hope, 1797–1802* (Oxford: Clarendon Press, 1924), p. 134.

[109] *Letters*, p. 191, note.

[110] Curtis to Spencer, 10 October 1800, *Spencer*, vol. IV, pp. 234–5.

[111] Barnard to Dundas, 21 September 1799, *RCC*, vol. II, p. 493.

[112] Curtis to Nepean, 4 January 1800, *RCC*, vol. III, p. 14.

[113] Curtis to Spencer, 10 October 1800, *Spencer*, vol. IV, pp. 232–3.

[114] Sir George Yonge to Dundas, 12 January 1801, *RCC*, vol. III, p. 406.

[115] House of Lords Debate on the Definitive Treaty of Peace, 13 May 1802, in *The Parliamentary History of England, from the Earliest Period to the Year 1803* (London: T. C. Hansard, 1816), vol. 36, p. 694.

Macartney, the former Governor, was outraged: 'If it ever gets into the French hands, which will ultimately be the case when once got out of ours, Adieu to the fabric, which for these 16 to 17 years past you have been endeavouring to raise in Asia.'[116] Macartney's right-hand man, John Barrow, was similarly adamant and not a little irritated:

It is however too evident that the French and not the Dutch will virtually possess this Colony, and that it is their intention to throw into it such a number of Troops from time to time before they make war against us, as will make it impregnable, and in so doing they will convert into a point of the greatest annoyance a place that would have secured to us our Indian possessions.[117]

Lord Castlereagh, one of Dundas's successors at the Board of Control, was painfully aware of the danger posed to the British Empire in India if the Cape were captured by the French. Unlike Dundas, he was dealing with a situation in which the Cape had been returned – ill-advisedly, in his opinion – to the Dutch:

If France and Holland (which on this point I must consider as the same) shall so far perceive their own interest as to establish the Cape of Good Hope as a free port, and thereby create complete commercial establishments, as an entrepôt between India and Europe, it must give a very fatal stroke to our India and China trade.[118]

'We are too blind to our own danger', Castlereagh warned. And he identified this threat as something that would 'give a direction to the Indian trade so pernicious to the interests of this country'.[119] His prognosis was gloomy but realistic 'if this revolution in the commerce of India takes place': 'I have not in my mind a particle of doubt that the whole fortunes of individuals resident in India will speedily be in the possession and under the power of foreign nations.'[120] The anonymous author of a tract published in 1805 recognised that, in British hands, the principal advantage to be derived from the Cape was 'of a negative kind'. In other words, a key motivating factor in taking it was to '[keep] others out of it'. In particular, it was important to exclude 'ambitious and enterprising people', by which he meant the French, 'who from such a port may harass our trade, and at some future period equip armaments against our eastern dominions'.[121] Robert Percival also highlighted the dangers of allowing the Cape to fall into the hands of the French by giving the colony up to the Batavian Republic. He pleaded that he had 'served my country in

[116] NAS, GD51/1/530/12, Macartney to Dundas, 25 April 1801.
[117] John Barrow to Macartney, 21 August 1802, RCC, vol. IV, p. 346.
[118] PRONI, D3030/L/1, Lord Castlereagh to Dundas, 24 September 1802.   [119] Ibid.
[120] Ibid.
[121] Anon., A Description of the Island of St Helena (London: R. Phillips, 1805), p. 232–3.

different quarters of the globe, and wherever it was my fortune to be stationed, I ever found her intriguing and perfidious enemies, the French, industriously labouring to accomplish her overthrow'.[122] There seemed little doubt to him that, in this scenario, other key British strategic locations would be subject to French attack. Britain did retake the Cape. But, once again, fears soon surfaced that it would come under assault from the French. The British fleet and garrison waited in anxious anticipation until news of Nelson's victory at the Battle of Trafalgar eventually reached Cape Town on 9 January 1806.[123]

Fears about the havoc the French could wreak were fully justified by the realities of the situation. As we have seen, the French were ready and willing to send support to the rebels in Graaff-Reinet in the hope of upsetting the fragile British administration, 500 miles away in Cape Town. More broadly, the French maritime threat to Britain was very real. In the first decade of the nineteenth century, French privateers devastated British commercial shipping in the Indian Ocean. Admiral Peter Rainier, commander-in-chief of the Navy's East Indies squadron, wrote despairingly that Indian Ocean waters 'now swarm with the enemy's privateers'.[124] British commerce was still under assault in 1807 when William Fawkener, from the Office of the Committee of the Privy Council for Trade, characterised it as 'a time when every possible attempt is making [sic] by the enemies of this country to cramp and narrow our commerce in every part of the world'.[125] Over £2.5 million worth of goods and bullion (£300,000 in two months in 1808), plundered from passing British East Indiamen, transformed Port Louis in Mauritius into a major emporium.[126] Less spectacular, but more practical from a military perspective, the 500 cavalry troops on the Ile de France were mounted on Arabian horses 'pillaged chiefly out of English or Arab merchant ships, legal and illegal prizes to their squadron'.[127] Lord Caledon was anxious about the island's influence on 'the continent of India, and its effects as to the comparative strength of the two countries of France and England'. Because of the danger to be apprehended around

---

[122] Robert Percival, *An Account of the Cape of Good Hope* (London: C. & R. Baldwin, 1804), p. 338.

[123] Hugh Popham, *A Damned Cunning Fellow: The Eventful Life of Rear-Admiral Sir Home Popham KCB, KCH, KM, FRS, 1762–1820* (Tywardreath: Old Ferry Press, 1991), p. 144.

[124] Peter Rainier to Spencer, 27 December 1800, *Spencer*, vol. IV, p. 156.

[125] BL, IOR, H/494, p. 506, William Fawkener to the Chairman and Deputy Chairmen of the East India Company, 17 December 1807.

[126] Gwyn Campbell, *An Economic History of Imperial Madagascar, 1750–1895: The Rise and Fall of an Island Empire* (Cambridge: Cambridge University Press, 2005), p. 61.

[127] Kelso to Cathcart, 20 March 1808, *Londonderry*, vol. VIII, p. 168.

the subcontinent, Caledon believed 'the conquest of the only French possession eastward of the Cape must have great weight'.[128] The smaller island of Bourbon was no better from a British perspective, as it offered 'the means of disturbing our possessions, or impairing the stability of our Indian empire'. Only by capturing it in 1810 did Britain manage to wrest 'from the vindictive hand of France one great instrument with which she proposed to strike at the vitals of Britain'.[129] Indeed, it was only by taking 'possession of the French post at Tamatave on Madagascar on 18 February' the following year, that Captain Lynde in HM Sloop *Eclipse* 'freed these seas from the last French flag'.[130]

By considering British fears of the French, we gain new perspectives on the value ascribed to this area for the wider British Asian empire. While the French threat to the Indian subcontinent itself waxed and waned, the gateway to the Indian Ocean was a constant source of concern for British ministers and East India Company men alike. The disruption of British commercial interests in Asia could be effected through Egypt, of course. But, increasingly, it was through the southern gateway region that the French saw their best chance of success.

For over half a century, British politicians, merchants and officials looked on anxiously as France reinforced its Indian Ocean islands and considered attacks on India, and as revolutionary ideas threatened to sweep through even the most apparently remote of locations.

Rival threats: United States

As British control over the southern gateway to the Indian Ocean became more formalised at the end of the eighteenth century, threats to its dominion there did not come solely from France. Of course, the whale-fishing vessels from the eastern seaboard of the United States offered a different menace to British hegemony: a commercial one. American trade was growing in importance. As one author remarked, 'of late the Americans have exported Cape wines to a considerable amount to their own country, as well as to different ports in Europe and in India'.[131] The Americans were active in developing their whale-fishing fleet in the last decades of the eighteenth century, and this alarmed some people into taking action.[132] In conducting a coastal survey of South-West Africa in

[128] Caledon to Castlereagh, 28 December 1808, *RCC*, vol. VI, p. 403.
[129] [Telfair], *Account of the Conquest of the Island of Bourbon*, pp. 25–6.
[130] BL, IOR, H/701, p. 457, Robert Farquhar to Secret Committee, 2 April 1811.
[131] KCL, DT2042 [John Bruce], 'Sketches of the Political and Commercial History of the Cape of Good Hope' (*c.*1796), p. 67.
[132] BL, IOR, G/32/165, p. 29, Brooke, 'Account of St Helena'.

1795, the commander of HMS *Star* was instructed 'to take possession of those bays in his Majesty's name, to warn off all foreign Ships from the Whale fishery, which has been much practised by the Americans'.[133] The following year, 1796, the Boston newspapers reported – erroneously as it turned out – that Britain had annexed the south-east coast of Africa, including Delagoa Bay, to exclude all foreigners from engaging in such activity.[134] And the American ship, *Argonaut*, was seized by the Royal Navy in Simon's Bay on 2 August 1796 'upon suspicion of being an illicit trader'.[135]

American interests also extended to the Ile de France.[136] In May 1784, Robert Morris wrote to Lafayette soliciting the latter's influence in opening the island up to American shipping. Morris suggested free trade would make Mauritius the entrepôt for Indian goods. Meanwhile, francophone settlers on Mauritius petitioned the court at Versailles to help them make their island just such a commercial centre. Shortly thereafter, restrictions were lifted.[137] The *Grand Turk*, belonging to Elias Hasket Derby, a leading Salem merchant, was the first New England ship to reach Mauritius in April 1786.[138] By 1810, 578 American vessels had called there.[139] It was, according to one source, 'the most successful of all our commerce to the East Indies'.[140] This link was formalised on 29 May 1794, when William Macarty, an American who had been a private commercial agent on the island since November 1790, was appointed US Consul by President Thomas Jefferson.[141] Personal and business links between American traders and French settlers promised to

[133] TNA, CO 49/1, John Blankett to Dundas, 23 December 1795. For further details, see Jill Kinahan, *By Command of Their Lordships: The Exploration of the Namibian Coast by the Royal Navy, 1795–1895* (Windhoek: Namibia Archaeological Trust, 1992), p. 27.
[134] Alan R. Booth, *The United States Experience in South Africa, 1784–1870* (Cape Town: A. A. Balkema, 1976), p. 200, n. 89.
[135] Charles Durnford and Edward Hyde (eds.), *Term Reports in the Court of the King's Bench*, 8 vols. (New York: Collins and Hannay, 1827), vol. VIII, p. 28. For full details of the case and the eventual ruling in favour of the plaintiffs, see pp. 26–38.
[136] See Larry W. Bowman, 'The United States and Mauritius, 1794–1994: A Bicentennial Retrospective', *American Neptune* 56 (1996), pp. 145–62.
[137] Alfred W. Crosby, 'American Trade with Mauritius in the Age of the French Revolution and Napoleon', *American Neptune* 25 (1965), pp. 5–17, p. 7. A decree of 30 November 1784 gave permission to American merchants to touch and trade at Ile de France. See Robert E. Peabody, *The Log of the Grand Turks* (London: Duckworth, 1927), p. 105.
[138] See Peabody, *Log of the Grand Turks*, pp. 57–62.
[139] Crosby, 'American Trade with Mauritius', p. 8.   [140] *Ibid.*, p. 14.
[141] Larry W. Bowman, 'The United States and Mauritius, 1794–1994: A Bicentennial Retrospective', *American Neptune* 56 (1996), pp. 145–62, p. 145. For further details on Macarty's appointment, as well as other information on American ties with the Ile de France up to 1810, see Auguste Toussaint (ed.), *Early American Trade with Mauritius* (Port Louis: Esclapon, 1954).

establish a powerful commercial base on the Ile de France. Martin
Bickham wrote to Stephen Girard in Philadelphia proposing that the
latter 'take a concern with me, at this place', thereby helping American
traders to gain access to 'the principal French settlements in India'.[142]

The wider American threat to the British position was perhaps most
thoroughly developed in the publication of a book, *The Cape of Good Hope
and Its Dependencies* by Captain Benjamin Stout, in 1798. The book, with
its original dedication to the American President, John Adams, suggested
that the United States should plant a settlement on the coast of Kaffraria,
the south-eastern part of today's Eastern Cape region of South Africa.
This presented a much more dangerous prospect than some ships pilfer-
ing fishing stocks. Stout was the master of an American ship, the *Hercules*,
which was transporting rice from Bengal to Britain under license from the
(British) East India Company. The ship ran aground near the
Umzimvubu River on 16 June 1796, some 500 miles from Cape Town.
Praising the friendliness of the Africans he encountered, Stout deployed
familiar tropes in presenting the landscape. He emphasised that the land
he encountered 'abounds in timber of the best quality; possesses many
excellent harbours; is blessed with the richest pasturage that feeds innumerable heads of the finest cattle ... their shores are frequented by fish of
every quality'.[143] The 'capabilities' of the country left Stout feeling that
'nothing is wanting to perfect the whole but the exertions of a wise and
liberal government'. And, to this end, he 'recommended the establishment of a colony from America in these parts' to the consideration of his
dedicatee, President Adams. While Stout recognised that the young
United States had much fallow and unexplored land of its own, he lauded
the economic value of a settlement in south-eastern Africa, which would
'amply repay American expense' since it would provide 'several articles
essential to their commerce which they cannot find at home'.[144] He
warned that if the United States neglected to do this, Britain would take
advantage, extending its influence up the coast from the Cape, controlling
Madagascar, and obtaining greater profit than from all its possessions in
the Indies, East and West combined.[145]

Stout's suggestion may have been somewhat fanciful. But, together
with trading incursions, it ensured that British naval men viewed the
newcomers warily. The first visit of the United States Navy to Table

[142] Martin Bickham to Stephen Girard, c.1802, in John Bach McMaster, *The Life and Times
of Stephen Girard, Mariner and Merchant*, 2 vols. (Philadelphia: J. B. Lippincott, 1918),
vol. I, p. 417.
[143] Benjamin Stout, *Narrative of the Loss of the Ship Hercules*, edited by A. Porter (1798;
revised edition, Port Elizabeth: Historical Society of Port Elizabeth, 1975), p. 12.
[144] *Ibid.*, p. 13.   [145] Haight, *European Powers and South-East Africa*, pp. 172–3.

Bay, with the arrival of the *Essex* in 1800, only served to increase British suspicions. The East India Company's agent at the Cape, John Pringle, was perturbed: 'The American frigate *Essex* has passed here on March 11th on its way to the Sunda Straits ... I am inclined to believe its real intention is ... in general to look for a proper place to form an establishment.'[146] Samuel Hudson referred, in a less than flattering tone, to the 'amazing influx of Americans ... this company is least coveted of any nation upon the habitable globe'.[147] And the outbreak of war between Britain and the United States in 1812 had worldwide ramifications. Admiral Sir Charles Tyler ordered the 'captain of the *Lion* to proceed off the Bank of Agulhas and endeavour to intercept some American ships expected from China'.[148]

The tiny island of Tristan da Cunha, nearly 1,800 miles from Southern Africa, might have afforded the Americans the kind of base Pringle thought they were seeking. Notwithstanding its remote situation, the Royal Navy was subsequently dispatched to take control. The presence of a few renegade Americans might have helped to persuade William Milne. He thought that the key inducement for taking possession of the island was to prevent other nations, especially the Americans, from using it 'as a refreshing stage to India'. Milne effectively grasped Britain's negative interest in the island: possession of Tristan was most valuable in denying the island to others, either as a means of escape or as a 'stage to India'.[149]

The Iberian malaise

Just as British control of the route to Asia through the southern Atlantic and Indian oceans was endangered by France and the United States respectively, so Britain, in turn, threatened the positions of other European powers in the region. In December 1807, Robert Dundas wrote from the Board of Trade to Lord Castlereagh, Secretary of State for War and Colonies by this stage, that 'the taking possession of the Portuguese settlements of Mozambique and Delagoa Bay on the east

[146] BL, IOR, G/9/6, pp. 272–3, John Pringle to William Ramsay, 30 March 1800. For the rather more civil official reception afforded the *Essex*, see TNA, WO 1/332, pp. 183–4, Yonge to Dundas, 29 March 1800. See also Booth, *United States Experience in South Africa*, p. 136.

[147] Cape Archives, A455, Dundas papers, file no. 20, quoted in McKenzie, *Making of an English Slave-owner*, p. 40.

[148] UWits, A124, Sir Charles Tyler, Journal, 6 March 1813.

[149] TNA, ADM 1/3029 Lt. M. 441 1816, William Milne, 16 October 1815, quoted in James Fichter, 'The British Empire and the American Atlantic on Tristan da Cunha, 1811–16', *Journal of Imperial and Commonwealth History* 36 (2008), pp. 567–89, p. 581.

coast of Africa' had been suggested to him by the Deputy Chairman.[150] They also discussed in great detail the capture of Portuguese East Africa, particularly of Delagoa Bay, from the Cape rather than from Bombay. Dundas was anxious to employ 'detachments from the Cape' because of the risk of Indian troops 'being anticipated from the Mauritius'.[151] In his reply, Castlereagh was also wary of 'a possible visit from the French at the Mauritius'. And fear of the French was never far from the surface even when dealing, ostensibly, with other European powers:

While the place remains in the hands of the Portuguese, the French have very little inducement, not being themselves capable of using it commercially, to lay hold of it; but if we were to take possession of it with means insufficient for its defence, it will then become an object to them to expel us and plunder the place.[152]

Although the plan to take Portuguese South-East Africa did not come to fruition, two weeks after this exchange, the Commissioners for India authorised the immediate occupation of Portuguese settlements and territories in India, either by arrangement with the Viceroy at Goa or by force of arms.[153]

The tottering Spanish Empire in America provided another possibility for expanding Britain's presence in the region and tightening its control over the route to India. The outbreak of war with Spain in 1739 had brought forth 'a flood of schemes for the exploitation, occupation or even dismemberment of Spain's colonial empire'.[154] Everything from the conquering of Chile and plundering of Lima, to the attacking of Panama and seizing of Manila was mooted.[155] In 1740, Edward Trelawney, governor of Jamaica, suggested that Britain should actively promote indigenous revolts in Spain's American colonies, thereby destroying Spain's empire and laying 'a foundation for the most extensive and beneficial trade with the inhabitants'.[156] Preparations were afoot again in 1748, when George Anson was influential in the Admiralty, for an expedition to the Falkland Islands, but were dropped in order to retain Spain's good will.[157] Two

[150] Robert Dundas to Castlereagh, 12 December 1807, *Londonderry*, vol. VIII, p. 93.
[151] *Ibid.*, p. 94.
[152] Castlereagh to Robert Dundas, 13 December 1807, *Ibid.*, pp. 94, 95.
[153] TNA, FO 63/58, Robert Dundas to George Canning, 23 December 1807.
[154] Glyndwr Williams, '"The Inexhaustible Fountain of Gold": English Projects and Ventures in the South Seas, 1670–1750', in John E. Grant and Glyndwr Williams (eds.), *Perspectives of Empire: Essays Presented to Gerald S. Graham* (London: Longman, 1973), pp. 27–53, p. 46.
[155] Barry Gough, *The Falkland Islands/Malvinas: The Contest for Empire in the South Atlantic* (London: Athlone Press, 1992), p. 6
[156] Peggy K. Liss, *Atlantic Empires: The Network of Trade and Revolution, 1713–1826* (Baltimore and London: Johns Hopkins University Press, 1983), p. 12.
[157] *Ibid.*, p. 16.

decades later, after British successes against Spain in the Seven Years War, ministers were emboldened to make another attempt on Spain's shaky dominions in South America. In 1768, British survey parties were reported captured on the coasts of Panama and Venezuela.[158] But Britain's trading interests in other parts of the globe, specifically the Indian Ocean, played an increasing part in such calculations.

A few years later, in 1780, a scheme proposed by Colonel William Fullarton found favour with ministers. Using information gathered from Robert M'Douall and Arthur Phillip (the future Governor of Botany Bay), both of whom served the Portuguese in Brazilian waters in 1770s, the plan involved capturing 'some advantageous ports', which 'should be fortified'. In considering the effect of this enterprise, Fullarton showed that he was thinking globally. The impact would be twofold:

> If these settlements were effected, it is evident that the trade of S[outh] A[merica] would be opened to our E[ast] Indian territories. If these settlements were not effected still the blow to Spain must be fatal because her richest possessions would be alarmed, their commerce and remittances interrupted, their ships destroyed, their towns plundered and the inhabitants incited to revolt.[159]

Crucially, Fullarton's plan introduced the Asian dimension into British designs. With Britain's commercial and strategic interests increasingly orientated towards protecting and consolidating the maritime route to the Indian Ocean, British politicians and military men were keen to take advantage of any chinks in the Spaniards' commercial empire in America.

By 1799, according to Manuel Gual, 'the colossal dominion of the Spanish Government' in America was 'ready to fall from its own weakness'.[160] One of the main causes of this was the revolutionary fervour evident across the Atlantic world. Its growth in South America encouraged Henry Dundas to urge his cabinet colleagues to sanction direct military intervention. Of course, the development of commercial connections was still crucial, as Dundas pointed out in March 1800 when he advocated 'the acquisition of the South American market to the manufactures and commerce of this country'.[161] But, just as with Fullarton's scheme, there were other considerations. The looming collapse of the Spanish Empire, and its replacement by something even more nefarious, cast a long shadow over Dundas's words. French control over South America would not just yield commercial advantages to Britain's enemy

[158] *Ibid.*, p. 20.
[159] BL, IOR, L/PS/1/6, William Fullarton, 'Proposal of an Expedition to South America by India, laid before the Cabinet by Lord North', 3 June 1780.
[160] 'Memorial of Manuel Gual', 2 May 1799, *Londonderry*, vol. VII, pp. 276–9, p. 278.
[161] TNA, PRO 30/8/243, p. 91, Henry Dundas, 'Memorandum for the consideration of HM's Ministers', 31 March 1800.

but strategic ones too. Having garnered information from Francisco de Miranda and other sources, Dundas asked ministers to consider 'the whole mischief that may be done, if this immense empire is to be permitted to revolutionise itself without guidance or control, or any direction given to their endeavours for independence'.[162] Mixed reaction from his cabinet colleagues put paid to any intervention, but the danger of revolutionary ideas spreading south of the Equator was just as real to contemporaries as the danger of their spreading west to the Caribbean colonies.[163] Some years later, in 1807, Louis Philippe, the exiled Duke of Orleans, reiterated Dundas's views, arguing that 'nothing but the timely and well directed interference of Great Britain can rescue that important quarter of the globe from falling a prey to Jacobinism, and save the world from the dreadful consequences which would inevitably follow that lamentable event'.[164] Orleans was more concerned with establishing a counterweight to Napoleon's France than protecting Britain's trade with Asia. Nevertheless, his intervention, as well as the plans and pronouncements of others, suggest that interpretations of British interest in South America based purely on economic grounds do not present the full picture. The security and expansion of Asian trade were also important. The prevention of French gains was critical. And the stalling of revolutionary fervour was increasingly emphasised. But revolutionary zeal, identified across South America, was also making an impact elsewhere; and these parts were controlled by Britain and played a crucial role in its control of the seaways to India.

Rising colonial sentiment

As we have seen in the case of the Spanish Empire in America, the eighteenth century witnessed a growing divergence between imperial centres in Europe and settler colonies, particularly in the Atlantic world. The rising forces of colonial and settler nationalism collided with ideas of political revolution, sending shockwaves around the Atlantic.[165]

---

[162] Henry Dundas, 'Memorandum for the consideration of the Cabinet', 3 October 1799, *Londonderry*, vol. VII, p. 285.

[163] For a contemporary summary of the British plans to conquer South America in the period, see Alexander Gillespie, *Gleanings and Remarks Collected During Many Months of Residence at Buenos Ayres* (Leeds: The Author, 1818), pp. 1–5.

[164] Louis Philippe, Duke of Orleans, 'Memoir on Spanish America, and the Viceroyalty of Mexico in Particular' (1807), *Londonderry*, vol. VII, pp. 332–44, p. 332.

[165] For recent considerations of this, see Thomas Bender, Laurent Dubois and Richard Rabinowitz (eds.), *Revolution! The Atlantic World Reborn* (New York: Giles, 2011); Janet Polasky, *Revolutions without Borders: The Call to Liberty in the Atlantic World* (London: Yale University Press, 2015).

Throughout the Atlantic world and across all European empires, old certainties were being questioned.

The South Atlantic was an area of the world where the shifting sands of imperial attachment and colonial sentiment could have an even bigger impact on the British Indian Ocean world. In the 1780s, British travellers commented on the difficulties of keeping colonial settler populations content in Southern Africa. George Forster, a traveller in the service of the East India Company and not to be confused with his namesake who accompanied James Cook to the Pacific, noted how the Dutch-speaking farmers and merchants 'make bad complaints of the oppressions of the government which they have represented to the [Dutch East India Company] directors in Europe in repeated memorials, but with no prospect of redress'.[166] Henry Rooke observed that the inhabitants of the Cape were 'much attached to the English, with whom they are greatly connected in time of peace'.[167] And Henry Pemberton noted that the Dutch settlers on the eastern frontier were 'extremely disaffected at present owing to their ports being shut up and other oppressions and exactions of the Dutch Government'.[168]

The experience of William Dalrymple gives an insight into the vacillating loyalties on colonial frontiers that could have much wider ramifications. Dalrymple travelled extensively in the eastern districts of the Cape. By virtue of speaking Dutch and French, he 'became intimately acquainted with many of the inhabitants' there. And his intelligence stretched as far as knowing (or claiming to know) 'their disposition towards England and France'. A local governor, 'Monsieur Vangraave', was reportedly 'in the French interest'.[169] Furthermore, he had orders from the Netherlands 'to favour the French nation in preference to the English'. The military were divided in their loyalties, with the two battalions serving at the Cape in 1785 seeming to adopt diametrically opposed positions. The regiment commanded by Colonel Murron, 'a Swiss who has been in the French service and is violent against the English and in the interest of France', presented one extreme. Although they were 'called Swiss', this did not fool Dalrymple: 'both officers and men' were 'French only paid by Holland'. Colonel Robert Jacob Gordon's regiment, on the other hand, comprised mainly Germans and Dutch. And Dalrymple was reassured that not only did Gordon have overall command of the troops in

---

[166] UWits, A154f, George Forster to Dundas, 22 January 1786.

[167] Henry Rooke, *Travels to Coast of Arabia Felix ... containing a Short Account of an Expedition undertaken against the Cape of Good Hope* (London: R. Blamire, 1783), p. 19.

[168] BL, IOR, G/9/1, p. 25, note, Pemberton, 'Narrative'.

[169] Presumably Dalrymple is referring to Cornelis Jacob van de Graaff, who arrived at the Cape as governor in early 1785.

the colony but he also had 'an English heart and is strongly attached to the Prince of Orange's interest'.[170] The civilian population also seemed more amenable to the British interest, at least in Dalrymple's opinion. In rather breathlessly cataloguing a list of grievances, thereby highlighting the apparently favourable disposition of colonial settlers to Britain, Dalrymple contributed to a commonly deployed rhetorical device among those keen to encourage a more proactive British presence in the region. In summary, 'the settlers are mostly Germans not in the Dutch interest but strongly in the English and ready to revolt from Holland if England would establish a port in the province'.[171] Of course, one needs to read Dalrymple's assessment in the context of his interest in establishing a British foothold in the eastern Cape.[172] Nevertheless, the scheme was accepted in principle by William Devaynes, Chairman of the East India Company, and it was subsequently laid before the government in October 1785. Ministers eventually decided not to act on the plan, however, choosing to avoid giving 'umbrage to the French or Dutch'.[173] Dalrymple's proposal illustrates the central role that considerations of colonial opinion played as travellers, merchants and politicians formulated policy towards the region in the late eighteenth century.

A few years later, John Blankett assessed the mood of the Dutch colonists again. 'The idea that prevails everywhere amongst the Dutch settlements', he told Lord Hawkesbury, is 'that their East India Company is in decline'. Blankett pointed out that this would inevitably precipitate calls for independence for the colony. But he qualified his remarks, acknowledging that 'the great ignorance of the colonists and their being separated in distant plantations from each other, may perhaps retard such an event, for a few years'. Nevertheless, the potential clearly existed for the colonists to break loose and 'any accidental aggravation or whatever may occasion a momentary passion will blow the embers to a blaze that the force of the Cape government is not sufficient to resist'.[174] For Blankett and others, the danger to the Dutch presented an opportunity for Britain to take greater control. However, as with South America, there were dangers too. And, by the time Blankett was writing, other forces were at work.

The American and French revolutions, and the political ideas they inspired, led to great upheaval and further complicated the picture across

[170] TNA, PRO 30/8/128, p. 78, William Dalrymple memorandum [c.1787]. For more on Robert Gordon, see Patrick Cullinan, *Robert Jacob Gordon, 1743–1795: The Man and His Travels at the Cape* (Cape Town: A. A. Balkema, 1992).
[171] TNA, PRO 30/8/128, p. 79, Dalrymple memorandum.   [172] See pp. 53–5 above.
[173] TNA, PRO 30/8/128, p. 79, Dalrymple memorandum.
[174] BL, Add. MS 38226, f. 113, Blankett to Lord Hawkesbury, 25 February 1790.

the region. As discussed above, South America was suffused with revolutionary sentiment. The Dutch colony in Southern Africa was similarly
affected. Francis Baring, in advocating the British capture of the Cape in
1795, observed the tendencies of the inhabitants who were 'very ill disposed towards their own government, and very favourably [disposed]
towards the French'.[175] In his 'Sketches of the Political and
Commercial History of the Cape of Good Hope', the John Bruce was
also aware of the danger posed by French ideas. For him, Dutch 'are
almost all converts to the French Revolutionary principles'.[176] John
Malcolm similarly concluded that:

French principles had been very generally disseminated, particularly in the country, where the ignorant farmers were wrought up to a frenzy by 2 or 3 designing
men. They talked of nothing but establishing their independence as a Republic,
making Cape Town a free port, being as they termed it, the friends of all nations,
but the slaves of none. They spoke of imitating the glorious examples set them in
Europe.[177]

The letter received by John Ross, a merchant in Hamburg, from
a kinsman serving on HMS *America* in 1795 gives an even clearer insight
into the attitudes of the Dutch settlers at the Cape towards the British on
the eve of the British occupation of the colony. This Ross was secretary to
the captain of the *America*, John Blankett. He travelled to Cape Town
with 'Lt Col. McKenzie of the 78th regt' and 'Captain Hardy', where they
were received by the governor of the Dutch colony. In an attempt to
persuade the Cape authorities to accept British suzerainty, the British
officers recounted the depredations of the French invasion of the
Netherlands that followed the Revolution, highlighting 'the scenes of
misery that people of rank and fortune had been reduced to, by being
obliged to fly their native country without any asylum'. Even though they
warned the governor and his entourage that 'this colony was threatened
with the like misfortune if not properly protected', they failed to elicit
a positive response. The principal explanation for this lukewarm reaction
was, according to Ross, the ambivalence of the settlers, who had little
liking for either their erstwhile masters in the United Provinces or the new
power in control of the territory. The governor 'described the agitated
state of the colonists and their want of attachment to any regular government'. He remarked 'that part of them were in open rebellion, and that

[175] Sir Francis Baring to Dundas, 4 January 1795, *RCC*, vol. I, p. 18.
[176] KCL, DT2042, Bruce, 'Sketches', p. 383. See also Johnson, *Imagining the Cape Colony*, p. 76.
[177] BL, IOR, H/738, p. 11, Sir John Malcolm, 'Account of the Cape of Good Hope in 1795'.

the majority would receive the French with open arms, [and] that the least idea of his accepting the British protection at present would occasion open revolt and much bloodshed'. Ultimately 'the native Africans [i.e. Dutch colonists] wanted independence ... they wished for neither French nor English but dreaded that protection from either of them would transfer the theatre of war to the Cape'.[178] The letter vividly captures the quandary into which colonial officials of all European powers in the region were plunged by the upheavals in Europe in the last decade of the eighteenth century. It also illustrates the fluxive nature of national identities and allegiances: to whom should polities and their populations turn when their natural loyalties were upset and irrevocably disrupted by the changing events in Europe? Apathy was, perhaps, the best result for which a European power could hope. James Prior, surgeon on *Nisus* frigate attached to the Cape station some decades later, commented on the vacillating and questionable loyalties of the Dutch settlers in South Africa before Britain was confirmed in possession of the colony. As far as Prior could make out, as long as 'the boors [i.e. the Dutch settlers]' could 'sell their cattle to advantage and remain exempted from strict legal restraints', they cared little whether 'the English or the Chinese possess the town'.[179]

The loyalties of the colony's inhabitants remained ambivalent throughout the early years of the first British occupation. Benjamin Stout was convinced, or was trying to convince his readers, that 'the inhabitants of the Cape, and the colonists in general, entertain a strong predilection in favour of the British'.[180] The example of 'Jan du Plieses' was cited by Stout in support of anglophone (either American or British) intervention. The farmer 'stated the hardships, which the colonists endured from the restrictive orders and persecuting conduct of the [Dutch, i.e. VOC] Government at the Cape':

He made no scruple in declaring that if any liberal and trading nation would form a settlement on the eastern or western coast, he would in conjunction with his neighbours, supply them with provisions to the extent of his ability, and trade with them, regardless of any order to the contrary he might receive from the Cape. Indeed, such are the sentiments of all the central and advanced colonists throughout the southern parts of Africa.[181]

But when he was detained at the Cape in March 1798, Richard Cleveland, an American merchant and ship's captain, questioned how far the inhabitants had accepted the change of administration:

[178] NAS, GD51/1/496, H. Ross to John Ross, 16 June 1795.
[179] Prior, *Voyage along the Eastern Coast of Africa*, p. 11.   [180] Stout, *Hercules*, p. 14.
[181] *Ibid.*, p. 49.

Notwithstanding the increase of buildings, and the rise in value of real estate, as well as various other advantages, felt by the inhabitants since they submitted to the English government, there was, nevertheless, observable in many an impatience of a foreign yoke, a feeling of being a conquered people, and a sense of degradation, which was very natural, and which would not be easily effaced.[182]

Fear of the French, combined with lack of confidence in those around them, convinced British administrators to keep a watchful eye on proceedings. Those in command of the British detachment chose not to place 'any confidence in the affections and loyalty of our new subjects', despite the fact that almost all of them had taken 'the oath of fealty to the King of Great Britain'. Instead, according to John Malcolm, they 'very wisely determined to leave all the regiments in garrison at the Cape, and to abandon all thoughts of prosecuting the expedition [to India] any further':

The whole of the military did not amount to many more than 3000 effective men, a force hardly sufficient to defend the Cape against a French invasion on the supposition that the inhabitants were well inclined, where there was good reason to suspect they were not, particularly those in the country where French principles had made wide progress.[183]

This assessment was confirmed by General James Craig. Observing how events in Europe affected the situation in Southern Africa, he remarked that the colony was 'in a state of considerable ferment'. The warring factions comprised those loyal to the Dutch government, as well as those variously in favour of French or British intervention. But 'by far the most numerous Party' were those who adopted 'the chimerical idea of existing by themselves as an independent state'.[184] Recognising that the Dutch authorities never had a strong hold over the settlers' affections, Craig noted that it had now sunk to a new low. The 'knowledge of what was going on in Europe has gained ground in this country', so that:

The temper of the people, predisposed by their sentiments with respect to their own rulers, has gradually become more and more susceptible of the impressions which designing persons have been busily employed in giving them, and it is certain that the great body of the people are at this moment infected with the rankest poison of Jacobinism.[185]

The following year Craig blamed 'the presence of the Dutch officers, numbers of whom notwithstanding my wish to the contrary had got on

---

[182] Richard J. Cleveland, *A Narrative of Voyages and Commercial Enterprises*, 2 vols. (Cambridge, MA: John Owen, 1842), vol. I, p. 35.
[183] BL, IOR, H/738, p. 4, Malcolm, 'Account of the Cape'.
[184] James Craig to Henry Dundas, 16 June 1795, *RCC*, vol. I, p. 53.
[185] Craig to Dundas, 22 September 1795, *RCC*, vol. I, p. 155.

shore', which had given 'encouragement to the ill-disposed' and occasioned 'a strong instance of Jacobinical insolence'.[186] Hercules Ross considered that the inhabitants were 'blind to their real interest' and were 'hostile' to the British. Ross was adamant that 'upon the whole a spirit of revolt against all regular government seems to prevail and Jacobinism has taken root here'.[187]

Except for the six principal merchants in Cape Town, Craig estimated that the entire population was hostile and would certainly join the French if they appeared in Table Bay. Jacobin ideas were rife in town and country alike. Samuel Hudson complained of 'Dutch Jacobins' at the Cape. He had no truck with such revolutionary sentiments, referring to the French who had spread such ideas as 'a hoard of public robbers who under the . . . mask of liberty and equality spread their pernicious doctrines to the ruin and destruction of all who listen to their infernal creed'.[188] And although Francis Dundas was 'perfectly at ease . . . from the profound quiet which reigns at the Cape', he cautioned that 'the circumstances of the times merit vigilance and attention' in case the French should attempt 'to find their way into this country with their revolutionary system, setting free the slaves, and arousing the poorer sort and the disaffected'.[189] Sir George Yonge informed Henry Dundas a few years later:

There is no longer any doubt if Jacobin emissaries having arrived here both from France and Germany as long ago as the year 1793 who propagated their doctrines with too much success at this place [Cape Town], and from that time there was not a family nor a farmer from among the Dutch boors or Hottentot that came to Cape Town which these emissaries did not seduce so that they returned having added to their spirit of independence the spirit of overturning all government calling themselves patriots.[190]

The well-documented rebellion in the district of Graaff-Reinet – between the Gamtoos and Great Fish rivers, about 400 miles east of Cape Town – has often been cited as one of the prime examples of revolutionary, levelling principles merging with settler demands for greater autonomy. The district had initially established its independence from the VOC's rule, and the settlers showed no sign of submitting to the new British regime (though they eventually did so in August 1796).[191] By April 1796, James Craig informed Henry Dundas that the burghers there were in

[186] UWits, A24, Craig to Dundas, 31 October 1796.
[187] B'hurst, MS.052/10, Hercules Ross to Dundas, 27 June 1795.
[188] National Library of South Africa, Cape Town, MSB 252, Samuel Hudson Diary, 25 November 1797, quoted in McKenzie, *Making of an English Slave-owner*, p. 40.
[189] B'hurst, MS.052/9, Francis Dundas to Henry Dundas, 3 March 1798.
[190] TNA, WO 1/332, pp. 170–1, Yonge to Dundas [March 1800].
[191] See Johnson, *Imagining the Cape Colony*, p. 117.

'open insurrection' against all authority and every form of government 'except what they have themselves formed, upon the Idea which they have conceived of that which exists in France'.[192]

Historians have tended to interpret the rebellion as being concerned with the material means of existence at the fractious frontier of a colonial outpost.[193] C. W. De Kiewiet, for example, emphasised the economic pressures faced by the burghers of the eastern districts affected by the unrest. For him, the connection between the French Revolution and the localised trouble was 'very slight'. The uprising was caused by 'what the burghers considered an unwarranted invasion upon their freedom' to deal with the local indigenous Africans.[194] Nevertheless, for our purposes, *perception* is crucial, and a genuine fear of the spread of French ideas was widely held by British officials and their families. The dreaded hand of France was everywhere in evidence. Lady Anne Barnard detected the early signs of outside interference in the middle of 1797. Writing to her old friend, Henry Dundas, she informed him about the 'gallant whaler', which 'with 24 men (as I hear) has taken a Dutch ship from Batavia laden with arms and ammunition'. Lady Anne acknowledged the 'finesse as well as courage' needed 'to effect this matter'. But the tone of her comments is mainly one of relief: 'I heartily rejoice we have got part and destroyed much of the powder, as the people of Graaf Renet (for which it was bound) are very ill affected.'[195] Lady Anne's husband, Andrew, was similarly wary of the settlers in these outlying districts who were 'disaffected to this Government or indeed to any other'. He laid the blame squarely on their 'having imbibed the cursed French principles of liberty and equality'.[196] John Pringle, the East India Company's agent at the Cape, confirmed the strange state of affairs:

The behaviour of the people here is very extraordinary, they have formed ideas of independence which is so absurd a scheme that it never occurred to me as likely to prove an obstacle to our designs, the Boers are doubtless kept in this delusion with a view to render them mere tools in the hands of those who for the moment enjoy their confidence and who will sacrifice them if possible to their own ends.[197]

And this situation rumbled on through the first British occupation. The Commander of the British Naval Squadron at the Cape, Sir Roger

---

[192] Craig to Dundas, 21 April 1796, *RCC*, vol. I, p. 368.
[193] For more on the historiographical import of the rebellion in Graff-Reinet, see Johnson, *Imagining the Cape Colony*, pp. 132–3.
[194] C. W. De Kiewiet, *A History of South Africa: Social and Economic* (Oxford: Clarendon Press, 1941), p. 31.
[195] Lady Anne Barnard to Dundas, 10 July 1797, *Letters*, p. 58.
[196] Andrew Barnard to Dundas, 21 September 1799, *RCC*, vol. II, p. 493.
[197] John Pringle to Brooke, 17 June 1795, *RCC*, vol. I, pp. 85–6.

Curtis, believed that the Dutch settlers were infinitely more prosperous under British rule than the previous regime. It was all the more exasperating, then, that they seemed not to appreciate this. Curtis attributed this to the fact that many of them were 'born and nurtured in Republican principles':

> Some lean towards the French; and it is said there is a small party who wish to become entirely independent of any European power, but, as it may be well imagined, so extravagant an idea has not many partisans.[198]

According to John Barrow 'Jacobinism, or subversion of all order, has industriously been propagated by the ill-disposed, among the ignorant part of the colonists, both in the town and the country districts'.[199] And Henry Lichtenstein maintained that the 'revolutions in France and Holland occasioned an universal ferment all over the colony'.[200]

It was not only the French who were responsible for spreading revolutionary ideas from Europe. Events in Ireland also had an impact on the stability of the British administration at the Cape, while the naval mutinies at Spithead and the Nore found their colonial equivalents in Southern African waters in October and November 1797.[201] The Barnards purchased 'a small estate about six miles from the Cape ... at a time when we feared the world was to be turned upside down'.[202] In the wake of the naval mutinies, and gripped with the terror of military insurrection at the Cape in August 1799, Lady Anne Barnard reported that one of the ringleaders of the conspiracy planned on using 'the brave boys from Vinegar Hill' to carry out his plans.[203] The extraordinarily febrile political climate in which British control at the Cape was initially established gives the lie to the idea that the British capture of the colony, as well as other areas in the region, was straightforward. Militarily, the conquest of the Cape, and subsequently of the French islands of the Indian Ocean, proceeded according to plan. But consolidating British control of the gateway to the Indian Ocean world was a much longer-term project, contingent on the acquiescence of a range of settler groups. For one writer, the solution was to send migrants

---

[198] Curtis to Spencer, 10 October 1800, *Spencer*, vol. IV, p. 235.

[199] John Barrow, *An Account of Travels into the Interior of Southern Africa, in the Years 1797 and 1798*, 2 vols. (London: T. Cadell and W. Davies, 1801–4), vol. I, p. 52.

[200] Henry Lichtenstein, *Travels in Southern Africa in the Years 1803, 1804, 1805, and 1806*, translated by Anne Plumptre (London: Henry Colburn, 1812), p. 373.

[201] Nicole Ulrich, 'International Radicalism, Local Solidarities: The 1797 British Naval Mutinies in Southern African Waters', *International Review of Social History* 58 (2013), pp. 61–85.

[202] US, BR19/1/2, Lady Anne Barnard to Lady Palmerston, 9 July 1800.

[203] 6 August 1799, *Diaries*, vol. I, p. 225.

from the British Isles (mainly 'distressed and underemployed people in Ireland') to the region, as well as forming a militia there. The perceived imbalance in the allegiance of European settlers would be rectified at one fell swoop. And, in doing so, the Cape 'would indeed thus very soon become quite an English colony, such a proportion of the inhabitants being English, as would entitle us to disregard the known jealousy of the Dutch towards our settlers'.[204] Of course, the success of this course of action implied that all of the British settlers had the same aversion to revolutionary principles as the writer. As the evidence of the naval mutiny of October 1797 proved, however, this was not always the case.

The French were having trouble with their colonies too. The dissatisfaction of the colonists was noted by Jacques-Henri Bernardin de Saint Pierre in 1769. The proximity of Ile de France to 'the Indies raised great expectations on their [the colonists] first coming. But before their establishment was effected they became discontented and much more so afterwards.'[205] Indeed, according Bernardin de Saint Pierre, 'discord reign[ed] all over the island' even at this stage.[206] In 1796, the agents of the Directoire in Paris, Monsieurs Baco and Burnel, arrived with a force of 1,200 soldiers to implement the decree abolishing slavery in the island. They were empowered to do so by force of arms if necessary. But they met stiff resistance from the colonists who countered by pointing to the island's constitution, adopted on 2 April 1791. It had conferred autonomy on the administration of internal affairs. Backed by the local militia, the Colonial Assembly expelled the agents of the Directoire and the island was regarded as being in a state of rebellion.[207] This news quickly reached the British settlements in the region. Lord Macartney told Robert Brooke that 'the people of Mauritius it is said are not at all pleased with the present rulers of France and that they are determined to reject the new governor expected from Europe and even to resist a French squadron that should attempt to compel their obediences'.[208] The following year, affairs were still 'in a very disturbed state'. As far as Macartney could gather, the colonists 'mean to resist, and some people are of the opinion that they would not be sorry to throw themselves under our protection'.[209] The regular French troops at Mauritius were sent to Batavia, Andrew Barnard reported to Henry Dundas, because their

[204] CRO, D LONS/L13/1/91, 'Importance of the Cape', pp. 2, 14.
[205] Jacques-Henri Bernardin de Saint Pierre, *A Voyage to the Island of Mauritius (or, Isle of France), the Isle of Bourbon, the Cape of Good Hope* (London: W. Griffin, 1775), p. 89.
[206] *Ibid.*, pp. 91–2.
[207] See Huguette Ly-Tio-Fane Pineo, *In the Grips of the Eagle: Matthew Flinders at Ile de France, 1803–1810* (Moka, Mauritius: Mahatma Gandhi Institute, 1988), pp. 29–30.
[208] RH, MSS.Afr.t.3, Macartney to Brooke, 30 December 1797.
[209] RH, MSS.Afr.t.3, Macartney to Brooke, 4 May 1798.

principles were 'too democratic for the government of that place, which still continues on the old system'. For their part, the inhabitants of the island lived 'in constant dread of a force from France coming out to enforce the order of the Directory for the emancipation of their slaves'.[210] One traveller, the Comte de Fouchécour, was convinced that the islanders were opposed to the Revolution. As someone under the protection of the British, his loyalties were ambiguous. Nevertheless, he told his wife that on Mauritius 'the majority of the inhabitants are for us', while the population on Bourbon was even more royalist than those on the larger island.[211] By 1800, Roger Curtis could confidently assert that 'the planters, which form a principal part of the inhabitants, are more moderate, and condemn the excesses the present unstable government of France is daily committing'.[212]

Such ruptures between imperial centre and colonial periphery presented opportunities for rivals, of course. In this instance, the strategically important island on the route to India could be acquired by Britain: 'Mon. Malartic the governor is an old man and I believe would be happy to give the island up to us without a shot being fired, provided that we could engage that at a peace it should not return again to the French.'[213] As they prepared to leave the Cape for India, Henrietta Clive informed her brother:

We are to have a convoy or rather if the truth is known, which is now a secret, that we are to go with a small fleet going to take the Isle de France. It seems the greater part of the people wishes to have the English in possession of the island and this secret expedition is to go with us.[214]

In the event, however, the expedition did not take place. And not everyone was convinced of the settlers' motives or their willingness to throw off their allegiance to France. Admiral Curtis, once again, was dubious. 'I still continue in my opinion', he wrote to Lord Spencer, that 'we can place no confidence in obtaining advantage from dissension among the inhabitants.'[215]

---

210 RH, GB 0162 MSS.Afr.s.1,2, Barnard to Dundas, 20 October 1799.
211 CRL, LAdd/215, Comte de Fouchécour to Comtesse de Fouchécour, 17 August 1799 [my translation].
212 B'hurst, MS.053, 'Account of the French Possessions in the Indian Ocean' (1800), p. 27.
213 RH, GB 0162 MSS.Afr.s.1,2, Barnard to Dundas, 20 October 1799.
214 Henrietta Clive to George Herbert, Earl of Powis, 17 June 1798, in Nancy K. Shields (ed.), Birds of Passage: Henrietta Clive's Travels in South India, 1798–1801 (London: Eland, 2009), p. 53.
215 Curtis to Spencer, 28 November 1800, Spencer, vol. IV, p. 239.

Meanwhile, the turmoil continued on Mauritius. In August 1803, Charles Decaen arrived in Port Louis determined to rein in 'les îles rebelles' to the rule of Napoleon's consular government.[216] He attempted to appeal to the nationalist sentiments of the colonists by arousing their hatred of the 'perfidy and pride' of the British, which threatened 'to disturb the peace of nations' and adversely affect the prosperity of the island.[217] But his words seem to have been ineffectual. Several years later, during his time on the island, John Kelso observed that 'there are various parties in the community, all impressed with different ideas relative to their situation as connected with the mother country'. The Scotsman perceived that 'a strong sense of the severity approaching tyranny of the Emperor's present mode of government and general proceedings chiefly and forcibly prevailed'. And he suggested that the settlers' attitudes towards the British were 'more favourable and pacific' than was generally supposed back in London.[218] Kelso was in no doubt:

The feelings of the Creoles are so totally estranged from the Napoleon principle of Government, and so sensible are they of the mildness and freedom of ours, that they only require an opening to embrace our cause with the utmost cordiality.[219]

According to an informant on the island 'the whole of the colonists are anxious for the blessing of a British government'.[220] Admiral Albemarle Bertie was of the same opinion. From close scrutiny of the available evidence and intelligence, it appeared to him that the majority of inhabitants 'would consider a change of masters as a desirable event, and that protected by an adequate force, they would declare themselves' for Britain.[221] His views were undoubtedly reinforced by conversations with Matthew Flinders, from whom he received an assessment of the loyalty of the island's inhabitants: 'Nearly the whole of the old inhabitants and such of the newcomers as possess many slaves and considerable landed property are doubtless disposed to be neuter.'[222] Perhaps the views of Antoine Bayard, one of Flinders's acquaintances, best expressed the ambivalent views of many islanders: 'Born creole, from father to son, the colony is the only country I have.'[223]

---

[216] Pineo, *In the Grips of the Eagle*, p. 35.
[217] Proclamation, 28 September 1803, quoted *Ibid.*, p. 53.
[218] Kelso to Cathcart, 20 March 1808, *Londonderry*, vol. VIII, p. 166.   [219] *Ibid.*, p. 172.
[220] Quoted in Pineo, *In the Grips of the Eagle*, p. 144.
[221] Bertie to John Wilson Croker, 8 March 1810, *RCC*, vol. VII, p. 266.
[222] Matthew Flinders, 'Questions relative to the Ile de France proposed July 14, 1810, by Vice Admiral Bertie at the Cape of Good Hope with my answers therein', quoted in Pineo, *In the Grips of the Eagle*, p. 150.
[223] Quoted *Ibid.*, p. 173.

When Robert Farquhar, future governor of the islands under British rule, sent Nesbit Willoughby with a proclamation, he sought to take advantage of this perceived ambivalence to French rule.[224] He requested that the message be disseminated that 'the English are about to appear … not as enemies but as your sincere friends'. He traduced the French, who were possessed of 'the insatiable desire which increases every day … to absorb kingdoms'. The British, on the other hand, were only interested in opening 'a favourable market at the colony and to all its good friends and allies': 'Our ships will come from all quarters into your roads to barter merchandise from Europe and India for those of your island; the only views of Britain are justice, commerce and plenty.' He finished off with a stinging indictment of the French regime: 'What has your government done for you? It has ruined your commerce and forced your fathers and children to take service without affording them the least subsistence.'[225] And, it seemed, at least to an extent, to have the desired effect. When the British eventually landed, 'the fidelity of the numerous and well disciplined militia upon which constituted the principal defence of the island was so paralysed that at the attack by our army the French General could not depend on them'.[226] In South America, Southern Africa and the south-west Indian Ocean, the predictable allegiances of settlers were under scrutiny and in flux. For European maritime powers keen to hold on to safe and secure shipping lanes, this development was worrying and unwelcome.

Home Popham and the South Atlantic

The British acquisition of the Cape Colony, St Helena and, after 1810, the French islands meant that the projection of British power could increasingly come from within the region itself. Perhaps the most meaningful expression of this increasingly dominant presence at the gateway to India came in the form of Sir Home Popham's attack on Río de la Plata. Ultimately, the failure of this expedition highlights the rising tide of creole sentiment in South America. But Popham's designs for British invention in South America – and the logistics by which it was effected – encapsulate, in many ways, the changing British relationship with the region as a whole, and its relationship to the British route to Asia. Its launch was underwritten by successful British intervention across the South Atlantic at the Cape, and the military operation was partially supported from other

[224] NUL, Mi 2F 9, Nesbit Willoughby to Samuel Pym, 19 August 1810.
[225] NUL, Mi 2F 6, 'Proclamation to the Inhabitants of the Isle of France', 28 July 1810.
[226] NUL, Mi 2F 839/21, 'Transcript of a Memorial to the Colonial Office' (1824).

British outposts, such as St Helena. Initial reports suggested – mistakenly – that locals were amenable to British intervention. In addition to the obvious economic gains to be expected from establishing a British foot-hold at the mouth of this important river, the expedition could prevent the spread of revolutionary fervour across the region and, ultimately, secure another key nodal point on the route to India.

Popham had shown interest in the region before, taking command of *Nautilus* and surveying the coast of South-West Africa.[227] However, in the early years of the nineteenth century, he became increasingly pre-occupied by the commercial advantages presented to Britain (and, as his critics were quick to point out, to him personally) of the Spanish Viceroyalty of Río de la Plata.[228] As noted above, the British government had made repeated plans to attack South America during the various wars of the eighteenth century. The ongoing struggle with Napoleon presented another occasion finally to wrest control of at least part of the region from the Spanish. Popham catalogued the potential advantages of such an acquisition, including the strategic ones. South America sent $50 million to Spain every year, and the loss of these provinces would necessarily destroy it as a maritime power.[229] And he dangled before Charles Yorke the prospect of 'annihilating the navy of Spain by cutting off its greatest nursery for seamen and its principal sources for foreign timber'.[230]

But there were other considerations. In making a well-known argument about the prospects for British commercial advantage by virtue of 'the geographical situation of that great continent, its population and resources', Popham introduced the connection between a strategic posi-tion in South America and the defence of trade with Asia. Admiral Christian had prophesied that the French would use bases in one ocean to launch assaults on British interests in another: the French force 'will rendez-vous at Rio-de-la-Plata and make the island of Ceylon their object'.[231] The expedition and subsequent political settlement proposed by Popham offered 'the greatest commercial advantages, not only to this

---

[227] See p. 52 above.

[228] It is worth pointing out, however, that Popham submitted a plan advocating the capture of Batavia in the East Indies in 1799, representing the 'tyranny' of the colonial power and the willingness of the locals in much the same terms as he was later to do in relation to South America. See UWits, A88/467, 'Plan for Capturing the Dutch settlement of Batavia, submitted by Sir Home Popham to Henry Dundas, Secretary of State for War' (1799).

[229] Christopher D. Hall, *British Strategy in the Napoleonic War, 1803–15* (Manchester: Manchester University Press, 1992), p. 97.

[230] TNA, PRO 30/8/345, pp. 82–3, Popham to Yorke, 26 November 1803.

[231] Christian to Spencer, 31 March 1798, *Spencer*, vol. IV, p. 168.

country but to our possessions in India, by opening a direct trade on each side of the continent, and drawing all the wealth of Spanish America from our enemies, which has always been their principal support in every war with Great Britain'.[232] His shrewd observation highlighted the entangled worlds of Spanish America and British Asia. Popham offered a practical way of establishing British control at Río de la Plata. In a memorandum of 1804, he suggested invading Buenos Aires and cited the opinion of Rufus King, the former American minister in London. King believed that outright conquest was the only way to save La Plata from the French, a fear that, as we have seen, energised much British activity in this region throughout the war. Indeed, a plan to occupy La Plata was approved by Pitt, before being postponed. But the expedition to retake the Cape of Good Hope in late 1805 offered, in Popham's mind at least, the prospect of finally establishing British control of the entire South Atlantic. Popham, in HMS *Diadem*, acted as Commodore and commander-in-chief of the expedition to the Cape. He even led a marine battalion onshore during the operation. But his ambitions did not end there.

Popham's opinions were seemingly borne out by intelligence received in Southern Africa, 'respecting the weak state of defence which Montevideo and Buenos Ayres were in'.[233] While at the Cape, an American ship, the *Elizabeth*, arrived in Table Bay. The ship's master, one Captain Waine, showed Popham newspapers and gazettes from Buenos Aires, which were apparently highly critical of the government.[234] Waine had been involved in the slave trade and was a frequent visitor to both Buenos Aires and nearby Montevideo.[235] South America in general, and Río de la Plata in particular, Waine told him, were rich in flour – then short at the Cape – and other provisions. Furthermore, the inhabitants would eagerly embrace liberation from their Spanish masters.[236] A small detachment of troops, perhaps as few as 500, would be enough to take the colony and Waine even offered to take part in the raid.[237] The American clearly also played on Popham's fear of the

---

[232] TNA, PRO 30/8/345, p. 82, Popham to Yorke, 26 November 1803.

[233] TNA, ADM 1/58, p. 240, Popham to Marsden, 13 April 1806.

[234] In relaying on intelligence received from a passing ship's captain, Popham followed a similar pattern to Robert Brooke who had received intelligence from 'one Captain Hogan of the ship Marquis Cornwallis' when he was developing a plan to attack the River Plate. See B'hurst, MS.062/37, 'Papers respecting the Eligibility of making an Attack on the Spanish Settlement on the River Plate, with Plans etc. annexed'.

[235] Gillespie, *Gleanings and Remarks*, p. 20.

[236] Popham, *A Damned Cunning Fellow*, p. 145.

[237] TNA, ADM 1/58, p. 244, J. Waine to Popham, 28 March 1806. The letter was published, as a letter from the 'Master of an American Ship' to Home Popham, in *Minutes of Court Martial, Holden on Board His Majesty's Ship, Gladiator* (London: Longman, Hurst, Rees and Orme, 1807), pp. 48–9.

French beating him to it.[238] Popham decided to act without recourse to his military and political superiors in London. For one thing, he was aware of the long-standing interest that William Pitt held in capturing the River Plate.[239] Initially, things seemed to proceed according to plan. Popham's ventures, though unauthorised, pleased George Canning, Secretary of State for Foreign Affairs, since Napoleon was closing European ports while the United States threatened to close its own. And, unlike other previous planned expeditions to South America, this one could take advantage of an expanded British presence in the region.

Popham made use of this principally for victualling and refuelling purposes, although he did manage to elicit some support from commanders on the ground in the form of manpower. For example, Sir David Baird, who had led the British reoccupation of the Cape, allowed him to have 1,200 men. Baird informed William Beresford, who led the army detachment:

From intelligence recently received of the present defenceless state and condition of the Spanish possessions at Rio de la Plata, and from being aware of the great advantages to be derived from the possession of them, as well to our nation at large as to this colony in particular, I have determined to embark a detachment from the forces under my orders, with the view of attempting the conquest of those possessions.[240]

Popham's squadron sailed eastwards from the Cape on 14 April and at St Helena Popham 'borrowed' a further 180 men.[241] Alexander Gillespie, a member of the expeditionary force, claimed that Robert Patton, the governor of the island, was 'acquainted with the plan of our future operations, and fearing our inability to execute it, he assumed the personal responsibility of ordering 180 men from his garrison, with all their appendages for the field'.[242] Popham's offer of carrying out some modifications to the island's semaphore system may have swayed Patton's decision.[243] In any case, at the end of the sorry affair, the governor's 'unauthorized zeal entailed upon him the forfeiture of his government'.[244]

---

[238] Liss, *Atlantic Empires*, p. 188.

[239] See 'Miranda and the British Admiralty, 1804–1806', *American Historical Review* 6 (1901), pp. 508–30; C. F. Mullett (ed.), 'British Schemes and Spanish America in 1806', *Hispanic American Historical Review* 27 (1947), pp. 269–78.

[240] David Baird to William Beresford, 12 April 1806, *RCC*, vol. VI, p. 390.

[241] Hugh Popham, 'Popham, Sir Home Riggs (1762–1820)', *Oxford Dictionary of National Biography*, Oxford University Press, 2004; online edn, January 2008 (www.oxforddnb.com/view/article/22541, accessed 25 October 2013).

[242] Gillespie, *Gleanings and Remarks*, p. 29.

[243] Popham, *Damned Cunning Fellow*, p. 148.

[244] Gillespie, *Gleanings and Remarks*, p. 29.

The precise target of this extraordinary expedition – an ambitious and unauthorised offshoot of the only large imperial expedition launched from Britain during the Napoleonic War – was Buenos Aires, the capital of the Viceroyalty of Río de la Plata.[245] Established as recently as 1776, this viceroyalty encompassed an enormous territory, incorporating present-day Argentina, Chile, Uruguay, Paraguay and Bolivia. The details of the short British occupation may be summarised briefly. On 25 June 1806, a small force under the command of Brigadier-General William Carr Beresford landed near Buenos Aires. With the addition of a marine battalion, this band totalled 1,635 men. It met limited resistance as the Spanish were taken by surprise and the governor fled. On 2 July the city surrendered, with Beresford taking possession. Rashly, Popham sent an open letter to the merchants of London reporting on the possibilities of this lucrative new market for their goods, and sending a consignment of over £1 million from the treasury of the Spanish administration. When the British public learned of Popham's victory dispatch on 13 September, the mood was typically euphoric. The Morning Post reported that 'late on Saturday night last a Gazette Extraordinary was published, containing the particulars of this brilliant achievement, which the firing of the Park and Tower guns had previously announced to the public joy'.[246] The day after the news was received in London, the Patriotic Fund at Lloyd's 'resolved that vases of £200 value each, with appropriate inscriptions, be presented to Major-General Beresford and Commodore Sir Home Popham for their gallant and disinterested conduct in this successful and important enterprise'.[247] Even the artist Joseph Farington reported a remark made at one of his soirées which reflected the wider public reaction:

[Crauford] Bruce thought the capture of Buenos Ayres a great acquisition to commerce ... He said it would be attended with the good effect of disseminating our manufactures into every corner of South America.

The convivial company agreed that the area could 'never again be held by Spain' and that the best policy 'to keep it out of the hands of the French would be to induce them to establish themselves under our naval protection, into free, independent, government'.[248] A victory procession was quickly arranged with the notional booty being ceremonially paraded to the Bank of England in a train of wagons.[249]

[245] See James Davey, In Nelson's Wake: The Navy and the Napoleonic Wars (London: Yale University Press, 2015), ch. 5.
[246] Morning Post, 15 September 1806.   [247] Popham, Damned Cunning Fellow, p. 152.
[248] 4 October 1806, in James Greig (ed.), The Farington Diary (London: Hutchinson, 1924), vol. IV, p. 25.
[249] See Charles Esdaile, Napoleon's Wars: An International History, 1803–1815 (London: Allen Lane, 2007), p. 262.

But the euphoria was destined not to last. Farington was prophetic: 'It would require too many troops for England to undertake to attach [Buenos Aires] to herself.'[250] Indeed, the British failure to consolidate this foothold in South America contrasts with successes elsewhere along the route to India. It suggests the power of local, colonial (or 'creole') sentiment and the difficulty of projecting British power into this region before the middle of the nineteenth century. The first signs of problems for the British conquerors came when a force of about 2,000 Spaniards was assembled under the leadership of Santiago Liniers, a French officer in Spanish service. They entered Buenos Aires on 10 August, overwhelmed Beresford's men, and forced their surrender. Beresford and his troops were marched off into the country, and Popham and his squadron could do nothing but blockade the River Plate and wait for reinforcements. When they eventually arrived, these reinforcements invaded Montevideo on 3 February 1807. But, after a second attempt on Buenos Aires on 5 July 1807, the British detachment gave up the Río de la Plata completely, agreeing to evacuate within ten days of 7 July.[251] Arriving as conquerors in La Plata, the British had not reckoned on arousing such creole patriotism and military resistance. In fact, the locals proved anything but amenable. The locals' 'well known impatience of that Government' [i.e. the Spanish colonial authorities] precipitated 'a spirit of insurrection and revolt leading to the most sanguinary excesses and which except by the presence of a very superior force might have been found impossible to control'.[252] General Whitelocke commented on 'the very hostile disposition of the inhabitants'.[253] An observer reported that in 1807 the creoles had become 'so enthused with military service they heard of new enemy disembarkations with jubilation'.[254] In some ways, this enthusiasm was partially as a result of the British approach which encouraged talk of all sorts of liberty – political and commercial. As one witness observed: 'A considerable number of rich people took it into their heads to make a revolution, in order to shake off the yoke of the Spanish Government, and to establish the independence of the country.'[255] A British officer there reported finding creoles were 'entirely turned toward independence, and the establishment of a republic or federal government similar to that of North America'.[256]

[250] 4 October 1806, in Greig (ed.), *Farington Diary*, vol. IV, p. 25.
[251] Fichter, *So Great a Profitt*, p. 313, n. 20.
[252] BL, Add. MS 37884, f. 223, William Windham to Robert Craufurd, 30 October 1806.
[253] Quoted in Ian Fletcher, *The Waters of Oblivion* (Stroud: Spellmount, 2006), p. 117.
[254] Liss, *Atlantic Empires*, p. 188.
[255] 'Private Annotations addressed to his Excellency the Minister of War, on the first Arrival of the English, under Major-General Beresford, at Buenos Ayres', 1 August 1806, *Londonderry*, vol. VII, p. 310.
[256] Quoted in Liss, *Atlantic Empires*, p. 189.

As a result of the debacle, Popham was ordered to return to Britain, whereupon he was brought to court martial for having launched his enterprise 'with no direction or authority whatever'.[257] One of the justifications for undertaking the assault was the protection of the route to India and the defence of Britain's position in the region. Popham tried to convince Sir David Baird and Robert Patton that a successful venture would benefit their respective territories. He told Patton 'that such an acquisition' would 'add to the commerce and safety of the island you govern, as well as be an additional safeguard to the trade of the East India Company'.[258] Sir David Baird was similarly persuaded that 'the possession of a settlement on the coast of South America, I consider pregnant with incalculable advantage, as well to our nation at large, as to this colony in particular'.[259] That the expedition was a failure highlights the strength of local settler opinion and, ultimately, the limits of all European power in the region.

Conclusion

For Britain, control of the gateway to the Indian Ocean was crucial for maintaining access to its growing Asian empire. But identifying places and acquiring control were not synonymous. A range of obstacles, principally in the form of French intervention, prevented complete British dominance. The fear of French invasion of India was only marginally more threatening than French attempts to build up its own Indian Ocean empire, to capture British outposts in the South Atlantic, or to support colonial rebels. What might be a feather in one country's control could very easily become 'a sword in the hands of France'.[260] The outbreak of the French Revolution complicated the picture even further, as 'the rankest poison of Jacobinism' threatened to infect whole swathes of the region.[261] Britain had to battle not only its traditional commercial and political foes, but also new groups of settlers seeking enfranchisement and liberty. Notwithstanding the failure of Home Popham's mission, the consolidation of the British position in the South Atlantic was relatively

---

[257] *A Full and Correct Report of the Trial of Sir Home Popham* (London: Richardson, 1807), p. 3. To the Admiralty, Popham may have been an officer who had acted improperly but to the merchants of the City of London, he was an adventurer who had made a bold attempt to open up new markets: they presented him with a sword of honour. Nevertheless, Popham faced a court martial at Portsmouth in March 1807. He defended himself vigorously, but was found guilty and severely reprimanded.
[258] Popham to Robert Patton, 13 April 1806, in *Minutes of Court Martial*, p. 47.
[259] Baird to Castlereagh, 14 April 1806, *Ibid.*, p. 58.
[260] TNA, WO 1/329, p. 48, Blankett to Nepean, 25 January 1795.
[261] Craig to Dundas, 22 September 1795, *RCC*, vol. I, p. 155.

successful. Even launching that assault employed troops from the British possessions in the region. And, as the reports of Captain Waine demonstrated, intelligence was crucial. Britain now had an intra-regional network of communications and information exchange at its disposal.

The preceding chapters have assessed the perceived strategic value of different parts of the region, as well as the interrelationships between trade and maritime possessions that characterised European engagement with it. Subsequent chapters explore more fully the ways in which these places were practically enveloped into the British Indian Ocean world: the exchange of news and information, the consolidation of political and military power, and the recruitment and deployment of troops. They investigate how this interconnected maritime 'world' at the southern reaches of the Atlantic and Indian oceans operated in practice, the ways in which it was increasingly incorporated into the British Empire in Asia, and the practical connections that linked it with the Indian subcontinent. Building on models developed by scholars of the Atlantic world, and being increasingly explored by those interested in Britain's Indian Ocean world, these chapters concentrate on the movement of people, information and ideas within and beyond this region. More specifically, they focus on the ways in which intelligence and military personnel – key factors in shoring up British interests in Asia during a period of war – were deployed in and around the region and drew it into the wider web of the British Empire.

4 'A constant and unreserved correspondence': networks of knowledge exchange

The field at Waterloo was not the only place where British power was being contested in 1815. Writing about the latest upheavals to afflict the northern frontiers of British India in the same year, Lord Moira wrote wearily to Lord Charles Somerset, the recently arrived governor at the Cape. Moira was confident that 'Your Lordship will have learned through the ordinary channels of intelligence the occurrence of a war between the East India Company and the State of Nepaul, and the untoward events which have attended the early operations of our arms.'[1] Moira's somewhat jaded tone aside, his correspondence with a 'brother' governor highlights some of the major themes of this chapter: the constant flow of news, intelligence and gossip shuttling around the British Empire, the means by which such information travelled, and the contingent nature of British power in the Indian Ocean at the time. Perhaps most obviously, in bringing such information and intelligence to the southern Atlantic and Indian oceans, Moira's letter embodies those very same 'ordinary channels' that he mentions.

The following two chapters focus on the ways in which transoceanic strategic, intelligence, military and scientific networks worked in practice. Tracing the arcs of these connections, and understanding how and why they operated, helps us further to understand the importance of this region as a gateway to that wider Indian Ocean world. The value of these connections was recognised at the time. Just as control of seaways and commercial channels was important, so commanding (and in some instances, curbing) the circulation of information was recognised as playing a crucial part in establishing and preserving the British position. Facts and information about the route, key strategic way stations, and the movements of European rivals were all eagerly sought. And there was no diminution in this exchange of information when Britain became more firmly established in the region. The links between India and the Cape were long-standing. As Richard Wellesley, another governor general of

[1] Lord Moira to Lord Charles Somerset, 9 February 1815, *RCC*, vol. X, p. 249.

India, reminded Sir George Yonge, one of Somerset's predecessors: 'My correspondence with the Earl of Macartney furnishes abundant proof of the advantages to be derived to the Public Service in India by the speedy communication from the Cape of Good Hope of intelligence affecting the interests of this empire.'[2] Robert Brooke put it rather more apologetically to Lord Macartney, 'I would not trouble you therefore with the accompanying papers were it not for the intelligence contained in them which possibly may prove useful.'[3]

Both of these examples point to the fact that it was not just people, goods and objects that circulated around the oceans of the world. Long-established commercial links helped to facilitate other types of exchanges. Networks of mobility are also, in a sense, networks of knowledge. Recently, there has been increasing scholarly interest in the circulation of knowledge between East and West.[4] As Simon Schaffer reminds us, 'the imperial vision hinged on reliable and potent knowledge'.[5] Information and intelligence gathering was a central part of the British war effort in the 1790s and 1800s.[6] Such activities were also of funda-mental importance to the British presence in the Indian Ocean. Britain's maritime empire was based on securing not just territorial 'keys' but also information.

As with other maritime spaces in the early modern world, the circula-tion of ideas, information, and intelligence characterised the southern Atlantic and Indian oceans. This chapter focuses on such patterns of movement in, through and around the region. Much of this information related to strategic and commercial concerns, but there were attendant interests in scientific and security matters. The area occupied a vital position for the gathering and circulation of intelligence.[7] For example, Major Francis Robson, a former captain on the Madras establishment and now lieutenant governor on St Helena, wrote to William Forsyth in London with news from the wider Asian arena:

---

[2] BL, Add. MS 13784, f. 82, Richard Wellesley to George Yonge, 15 September 1800.
[3] B'hurst, MS.062/16, Robert Brooke to Lord Macartney, 3 June 1797.
[4] See, for example, Bernard Lightman, Gordon McOuat and Larry Stewart (eds.), *The Circulation of Knowledge between Britain, India and China: The Early-Modern World to the Twentieth Century* (Leiden: Brill, 2013); Timothy Davies, 'English Private Trade on the West Coast of India, c.1680–c.1740', *Itinerario* 38 (2014), pp. 51–73.
[5] Simon Schaffer, 'Visions of Empire: Afterword', in D. P. Miller and P. H. Reill (eds.), *Visions of Empire: Voyages, Botany and the Representations of Nature* (Cambridge: Cambridge University Press, 1996), pp. 335–52, p. 336.
[6] Robert R. Dozier, *For King, Constitution, & Country: The English Loyalists and the French Revolution* (Lexington, KY: University Press of Kentucky, 1983), pp. 39–47.
[7] For further examples, see undated intelligence reports, signed by Andrew Mitchell. B'hurst, MS.052/11–12.

Admiral Rainier has taken Amboyna and Banda so that the whole of the spice islands are now in our possession. I cannot enumerate to you the exact value of these places but it is publickly said that in cash and spices [it] is worth more than two millions sterling so that our good friends the Dutch have nothing left but Batavia, where at present a most dreadful sickness prevails.[8]

And the flow of information was not unidirectional. During the first British occupation of the Cape, the presence there of the American ship *Betsy*, bound for Batavia, provided Andrew Barnard with an opportunity to forward some 249 letters to the Dutch governor of Batavia. These were discovered in the administrative offices 'upon the surrender of this colony to the arms of His Britannic Majesty'. Barnard acknowledged:

These letters are of course of a very old date but they are forwarded as they possibly contain information interesting to individuals or documents of importance to many inhabitants of your Presidency.

And the British administration hoped that its munificence would be rewarded, with Barnard anticipating that the governor would 'direct such an act of justice to be reciprocated if any letter under similar circumstances destined for this place should be laying with you'.[9] As this last example underlines, information was also exchanged between different empires. Samuel Hood Linzee, commander of HMS *L'Oiseau*, assured the Governor of Mozambique that 'should you have any information relative to the trade of the enemy's ships belonging to the republic of France particularly of the Isle of France and Bourbon, I shall be obliged to Your Excellency for it'.[10]

Building on some of these examples, the discussion that follows investigates the region's crucial role as an information nodal point, conveying intelligence from India to Britain and vice versa. It explores the ways in which information arrived in the region, the channels through which it streamed, and the effects that it had on the British presence there, suggesting that flows of information were crucial means of imbricating the region in a wider Indian Ocean world and confirming it as a critical element of Britain's maritime empire. Jill Geber has drawn attention to the fact that the proximity of the Cape, its status as a British colony and its strategic location encouraged mutual military and administrative support between the Cape and India.[11] In arguing for its capture in the first place,

---

[8] RBG, FOR/1/2, p. 70, Francis Robson to William Forsyth, 12 October 1796.
[9] RH, MSS.Afr.t.2, Andrew Barnard to the Governor of Batavia, 1 August 1798.
[10] AHU, Conselho Ultramarino (CU), Moçambique (Moç.), CX83/7, Samuel Hood Linzee to Governor of Mozambique, 5 July 1799.
[11] Jill Geber, 'The East India Company and Southern Africa: a guide to the Archives of the East India Company and the Board of Control, 1600–1858', Ph.D. dissertation, University of London, 1998, pp. 104–5.

and in assessing its worth to the nation, the fact that the Cape belonged to commercial, political and military networks that spanned the Indian Ocean was a key consideration. By focusing on the wider maritime region as a conduit for receiving, transmitting and generating information, we can more fully understand its role in these networks. In examining the physical distribution and dissemination of information and ideas, the chapter emphasises the *central* location of this 'peripheral' space in the circulation of such information.

The discussion is arranged under several broad themes. The first half of the chapter explores the movement of information to, from and through the region. It considers how it travelled, the kinds of channels through which it passed, and the role played by state- and semi-state-sponsored spying and espionage in curbing as well as facilitating such flows. The second part considers the effects of these information movements on Britain's strategic and political position in the Indian Ocean. The circulation of news had consequences for individuals in the region, keeping them abreast of developments in the wider British world. But it was also vital for the maintenance of British power there too. Conversely, of course, the ever-present and nagging fear of intelligence falling into enemy hands also characterised the region and influenced its place in the wider British Empire. These fears were amplified when information exchanges threatened to precipitate disaster from within, as almost happened during the naval mutiny at the Cape in 1797. The discussion concludes by acknowledging that military and strategic intelligence were not the only forms of information exchanges taking place. The final section explores, therefore, the ways in which scientific ideas cemented the British position in the region.

Moving information: personal connections and official channels

The business of government, the security of the empire, the mechanics of trade and the maintenance of personal and familial ties all relied on successful correspondence. Information about the progress of wars, news of naval victories, and tidings about a whole host of other matters crisscrossed the maritime world of Britain's late eighteenth-century empire, inscribing patterns of news and information exchange that mirrored wider developments and imperial connections. How did news and information flow around this world? Sometimes information was acquired serendipitously from naval officers and seamen. This was certainly the case with someone like John Turner, who was apparently cast away on the east coast of Africa, before returning with news of capacious

bays and curious animals.[12] Nevertheless, the 'usual channels' mentioned
by Lord Moira invariably involved connections forged by ships. Given its
central location on the maritime highway between Britain and India, the
southern arc of the Atlantic and Indian oceans received its fair share of
updates from passing ships. Lady Anne Barnard remarked on how 'our
Bay is now covered with ships and we welcome them with the greater
pleasure that they have brought us so much good news of late'.[13]
Although news exchanges relied on ships, the information itself could
be carried in a variety of media – from official dispatches to private letters
and personal conversations – which combined to create a richly textured
nexus of information exchange.

Of course, much of the strategic and commercially sensitive information circulated via government or quasi-governmental channels. The East
India Company was a key sponsor of information gathering and distribution in this regard. As with other aspects of this maritime space, the
archives of the East India Company are a crucial resource. Betty Joseph
observes that the Company's 'official record' acted as 'an instrument of
governance', and this is particularly the case in relation to information
exchanges.[14] When the *Swallow* was sent to Africa on a surveying mission
in 1783, for example, the Company placed a premium on securing the
information and getting it back to Britain:

You will as soon as you have examined it proceed directly to St Helena where you
will deliver to our Governor there [a] copy of your journal & all charts, plans and
views taken or made during your voyage which you will keep ready for that or any
other occasion that may offer of transmitting them to us.[15]

Information regarding the Company's territories in India necessarily
passed through the region, giving those *in situ* an opportunity to congra-
tulate the East India Company on good news, or otherwise to analyse and
interpret the runes for those back in London. The authorities on St
Helena, for example, had 'the honor of again addressing you by the Fox
Packet, Capt. Court, that arrived here 8 instant from Bengal'. The ship
was 'dispatched home with the pleasing account of peace with the
Marattas, and a confirmation of the death of Hyder Ally'. The St
Helenians were convinced that the victory over the 'Marattas' would be

[12] UWits, A88/100, Thomas Pringle to Macartney, 3 July 1797.
[13] Lady Anne Barnard to Macartney, 25 January 1799, in Dorothea Fairbridge (ed.), *Lady Anne Barnard at the Cape of Good Hope, 1797–1802* (Oxford: Clarendon Press, 1924), p. 83.
[14] Betty Joseph, *Reading the East India Company, 1720–1840* (Chicago: University of Chicago Press, 2004), p. 6.
[15] TNA, CO 77/25, p. 125, 'Heads of Instructions given by the Secret Committee to the Captain of the Swallow', September 1783.

particularly beneficial 'as we flatter ourselves it will be a means of restoring yours and the nation's future power throughout all Indostan, as well as re-establishing tranquility in the Carnatic'. Their basis for such an analysis was, however, somewhat dubious: 'We understand that Tippoo Saib, Hyder's successor[,] has already shewn less hostile intentions to the English than those pursued by his father; permitting the British subjects in the towns that were taken a free communication with the Presidency of Madras.'[16]

But there was a healthy exchange of information and intelligence between merchant ships and government departments. It is important not to underestimate the personal element involved here. As Natasha Glaisyer points out, 'a single letter writer could form the hub of an enormous network of correspondents'.[17] Correspondence between personal contacts, family and friends was a vital means of transmitting information.[18] The networks facilitated by such information and knowledge exchanges helped to overcome problems of physical distance in the British Empire in the eighteenth century, and they also created bonds between different parts of the empire.[19] But they also give a sense of the precarious nature of the connections, dependent as they were on ships reaching their destination safely, avoiding both enemy vessels and natural perils.[20] Informing Elias Hasket Derby of their activities at the Cape, William Vans and Ebenezer West adopted a cautious approach: 'We wrote you several letters from Cape [of] Good Hope (via England, West Indies and by Capt. Carpenter), but as letters often miscarry we again give you the ruff [recte rough] disposal of goods at the Cape.'[21] Thomas McRitchie, on St Helena, chastised William Forsyth, the superintendent of the royal gardens in London, for his silence: 'I have never received a letter from you these two years past.' He did acknowledge, however, how uncertain the whole operation was: 'I wrote you a letter on receiving my box with the shawls and shoes but as I sent it by a private

[16] BL, IOR, H/175, p. 629, Extract of letter from Governor and Lieutenant Governor of St Helena to the Secret Committee of the Court of Directors, 17 May 1783.

[17] Natasha Glaisyer, 'Networking: Trade and Exchange in the Eighteenth-Century British Empire', *Historical Journal* 47 (2004), pp. 451–76, p. 473.

[18] For a detailed discussion of this phenomenon, especially as it pertained to the North Atlantic, see Lindsay O'Neill, *The Opened Letter: Networking in the Early Modern British World* (Philadelphia: University of Pennsylvania Press, 2015).

[19] Craig Bailey, 'Metropole and Colony: Irish Networks and Patronage in the Eighteenth-Century Empire', *Immigrants & Minorities* 23 (2005), pp. 161–81, p. 161.

[20] For more on the practicalities of sending information around the region in letters, see UWits, A88/143, List of letters from Earl Macartney delivered by Mr John Murray to Commodore Douglas, St Helena, 18 September 1797.

[21] William Vans and Ebenezer West to Elias Hasket Derby, 22 April 1786, in Robert E. Peabody, *The Log of the Grand Turks* (London: Duckworth, 1927), p. 69.

person you very probably have never received it.'[22] So too did Lady Anne Barnard in writing to her old flame, Henry Dundas. She sent the same letter twice, 'once by an excellent conveyance and once by a moderate one but I have had enough of experience of the many accidents which letters are exposed to, to be sure that at such a distance there is no fear of your receiving too many'.[23] Her opinion was born of bitter experience, when letters from her sister, Margaret, and 'others very precious to me are gone on to visit Bengal'. By missing landfall at the Cape, the epistles were destined to continue along the route plied by ships to and from the subcontinent. Lady Anne was left to lament the fact that 'they will return to England and I may possibly have them a twelvemonths hence'.[24]

Even in the official arena of information gathering and exchange, personal connections were important. Interpersonal networks, in which exchanges of information played such a vital role, were (and were acknowledged as) central to the administration of the empire until 1815 and beyond.[25] For example, Richard Lewin, 'Resident' at the Cape for the Government of Madras in the early 1780s and detailed to gather as much useful intelligence as possible, recommended that such a connection be established with 'Messers Clifford and Teysett'. They were 'agents for the Hon Co. in Amsterdam', and it occurred to Lewin that:

some advantages might be derived to the Publick service from the establishment of a correspondence between that house and me, as they may have it in their power occasionally to transmit to me, by the Dutch ships that sail from thence, intelligence which may be highly useful to the Hon. Company's presidencies in India, and which cannot otherwise be so safely and speedily conveyed.[26]

The value of personal communication was underlined during the first British occupation when Lord Macartney wrote to Henry Dundas about 'the Three Sisters, an American Vessel which left Bengal on the 7th of February last, [which] stopped at this place on her way to Boston'. The ship had called at Bourbon, and embarked from that island with a 'M. Vergoz with his wife and several children'. Macartney gave them permission to come on shore at the Cape 'in order that I might have an

---

[22] RBG, FOR/1/2, p. 48, Thomas McRichie to Forsyth, 14 June 1792.

[23] NAS, GD51/9/218, Lady Anne Barnard to Dundas, 12 November 1801.

[24] US, BR19/1/2, Lady Anne Barnard, to Mary, Viscountess Palmerston, 9 July 1800.

[25] See Kirsten McKenzie, 'Social Mobilities at the Cape of Good Hope: Lady Anne Barnard, Samuel Hudson, and the Opportunities of Empire, c.1797–1824', in Tony Ballantyne and Antoinette Burton (eds.), Moving Subjects: Gender, Mobility, and Intimacy in an Age of Global Empire (Urbana, IL: University of Illinois Press, 2008), pp. 274–95, p. 276.

[26] BL, IOR, H/153, pp. 568–9, Richard Lewin to Peter Michell, 30 January 1781.

opportunity of obtaining some information relative to the place which they came from'. The governor was not disappointed:

What I have been able to learn is that by a vessel privately sent from Bourdeaux by some merchants who are interested in the affairs of the Isles of France and Bourbon, news had been lately received there that the French Government, exasperated at the abrupt dismission [*sic*] of their Commissioners, had come to a resolution of immediately dispatching some Ships of War and a considerable number of troops.[27]

Macartney's interest in military matters was a recurring theme, and the security situation in the region dominated the movement of information and intelligence, as well as people and troops. Personal communication networks could even cut across apparently immutable lines of national allegiance. When Matthew Flinders arrived at the Cape in June 1810 after six years in captivity on the Ile de France, for example, he lost no time in writing to his 'particular friend' on the island, Charles Desbassayns, 'that there was a prospect of your island being almost immediately annexed to the British dominions'.[28]

Moving information: spying and espionage

The security concerns of British politicians and merchants were underscored when Peter Rainier wrote to Lord Spencer in July 1799. Rainier, the commander-in-chief of the Royal Navy's East Indies station, seemed to be passing on straightforward, workaday information to his superior at the Admiralty. The letter informed Spencer that 'the Sceptre sails for the Cape the day after tomorrow with a convoy of three valuable ships of the Company. The other three ships belonging to the Cape Station will be sent back as soon as possible.'[29] In its concern with merchant ship movements, this news was hardly extraordinary. What made the letter different from a commonplace piece of correspondence, however, was the fact that it was written in cipher. The use of such subterfuge was not unusual at a time when ships – both naval and merchant – were almost constantly at risk of capture.[30]

Particularly during wartime, secrets, information and intelligence were the order of the day.[31] William Huskisson, Undersecretary at War, was

[27] RH, MSS.Afr.t.4, Macartney to Dundas, 1 May 1798.
[28] Marina Carter, *Companions of Misfortune: Flinders and Friends at the Isle of France, 1803–1810* (London: Pink Pigeon Press, 2003), p. 125.
[29] BL, Add. MS 75834, Peter Rainier to Lord Spencer, 30 July 1799.
[30] See Margaret Bradley, *Daniel Lescallier, 1743–1822, Man of the Sea or Military Spy? Maritime Developments and French Military Espionage* (Lewiston, NY: Mellen, 2005).
[31] Michael Durey, 'William Wickham, the Christ Church Connection and the Rise and Fall of the Security Service in Britain, 1793–1801', *English Historical Review* 121 (2006),

keen to meet with David Scott of the East India Company 'as I have a great deal of secret intelligence to communicate to you, which will be despatched to Portsmouth tomorrow evening, and sent to the Cape and India by a fast sailing cutter the next day'.[32] And subterfuge was rife in the Indian Ocean itself. Robert Brooke was delighted to report that when the *Polyphemus* called at St Helena, its passengers included 'a Major Tench, a very ingenious man whose letters from France you may have seen as also those that pass under the name of Giffard. From him I heard much respecting the political state of Europe.'[33] Meanwhile, Captain Teller, an American, came to Port Louis in May 1800 disguised as a Dane.[34]

The ways in which secret – perhaps more accurately described as sensitive – information moved around this part of the Indian Ocean world highlights its practical value. In August 1771, Lord Harcourt reported to Lord Rochford that intelligence, recently received from the Dutch commanding officer at Cape Town, alerted him to the fact that some 7,000 French soldiers had gone to the Ile de France.[35] Other reports around the same time suggested that the French were garrisoning the Seychelles.[36] Such intelligence could be gathered by the crew of passing ships or from sympathetic locals. But the use of 'agents' was also an option.

The admirably detailed nature of the intelligence sent to Lord Rochford by Mr Petrie from the Cape on 26 October 1775 gives an insight into the ways in which such information was procured. It was not received until 28 April 1776. But Petrie gives a sense of the ways in which intelligence swirled around, as well as the different agendas it could be made to serve:

The following particulars have come to my knowledge by the means of the commandant of the troops here, Major Du Prehn, formerly in the service of Brunswick and known, I believe, to some at the English Court. They were communicated to him, by the French Engineer, and as they correspond with the accounts from other quarters they may, I imagine be depended upon.[37]

pp. 714–45, p. 714. For further information on this in the British domestic and European context, see Elizabeth Sparrow, 'Secret Service under Pitt's Administration, 1792–1806', *History* 83 (1998), pp. 280–94.

[32] CRL, LAdd/1122, William Huskisson to David Scott, 14 April 1796.

[33] B'hurst, MS.062/23, Brooke to Macartney, 14 December 1797.

[34] Alfred W. Crosby, 'American Trade with Mauritius in the Age of the French Revolution and Napoleon', *American Neptune* 25 (1965), pp. 5–17, p. 12.

[35] Nicholas Tracy, *Navies, Deterrence, and American Independence: Britain and Seapower in the 1760s and 1770s* (Vancouver: University of British Columbia Press, 1988), p. 100.

[36] BL, IOR, H/105, p. 383, Philip Pittman to Thomas Hodges and Council at Bombay, 8 December 1770.

[37] BL, IOR, H/120, p. 151, Mr Petrie to Lord Rochford, 26 October 1775.

Allowing such information to circulate could, of course, serve other ends. 'The Colonel of Engineers concluded the subject by saying that he believed their court did not mean war but were determined to preserve the respect due to the French flag in all parts of the world, and made mention of some insults which had been offered to their nation in Bengal and in different parts of India by the servants of the English Company', wrote Petrie.[38]

The French had a spy at the Cape in the 1770s. Monsieur Pacheron 'resides at the Cape as a commissary buying up all kinds of provisions, salting meat and baking biscuit for the [French-controlled] islands' in the Indian Ocean. But the anonymous correspondent was sure that there was more to Pacheron's job description than that of an agent victualler for outlying French colonies: 'This man is a spy and seems to be left there on purpose to get intelligence of the motions of the English.'[39] The strategic importance of places like the Cape meant that accurate information on troop and personnel movements was at a premium. It also made for a somewhat febrile atmosphere of claim and counterclaim, as alluded to by Samuel Appleby. He reported that the residents at the Cape were 'greatly surprised to hear the Hawke [his ship] was to return to India, and as it was a thing intirely new, [they] immediately concluded I was on the look out after the French'. The machinations of the local French agent, Monsieur de Roche, worked against Appleby. By 'oblique hints', the Frenchman 'insinuated otherwise' and:

gave the Dutch to understand that I was there to look out after them and that the additional force sent to the squadron from England must be owing to some scheme the English Ministry had formed against their settlements and did not fail to say Ceylon was certainly the object.[40]

As a result, Appleby found it almost impossible 'to get any question answered by a Dutchman relative to anything I wanted to ask, and I believe the Governor thought there might be some truth in this history as he never showed the least civility either to Mr Finch or me'.[41]

Despite Appleby's indignation, the reaction of the Dutch colonists was unsurprising. Indeed, their reticence proved to be well founded when, in 1780, Richard Lewin, a Company official at Fort St George, travelled in the *Nymph* to take up his appointment as 'in quality of Resident' at the

---

[38] *Ibid.*, p. 152.

[39] BL, IOR, H/107, p. 37, Intelligence from the Cape concerning French provisioning, extract of letter from George Patterson, Cape of Good Hope, 8 July 1772.

[40] TNA, ADM 1/163, p. 243, Samuel Appleby to Robert Harland, 31 December 1772.

[41] *Ibid.*, p. 244.

Cape for the government of Madras.[42] Everything seemed above board:
Lewin was awarded a salary of 200 pagodas per month and carried a letter
to be delivered to the Dutch governor upon his arrival. But Lewin was
expected to engage in more useful activities than the usual pleasantries, as
his instructions from Madras made plain:

> Your principal business in this character [i.e. as Resident] will be to procure the
> most authentic intelligence respecting the motions and designs of our enemies,
> and to transmit the same by the earliest conveyances to the Court of Directors,
> and to the several Presidencies in India, and to Sir Edward Hughes. You are also
> by every means in your Power to procure such assistance as may be wanted by any
> of His Majesty's or the Company's Ships, which may put into the Cape, and to
> make such public applications to the Governor on this head, from time to time, as
> you shall find expedient.[43]

Lewin certainly had no qualms about his role. Upon his arrival, he
reported that 'the Select Committee of Fort St George' have 'appointed
me to reside at this place for the purpose of transmitting intelligence as
well to the Hon. the Court of Directors as to the several presidencies in
India, and to the Commander-in-Chief of His Majesty's naval force'. And
he lost no time in 'addressing you in conformity to the instructions
I received with my appointment'.[44]

John Pringle was the East India Company's commercial agent at the
Cape but his remit extended beyond purely commercial activities.[45]
The Governor of the Ile de France was adamant that Pringle played
a key role in bringing about the change of government at the Cape.
Decaen observed:

> Mr Pringle, the agent of the English company, lived at the Cape for twelve years
> before the conquest of this colony; he has contributed a lot to the ease of this
> conquest in working the spirit of the leaders and corrupting them by various
> means.[46]

---

[42] Little is known about Lewin. His death was reported in 1832. See *Gentlemen's Magazine*
102 (1832), p. 573.

[43] The President and Council of Madras to Richard Lewin, 16 October 1780, in Thomas
Herbert Lewin (ed.), *The Lewin Letters: A Selection from the Correspondence and Diaries of
an English Family, 1756–1884*, 2 vols. (London: Archibald Constable & Co., 1909), vol. I,
pp. 21–2.

[44] BL, IOR, H/153, p. 565, Lewin to Peter Michell, 30 January 1781.

[45] Perhaps Pringle's most extraordinary claim to fame is his involvement in the transfer of
British-style accounting to Southern Africa. See Grant Samkin, 'Trader Sailor Spy:
The Case of John Pringle and the Transfer of Accounting Technology to the Cape of
Good Hope', *Accounting History* 15 (2010), pp. 505–28.

[46] Quoted in Huguette Ly-Tio-Fane Pineo, *In the Grips of the Eagle: Matthew Flinders at Ile
de France, 1803–1810* (Moka, Mauritius: Mahatma Gandhi Institute, 1988), p. 122 (my
translation).

In response, the governor appointed a French agent, M. Broussonet, to do something similar.

Spying was particularly useful in relation to the Ile de France. To this end, Captain Lockhart Russell was sent by the Bengal Presidency in the early 1770s to obtain more information about the seemingly inexorable build-up of defences on the island and what it meant for British India. Ultimately his extraordinarily detailed report ended up with the Company in London, from where it was forwarded to Whitehall for 'Lord Rochford's inspection'.[47] Russell, a captain in a regiment of Engineers, described the difficulty and danger of approaching the island during a hurricane in March 1772. But this did not prevent him from recording precisely how the French had built up their garrison since 1768, their receipt of a shipload of specie from the Spaniards at Manila, and their arrangements with Hyder Ali and other princes in India.[48] These machinations pointed to one thing:

> The result of these politics was the forming of an expedition, which aimed at totally extirpating the Company from their possessions in India, by landing twenty thousand Europeans about July or August 1771 at Pondicherry, who were immediately to take the field.[49]

One of the most interesting features of the report, however, is the lengths to which Russell went to obtain this information as well as the attempts of the French to prevent this from happening. Under the pretence of not wanting to disturb the Governor at night, Russell managed to ensure that he landed in the daylight: 'While dark they would have hurried me into the country to prevent my seeing the defences of the place, I therefore resolved if I was to march it would be with my eyes open in the broad day.'[50] Elsewhere, the French tried to conduct British visitors by 'round about ways at a distance from the town, into a country retreat called the Reduit, surrounded with mountains, which wholly eclipses their view of any part of the island, and wholly cuts off their correspondence with those of the country who could give such information as they might be desirous of gaining'.[51] Eventually, Russell managed to gain free rein to roam about the island, an opportunity he seized with characteristic alacrity: 'From this time I rambled at large, and I confess took full advantage of my licence by going everywhere I thought I could improve my knowledge of the strength of the place, the avenues of access most favourable to attacking Port Louis on some future occasion and such

---

[47] BL, IOR, H/106, p. 187, Chairman and Deputy Chairman to Mr Sutton, 5 August 1772.
[48] BL, IOR, H/106, pp. 191–232, 'Report of Capt. Lockhart Russell to the Court of Directors of the East India Company', 24 July 1772.
[49] *Ibid.*, pp. 210–11.   [50] *Ibid.*, p. 198.   [51] *Ibid.*, pp. 200–1.

like.'[52] Despite this lapse, the French authorities were generally alive to the threat carried by people like Russell and attempted to guard the secrets of their island's fortifications jealously. In writing to Warren Hastings and the Council at Fort William, Sir Edward Hughes informed them of the arrival of the *Swallow* at Bombay. On its passage, Captain Piggott had found it 'necessary to anchor at Mauritius to repair some defects in the sloop which could not be done at sea'. But if he was expecting a warm welcome, Piggott must have been sorely disappointed:

The Governor Monsieur Temay gave him a reception which amounted to rudeness, upon a pretended supposition of his coming there as a spy, & went so far as to order him away before he could have what was necessary.[53]

Monsieur Temay's coldness towards Piggott may have been ungentlemanly but it was almost certainly well founded. Whatever Piggott's motivations, Hughes added, 'the enclosed intelligence will best inform you, Sir and Gentlemen of the state of affairs at the French islands'.[54]

Temporary visitors to the island were a problem for the French authorities. But more permanent residents were much more troublesome. In the first decade of the nineteenth century, John Kelso, the 22-year-old son of a Scottish military officer, made his way to Calcutta to work for an uncle who was in business in Bengal. Like many Europeans in India, Kelso found that the climate 'disagreed with his health'. In search of relief, he made his way to Prince of Wales (now Penang) Island. But before he could reach Malaya, he was 'captured by the French, and carried to the Isle of France'. It was 'during his confinement there' and 'from a laudable zeal for the interests of his country' that he gathered impressions and observations, submitting a plan of assault to the government in London.[55]

Perhaps the most renowned 'spy' in the region, however, was Matthew Finders. Flinders is most famous as the naval officer and hydrographer who surveyed vast stretches of the Australian coast in HMS *Investigator*. But the loss of his ship on this mission forced Flinders to make for Britain in a schooner, the *Cumberland*, in search of a replacement vessel. In crossing the Indian Ocean, however, the *Cumberland* proved very leaky and forced Flinders to call at the Ile de France in 1803 for urgent repairs. Flinders was under the mistaken impression that the passport issued to him by the French government before he left Britain would suffice. But his appearance aroused the suspicions of the governor,

---

[52] *Ibid.*, p. 205.
[53] BL, IOR, H/124, p. 515, Sir Edward Hughes to Bengal Council, 7 February 1776.
[54] *Ibid.*, p. 516.
[55] David Boyle to Lord Melville, 19 March 1808, *Londonderry*, vol. VIII, p. 163.

Decaen. Although he was a man of science, Flinders was also a serving naval officer, whose skill in charting and mapping could pose a threat to the island's security. The situation was enflamed by a number of factors, all of which involved the circulation of information (or misinformation) along the maritime routes of empire. First, Decaen had read the intelligence report by Péron, the scientist who had accompanied Baudin's rival French expedition to Australia, on the development of Port Jackson and the use that Britain could make of the colony to expand its interests in the Pacific. Second, Decaen had also intercepted documents which informed him of the strengthening of the British naval force in eastern waters.[56]

As a result, Decaen was convinced that Flinders was there to reconnoitre a British invasion of the island.[57] And, even though he was technically innocent of this charge, Flinders *was* still interested in acquiring valuable information about this stopping-off place. Calling at the Ile de France would, according to Flinders, 'enable me to acquire a knowledge of the periodical winds, and of the present state of the French colony, how far it and its dependencies in Madagascar might be useful to Port Jackson, and how far it would be a convenient place for me to touch at in my future expected voyage'.[58] This somewhat ill-advised candour persuaded Decaen to order Flinders's detention, and it would be another six years before Flinders could resume his journey to Europe. In the immediate aftermath of his arrest, the crucial importance of information in establishing and maintaining the balance of power in the region was underlined. Two boxes and a trunkful of documents were collected from Flinders's ship, while all charts, letters, documents and journals were confiscated.[59] When these documents were inspected, they were found to contain dispatches directed to the Secretary of State from Philip Gidley King, the governor of New South Wales, and Lieutenant-Colonel Paterson, the commander-in-chief in Port Jackson. Ultimately, Decaen indicted Flinders on charges of stopping at the island 'to make himself acquainted with the periodical winds, the port, and the present state of the colony'.[60]

Flinders always maintained that he had been held unlawfully and treated abominably. But there were many people on the island who agreed with their governor in regarding him as a security risk. After the British conquest of the island in 1810, for example, a faction of the French inhabitants accused Flinders of spying, perhaps seeking a scapegoat for their misfortune. Adrien d'Epinay, author of *Renseignements pour servir à*

---

[56] For further details, see Pineo, *In the Grips of the Eagle*, p. 72.   [57] *Ibid.*, pp. 78–82.

[58] Matthew Flinders to Charles Decaen, 21 December 1803, in Matthew Flinders, *A Voyage to Terra Australis ... in the Years 1801, 1802 and 1803*, 2 vols. (London: G. & W. Nicol, 1814), vol. II, p. 368.

[59] Pineo, *In the Grips of the Eagle*, pp. 72–5.   [60] *Ibid.*, p. 74.

l'histoire de l'île de France jusqu'à l'année 1810, claimed that the naval officer made soundings along the coast at night, which he transmitted to Bengal.[61] And, although he seems generally to have abided by the terms of his confinement, there is some evidence of Flinders's testing their limits. In August 1809, for example, when fellow captive Captain Lynne was due to leave for the Cape of Good Hope as part of a prisoner exchange, Flinders made plans to communicate with the British squadron there. Should Lynne send back any 'interesting and confidential' missives, Flinders suggested that Felix Froberville, then a prisoner at the Cape, who could be sworn to secrecy, might be asked to carry them.[62] When he was eventually released, Flinders arrived at the Cape where he was quizzed by Admiral Albemarle Bertie about any information he might have 'relative to the colony and Bourbon'.[63] In spite of his self-deprecating tone, Flinders knew the value of his information:

I know not whether the sketch of the port and town of Port Louis, and the information upon the finances and strength of the island, and the dispositions of the inhabitants, which I gave to Admiral Bertie at the Cape, were of any advantage in making the dispositions, and in the attack; but I believe that everything proved to be as I pointed out.[64]

And there is some indication to support the idea that Flinders made a map of Madagascar during his time in captivity, which was communicated to the British expedition before the assault on that island. After the surrender of Tamatave, Robert Farquhar proposed to exploit the resources of the 'Grande Ile' and he wrote to Lord Bathurst asking for a copy of the document, 'which will be of the greatest assistance in enabling me to draw from Madagascar those resources it is so well calculated to afford'. The new British governor of Mauritius commended Flinders's 'intelligence and industry' which were 'seldom to be met with' before elaborating on the product of these virtues.[65] According to Farquhar, Flinders created:

a map of Madagascar from the materials to which his connections here and the general estimation in which his character was held gave him easy access. I have also been informed that he made some valuable extracts of the voyages and travels into that important island.[66]

---

[61] *Ibid.*, p. 132.   [62] Carter, *Companions of Misfortune*, p. 50.   [63] *Ibid.*, p. 125.
[64] Matthew Flinders to Josias Rowley, February 1811, in Carter, *Companions of Misfortune*, p. 134.
[65] Robert Farquhar to Lord Bathurst, 25 February 1813, in Pineo, *In the Grips of the Eagle*, p. 131.
[66] *Ibid.*

Whatever his activities while at the Ile de France, the example of Matthew Flinders provides us with an insight into the circulation of clandestine information and intelligence. Perhaps the most important point is the fact that there was a great deal of information available: the blockading squadron had ample opportunity to survey the coast, and Flinders stated that, after his arrival at the Cape, he spent much time improving 'the rough maps of the port drawn by other naval officers'.[67] Records of the British expeditionary force indicate that the cruising ships – notably the officers aboard the *Nisus* – took numerous depth soundings around Mapou Bay just prior to the disembarkation. And there was a robust trade in documents and information about the island to be found at the Cape. A few years earlier, the Comte de Fouchécour suggested that 'he could perhaps obtain some documents upon these islands' when he arrived at the Cape.[68] In other words, the case of Flinders points to a wider phenomenon of information and intelligence circulation in the southern Atlantic and Indian oceans. With Flinders, and many of the other 'spies' discussed above, the impact of their activities was obvious. But the movement of information had wider ramifications for the British presence here, carrying personal as well as professional news to and from British settlers and administrators residing in the region and locating this maritime space at the hub of multiple flows of information and intelligence.

News flows: effects and consequences

The effects of such movements of information on the British position in the South Atlantic and Indian Ocean were manifold. As Decaen's reaction to Flinders demonstrates, the strategic and military value of information was paramount. However, the letters and personal communications that travelled to and through the region were useful on a variety of levels. Perhaps most obviously, they provided emotional succour for individuals. Lady Anne Barnard remarked that receiving Lady Palmerston's letter 'and a group of others mostly from my sister who I had not heard from before since [*sic*] I left London gave me such a sensation of joy as I have not experienced for some time'.[69] For Lady Anne, those who resided in 'far distant countrys' were particularly reliant on correspondence. 'No one can have an idea of the pleasure a letter affords from a friend', she maintained, 'till the knowledge is dearly earned by distance'.[70]

---

[67] Carter, *Companions of Misfortune*, p. 165.
[68] CRL, LAdd/211, 'Memorandum of transactions of the Comte de Fouchécour', 1798–99.
[69] US, BR19/1/1, Lady Anne Barnard to Mary, Viscountess Palmerston, 9 December 1797.
[70] US, BR19/1/2, Lady Anne Barnard to Mary, Viscountess Palmerston, 9 July 1800.

In another letter, she wrote of 'how we long for the next ships to tell us about a thousand matters we are anxious to hear of'.[71] And it worked in reverse: the same applied to those in Europe. Lady Anne's father-in law, Thomas Barnard, Bishop of Limerick, reported to his nephew, with obvious delight, that he had received 'a letter last Sunday from our Hottentot Friends' – his son and daughter-in-law at the Cape.[72]

This personal morale boost was matched by the lift that good news offered to national sentiment: news of the Battle of the Nile spread like wildfire around the Indian Ocean, for example.[73] Lady Anne took great pleasure in the 'good news' brought by passing vessels. Her position at the southern tip of Africa, at an information crossroads, is highlighted by the nature and variety of the information that she reported to Macartney:

To the defeat of Buonaparte's fleet and to his being obliged to return to Alexandria, there is added the successful negotiations of Colonel Kilpatrick in India, where everything seems to clear up, over which threatening clouds had lowered.[74]

When Buenos Aires was captured in 1806, St Helena was one of the first places to hear about Popham's daring raid. The *St Helena Gazette* assured its, admittedly limited, readership that 'the public Treasure found there' was 'immense': 'It is supposed a subaltern's share will amount to 2000 *l* exclusive of what will arise from the sale of the Royal Stores'. And all this had been achieved with 'very little more loss than what has already been stated' (i.e. 'Captain Le Blanc of the 71st lost a leg and a private of the St Helena Light Company was killed'). With barely concealed delight, the newspaper reported on the '2,000,000 of Spanish Dollars' that had been 'forwarded to England in the Narcissus Frigate on account of the Captors'.[75] The example of Sir Thomas Reynell, on a military tour of South Africa in the second decade of the nineteenth century, corroborates this assessment. The arrival of a large bag in the camp 'was not a little enhanced by finding it to contain a vast number of English letters and papers of a late date, brought out by HMS Acorn, that left England early in the month of September'. Commenting on the effects of reading about

[71] UWits, A557f, Lady Anne Barnard to Dundas, 23 May 1801.
[72] Thomas Barnard to Captain Andrew Barnard, 3 August 1797, in Anthony Powell (ed.), *Barnard Letters, 1778–1824* (London: Duckworth, 1928), p. 81.
[73] Jonathan Duncan to Secret Committee, Bombay, 3 November 1798, quoted in Mabel V. Jackson Haight, *European Powers and South-East Africa: A Study of International Relations on the South-Eastern Coast of Africa, 1796–1856* (London: Routledge & Kegan Paul, 1967), p. 122.
[74] Lady Anne Barnard to Macartney, 25 January 1799, in Fairbridge (ed.), *Lady Anne Barnard at the Cape of Good Hope*, p. 83. Major James Achilles Kirkpatrick negotiated with the Nizam of Hyderabad.
[75] BL, IOR, G/32/163, *St Helena Gazette Extraordinary*, 4 September 1806.

British success in the Peninsular War, Reynell pronounced that it was 'hardly possible to imagine the pleasure of receiving such intelligence after being as we were so long in arrear of news from Europe, and in a situation so remote and ... cheerless'.[76]

But the importance of news to those in the region itself was matched by its significance for strategists and politicians in Britain and India. One of the principal benefits of reliable intelligence and information exchange was its role in establishing and maintaining Britain's naval supremacy in these waters.[77] Eyewitnesses on the water or on the ground gave correspondents important details about rivals' positions. The recognition that trade (and, he might have added, reliable information) was inextricably bound up with the successful control of shipping lanes and commercial entrepôts is evident in the report sent from the Cape by Captain Charles Purvis, of the *Valentine*:

There are at this time six French transport ships in Table Bay and more expected out, besides two that have already passed the Cape bound to Mauritius. I should conceive by the number of French on shore, and the vast crouds on board their ships that their number exceeds the enclosed intelligence. Perhaps the court of directors may have had notice of this force before. However, I look upon it as my duty to give them this intelligence which if of any use will give the greatest satisfaction to their most obedient humble servant.[78]

A more concrete example of the value of such information was offered by the governor of St Helena a few years later. 'Intelligence received of an expedition being intended against the island' encouraged him to reinforce 'the interior passes leading up to the hills as strong as possible to make up for my want of numbers' and generally prepare the island's defences.[79]

Given the nature of the sailing conditions, information flows frequently followed a circuitous route. This was certainly the case with news gathered at the Cape by Samuel Appleby about French fortifications and troop numbers on the Ile de France. Captain Appleby was dispatched by Robert Harland in October 1772 to give an 'account of the French ships' that he found there.[80] Appleby reported that 'they seem from their present inconsiderable force to have laid aside all the designs they had formed against India'. Nevertheless, he warned:

---

[76] B'hurst, MS.059, Sir Thomas Reynell, 'Journey through the Settlement of Cape of Good Hope', 10 December 1813.

[77] Tracy, *Navies, Deterrence, and American Independence*, p. 12.

[78] BL, IOR, H/102, p. 471, Extract of a letter from Capt. Charles Purvis of the Ship *Valentine*, 23 March 1770.

[79] B'hurst, MS.062/14, Brooke to Macartney, I June 1797.

[80] TNA, ADM 1/163, p. 242, Appleby to Harland, 31 December 1772.

This armament being over it does not seem they intend to be at rest, but mean to give the English as much trouble as possible till any favourable opportunity offers for them to put their schemes in execution.[81]

It took some time for this information to get back to Britain, however. In September 1773, Robert Harland reported to the Admiralty that he had arrived at Fort St George in April 1773 where he expected to meet Appleby in his ship, the *Hawke*. Unfortunately, it was 'obliged to go to Trincomalee to get some repairs done to her'. As a result, Harland had to be content with the letters left by Appleby for him 'with such intelligence as he had been able to collect, of which I send you a copy'.[82] According to a note on the file, Harland's letter was not received until 9 May 1774.

Acquiring, and acting upon, intelligence was particularly important during the long Revolutionary and Napoleonic Wars. George Keith Elphinstone admitted to Lord Spencer that his success in capturing the Cape was 'entirely owing to your activity and frequent communication of good information that has enabled us to perform a service of much consequence to the security of this place, and all our eastern commerce'.[83] The existence of knowledge-exchange networks between the Indian subcontinent and the British possessions south of the Equator was described by Richard Wellesley, governor general in Bengal, to the new naval commander at the Cape:

A constant and unreserved correspondence on every question affecting the mutual interests of India and the colony of the Cape of Good Hope subsisted between the Earl of Macartney, the late Sir Hugh Christian and me. Sir Hugh Christian constantly advised me by every opportunity of the strength, condition and distribution of the squadron under his command.

As Wellesley observed to Curtis: 'This intercourse was productive of important benefits to the public service.'[84] The importance of information is captured in the delight with which it was reported that a French schooner of just four guns and fifteen men had fallen into British hands in the run up to the British assault on the French Indian Ocean islands. The cargo was not silver or gold but rather consisted of 'nearly 600 letters (public and private) disclosing for the first time the military resources, the condition of the mercantile interests and the views of the inhabitants of both islands'.[85]

[81] *Ibid.*, p. 243.
[82] TNA, ADM 1/163, p. 239, Harland to Philip Stephens, 20 September 1773.
[83] BL, Add. MS. 75856, f. 289, George Keith Elphinstone to Spencer, 19 August 1796.
[84] Wellesley to Sir Roger Curtis, 24 October 1800, *Spencer*, vol. IV, p. 163.
[85] NUL, Mi 2F 839/12, pp. 9–10, 'Account of the Career of Sir Nesbit Willoughby, 1790–1832' [c.1832].

This example highlights again the crucial part played by maritime connections in the circulation of intelligence. The Royal Navy in particular played a key role in procuring or intercepting vital information at this time. In August 1805, John Barrow ordered Home Popham to send a frigate 'to cruise on the east coast of South America between Rio de Janeiro and Rio de la Plata ... for the purpose of procuring intelligence of the enemy's motions'.[86] And on approaching the Cape, Popham sent Captain Ross Donnelly, commanding HMS *Narcissus*, off in search of intelligence. More specifically, Donnelly was instructed to direct his vessel to St Helena, where the governor 'has been regular in his examination of all neutral vessels from the Cape' and who 'will put you in possession of such intelligence as he has procured'. Popham encouraged the officer to perform whatever 'mere deceptions and expedients' were necessary.[87] After that, Donnelly was to make for Cape Town – under false colours if necessary – to gather all the intelligence he could about the garrison and shipping in Table Bay.[88] And Popham's attack on South America was partially based on 'intelligence respecting the weak state of defence which Montevideo and Buenos Ayres were in', procured 'from the master and owner of an American ship'.[89] From his long letter explaining his actions to William Marsden at the Admiralty, it is clear that Popham had been collecting information about the Spanish colonies for some considerable time.[90] The American Captain Waine's enthusiasm complemented information supplied by 'Mr Wilson, an eminent merchant in the City of London', an English carpenter who had been eleven years in Montevideo, and another unidentified Englishman who had been eight years in Buenos Aires, two of them as interpreter in the Customs House.[91]

In the southern Indian Ocean a few years later, Commodore Rowley reported to the Admiralty that he had deployed some of the squadron to Madagascar and the French Islands to obtain intelligence. The *Laurel*, the *Harrier* and the *Grampus* had called at Madagascar for 'refreshments and water' before 'reconnoitering the harbour of Port

---

[86] John Barrow to Home Popham, 2 August 1805, in *Minutes of Court Martial, Holden on Board His Majesty's Ship, Gladiator ... for the Trial of Sir H. Popham* (London: Longman, Hurst, Rees and Orme, 1807), pp. 17–18.

[87] Popham to Ross Donnelly, 4 October 1805, *RCC*, vol. V, pp. 246, 247.

[88] Hugh Popham, *A Damned Cunning Fellow: The Eventful Life of Rear-Admiral Sir Home Popham KCB, KCH, KM, FRS, 1762–1820* (Tywardreath: Old Ferry Press, 1991), pp. 138–9.

[89] Popham to William Marsden, 13 April 1806, *RCC*, vol. V, pp. 395, 397.

[90] TNA, ADM 1/58, pp. 240–3, Popham to Marsden, 13 April 1806; TNA, ADM 1/58, p. 244, J. Waine to Popham, 28 March 1806. See also Popham, *Damned Cunning Fellow*, p. 145.

[91] Popham, *Damned Cunning Fellow*, p. 145.

Louis'.[92] Indeed, the British capture of Mauritius was dependent on intelligence. The proclamation issued by Robert Farquhar was partially done to counteract information being distributed by 'plotters' who 'have tried to lessen our characters in your eyes'.[93] And, following his successful distribution of the proclamation, Nesbit Willoughby was happy to report that he had 'gained from some of the most respectable inhabitants and well wishers to the English the most satisfactory information'.[94]

Of course, such networks of communication in the region, and their extension across the watery expanse of the Indian Ocean, were not exclusive to the British.[95] And, although the acquisition and distribution of knowledge are increasingly recognised as fundamental elements in the construction and maintenance of the British presence here, it is important not to forget that this power was often contingent, relying on others, or under threat from indigenous and European rivals. Indeed, local indigenous powers were adept at gathering, deploying and protecting information. An ability to garner information is conveyed in an incident recounted by Sir William Jones. On his way to assume his legal appointment in India, Jones was taken aback by the perspicuity of the local ruler on Anjouan:

I was astonished at the questions which Alwi' [the local ruler] put to me concerning the late peace and the independence of America; the several powers and resources of Britain and France, Spain and Holland; the character and supposed views of the Emperor; the comparative strength of the Russian, Imperial, and Othman armies, and the respective modes of bringing their forces to attention.[96]

While responding candidly to his hosts, Jones recognised the potential value of such information admitting that 'I answered without reserve, except on the state of our possessions in India'.[97] Letters from south India and addressed to the chief minister at Kandy display a similar concern for circumspection. Their discussion on maritime trade was written in Arabic-Tamil to prevent information falling into the hands of the

---

[92] TNA, ADM 1/60, Josias Rowley to William Wellesley-Pole, 2 July 1808. See John Frederick Day, 'British Admiralty control and naval power in the Indian Ocean, 1793–1815', Ph.D. thesis, University of Exeter, 2012, p. 187.

[93] NUL, Mi 2F 6, 'Proclamation to the Inhabitants of the Isle of France', 28 July 1810.

[94] NUL, Mi 2F 9, Nesbit Willoughby to Samuel Pym, 19 August 1810.

[95] In this regard, see Robert Ross and Alicia Schrikker, 'The VOC Official Elite', in Nigel Worden (ed.), *Cape Town between East and West: Social Identities in a Dutch Colonial Town* (Hilversum: Uitgeverij Verloren, 2012), pp. 26–44, pp. 36–7.

[96] William Jones, 'Remarks on the Island of Hinzuan or Johanna', in *The Works of Sir William Jones*, edited by Anna Maria Jones, 13 vols. (London: J. Stockdale, 1807), vol. IV, pp. 269–313, pp. 287–8.

[97] *Ibid.*, p. 288.

British.[98] The Indian Ocean was a space, in other words, where intelligence was an important currency to be guarded carefully and exchanged cautiously.

Dangerous intelligence: subversion

As we have seen, the competition offered by European rivals was intense, making it equally as important to prevent intelligence or useful information from falling into the hands of the enemy. So when the *Grampus* was captured by French ships in 1759, the second mate, Thomas Smallwood, was happy to report to the ship's owner that at least 'we threw the Company's & King's packets overboard and all letters'.[99] It was perhaps for the same reason that, in reporting the capture of the *Osterley* two decades later at the hands of the French, two crewmen gave a particularly grim account. In addition to offering a sense of the way in which intelligence operated and how it circulated around this oceanic region, their account also emphasised the crucial role played by information exchanges:

The Hon. Co's packets were all sunk with an anchor early in the morning of the engagement. We are however very sorry to observe that the French had the best intelligence of all our transactions at Bengal even to the names of the ships and days appointed for their sailing. And we were exceedingly shocked and surprised to hear the commodore and his officers vauntingly declare that the Elizabeth was the property of an Englishman now at Fort St George.[100]

Thomas Barnard, Bishop of Limerick, believed that letters from his son, Andrew, fell foul of exactly this sort of action:

I got several letters from the Cape and one from Lord Macartney since you left us. I cannot assign any cause for the numerous letters we have written not reaching them. I suppose the French have taken them, and will publish them in revenge for our printing the intercepted private correspondence of Buonaparte's officers.[101]

The doleful effects of the movement of intelligence were brought home as the failure of George Johnstone's expedition to the Cape in 1781 was attributed by Henry Rooke to the fact that 'we had been expected at the

[98] Sujit Sivasundaram, *Islanded: Britain, Sri Lanka, and the Bounds of an Indian Ocean Colony* (New Delhi: Oxford University Press, 2013), p. 38.

[99] BL, IOR, H/95, p. 153, Extract of letter from Thomas Smallwood to Samuel Braund, 26 May 1759.

[100] BL, IOR, H/143, pp. 189–90, Edward Parry and Daniel Barwell to Court of Directors, 17 March 1779.

[101] Thomas Barnard to Isabella Barnard, 22 June 1800, in Powell (ed.), *Barnard Letters*, p. 124.

Cape for some time'.[102] And one of the advantages offered by St Helena, for example, was the secrecy and consequent security that it offered: 'It is perhaps the only spot throughout the widely extended dominions of this empire, whence an expedition could sail with an absolute certainty of keeping its destination secret.'[103]

All of the European powers worried about sensitive information falling into their rivals' hands. According to Jacques-Henri Bernardin de Saint Pierre, the Dutch forbade the publication of plans of their colonies for precisely this reason. Instead, plans were given in manuscript form to each master of a vessel at the outset of a voyage. At the conclusion of the journey, it was the master's responsibility to deliver them 'into the proper office at their admiralty'.[104] Robert Gordon, the commander of one of the Dutch garrisons at the Cape, travelled widely in the colony. But, to the consternation of many men of scientific bent, the fruits of Gordon's researches were not widely known.[105] Thomas Pennant blamed national rivalries, or rather Dutch intransigence, for the failure to publish: 'the jealousy of the Dutch prevents us from reaping any benefit from his travels'.[106] Security concerns were almost certainly a major contributing factor to this state of affairs. The campaign to acquire Gordon's journals, papers and natural history drawings was partially based on the commercial advantages to be derived from them. John Pinkerton, in his attempts to persuade the government of their value, was convinced of their 'great importance to this commercial country, and the interests of its oriental colonies'.[107] It was presumably for this same reason that Bernardin de Saint Pierre was reluctant to publish too many details about the defence of the Ile de France, 'lest what he proposed as a means of its defence, might be of advantage to an enemy about to attack it'. His caution was, apparently, based on bitter experience: 'This ought to have occurred to those who have published plans and charts of our colonies, of which our enemies have more than once availed themselves to our disadvantage.'[108]

Despite the protestations of people like Pennant, the government in London was equally worried about the information contained in

---

[102] Henry Rooke, *Travels to the Coast of Arabia Felix ... containing a Short Account of an Expedition Undertaken against the Cape of Good Hope* (London: R. Blamire, 1783), p. 17.

[103] William Innes Pocock, *Five Views of the Island of St Helena from Drawings Taken on the Spot* (London: S. and J. Fuller, 1815), p. 12.

[104] Jacques-Henri Bernardin de Saint Pierre, *A Voyage to the Island of Mauritius (or, Isle of France), the Isle of Bourbon, the Cape of Good Hope, &c.: with observations and reflections upon nature, and mankind by a French officer. Translated from the French by John Parish* (London: W. Griffin, 1775), p. 181.

[105] See pp. 132–3 above.

[106] NMM, P/12/16, p. 17, Thomas Pennant, 'Outlines of the Globe'.

[107] John Pinkerton to William Windham, 14 May 1806, *RCC*, vol. V, p. 421.

[108] Bernardin de Saint Pierre, *Voyage to the Island of Mauritius*, p. 181.

correspondence falling into the wrong hands. The risk of enemy inter-
ception was of paramount concern. Almost immediately after his arrival
at the Cape, Lord Macartney put into action one of his key instructions: to
caution inhabitants of the new British possession about the danger of
intelligence falling into enemy hands and to urge them to take the utmost
care in the conveyance of foreign correspondence. The thirty-sixth article
of his instructions warned that 'during the time of war our enemies have
frequently got intelligence of the state of our settlements and plantations
by letters from private persons to their correspondents in Great Britain,
taken on board ships coming from such settlements and plantations,
which has been of dangerous consequence'.[109] When he arrived,
Macartney lost no time in putting this advice into effect:

All merchants, inhabitants and others are hereby required and commanded to be
very cautious in giving any accounts or information of the affairs or circumstances
of said settlement; and the harbour master and all others whom it may concern are
moreover to give directions to all masters of ships or other persons to whom they
may entrust any letters that they may put such letters into a bag with sufficient
weight to sink the same immediately in case of imminent danger from the enemy,
and the merchants and inhabitants [likewise].[110]

On receiving his commission as governor, Sir George Yonge was specifically warned, in the same terms as his predecessor, that the sending of
letters posed a real threat to national security. Yonge was reminded to warn
all merchants and settlers about the damage they could cause by loose talk
and looser correspondence.[111] And when the Cape fell into British hands
again in 1806, another proclamation was issued 'to prevent the evils that
must arise from an improper introduction of strangers into this colony'.[112]

The dangers posed by European rivals, principally the French, were the
perennial focus of much of the information gathered from the Cape and
elsewhere in the region. An American vessel, the *Caroline*, a cutter of only
38 feet, was seized as it entered Table Bay in 1798, suspected (correctly)
of carrying dispatches from the Directoire in Paris to the Ile de France.
Richard Cleveland, its youthful skipper, subsequently remarked on how
they 'had scarcely dropped our anchor when we were boarded by a man-
of-war's boats' and Cleveland was 'immediately hurried ... ashore, in my
sea garb, to see the Admiral [Sir Hugh Christian]'.[113] The attitude of the

[109] Instructions to Lord Macartney, 30 December 1796, *RCC*, vol. II, pp. 18–19.
[110] RH, MSS.Afr.t.4*, Proclamation, 16 May 1797.
[111] PRONI, D2431/14, pp. 56–7, 'Instructions from Henry Dundas to Sir George Yonge,
29 May 1799'.
[112] 'Proclamation', 25 February 1806, *RCC*, vol. V, p. 354.
[113] Richard J. Cleveland, *A Narrative of Voyages and Commercial Enterprises*, 2 vols.
(Cambridge, MA: John Owen, 1842), vol. I, p. 26.

naval and civil authorities was part of the febrile atmosphere more generally, as speculation abounded among 'the good people of the Cape' about the 'real object' of Cleveland's enterprise:

While some among them viewed it in its true light, that of a commercial speculation, others believed, that, under this mask, we were employed by the French government for the conveyance of their despatches; and some even went so far as to declare a belief, that we were French spies, and as such deserving of immediate arrest and confinement.[114]

The process of preventing the exchange of information was simple: the thorough search of the vessel and examination of all papers and documents on board. And the result was predictable: 'My journal, book of accounts, and private letters and papers were submitted to his inspection; and the letters I had for French gentlemen in the Mauritius were all broken open.'[115] Nevertheless, Cleveland was able to conceal the messages successfully and, after a clumsy attempt to lure him into a customs violation, Lord Macartney allowed him to sell his vessel and cargo to the commander of the naval squadron. However, Cleveland himself was not able to leave the Cape for four months, by which time the dispatches were useless.[116] The perceived threat posed by 'neutral' ships carrying dispatches or information was reiterated in another example offered by Cleveland. Calling at the Cape on its way from Boston to India, the *Jefferson* of Boston roused the suspicions of the government and, 'not satisfied with the examination of the log-book and papers, they caused her to be entirely unladed'.[117]

The problems posed by French intelligence did not just extend to French ships. Lord Macartney wrote to the commander of the fleet on the Cape station, Admiral Pringle, and commended his actions in detaining 'the Danish ship bound to the Isle of France till our India fleet shall have passed'. Macartney authorised Pringle 'to embargo all other ships proceeding to the eastward as long as you think there is a likelihood of their conveying any intelligence to the enemy that might endanger the safety of the Indiamen in their passage to the Bay of Bengal'.[118] Henry Dundas cautioned Macartney that 'many serious inconveniences may arise from the too great or improper concourse of foreigners, and particularly of French and Dutch to the Cape'. The governor was warned 'to be particularly watchful of such, and to permit none not thereto belonging

---

[114] *Ibid.*   [115] *Ibid.*, p. 28.
[116] Alan R. Booth, *The United States Experience in South Africa, 1784–1870* (Cape Town: A. A. Balkema, 1976), pp. 18–19.
[117] Cleveland, *Narrative of Voyages*, vol. I, p. 35.
[118] RH, MSS.Afr.t.2, Macartney to Pringle, 17 June 1797.

before the capture ... to establish themselves there without their being authorised by a license signed by the proper office here in England, or where you shall see other good cause for granting such permission'.[119] Dundas's advice proved prophetic. Barely ten months later, Macartney informed him that the whaling ship, the *Fonthill*, had just left the Cape with Jacob de Freyn, 'a Dutch prisoner', on board. Clearly heeding the warnings, Macartney judged it 'best for the Public Service' to send de Freyn to Britain and, at the same time, 'to recommend that he should not be speedily released or exchanged, as he is a very shrewd dangerous fellow and commanded the Dutch Brig taken at Delagoa Bay, that was fitted out from Batavia, and sent with a design of exciting insurrection at Graaff Reinet'.[120] In another episode, William Huskisson warned Macartney about a 'Captain de Jong late in the service of the United Provinces'. He was proceeding to the Cape to arrange his affairs, but Huskisson intimated that 'it may be necessary to observe a certain degree of circumspection with regard to the conduct and employment of this gentleman during his residence at the Cape, although there is no positive ground for supposing that he is disaffected to the present established government of that settlement'.[121] A few years later, Sir George Yonge was adamant that Comte de Fouchécour required a passport as otherwise he would not be allowed to land at the Cape.[122]

In March 1800, Francis Dundas, the acting governor of the Cape, was forced to issue a proclamation in an effort to check the circulation of rumours and false intelligence. He warned the public against 'the propagating of vague and ill-founded reports which have from time to time originated from the dissipated people of this country, especially upon the subject of the late disturbances in the country districts', and threatened them with harsh penalties.[123] At the same time, Lady Anne Barnard reported a more concrete threat. Among the prizes brought into harbour by the Royal Navy that year was the *Frederick*, a vessel sailing under the Prussian flag. Despite its apparent identity, the ship's crew as well as its cargo and passengers, were discovered to be French. One of these passengers, 'Mr Prediguer', was returning to Batavia from Europe with secret information, which British authorities believed included a plan to reconquer the Cape. Prediger and his party were arrested at the Cape and sent

---

[119] UWits, A88/b6, Dundas to Macartney, 14 January 1797. In this, Dundas was probably following the advice of Lord Liverpool, who had suggested that the governor of the Cape should have the power 'to prevent any person settling there in future except natural-born British subjects'. See UWits, A88/34, Lord Liverpool to Dundas, 27 August 1796.
[120] RH, MSS.Afr.t.4, Macartney to Dundas, 14 October 1797.
[121] UWits, A88/b14, Huskisson to Macartney, 25 March 1797.
[122] UWits, A574f, Sir George Yonge to Monsieur Le Viscomte de Vaux, 9 April 1799.
[123] Fairbridge, *Lady Anne Barnard at the Cape of Good Hope*, p. 185.

to Britain for trial (although Prediger died during the course of the
voyage). Proving its value to Britain's Asian empire, the British authorities in India were warned about the alleged French threat to their
possession.[124]

Dangerous intelligence: mutiny

News from home did not only bring tidings of naval victories, but could also
transmit much more dangerous information. One of the most powerful
things to circulate around the oceans was also one of the most intangible:
revolutionary sentiments.[125] Robert Brooke on St Helena, for example, was
'alarmed at the late accounts from Ireland and at that turbulence of spirit
that seems to have spread like a contagion all over the world'.[126] And the
political potency of information and ideas was recognised in even the most
mundane and domestic of contexts. When Lady Anne Barnard described an
auction of prize goods from captured French ships at the Cape in the
southern hemisphere spring of 1800, for example, the sale of a piece of
wallpaper proved controversial because of the revolutionary imagery it
carried. Its 'large patterns and beautiful borders' were 'wickedly imagined
and artfully calculated to sow even by the medium of a papered wall the
seeds of the French principles'. So dangerous could the circulation of ideas
be that it was promptly 'suppressed altogether'.[127]

But sale of wallpaper was by no means the most serious threat faced by
the British Empire in the region. In contrast, the mutinies that broke out
in the Royal Navy fleet at the Cape in late 1797 powerfully demonstrate
the ways in which information acted upon local concerns and catalysed
specific grievances.[128] The Navy's ships and men carried ideas and intelligence, its networks of shipping and communication linking the metropolis and colonies and colonies with each other.[129] In the case of mutiny,
of course, this merely increased the risk of spreading the contamination.
Accounts of the mutinies at Spithead and the Nore arrived at the Cape on

---

[124] 19 October 1800, *Diaries*, vol. II, p. 252, n. 44.
[125] For a recent discussion of this phenomenon, specifically in relation to the Atlantic, see
Janet Polasky, *Revolutions without Borders: The Call to Liberty in the Atlantic World*
(London: Yale University Press, 2015).
[126] B'hurst, MS.062/5, Robert Brooke to unknown recipient, undated [c.1796].
[127] Undated diary entry [late September 1800], *Diaries*, vol. II, p. 256.
[128] The mutiny is fully documented, often hour by hour, in the correspondence of Lord
Macartney in UWits, A88/149–65.
[129] For a more detailed discussion of the Royal Navy in Southern African waters in the
period, see John McAleer, 'Atlantic Periphery, Asian Gateway: The Royal Navy at the
Cape of Good Hope, 1785–1815', in John McAleer and Christer Petley (eds.),
The Royal Navy and the British Atlantic World, c.1750–1820 (Basingstoke: Palgrave
Macmillan, 2016), pp. 183–206.

31 August via the East Indiaman *Arniston,* which left England on 5 June, bound for China.[130] In early September 1797, Macartney informed his friend and colleague from his days at Madras, Major General William Sydenham, that 'you will hear by these ships various rumours of tumults, mutinies and distresses of all kinds at home'.[131] At the same time, he wrote to Robert Brooke on St Helena with reassuring news that 'the mutiny at Sheerness was likely to be soon terminated'.[132]

But events were to confound Macartney's optimism. Sailors in the British squadron at the Cape knew about the Nore mutiny before their superiors, indicating the lines of communication along which revolutionary information spread globally.[133] A body of recent scholarship has shown that news and memories of other mutinies affected sailors considering such a course of action.[134] Thomas Pringle, the naval commander on station, was 'most anxious to hear particulars of the mutiny in the fleet' because 'its consequence must entirely depend upon its cause, if it has proceeded from small pay that may be removed for the present but if from improper insinuations of villainous doctrines it may go to much mischief'.[135] Pringle eventually received intelligence from Evan Nepean, dated 3 May, 'acquainting me that disturbances of a very serious nature had taken place among the crews of the ships at Spithead, in order that being aware of the circumstances, I may be prepared to take the most vigorous and effectual measures for counteracting any attempt that might be made by ill designing persons to excite a Spirit of Mutiny among the Ships of the Squadron under my Command'.[136] But it arrived too late. Notwithstanding the belated warning, Pringle remarked ruefully that 'by my letter of the 13th of October in the Dane Ship *Bornholm* their Lordships will see that their intelligence of the mutiny at Spithead was very unfortunately much too late to enable me to take the precautions therein mentioned'.[137]

The news electrified the situation at the Cape. On 2 October, 'some strong symptoms of mutiny appeared on board' the *Vindictive,* which was

---

[130] RH, MSS.Afr.t.3, Macartney to Brooke, 14 October 1797.
[131] RH, MSS.Afr.t.3, Macartney to William Sydenham, 12 September 1797.
[132] RH, MSS.Afr.t.3, Macartney to Brooke, 7 September 1797.
[133] Niklas Frykman, Clare Anderson, Lex Heerma van Voss and Marcus Rediker, 'Mutiny and Maritime Radicalism in the Age of Revolution: An Introduction', *International Review of Social History* 58 (2013), pp. 1–14, p. 10.
[134] See Niklas Frykman, 'Connections between Mutinies in European Navies', *International Review of Social History* 58 (2013), pp. 87–107; Jonathan Neale, 'The Influence of 1797 upon the Nereide Mutiny of 1809', in Ann Veronica Coats and Philip MacDougall (eds.), *The Naval Mutinies of 1797: Unity and Perseverance* (Woodbridge: Boydell & Brewer, 2011), pp. 264–79.
[135] UWits, A88/135, Pringle to Macartney, 31 August 1797.
[136] TNA, ADM 1/56, Pringle to Evan Nepean, 15 November 1797.   [137] *Ibid.*

overcome 'by the prudence and spirit of her commander', Captain Gardner.[138] The ship was separated from the rest of the squadron as a precaution to prevent the mutiny spreading, but this only served to enflame the situation. Another warning of disquiet came a few days later, on 5 October, when an unsigned letter was dropped on the deck of the *Tremendous*. Addressed to Captain Stephens, it claimed that sailors on the *Rattlesnake* were being abused, and that to 'keep disturbance from the fleet' this should be righted on every ship and that there must be no 'bad usage' or mistreatment of the crew. Stephens did not react and, on 7 October, a jacket was attached to the jib-boom of each naval ship lying in Simon's Bay. With a round of cheers, the *Tremendous, Trusty, Imperieuse, Braave, Rattlesnake, Chichester, Star* and *Suffolk* rose in general mutiny.[139]

Although the demands of the ships' crews included the removal of some commissioned and warrant officers, the poor quality of the provisions, especially of bread and biscuit, provided a common grievance. The failure of the wheat harvest at the Cape in 1797 and the absence of supplies requested from the Victualling Board gave a focus for dissatisfaction.[140] Admiral Pringle managed to curtail the disturbance by entering into dialogue with his sailors on the reasons for the poor quality of the provisions, as well as the steps being taken to improve things. He also agreed to examine all cases concerning alleged abuses.[141] This had the necessary effect and, on 12 October, Pringle 'issued a proclamation of pardon and amnesty and we hope that there is now an end to this unpleasant business'. Lord Macartney recalled that the 'disturbances continued until Thursday last when the Royal Standard was hoisted on board the Flag Ship as a signal that good order and discipline were re-established in the fleet'.[142] But, at the end of October, Francis Dundas wrote to London bemoaning the fact that the first outbreak of mutiny was not as 'effectually' quelled as he thought. 'One or two of the men of war' were 'in a state of mutiny, and in all of them, I am sorry to say, the officers appear to have lost the greatest part of

[138] RH, MSS.Afr.t.3, Macartney to Brooke, 14 October 1797.
[139] Nicole Ulrich, 'International Radicalism, Local Solidarities: The 1797 British Naval Mutinies in Southern African Waters', *International Review of Social History* 58 (2013), pp. 61–85, p. 72.
[140] A shortage of food supplies for British sailors and soldiers at the Cape was a recurring theme. Elphinstone's expedition to capture the Cape in 1795 had also suffered severely and was only relieved when wheat arrived from India that was originally destined for Britain. See Roger Knight, *Britain against Napoleon: The Organisation of Victory, 1793–1815* (London: Penguin, 2014), p. 172.
[141] John Frederick Day, 'British Admiralty control and naval power in the Indian Ocean, 1793–1815', Ph.D. thesis, University of Exeter, 2012, p. 151.
[142] RH, MSS.Afr.t.3, Macartney to Brooke, 14 October 1797.

their authority'. Although Dundas reported that Pringle was 'taking the proper steps for bringing the deluded seamen to a sense of their duty', he feared that 'measures far more rigorous than those hitherto adopted will be necessary before that very reasonable end can be accomplished'.[143]

As Nicole Ulrich has noted, the similarities between the mutinies in Simon's Bay and at Spithead – in terms of both the sailors' organisation and the nature of the crews' grievances – are remarkable.[144] The sailors clearly alluded to this fact themselves in their catalogue of grievances. They claimed that 'the people of this squadron has heard something of the conduct of His Majesty's Fleet in England, and the regulations that has taken place in consequence with regard to extra allowance of pay and provisions'.[145] Lord Macartney's explanation for the outbreak of mutiny was certainly straightforward. In 'complaining of grievances, depriving the officers of their commands, [and] appointing committees and delegates', the sailors at the Cape were 'imitating all the rebellious formalities of the naval mutineers in England'.[146] Macartney recognised that news travels and that the mutinies in Britain had inspired similar protests in South Africa: 'It appears solely to have proceeded from mere wantonness in the sailors and a vanity of aping their fraternity in England.'[147] Pringle concurred. The mutineers' conduct was 'nearly the same with that which is reported to have lately taken place in His Majesty's fleet in England, and I fancy was instigated by it, the information of which had been brought about a month ago'.[148]

Given the connected nature of these naval networks, and without some deterrent, the canker of mutiny could quickly spread.[149] Macartney warned Robert Brooke on St Helena: 'I am therefore not without apprehension of something similar having happened in the ships of war that convoyed the fleet from hence to St Helena, especially as the time is now elapsed within which we expected some of them to return.'[150] And he confided to Dundas that 'almost at the moment [the mutiny] was hatching at this place a similar contagion had caught the ships at St Helena'. He feared even greater consequences:

---

[143] B'hurst, MS.052/8, Francis Dundas to Henry Dundas, 29 October 1797.
[144] Ulrich, 'International Radicalism, Local Solidarities', p. 72.
[145] TNA, ADM 1/56, 'General Statement of the Grievances complained of by the Different Ships' Crews of the Squadron' [October 1797].
[146] RH, MSS.Afr.t.3, Macartney to Brooke, 14 October 1797.
[147] B'hurst, MS.052/2, Macartney to Dundas, 13 November 1797.
[148] TNA, ADM 1/56, Pringle to Nepean, 13 October 1797.
[149] Pringle was convinced that 'official information' about the measures taken 'relative to the late mutinies in England … would have prevented any thing of the kind taking place here'. TNA, ADM 1/56, Pringle to Nepean, 15 November 1797.
[150] RH, MSS.Afr.t.3, Macartney to Brooke, 14 October 1797.

I should not be at all surprised to hear of some disturbance of the same kind in Admiral Rainier's squadron, as soon as it is informed of what has passed here and elsewhere.

Macartney was particularly colourful when describing the potential ramifications of the mutiny for Britain's wider interest, freighting his remarks with erudite allusions to history and poetic references:

This spirit of sea mutiny seems like the sweating sickness in Edward the 4th's reign, a national malady which, as we are assured by the historians of the day, not content with its devastations in England visited at the same time every Englishman in foreign countries at the most distant parts of the globe:

> The General Air
> From Pole to Pole, from Atlas to the East
> Was then at enmity with English Blood.[151]

Although Macartney's fears were not realised and, eventually, normal service was resumed, the outbreak of mutiny offers powerful proof of the malign effect that information flows could potentially have on the British presence in the region. But the movement of information and ideas to, from and through this oceanic space was not restricted solely to strategic considerations or military matters. The next section explores the ways in which consolidation of the region in Britain's maritime empire could also be advanced by the circulation and exchange of scientific expertise.

Circulating scientific ideas

Historians have long recognised the important role that scientific knowledge – and the ideas, institutions and systems associated with it – played in consolidating European empires in the early modern period.[152] Jim Endersby has remarked that 'correspondence networks', such as those forged by plant collectors, were 'the single most important tool of the imperial scientific endeavour'.[153] The study of such informal scientific networks in relation to this gateway region demonstrates the ways in which it was connected to other places in the Atlantic and Indian oceans, and the effects of such connections – economically and ecologically, politically and strategically. It was not

---

[151] B'hurst, MS.052/2, Macartney to Dundas, 13 November 1797.
[152] There is an extensive and ever-expanding literature on the broad theme of science and empire. For an introduction, see Robert A. Stafford, 'Scientific Exploration and Empire', in Andrew Porter (ed.), *The Oxford History of the British Empire, Volume 3: The Nineteenth Century* (Oxford: Oxford University Press, 1999), pp. 294–319.
[153] Jim Endersby, *Imperial Nature: Joseph Hooker and the Practices of Victorian Science* (Chicago: University of Chicago Press, 2008), p. 84.

merely as colonial outposts or peripheries that these way stations were imbricated in Britain's maritime empire. Sitting at the heart of a maritime crossroads, the area partook of something akin to Roy MacLeod's concept of the 'moving metropolis', where local centres assumed a measure of autonomy and authority while remaining within a framework of empire.[154] Studying the movement of expertise and physical scientific specimens demonstrates the central position of the region in Britain's reshaped maritime empire.

By the early nineteenth century, as Felix Driver and Luciana Martins have observed, the idea of circulating plants around the world was well established.[155] And this also applied in the southern gateway region: the physical movement of plants and scientific specimens connected it with other regions. It is important to remember that such networks were in existence before the British rose to prominence in the South Atlantic.[156] Connections facilitated by the Dutch East India Company (VOC) brought knowledge of the Cape's flora, fauna and indigenous inhabitants to the wider world.[157] In 1779, for example, the Cape Fiscal, W. C. Boers, sent 150 plant specimens to the *Bataviaasch Genootschap voor Kunsten en Wetenschappen* in Batavia as a contribution to its natural history collections.[158] As Sir George Yonge acknowledged, these scientific activities and agendas had been pursued by other countries long 'before we began our career'.[159]

Nevertheless, the growth of British power in Asia had a direct impact on the ecology of the southern Atlantic and Indian oceans, through the

---

[154] See Roy MacLeod, 'On Visiting the "Moving Metropolis": Reflections on the Architecture of Imperial Science', in Nathan Reingold and Marc Rothenberg (eds.), *Scientific Colonialism: A Cross-Cultural Comparison* (Washington, DC: Smithsonian Institution Press, 1987), pp. 217–49.

[155] Luciana Martins and Felix Driver, '"The Struggle for Luxuriance": William Burchell collects Tropical Nature', in Felix Driver and Luciana Martins (eds.), *Tropical Visions in an Age of Empire* (Chicago: University of Chicago Press, 2005), pp. 59–74, p. 61.

[156] In this regard, see Alette Fleischer, 'The Company's Garden and the (Ex)change of Nature and Knowledge at Cape of Good Hope (1652–1700)', in Lissa Roberts (ed.), *Centres and Cycles of Accumulation in and around the Netherlands during the Early Modern Period* (Zurich: LIT, 2011), pp. 101–27, pp. 111–13.

[157] Gerald Groenewald, 'Southern Africa and the Atlantic World', in D'Maris Coffman, Adrian Leonard and William O'Reilly (eds.), *The Atlantic World* (Abingdon: Routledge, 2015), pp. 100–16, pp. 107–8. For further examples of this phenomenon, see Siegfried Huigen, *Knowledge and Colonialism: Eighteenth-century Travellers in South Africa* (Leiden: Brill, 2009). The case of the French on the Isle de France is discussed in Lissa Roberts, '"*Le centre de toutes choses*": Constructing and Managing Centralization on the Isle de France', *History of Science* 52 (2014), pp. 319–42.

[158] Ross and Schrikker, 'VOC Official Elite', p. 41.

[159] BL, IOR, Western Manuscripts, MSS Eur D809, Yonge to William Roxburgh, 8 December 1791.

transfer of plants and seeds and the founding of gardens.[160] Robert
Percival remarked that the gardens in Cape Town, much neglected by
the Dutch authorities in the last days of their administration there, still
offered a wide variety of plants, originating from across the globe ('from
Europe, many from India, Otaheite, and other parts of the world'),
including 'the tea plant, and bread fruit tree'.[161] St Helena was also
situated at a number of oceanic crossroads. For example, William Bligh
exchanged indigenous St Helenian trees for some breadfruit and other
plants on his way from the Pacific to the Caribbean.[162] Maritime routes
and connections facilitated the transfer of material from India to St
Helena.[163] The potential of its location was noted by some of the island's
eminent residents:

We think the situation on this island is peculiarly well adapted to render it an
intermediate nursery for the preservation of such plants as may not have strength
to endure the whole course of a voyage to Europe or to the Eastern world.[164]

The 'Superintendent of Improvements', Henry Porteous, tried 'productions of the warm climate of India':

Conformable to my orders, I am now naturalizing all the trees and shrubs which
came from India in the garden in James's Valley, where in a short time I trust there
will be a fine collection, as those already procured and planted grow very well ...
we soon hope to propagate a much greater variety of trees and shrubs here, as the
soil and climate seem so peculiarly well adapted to Eastern productions.[165]

The complex logistics involved in arranging such transfers may be seen
from a series of letters that organised the transportation of plants from
Madras to the island in 1790. Captain Thomas Foxall, of the *General
Goddard*, was entrusted with the precious cargo with the particular
request 'that you pay every attention to the preservation thereof during

---

[160] This argument is advanced in the ground-breaking work of Richard Grove. See his *Green Imperialism: Colonial Expansion, Tropical Island Edens and the Origins of Environmentalism, 1600–1860* (Cambridge: Cambridge University Press, 1996).

[161] Robert Percival, *An Account of the Cape of Good Hope* (London: C. & R. Baldwin, 1804), pp. 118–9.

[162] Donal M. McCracken, *Gardens of Empire: Botanical Institutions of the Victorian British Empire* (London: Leicester University Press, 1997), p. 13

[163] For more details on agitation for the establishment of a formal Company botanic garden on St Helena in the 1780s, see Grove, *Green Imperialism*, pp. 339–40.

[164] St Helena Planters' Society to James Anderson, 14 June 1788, in James Anderson, *Correspondence for the Introduction of Cochineal Insects from America, the Varnish and Tallow Trees from China, the Discovery and Culture of White Lac, the Culture of Red Lac. And also for the Introduction, Culture and Establishment of Mulberry Trees and Silk Worms ...* (Madras: Joseph Martin, 1791), pp. 4–5.

[165] Henry Porteous to Robert Brooke and the Council of St Helena, 1 April 1788, in Anderson, *Correspondence*, p. 7.

the passage to that island'.[166] On 9 April, the planters on St Helena reported the safe arrival of 'the twelve nopal plants sent hither by Dr Anderson; also a plant of the Bread Fruit Tree consigned to us from Mr Roxburgh of your settlement; and we have the pleasure to inform you that they are in a very thriving situation'.[167] William Roxburgh was an active correspondent, sending a long list of plants to the island.[168] Judging by travellers' accounts, St Helena's role as a nursery for Asian plants was a success. An Indian traveller on his way to Britain, Mirza Abu Taleb Khan, described the island as a sort of botanical crossroads, nurturing trees and plants from both Europe and Asia.[169] And when Roxburgh called in 1814, he identified a host of plants introduced from elsewhere, such as 'Cordia macrophylla, a large tree from Bengal', 'Daphne odora . . . from China' and 'Mespilus japonica'.[170]

Ile de France was also a hub of scientific knowledge in the southern hemisphere. It supplied botanical, zoological and geological specimens to Europe, including banana plants, *Musa cavendishii*, and sugar cane species. When he returned to Europe in 1819, Charles Telfair had to charter almost an entire vessel to transport the equipment and plants he had acquired there. And he was not just taking from the island.[171] Through horticultural experiments and the importation of seeds from India, Australia, Africa and China, Telfair added considerably to the indigenous flora of Mauritius and connected it with the wider world of early nineteenth-century botanical endeavour.

There was more to this interest in plants and seeds than amateur curiosity, however. It was underpinned by a concern for the economic possibilities offered. The activities of botanical collectors were part of 'a mercantilist framework'.[172] James Anderson, physician-general at Madras, recognised the links that could be forged between the subcontinent and St Helena. In order to encourage the botanical connections he put some 'seeds in a box which I have likewise committed to Capt.

---

[166] Robert Clerk to Thomas Foxall, 11 January 1790, *ibid.*, pp. 11–12.

[167] Extract of a letter from St Helena, 9 April 1790, *ibid.*, p. 16.

[168] RBG, WJB/1/3/23, 'An Alphabetical List of Plants seen by Dr Roxburgh growing on the Island of St Helena in 1813–14', p. 316.

[169] Mirza Abu Taleb Khan, *Travels of Mirza Abu Taleb Khan in Asia, Africa, and Europe, during the Years 1799, 1800, 1801, 1802, and 1803*, translated by Charles Stewart (London: Longman, Hurst, Rees, Orme, and Brown, 1814), p. 97.

[170] RBG, WJB/1/3/23, 'Alphabetical List of Plants seen by Dr Roxburgh', pp. 303, 305, 313.

[171] Marc Serge Rivière, 'From Belfast to Mauritius: Charles Telfair (1778–1833), Naturalist and a Product of the Irish Enlightenment', *Eighteenth-Century Ireland* 21 (2006), pp. 125–44, p. 136.

[172] David Philip Miller, 'Introduction', in Miller and Reill (eds.), *Visions of Empire*, pp. 1–18, p. 5.

Gregory's care'. He sent these to the tiny Atlantic island outpost 'with a view to establish sufficient firewood, and to serve as a shelter and support to the vine of the yam; although some are fit for other purposes, as you will see by the remarks attached to the enclosed list of them'.[173] And there was a burgeoning exchange in botanical and horticultural specimens between outposts in the southern Atlantic for the purposes of economic advantage. Captain Seaver informed the governor of the Cape that he planned to take 'such seeds and plants with other necessaries as may be possible to be put on board so small a vessel, for the purpose of forming an establishment, on the said Island [Tristan da Cunha] to refresh, and succor any Vessels which may occasionally pass in that track of sea'.[174] Meanwhile, the authorities on St Helena were always keen for specimens from the Cape. In 1814, they wrote to the Cape with 'descriptions of the best sort of timber in the neighbourhood of Plettenberg Bay', requesting that means be taken 'for procuring and transmitting to us the seeds of the plants that are enumerated':

Fir; Stinkwood or native oak; Izen or iron wood; Red and white els; Hassagai; Saffron wood; White and hand pean; Essen or ash; White bosh hout; Door boom . . .and above all the Cape yew.[175]

The East India Company agent at the Cape, John Pringle, sent 'the list of forest tree seeds', to the governor, Sir John Cradock, who subsequently dispatched them to St Helena in response to this request.[176]

A key figure in expanding the botanical networks of the Cape was William Roxburgh, superintendent of the East India Company's Botanic Garden at Calcutta. Roxburgh's time in Southern Africa, and his enduring interest in connecting it with the gardens in the subcontinent, indicates that the region was linked not just with London, but that it was also part of a wider Indian Ocean network. William Roxburgh's presence at the Cape indicates how this alternative network might have worked in practice and the means by which the region was connected not just with London, but that it was also potentially part of a wider Indian Ocean network. Roxburgh already had a wide spectrum of connections,

[173] James Anderson to St Helena Planters' Society, 4 February 1789, in Anderson, *Correspondence*, p. 9.
[174] Cape Records CO 3885, Memorials Received 1811, V, No. 1, Seaver to Henry George Grey, 3 September 1811, in James Fichter, 'The British Empire and the American Atlantic on Tristan da Cunha, 1811–16', *Journal of Imperial and Commonwealth History* 36 (2008), pp. 567–89, p. 576.
[175] BL, IOR, G/9/13, pp. 37–8, M. Wilks, J. Skelton, H. W. Doveton, Robert Leeck to Cape of Good Hope, 14 February 1814.
[176] BL, IOR, G/9/20, p. 31, John Pringle to Sir John Cradock, 4 April 1814.

many of which bypassed London: by 1793, he was distributing teak seed, Bengal hemp, Virginia tobacco, Cerulean indigo and Arabian coffee, and sending plants to England, St Helena, the West Indies and different parts of India.[177] Roxburgh called at the Cape on his way to Britain for health reasons in 1798, bringing 'many fine plants in the highest order on shore with me here'. But he lost no time in collecting 'many seeds, specimens etc.' for use elsewhere.[178] And Roxburgh soon recognised the region's potential for advancing the work of his own institution. While politicians and officials identified the potential for the recruitment of troops, Roxburgh saw the chance to acquire some useful additions to his botanical establishment.[179] So, when Lieutenant John Owen was dispatched by the Bengal Presidency to the Cape to recruit soldiers for its army from the defeated Dutch garrison in 1797, Roxburgh lost no time in contacting the army man. As Owen recalled, Roxburgh wrote to him, asking him 'to make a collection of any curious plants, flowers, bulbs, or seeds I might meet with during my residence at the Cape of Good Hope, and forward them' to Sir John Shore, the governor general at Fort William.[180] Later, when Roxburgh travelled to Britain, he left his son, John, at the Cape to collect for his father's garden in Calcutta.[181]

The consolidation of these scientific networks by the establishment of botanical gardens offers further proof of the ways in which the region was connected to Britain's maritime world. The development of botanical sites and agricultural stations reflected a demand for empirical and theoretical knowledge about the earth's flora.[182] According to Patricia Seed, acts of planting and building were key means by which British rights of possession overseas were established: 'As a sign of possession the garden represented the entire colonial ambition to possess the land by establishing a part of the project in a central and visible way.'[183] Gardens around the empire nurtured 'economic botany and a move towards the development of a complex network of plant exchange between the colonies and

[177] Adrian T. Thomas, 'The Establishment of Calcutta Botanic Garden: Plant Transfer, Science and the East India Company, 1786–1806', *Journal of the Royal Asiatic Society* 16 (2006), pp. 165–77, p. 172.
[178] BL, Add. MS 33980, f. 137, Roxburgh to Sir Joseph Banks, 24 April 1798.
[179] On the recruitment of troops, see pp. 204–13 below.
[180] BL, IOR, P/4/50, pp. 255–6, John Owen to Sir John Shore, 6 February 1797, in Public Consultations at Fort William, 3 May 1797, paragraph 87, quoted in Tim Robinson, *William Roxburgh: The Founding Father of Indian Botany* (Chichester: Phillimore, 2008), p. 210.
[181] BL, Add. MS 33980, f. 261, John Roxburgh to Banks, 6 January 1801.
[182] Nuala C. Johnson, *Nature Displaced, Nature Displayed: Order and Beauty in Botanical Gardens* (London: I. B. Tauris, 2011), p. 15.
[183] Patricia Seed, *Ceremonies of Possession in Europe's Conquest of the New World, 1492–1640* (Cambridge: Cambridge University Press, 1995), p. 29.

home', and between colonies.[184] As Richard Drayton has remarked, the associated ideology of 'improvement' was 'a concern shaping activity at the empire's periphery as well as at its centre'.[185]

Robert Percival commended Macartney for ordering the garden at the Cape 'to be replanted and laid out', while simultaneously procuring 'a great number of very curious plants from Asia, Europe, Africa, and South America; most of which thrived very well'.[186] William Roxburgh hoped that the Botanical Garden would be reinvigorated by the British. As with Macartney's improvements, Roxburgh also brought plants to supply the garden. When he arrived at the Cape, he brought 'many fine plants in the highest order on shore with me here'. With these specimens, Roxburgh hoped 'to induce Lord Macartney to establish or recommend establishing a small Botanic Garden here'. He was firmly of the opinion that, 'should the Cape remain with us on concluding a peace, the culture of Hemp and Tobacco ought I think to be particularly attended to. I dare say flax will also grow exceedingly well here.' Roxburgh's vision for the Botanical Gardens was more wide-ranging than simply as a place from which to gather specimens. He was more attuned to the Banksian view of the value of botanical gardens: 'We may then, if this place remains in our possession, soon hope to see all the plants of the East carried westward and those of the West brought East.'[187] Roxburgh saw the Cape sitting at the heart of a network, supplying and being supplied from further afield:

Since we have been in possession of the Cape of Good Hope, it has often occurred to me that a small Garden establishment there would be of infinite use. In the first instance as a resting place for plants to recoup at from India to Europe and the West Indies; and from these countries again to our colonies to the Eastward of the Cape, and for forwarding the plants of the Cape itself, as well as for introducing others into that colony should we retain it; or even should it be restored to the Dutch at the close of the War.[188]

In this scheme, the Cape would become the centre of its own network, bypassing London and creating an alternative hub of botanical activity.

Yonge's grand designs for 'founding theatres and masquerade rooms', as Marquess Wellesley described them, have found disfavour among contemporaries and later historians alike.[189] But among his various

[184] Johnson, *Nature Displaced, Nature Displayed*, p. 6.
[185] Richard Drayton, *Nature's Government: Science, British Imperialism and the Improvement of the World* (New Haven: Yale University Press, 2000), p. 113.
[186] Percival, *Account*, p. 119.
[187] BL, Add. Ms 33980, f. 138, Roxburgh to Banks, 24 April 1798.
[188] Roxburgh to Banks, 10 December 1796, quoted in Robinson, *William Roxburgh*, p. 210.
[189] Quoted in J. K. Laughton, 'Yonge, Sir George, fifth baronet (1732–1812)', rev. Jonathan Spain, *Oxford Dictionary of National Biography*, Oxford University Press,

schemes were plans relating to agricultural improvements and scientific advances, which located plant exchanges and botanical research at the heart of his strategy for the colony's development. Yonge had already been involved in similar initiatives for establishing a garden at St Helena when he was Secretary at War in London.[190] And his schemes for the Cape were equally ambitious and would have connected it with other areas in the empire on an economic and commercial footing, circumventing the imperial metropolis in a similar way to that imagined by Roxburgh. In the same way as Sir Joseph Banks considered Kew as 'a great botanical exchange house for the empire', Yonge envisaged something similar for the Cape.[191] And Yonge's vision was one that bypassed London. He reminded Sir Stephen Lushington that he 'had the honour of having His Majesty's Botanical Garden at St Vincent under my care for several years'.[192] Yonge remarked on the potential global connections that flowed from this. He was, he wrote, commanded to facilitate connections with the Cape, just as 'directions having likewise here been given for the Duke of Portland's Office to form a connexion between the Cape and the South Waters'. According to Yonge, the last piece in the jigsaw was for 'the East India Company to give a sanction to a similar cooperation with their settlements in India'. Yonge's plans were linked to wider questions of what purpose the Cape might serve as a hub of empire:

It appears to me, that, by this means the Botanical Garden at the Cape may become what the situation and valuable productions render it particularly qualified for: the centre of union, correspondence and connexion with every part of the globe, for the purposes of useful science, more especially as I understand there is an easy and immediate communication with the West Indies from the Cape, the voyage . . . not exceeding a month or six weeks sail at the most.[193]

Yonge envisaged a connection between these different botanical establishments with the mutually beneficial result that, 'by a communication of the contents of each garden, mutual aid may be given to all'. These connections – or, more accurately, the gardens comprising them – could potentially contribute 'not only to articles of ornament but of domestick viability of food, of medicine and of commerce'. Yonge wanted 'to extend this plan' which would, 'by means of a connexion in the every [sic] part of the globe', offer countless benefits to 'mankind in general'.[194] To that end, Yonge

---

2004; online edn, May 2009 (www.oxforddnb.com/view/article/30223, accessed 15 July 2015).

[190] See Grove, *Green Imperialism*, p. 340.
[191] Quoted in Endersby, *Imperial Nature*, p. 233.
[192] See Richard A. Howard, 'The St Vincent Botanic Garden: The Early Years', *Arnoldia* 57 (1997), pp. 12–21.
[193] BL, IOR, E/1/100/204, Yonge to Sir Stephen Lushington, 10 May 1799.   [194] *Ibid.*

requested permission from Lushington, and ultimately the East India Company, to correspond with other people in the Company's dominions.

Clearly this permission was granted because, on 29 May 1799, the authorities in Bombay reported:

It being the intention of Sir George Yonge the Governor of the Cape to restore and improve the Botanical Garden there, we direct that he be provided with a catalogue of the plants at Bombay, and that Dr Helenus Scott be requested to correspond with His Excellency from whom he will receive every assistance which can lend to the encouragement of such productions and to the promotion of science.[195]

The establishments in Bengal and at Fort St George followed suit within a week, ordering catalogues of the plants in their respective gardens to be sent to the Cape, as well as directing their respective Botanical Superintendents to get in touch with Yonge.[196] Exchanges of plants and specimens continued to take place between the Cape and India throughout the following year. On 2 September 1800, for example, more than one hundred kinds of seed were sent from Calcutta to the Cape:

The reply of the Gov-Gen in Council is recorded in the proceedings noted in the margin, and we beg leave to inform you that in consequence of our orders to the superintendent of the Botanical Gardens at this Presidency [Bengal], he has shipped on the Princess Mary, now under dispatch, two chests of plants and a box containing above one hundred kinds of seeds, accompanied by a catalogue of the plants at present growing in the Hon'ble Company's Botanic Gardens in Bengal for the information of His Excellency the Governor of the Cape.[197]

Seeds were sent to the Cape from Madras the following month: 'We have embarked on the Queen a supply of seeds and plants for the Cape of Good Hope, which have been collected by the superintendent of the Nopalry.'[198] Yonge wrote to Wellesley in India, recording his appreciation, and saying that he was:

much obliged to the Court of Directors for the liberal manner in which they sent orders to assist the Botanical Garden here, from a love of science which does them honor, and I need not say how much I feel the kindness with which you have been pleased to lend assistance, which has been of great service to the institution & I trust in the end will be of public utility.[199]

---

[195] BL, IOR, E/4/1014, p. 411, Public Letter, Bombay, 29 May 1799, paragraph 33. The reference is to Dr Helenus Scott (1757–1821) of the Bombay Medical Service.
[196] See BL, IOR, E/4/648, p. 640, Public Letter, Bengal, 5 June 1799; E/4/885, p. 537, Public Letter, Fort St George, 5 June 1799, paragraph 49.
[197] BL, IOR, E/4/60, Public Letter, 2 September 1800, paragraph 24.
[198] BL, IOR, E/4/327, Public Letter, 9 October 1800, paragraph 126.
[199] BL, Add. MS 13785, f. 47, Yonge to Wellesley, 24 January 1801.

Conclusion

Networks of news and information exchanges connected the southern reaches of the Atlantic and Indian oceans with the wider British maritime empire. For some people, these channels of communication offered the opportunity to receive personal news, trading updates and family gossip. For others, they stretched beyond national boundaries, facilitating the interchange of scientific ideas and specimens with like-minded individuals. But, as we have seen, for many people the value of information (and its exchange) resided in its strategic and political significance, and whether it would support or undermine the prevailing order.

For many contemporary commentators, the importance of the region remained synonymous with its strategic importance. For them, its primary value lay in its position astride the sea route to the East, a series of Indian outposts providing forward defensive positions, depriving the enemy of crucial bases for the invasion of the subcontinent and diminishing the depredations of enemy privateering at source. No less a man than the King used the terms to describe Britain's overseas interests in the region. In 1804, George III told Henry Dundas that he 'has ever looked upon the Cape of Good Hope as the key to our possessions in the East Indies and therefore on the late peace ever feared the evils that might arise from giving [up] that most essential place. Perhaps there never was a time when it might with more advantage be again in our hands.'[200] British control offered positive strategic advantages, permitting the use of these places as support bases and revictualling stations for vessels in the Indian and China trades. But they also provided places for garrisoning troops, whence they could be drawn to India in the event of any sudden emergency. Lord Castlereagh, for example, ordered that the Cape should, if necessary, be completely denuded of troops to deal with such a crisis.[201] The use of the region as a place from which to source and deploy troops forms the subject of Chapter 6. Encapsulating the rhetoric of strategic advantage *and* the practical logistics required, this chapter offers a suitable conclusion to this examination of the ways in which this region at the southern edges of the Atlantic and Indian oceans was enfolded into the Britain's wider maritime empire.

---

[200] BL, Add. MS 40100, f. 321, George III to Viscount Melville [Henry Dundas], 16 July 1804.

[201] Christopher D. Hall, *British Strategy in the Napoleonic War, 1803–15* (Manchester: Manchester University Press, 1992), p. 125.

5   'The great outwork and bulwark of India': troops, military manoeuvres and defending the eastern empire

Reflecting on his time with the British expedition to South America, Alexander Gillespie remarked that a maritime power 'has always the exclusive means of projecting and accomplishing great designs by a judicious direction' of troops.[1] The 'calculated mobilisation of sea-power' to transport troops is, as James Davey has reminded us, evidence of 'how Britain used its naval supremacy' in the period. At regular intervals during the Revolutionary and Napoleonic Wars, Britain succeeded in moving armies quickly and efficiently across Europe, and this ability to move forces in large numbers was a significant advantage to Britain throughout the conflict with France.[2] These impressive feats had added significance in non-European contexts, where the distances over which troops had to be transported were greater and where smaller numbers of men could more meaningfully influence the outcome of military engagements and effect wider strategic objectives. This theme has not gone unnoticed by historians of Britain's activities in the wider world. For example, scholars have focused on the role of troop movements in the Atlantic Ocean in the late eighteenth century, particularly in the Caribbean theatre.[3] Surprisingly little attention, however, has been paid to the Indian Ocean context, with most studies concentrating squarely on the (admittedly large and complex) topic of troops, armies and military matters in the Indian subcontinent.[4] But this relative dearth of research on the way in which the British military edifice in India was supported by the wider maritime region, and the connections it offered, is even more

---

[1] Alexander Gillespie, *Gleanings and Remarks collected during Many Months of Residence at Buenos Ayres* (Leeds: The Author, 1818), p. 7.

[2] James Davey, 'The Repatriation of Spanish Troops from Denmark, 1808: The British Government, Logistics, and Maritime Supremacy', *Journal of Military History* 74 (2010), pp. 689–707, pp. 690–1.

[3] Siân Williams, 'The Royal Navy in the Caribbean, 1756–1815', Ph.D. thesis, University of Southampton, 2014, p. 62. For further details, see Mike Duffy, *Soldiers, Sugar and Seapower: The British Expeditions to the West Indies and the War against Revolutionary France* (Oxford: Oxford University Press, 1987).

[4] For a notable exception, see the work of Edward Ingram cited in Chapter 2, n. 51, p. 46.

surprising in relation to the southern 'gateway' region and its position at the crossroads of oceanic systems. Yet contemporaries were well aware of the importance of military considerations in the consolidation and extension of British power in the Indian Ocean.

The 'great designs' that people like Gillespie had in mind in relation to the southern Atlantic and Indian oceans involved, as we have seen, consolidating the British colonial and naval presence around this strategic gateway, and ensuring that European rivals did not steal a march. If movements of ideas and intelligence connected this southern oceanic region to both the Indian subcontinent in the East and the British Atlantic world in the West, then securing that connection depended on even more practical considerations: the movement, recruitment and deployment of troops. The distribution and organisation of troops across the region were the natural corollaries of the circulation of intelligence and information. The link with India, in particular, was crucial. Many scholars have observed the way in which Indian military power became a vital complement to British naval power in building the British Empire east of the Mediterranean.[5] But this military link, and the power it offered, had to be sustained by conveying fresh troops from Europe via existing maritime channels, as well as the recruitment of troops from places along the way. As the British presence there became more secure, and the region became knitted more closely into wider British imperial and commercial maritime networks, the role of the South Atlantic and southern Indian Ocean area in satisfying British troop requirements – whether through 'seasoning', recruitment or immediate transfer in times of emergency – became one of the key themes linking it to the wider Indian Ocean. Examining this phenomenon provides an intriguing example of how this oceanic system worked in practice. To defend British Indian interests, Dutch and German soldiers garrisoned at the Cape signed up for service in India and European troops were landed and 'seasoned' in Southern Africa prior to serving in the subcontinent. Plans were hatched in London for deploying Indian sepoys in Africa and the Caribbean, exploiting the region as a crucial way station, and regiments serving at the Cape and St Helena were used to quell mutinies or lend additional support to campaigns in South America, Egypt and India. For all of these reasons, this southern gateway was vitally connected to Britain's central Indian Ocean concern: India itself.

This chapter examines the pivotal role played by this region in supplying Britain's Indian empire with troops: either recruited from existing

---

[5] David Washbrook, 'The Indian Economy and the British Empire', in Douglas M. Peers and Nandini Gooptu (eds.), *India and the British Empire* (Oxford: Oxford University Press, 2012), pp. 44–74, p. 54.

garrisons or transferred in the case of security emergencies. In doing so, it underscores the centrality of military matters in all contemporary commercial calculations in the region. The discussion is arranged in three principal sections. First, it explores the specific advantages offered to the military by a strong British presence in the region. Second, the use of the Cape in particular as a place from which to recruit troops and its role as a base to land and muster troops for deployment elsewhere is examined. Finally, the rapid deployment of troops stationed at the Cape in cases of emergency in India is discussed.

Military connections were forged by the maritime route taken by British ships around the Cape. At its most basic, this meant that military reinforcements intended for India frequently stopped off at places in the region that were under (or about to be under) British control. For example, George Moore, a young cadet travelling to India to take up his appointment in the East India Company's Bengal Army, witnessed the second British capture of the Cape in 1806. More than this, however, his letter home illustrates the active involvement of such 'Indian' troops in the region. Moore and his colleagues volunteered to assist as General Sir David Baird prepared to retake the Cape and were stationed on the beach in South Africa before resuming their voyage to India.[6] Most of the voyages between these oceanic worlds were less eventful for the soldiers and officers involved. The example of the 89th Regiment illustrates the movement of troops very well, and the ways in which such movements trace the strategic, economic and political connections between places in the region. The first battalion of the regiment sailed from Britain for Buenos Aires on 23 February 1807 to take part in the ill-fated schemes of Home Popham. After five months at sea, the soldiers arrived in time to learn that the British forces already on the ground were being evacuated, whereupon they were ordered to the Cape. The regiment arrived in Africa in October 1807. Less than a year later, in September 1808, the regiment embarked for Ceylon.[7] But all of the movements of troops discussed in this chapter were critical in inscribing and establishing what Durba Ghosh and Dane Kennedy refer to as 'the multiple networks of exchange that arose from the imperial experience'. These networks connected colonies and other areas of British imperial activity to each other, as well as to Britain.[8] This chapter shows the ways in which that military 'network', or system of connections, operated on the practical level of

[6] NAM, 1998-08-23, George Moore to Sarah Moore, 6 February 1806.
[7] NAM, 1966-02-07, Pay Warrant book, 1807.
[8] Durba Ghosh and Dane Kennedy, 'Introduction', in Durba Ghosh and Dane Kennedy (eds.), *Decentring Empire: Britain, India and the Transcolonial World* (London: Sangam Books, 2006), p. 2.

troop movements and regimental deployments. It uses the particular circumstances of these organised movements of personnel to explore the connections between the East India Company's control of large swathes of the Indian subcontinent and the British presence in the South Atlantic, Southern Africa and the south-western Indian Ocean. It demonstrates how the empire in India was crucially reinforced and defended by the strengthening of the British presence thousands of miles away, and how administrators, politicians and military officers conceived of military resources in a 'transoceanic' and imperial context.

The tangible benefits of the Cape, in particular, were noted by many contemporaries. Troops stationed in Africa were very much 'looked upon as part of the Indian force'.[9] The ability to recruit soldiers and deploy regiments between the two places was one of the 'mutual advantages to be derived from an intercourse between India and the Cape'.[10] As Richard Wellesley pointed out, this was one of the benefits offered by a territorial foothold on the African continent: 'As a military station I believe it to be one of the most advantageous which can be imagined to a power compelled to maintain a large European force in India.'[11] For John Barrow, the 'geographical situation' of the Cape offered a place 'to assemble in time of war for convoy', as well as 'to re-establish the health of their sickly troops, worn down by the debilitating effects of exposure to a warm climate; and to season, in the mild and moderate temperature of Southern Africa, such of these from Europe as may be destined for service in the warmer climate of their Indian settlements'.[12] One of the colony's early governors, Sir George Yonge, also recognised the advantage of having the ability to mobilise troops from a base in the near vicinity in case of emergency in India: 'Among the many important advantages which give an inestimable value to this Dominion of the Crown, that of its being by its situation a Depot and a point of departure from whence

---

[9] NAS, GD51/3/1/34, Richard Wellesley to Henry Dundas, 28 February 1798.
[10] Council at Fort St George to Lord Macartney, 25 June 1797, *RCC*, vol. II, p. 104. The actual numbers recruited from the Cape in the period is difficult to assess accurately as references to projected numbers of troops and double counting are rife in the sources. However, it would seem that individual campaigns could recruit several hundred at a time to supplement existing garrisons in India, which numbered 18,000 Europeans in the 1790s. Some 375 recruits were signed up by Owen in 1795 and 1796 (BL, IOR, E/1/94/81, p. 81; F/4/3/634; G/9/6, pp. 7–8, 24–5), 270 enlisted in 1806 (John Grainger, 'The Conquest of the Cape, 1806', *Army and Quarterly and Defence Journal* 123 (1993), pp. 320–1) and, in 1809, Lord Caledon sent 416 to India (BL, IOR, G/9/10, p. 126, Caledon to Pringle, 22 October 1809). Although the number of troops recruited directly from the region at any one time was small, their potential to provide important support was highly valued.
[11] NAS, GD51/3/1/34, Wellesley to Dundas, 28 February 1798.
[12] John Barrow, *An Account of Travels into the Interior of Southern Africa, in the Years 1797 and 1798*, 2 vols. (London: T. Cadell and W. Davies, 1801–4), vol. I, pp. 1–2.

India may be with speed defended and assisted is not one of the least considerations.'[13] By providing a stable location to muster and launch troops, the Cape was a key military benefit for British and East India Company authorities. During the first decade of British occupation, the tactical benefits derived from the Cape in terms of moving troops between India and Africa were defined under two broad categories: a place from which to recruit and deploy troops, and as a pool of military manpower to be drawn upon in the case of a security emergency in India. Robert Percival was blunt in his assessment: 'If this station should be found to afford the government an opportunity of maintaining a force in a most central and convenient position, and yet at a reduced expence, no one will dispute that this consideration alone is sufficient to render the possession of the colony an object of the most desirable nature.'[14]

Military matters underwrote everything. The threat of violence – real or imagined, in wartime or peacetime – was equally as important a facilitator of the movement of people and goods, issues central to most maritime histories, as the operations of commerce.[15] The anonymous author of a tract published in praise of St Helena in 1805 recognised that strategic advantage went hand in hand with military support. To make a port like Cape Town or an island like St Helena 'a place of importance to this country, whether as a barrier to our East India territories, or as a port from which to direct our attacks against the colonial possessions of other powers, great sums must necessarily be expended in its improvement, and in the maintenance of large and adequate garrisons'.[16] Of course, the region's prime position could also be a drawback too, as Lord Macartney pointed out. By allowing the French to hold the Cape, Macartney observed, Britain would be permitting them 'to train and season bodies of troops here sufficient at a favourable opportunity to pour into the southern peninsula of India and I fear to achieve the conquest of it'.[17] He was even more concerned three years later when the future of the Cape was under further threat – this time the danger came less from French arms than from the machinations of European power politics. Writing to Henry Dundas, and indignant about the potential return of the Cape under the Treaty of Amiens, Macartney observed that its location offered significant advantages to its occupier. He pointed out the worst-case scenario of

---

[13] BL, Add. MS 13785, f. 42, Sir George Yonge to Wellesley, 24 January 1801.
[14] Robert Percival, *An Account of the Cape of Good Hope* (London: C. & R. Baldwin, 1804), pp. 337–8.
[15] Nicholas Purcell, 'Tide, Beach, and Backwash: The Place of Maritime Histories', in Peter N. Miller (ed.), *The Sea: Thalassography and Historiography* (Ann Arbor, MI: University of Michigan Press, 2013), pp. 84–108, p. 86.
[16] Anon., *A Description of the Island of St Helena* (London: R. Phillips, 1805), p. 231.
[17] RH, GB 0162 MSS.Afr.s.1,2, Macartney to William Richardson, 28 February 1798.

Britain being 'driven out of the continent of India'. In such a situation, 'we might by properly stationing our force at the Cape and Ceylon still retain a formidable rank in the east, still command its great avenues and preserve and secure our commerce to China'.[18] It was clear then that defending trade and preserving strategic positions in the Indian Ocean were crucially affected by the number, quality and location of troops that could be called upon.

Troops: recruitment and deployment

The specific military benefits of a secure British presence in the southern gateway region were acknowledged from the middle of the eighteenth century, long before that presence had been consolidated. This was partially as a result of expanding East India Company commitments in the Indian subcontinent, and the defensive requirements that went with that. Although large swathes of India had come under Company control by the middle of the eighteenth century, a Company army that rivalled the regular Crown forces and was recruited directly from the British Isles was not politically feasible. Of course, the Company garnered much of its military strength through recruitment drives in India among the professional indigenous soldiers or sepoys.[19] By 1761, in the course of the Seven Years War, the Company had some 23,000 sepoys under arms.[20] But European troops were still regarded as vital in buttressing Company rule in India, and it found itself unable to recruit the soldiers it needed to cover its expanding territorial responsibilities in the subcontinent. As a result, beginning in 1754, units of the regular army were sent to India to supplement the Company's troops.[21] Of course, any other avenues that might add to this supply without causing political problems in Britain were to be welcomed. Initially, however, just managing to disembark healthy European troops on Indian shores was a boon.

---

[18] NAS, GD51/1/530/12, Macartney to Dundas, 25 April 1801.

[19] There is a rich literature on European armies in India. Seema Alavi, *The Sepoys and the Company: Tradition and Transition in Northern India, 1770–1830* (New Delhi: Oxford University Press, 2006); Peter B. Boyden and Alan J. Guy (eds.), *Soldiers of the Raj: Indian Army, 1600–1947* (London: National Army Museum, 1998); Gerald J. Bryant, 'The East India Company and its army', Ph.D. thesis, University of London, 1975; Gerald Bryant 'Officers of the East India Company's Army in the Days of Clive and Hastings', *Journal of Imperial and Commonwealth History* 6 (1978), pp. 203–27; David Omissi, *The Sepoy and the Raj: The Indian Army, 1860–1940* (Basingstoke: Macmillan, 1994).

[20] P. J. Marshall, *The Making and Unmaking of Empires: Britain, India, and America c.1750–1783* (Oxford: Oxford University Press, 2005), p. 129.

[21] Arthur N. Gilbert, 'Recruitment and Reform in the East India Company Army, 1760–1800', *Journal of British Studies* 15 (1975), pp. 89–111, p. 91.

Logistics and the general difficulties of supplying troops to India from Europe were legion.[22] The problems of supplying and sustaining the army in India were exacerbated by the high death rate caused by the long and treacherous sea voyage to Asia and the debilitating effects of tropical diseases that hampered the Company's forces when troops arrived there.[23] The embarkation lists of the Company give some idea of the effect of the passage to India on raw European recruits. There are cases where most of the men perished en route. In 1760, for example, out of fifty-three officers and men on the *Osterly*, thirty-three died at sea. In the same year, forty-three of the sixty-one men on the *Worcester* never reached India.[24] The importance of 'getting out the forces to India with expedition, and in good airy ships' was recognised at the very highest level. At the end of the century, it struck Henry Dundas 'more forcibly than every other consideration'.[25] Even those who survived the passage to India and their first few months in the subcontinent's unforgiving climate, measured up poorly against the military manpower of other European nations. For example, in 1775, one informant told Lord Rochford, the Secretary of State, that British recruits could not be compared with their French equivalents at the Ile de France:

Such of the troops as I saw at Mauritius were able-bodied, well accoutred and appeared infinitely better in every respect under arms than our soldiers in the East Indies. The recruits in general sent out [by] your East India Company seem to be from the very dregs of the people, under size and hardly able to support their flintlocks; whereas the soldiers at Port Louis are stout, hardy-looking men and to appearance from five feet eight to five feet ten in height.[26]

Despite advances in medical knowledge and more attention being paid to things like climate, nutrition and clothing – outfits for the 84th Regiment at the Cape were returned to Europe on account of their 'not being fit for this climate', for example – unfamiliar and unforgiving conditions took their toll on European troops in the East.[27] Even in the healthiest of seasons, an eighth of the European troops in the subcontinent was estimated to be unfit for service due to illness.[28] The terrifying mortality rate of those travelling to India, combined with the scarcely less depressing

[22] In this regard, see the series of letters to and from William Huskisson, Undersecretary at War between 1796 and 1798, trying to sort out troop transports to the Cape and India. CRL, Ladd/1114–28.
[23] Gilbert, 'Recruitment and Reform in the East India Company Army', pp. 91–2.
[24] *Ibid.*, p. 92, n. 7.   [25] CRL, LAdd/1122, Huskisson to David Scott, 14 April 1796.
[26] BL, IOR, H/120, p. 149, Mr Petrie to Lord Rochford, 26 October 1775.
[27] RH, MSS.Afr.t.2, H. Ross to John Pringle, 10 November 1797.
[28] Erica Wald, *Vice in the Barracks: Medicine, the Military and the Making of Colonial India, 1780–1868* (Basingstoke: Palgrave Macmillan, 2014), p. 19.

picture of military life (and death) in the subcontinent surely served further to discourage Europeans from signing up for service. This seems to have been at least a contributing factor in the mutinous behaviour of a regiment of Seaforth Highlanders in 1778, who rose up at the prospect of being sent to serve the Company in India.[29] Given all of these circumstances, then, it is little wonder that some of the benefits presented by the South Atlantic and southern Indian Ocean region more generally were specifically reimagined and represented for military men.

The beneficial effects of the region for those recuperating from illness or travelling has a long and enduring history, stretching back before the establishment of permanent European settlement there. This continued into the second half of the eighteenth century. For Sir Robert Harland, in command of the Royal Navy in the Indian Ocean, the Cape was 'the first [i.e. best] place in the world that ever I have seen for seamen to shake off the disease of a voyage'.[30] After landing at a bay some 500 miles east of the Cape of Good Hope, Lieutenant Henry Pemberton was struck by the apparent health and longevity of the people: 'Some Dutchmen and women whose prodigious stature and florid complexion announced the most perfect state of health. Sickness and disease are little known to these happy regions.'[31] Arguing for the establishment of a permanent British settlement in the area, Pemberton extolled the health benefits and its consequent advantages for East India Company trade. But it was of particular use for soldiers and sailors, offering 'a most salubrious climate for departing of European troops till their service might be wanted in India and for the restoring to vigour and health the convalescent of our more eastern settlements'.[32] He observed that it would be extremely useful to have access to a port which afforded 'every kind of refreshment and restoring health to the broken constitution of an Indian Sailor'. It would, he remarked, afford 'an healthful dispository [sic] for the European soldier, until his services might be wanted in India and at most but 7 weeks sail from Bombay and 8 weeks from Madras'.[33] William Dalrymple agreed. This area provided all sorts of refreshments and, 'in case of the scurvy' breaking out on a ship, its settlement would allow for a much sooner landfall than Johanna in the Comoros Islands.[34]

---

[29] See BL, Add. MS 42071, Humberston-Greville letters on the rising of the Seaforth Highlanders, September 1778.

[30] UWits, A30, Robert Harland to Philip Stephens, 24 October 1774.

[31] BL, IOR, G/9/1, pp. 20–1, Henry Pemberton, 'A Narrative with a Description and Drawing of Croem or Crontz Riviere Bay Situate on the South East Coast of Africa' [1785].

[32] Ibid., p. 25.   [33] Ibid., pp. 21–2.

[34] TNA, PRO 30/8/128/65, William Dalrymple to William Pitt, quoted in Diana Dalrymple to William Pitt, n.d.

Even after reduction in voyage lengths, improved nutrition supplies and progress in prophylactic measures against scurvy, places like the Cape and St Helena were still considered suitable recuperation stations, particularly for those serving in India. It proved particularly popular with individuals who were given leave from their postings in India in order to recover their health. In 1815, Andrew Hudleston, a servant of the East India Company in Madras, wrote to his parents telling them of his cousin William Hudleston's liver complaint: 'He was attacked shortly after my arrival by a fit of the liver which at first appeared very slight, but took an unfavorable turn so as to confine him to the house for two months.' In order to help progress his recovery, William 'was advised to take a short trip to the Cape of Good Hope in order that his cure might be complete'.[35] Members of the army in particular were thought to benefit. In 1835, Captain F. B. Doveton left Madras for Southern Africa in order 'to renovate my frame'.[36] In a similar vein, an East India Company committee recommended that 'Brevet Captain William O'Reilly of the Madras Establishment be permitted to continue his residence at the Cape for the recovery of his health'. It authorised the Company's agent at the Cape to issue 'furlough pay' until 30 March 1825, after which time O'Reilly's thirty-month sabbatical from his duties at Madras expired and no more payments were to be made.[37]

As a consequence, the climatic advantages offered by places like Southern Africa and the surrounding maritime littoral were frequently repackaged and represented as military considerations. Richard Wellesley's assessment of the strategic and economic value of the Cape, where he stopped on the way to India, was coloured by reflecting on the effects of climate and environment on troops: 'The climate is remarkably healthy; so much so that the appearance both of the officers and soldiers stationed here bears striking testimony to the fact.' The contrast with the wane army recruits from home was remarkable: 'You will hardly see regiments in England of so healthy an appearance as those which have been here for any time.' And there was another consideration, which, for someone with potentially pressing interests in India like Wellesley, was even more attractive:

The heat is however frequently very severe, so that a soldier who has been here for a year or two is well accustomed to be exposed to a very ardent sun, and receives a sort of preparation for the climates of India. The advantage of this circumstance

---

[35] CRO, D HUD 13/3/1, Andrew F. Hudleston to parents, 2 February–10 March 1815.
[36] Quoted in John McAleer, *Representing Africa: Landscape, Exploration and Empire, 1780–1870* (Manchester: Manchester University Press, 2010), p. 41.
[37] BL, IOR, D/10, pp. 104–5, 13 October 1824.

has lately been proved in India, where the regiments, which had passed through the seasoning of this climate, have arrived and continued in much better health, than those which proceeded thither directly from Europe, or which remained here but for a very short period of time.[38]

In short, now that it was in British hands, troops travelling from Europe to India could expect to derive much benefit from stopping at the Cape. In outlining the actions he was taking to send troops to India, to reinforce the campaign against Tipu Sultan in the south of the subcontinent, Lord Macartney was happy to inform Henry Dundas about their health and vigour. Those troops 'now under orders for embarkation are remarkably healthy'. And their healthy bodies matched their qualities in other ways as they were, Macartney preened, 'in every respect well appointed, and strongly animated with the ardor and spirit of enterprise which mark the true character of British Soldiers'.[39] A few years later, Francis Dundas was delighted to confirm that the troops that sailed for Madras were 'in perfect health and good condition in every particular'.[40] After his earlier encomia for the Cape, Wellesley later hoped to benefit from precisely the same circumstances when he wrote to request troops for service in India in 1800. He hoped that Sir George Yonge would 'necessarily feel the expediency of composing the reinforcements which you send in consequence of this letter of the most experienced and seasoned troops now at the Cape'. As Wellesley commented:

The usual course of service has been to season the King's Troops in the climate of the Cape for eventual use in India. Under this system part of the force I received from Earl Macartney was immediately employed in active service, and was distinguished at the siege and assault of Seringapatam.[41]

Given the levels of sickness and mortality on troop ships and in India, respite from the journey and an opportunity to acclimatise to the heat were important considerations to be borne in mind. Robert Brooke was adamant:

By sending out the recruits there in the first place and drafting the soldiers wanting annually for India from thence you would always keep up the garrison, and forward me with good constitutions for service in the warm climate of the East.[42]

Robert Percival, who spent some time at the Cape recovering his health after serving in India, observed: 'The effects of the Cape in recruiting men

[38] NAS, GD51/3/1/34, Wellesley to Dundas, 28 February 1798.
[39] RH, MSS.Afr.t.3, Macartney to Dundas, 18 September 1798.
[40] B'hurst, MS.052/7, Francis Dundas to Henry Dundas, 2 November 1799.
[41] Wellesley to Yonge, 24 October 1800, *RCC*, vol. III, p. 343.
[42] B'hurst, MS.062/36, 'Hints regarding the Cape by Governor Brooke' [c.1798].

after a long sea voyage with astonishing rapidity are well known; and its
property of seasoning troops for warmer climates has been proved in
many instances.'[43] And he concurred with Wellesley and others: 'Those
regiments who have been first retained for a couple of years at the Cape,
before they were sent on to India, were much better able to endure that
climate than those who were sent out immediately.'[44] He painted an
almost paradisiacal picture of the region as the perfect place for soldiers
to recuperate and 'season': 'Besides the advantages of its centrical position, the qualities of the climate of the Cape, in seasoning soldiers for
service in the warm latitudes, joined to the cheapness with which an army
may be maintained here, are sufficient motives for making it out as a most
desirable military station.' It was certainly much more attractive than
either the West Indies or the East Indies with the 'pestilential nature of
the climate' in both places.[45] He continued:

The invigorating effects of the climate of the Cape have been proved in innumerable instances. Many of our officers who came thither from India with constitutions so enfeebled, that their cure seemed beyond the reach of medicine, were in
a very short time so restored at the Cape as to be able to return in perfect health to
their regiments.[46]

Another writer was equally as effusive: 'The Cape is notoriously a most
healthy climate where men retain in a great degree their European vigour,
which vigour is improved by the excellence of the provisions and the
wholesomeness of the wine.'[47] And Lady Anne Barnard corroborated
these views by remarking that the troops stationed in Southern Africa 'are
esteemed to be in fine order – to me they appear well dressed – well
matched men and better looking than any of the lately raised regiments
that I saw in England.'[48] The advantages were not just confined to
soldiers. Sir Home Popham suggested that 'they must equally apply to
sailors, and hence a question of great importance would arise, namely
whether it may not be more expedient to keep the greater part of our naval
armament for the eastern hemisphere at the Cape rather than in India'.[49]
    These views about the climatic benefits resurfaced when Britain took
the Cape for a second time, after the collapse of the Peace of Amiens.
In 1806, Lieutenant-Colonel Lamington Baillie, of the Bengal Cavalry,
employed similar terms as those used by Barrow, Wellesley and Percival.

[43] Percival, *Account*, p. 337.   [44] *Ibid.*, p. 139.   [45] *Ibid.*, p. 336.   [46] *Ibid.*, pp. 336–7.
[47] CRO, D LONS/L13/1/91, 'Importance of the Cape of Good Hope Considered'
(c.1815–16), p. 22.
[48] Lady Anne Barnard to Dundas, 10 July 1797, *Letters*, p. 54.
[49] B'hurst, MS.310, Home Popham, 'Thoughts of the Naval, Military, Commercial and
Colonial Importation of the Cape of Good Hope, with Suggestions for Affording Relief to
the Distressed and Unemployed Peasantry of Ireland' (c.1816), pp. 5–6.

He drew on the climatic advantages of the Cape in order to advocate a proactive recruitment policy among soldiers serving in the Dutch garrison:

The superiority for immediate service in India of the seasoned soldier of the Cape, to the recruit proceeding directly from England[,] has been found by repeated experiment and I believe it is equally certain that the deficiencies in the Company's European Corps abroad may be supplied from the same place not only more promptly but at a considerably lighter expence than from this country.[50]

As one contemporary pointed out, Barrow's account 'clearly explains the advantages of this position to season the young recruits for India', and made the case for keeping 'the greater part of our naval armament for the East Hemisphere at the Cape rather than in India'.[51] This writer went further than Barrow in seeing the advantages that the region could offer. The 'salubrity of the climate' was 'exemplified in the small degree of mortality among the troops and in the vigor and stability of their constitutions', which was also replicated in naval personnel.[52] They saw no drawbacks in a place that promised to be 'a most suitable repository for such recruits effectually to season them for a southern clime and to fit them for soldiers'.

The healthiness of the climate, the cheapness of provisions ... combined with the convenient situation of the colony for speedy intercourse with most parts of the world, particularly the East and West Indies, peculiarly recommend the adoption of this plan; besides if such an establishment were formed this depot might in conjunction with the colonial militia already alluded to answer any immediate purpose of defence.[53]

And these views were given practical expression in 1815, when Lord Moira asked troops to be sent from the Cape Colony to the subcontinent. He recommended 'the expediency of selecting those corps which are most efficient in point of numbers, and which have served for the longest period in the colony, as being likely from the latter circumstance to be more immediately fit for active service in India'.[54]

Although Southern Africa garnered most attention, other places in the region could offer similar benefits, and the same themes were evident in the writing about them. The Ile de France, for example, provided similar recuperation possibilities, according to Jacob Haafner. 'The sojourn of the troops' at this 'intermediate station' allowed them to 'recover from the

---

[50] BL, IOR, E/1/113, p. 153, Lamington Baillie to East India Company, 8 April 1806.
[51] CRO, D LONS/L13/1/91, 'Importance of the Cape', pp. 21–2.   [52] *Ibid.*, p. 22.
[53] *Ibid.*, p. 35.
[54] Lord Moira to Lord Charles Somerset, 9 February 1815, *RCC*, vol. X, p. 250.

weariness inculcated by the voyage, and ... gradually accustom themselves to the hotter climate'.[55] And the papers of William Windham include the views of Sir George Young on the merits of Madagascar. Among the many boons presented by this island, Young proposed it as a place where 'our troops may be inured to the discipline of a camp and have the great benefit of a gradual seasoning to the climates of India'.[56]

Given the longevity of the British presence at St Helena, it is unsurprising that it was presented as offering similar assistance in terms of health and well-being. The governor, Robert Brooke, an East India Company appointee who had seen action in India and its effects on men, advocated the island as a place for military personnel to rest and recuperate. He believed that it 'may be rendered still further useful ... were it to be considered and made use of as a place well adapted to collect and train up men at, for land and sea service in the East'. St Helena's strategic position gave it another potential advantage as troops stationed here could be employed 'occasionally on secret expeditions' in order to 'disconcert the distant enemy of Great Britain'.[57] The latter comment was one that, as we will see, applied across this oceanic region, especially in times of dire need. But in relation to its promise as a recuperation station, the authorities obviously took heed of Brooke's advice. In the first decade of the nineteenth century, the 'decency and order' of the garrison was 'observed by every passing stranger'.[58] Even more impressively, 'numbers of discharged soldiers, returning from India' were 'perfectly restored to health on the passage to St Helena' and 'now offered with alacrity to renew their time of service'.[59] The climatic and situational benefits offered by St Helena, therefore, 'enabled the Governor to forward drafts to India, amounting, at different periods, to the number of twelve hundred and ten men, all of them disciplined soldiers, prepared for a hot country by a seasoning in the medium climate of St Helena'.[60] Another writer stated St Helena's case even more categorically: 'The sickly crews of ships that touch here, very shortly recover.' The bracing mid-Atlantic air apparently had the same effect on 'the invalids, who are discharged from different regiments of India'. The author of this tract suggested that

---

[55] 'Jacob Haafner's description of Mauritius', in Shawkat Toorawa (ed.), *The Western Indian Ocean: Essays on Islands and Islanders* (Port Louis: Hassam Toorawa Trust, 2007), pp. 77–86, p. 78.

[56] HRO, 38M49/5/61/20, 'Observations on the Island of Madagascar by Colonel Sir George Young' (c.1806–7), p. 5.

[57] BL, IOR, G/32/165, p. 32, Robert Brooke, 'Account of St Helena with Various Observations Annexed' [1792].

[58] Thomas H. Brooke, *A History of the Island of St Helena: From Its Discovery by the Portuguese to the Year 1806* (London: Black, Parry and Kingsbury, 1808), p. 293.

[59] *Ibid.*, p. 294.   [60] *Ibid.*

many who were 'sent home as incurable and unfit for service ... during their stay at St Helena recover so fast, that they again enlist here, and continue to enjoy good health'.[61] The guarantee of personal first-hand experience was even brought to bear:

Of this the writer saw some remarkable instances, in men whom he had known in India, and who were there reduced to such a state of weakness, or were afflicted with such diseases, that their recovery and even their existence in that climate seemed impossible: Yet these men had recovered completely, and appeared sufficiently strong and vigorous for any military duty.[62]

All of this clearly pointed to the myriad benefits to be derived from using St Helena as a key recruitment and recuperation station. The facts outlined, this author felt, deserved 'the attention of the East India Company, as it shews how the military part of this settlement may be recruited with more convenience, and at far less expense, than by sending soldiers immediately from Europe'.[63] But it was not just as a way station for British troops that the region at the southern extremity of the Atlantic and Indian oceans became an intimate part of the Indian Ocean military network. It also offered the chance to find fresh infusions of troops via recruitment drives in the region itself.

Recruitment: gateway to India

The providential geographical position and disease environment of the region made it an ideal location at which to rest and recuperate troops on their way to and from India. But the British requirement for military reinforcement meant this was not enough. The British East India Company's expansion in the subcontinent in the second half of the eighteenth century necessitated a much greater military supply. Despite an expansion in military manpower, this was never sufficient.[64] By 1776, the manpower situation was desperate. The Company's Secret Committee repeatedly requested 'that an additional force may be sent to the East Indies for the effectual support of the Company's trade and settlements there'.[65] Despite reassurances from Lord North, the Company's representatives were becoming increasingly distressed, pointing out 'the very great difficulties that occur in raising a sufficient number of recruits to compleat the military establishments at the Company's several presidencies'. This

[61] Anon., *Island of St Helena*, p. 117.   [62] *Ibid.*   [63] *Ibid.*, pp. 117–18.
[64] James H. Thomas, 'The Isle of Wight and the East India Company, 1700–1840: Some Connections Considered', *Local Historian* 30 (2000), pp. 4–22, p. 9.
[65] BL, IOR, H/84, p. 54, Extracts from the minutes of the Secret Committee, 13 January 1776.

was compounded by 'the obstructions attending the execution of the plan for acquiring volunteers from amongst the American prisoners proposed to be shipped at Gibraltar'. The upshot was that the Company had around seven hundred men 'when by the last return a recruit of not less than 2700 men will be wanting to put those establishments upon their settled quota in order to be prepared to defend the Company's valuable possessions in the East Indies against a surprise or sudden attack that may be made by any European power'.[66] As if to reinforce the point, the authorities in Bombay warned London that 'the present reduced state of our European Military is a matter worthy of your most serious attention'. The situation was so dire, in fact, that 'unless you can devise some method to send us a speedy recruit those corps will soon by the common casualties of the service be nearly extinct'.[67] This became a common refrain.[68] Barely a decade later, when Lord Cornwallis arrived to take up the reins as governor general, the same situation pertained. Cornwallis lost no time in complaining to the Company, and to prominent individuals, about the quality of the recruits sent out to India. On 10 November 1786, for example, he wrote to the Duke of York, a future Commander-in-Chief. While the Company's artillery troops were 'very fine', Cornwallis warned that the European infantry, 'on whom the defense of these valuable possessions may one day depend, are in a most wretched state'.[69] The following year, Cornwallis wrote a much more detailed report excoriating the state of European troops in India. He professed himself satisfied with the native troops but expressed dismay at the poor condition of the Europeans in the Company's service, who were 'men worn out by long service, intemperance and infirmities and of others so diminutive in size as to be totally unequal to the duties of the field'. He was clear in his opinion that 'a respectable body of well disciplined and serviceable Europeans is indispensably necessary for the security of your own possessions and for the maintenance of the national honour in India'.[70]

[66] BL, IOR, H/84, p. 55, Extracts from the minutes of the Secret Committee, 13 November 1776.

[67] BL, IOR, H/84, p. 59, Governor and Council of Bombay to the Court of Directors, 22 December 1776.

[68] The situation was not even ameliorated by various acts of parliament such as 'An Act for Better Recruiting the Forces of the East India Company' in 1799, which gave the Company the right to train and exercise its recruits in England, to draw from the King's recruits as a source of manpower, and to subject them to martial law both before and during the voyage to India. See Thomas, 'Isle of Wight and the East India Company', p. 11.

[69] Lord Cornwallis to Duke of York, 10 November 1786, in Charles Ross (ed.), Correspondence of Charles, First Marquis Cornwallis, 3 vols. (London: John Murray, 1859), vol. I, p. 235.

[70] BL, IOR, F/4/3, p. 634, Cornwallis to the Court of Directors, 16 November 1787.

Despite the British reliance on indigenous troops, European soldiers – numbering some 18,000 in 1790 – were still regarded as providing the 'steel core' of the army.[71] The authorities were always keen to ensure that armies were 'composed in as large a portion as is practicable of European troops'.[72] But there were very few recruits coming from Europe. The report of a 'Joint Committee of Correspondence and Shipping' highlighted the fact that between 1797 and January 1799 only eighty-five recruits officially embarked from Britain.[73] Nevertheless, the same report also pointed to another source of manpower for Britain's Asian interest: the South Atlantic and, in particular, Southern Africa. This region was to become a crucial element in maintaining British power in India, not only by providing healthy stopping-off points but by offering fresh reinforcements too. The committee's report shows how the Company tried to compensate for the weak supply of recruits by enlisting foreign troops stationed in Africa for service in India.[74] Of course, recruiting British soldiers from these places would not add to the overall military tally. As a result, recruiting in the region also involved capturing, persuading, bribing or otherwise inveigling foreign troops to sign up for British service in India.[75] As such, these recruiting drives were inflected by European rivalries. This became a running theme throughout the early years of the nineteenth century and helped to cement the place of the Cape, St Helena and elsewhere as fundamental parts of the British Indian Ocean world.

The authorities on St Helena, for example, also helped India in times of need. The island's governor, Robert Brooke, was always 'ready to throw in my mite' for the greater good.[76] The prospect of recruiting directly came in the 1790s, when British forces operating from St Helena captured a Dutch fleet. Thomas Brooke reported that 'between seventy and eighty of the prisoners who were found to be Danes, Norwegians, and

[71] Wald, *Vice in the Barracks*, pp. 7–8, 21. On the issue of recruiting indigenous troops, see P. J. Marshall, 'The British in Asia: Trade to Dominion', in P. J. Marshall (ed.), *The Oxford History of the British Empire. Volume II: The Eighteenth Century* (Oxford: Oxford University Press, 1998), pp. 487–507, p. 499. By the middle of the eighteenth century, the British recruited Telugu-speaking people for the Company's Madras regiments, while northern Indian Rajputs and so-called military Brahmins were recruited for Bengal.
[72] Moira to Somerset, 9 February 1815, *RCC*, vol. X, p. 250.
[73] Gilbert, 'Recruitment and Reform in the East India Company Army', p. 107.
[74] TNA, WO 1/893, pp. 397–421, Report of a Joint Committee of Correspondence and Shipping, 3 January 1799.
[75] The use of non-British troops in serving the empire is now beginning to attract attention from scholars. For an excellent recent study, see Stephen Conway, 'Continental European Soldiers in British Imperial Service, c.1756–1792', *English Historical Review* 129 (2014), pp. 79–106.
[76] B'hurst, MS.062/25, Robert Brooke to Macartney, 26 December 1797.

Swedes, and were desirous of changing masters, enlisted in the Company's service'. And it was not just the Europeans who were willing to sign up: 'The Malays, also, considered their capture by the English as a release from slavery; and readily agreed to take an oath of fidelity, and enter the British service.'[77] In the end, around one hundred men were sent to India and Brooke hoped 'to enlist several more and to be able to detach a large party of Europeans and two companys [sic] of Malays that I have trained in by the first ships that touch here on their passage to the East'.[78] Lord Cornwallis in India told Brooke that he was 'truly sensible of the earnest and meritorious zeal with which you have been actuated in preparing and embarking for the service of this country so considerable a part of the force of your island'.[79] He elaborated from his military headquarters at Choultry Plain, near Madras: 'The party of 250 men, which you sent on board the Canton, arrived here in high health and excellent order, and have proved a timely and valuable recruit; upwards of seventy were drafted into the artillery, and Colonel Geels reports very favourably of them.'[80]

This pattern was writ large further east, at the Cape, which offered the most fruitful recruiting ground for the Company. By 1760, 75 per cent of the soldiers stationed at the Cape came from German states.[81] The danger of disaffection and desertion can be gauged from the fact that, in times of war, troops were removed from Robben Island on account of their questionable loyalties. Following the capture of the former Dutch outpost, it also offered the potential to provide an instant boost to British armies in India by recruiting from European troops – 'transient' mercenaries rather than colonial settlers, indigenous people or free blacks – already serving in Dutch regiments there. The defensive forces at the Cape numbered some 3,631 men.[82] As a consequence of the dearth of recruits back in Britain, the Cape, as a European settlement with a garrison, was quickly recognised as a potentially rich recruiting ground for the East India Company's armies in India. The dubious loyalty of various European colonists perceived by many was also, apparently, identified in military regiments. Even before it was captured, there had been rumours about discontent in the ranks of the Dutch army and navy,

[77] Brooke, St Helena, p. 314.
[78] B'hurst, MS.062/5, Robert Brooke to unknown recipient, undated [c.1796].
[79] Cornwallis to Robert Brooke, n.d. [c.1796], in Brooke, St Helena, p. 294.
[80] Cornwallis to Robert Brooke, 14 September 1796, in Brooke, St Helena, p. 295.
[81] Nigel Penn, 'Soldiers and Cape Town society', in Nigel Worden (ed.), Cape Town between East and West: Social Identities in a Dutch Colonial Town (Hilversum: Uitgeverij Verloren, 2012), pp. 176–93, p. 178.
[82] P. W. Marnitz and H. D. Campagne, The Dutch Surrender of the Cape of Good Hope, 1795 (Cape Town: Castle Military Museum, 2002), p. 12.

and the potential to recruit disgruntled soldiers and sailors. Robert Percival noted how 'the Dutch ships were in a very bad condition for fighting, the crews were extensively disaffected, being merely composed of requisition-men forced into the service'. This questionable loyalty was compounded by the fact that 'few were natives of Holland, the far greater part being Hanoverians, Prussians, and Germans'.[83]

Before its formal acquisition in 1795, preparations were under way to sign up as many recruits as possible. In addition to readying an invasion force, James Craig asked for guidance regarding the 'three German Regiments in the pay of the States-General' of the Netherlands. He wondered if it might not be useful 'to take these regiments into British pay'.[84] In the short term, this would have obvious benefits in helping to secure the British position in Southern Africa. The response from army headquarters in London was positive. According to the latest information available, 'the principal force at the Cape' consisted of 'the remains of two Regiments of Mecklenburgh Strelitz, which have for a certain limited time been taken into the Pay of the Republic'. It was believed that these men might have some grievances that could be exploited. For example, it was considered 'by no means improbable from the events which have taken place that the payment of their subsistence is now in arrears'. Craig's orders were not just the reduction of the Cape's military establishment but its redeployment in the service of its new master:

If by holding out to the officers and men the liquidation of such arrears, should any be due to them, and by taking them into the pay of Great Britain, you can engage them for the service of this country on the terms on which they are now employed, it will be highly expedient that it should be done, and you will consider yourself at liberty to hold out such conditions to them.[85]

Craig and his colleagues were successful. When the British arrived, the leader of the naval fleet, George Elphinstone, persuaded many of the garrison to enlist in 'the Marines, and I ordered them to be enlisted with a bounty of two pounds, and shall clothe them as soon as possible, they have served faithfully, and are excellent German soldiers'.[86] Apparently many of these disaffected European soldiers 'seemed quite happy on being taken by us, and several entered immediately into our service'.[87] And the paucity of manpower in India quickly led to the

---

[83] Percival, *Account*, p. 35.
[84] 'Memorandum drawn up by Major-General James Craig', 22 February 1795, *RCC*, vol. I, p. 32.
[85] [Office of the Commander-in-Chief] Horse Guards to James Craig, 23 February 1795, *RCC*, vol. I, pp. 32–3.
[86] George Keith Elphinstone to Dundas, 12 September 1795, *RCC*, vol. I, p. 121.
[87] Percival, *Account*, p. 35.

identification of Southern Africa as a prime area for supplying troops. The Company's authorities at Fort William wrote to General Craig, for example, pleading for reinforcements:

The force of the European troops in Bengal is so reduced, and the prospect of obtaining an early augmentation of it from Europe so uncertain, that it is our indispensable duty to state these circumstances to Your Excellency, in the expectation that you may be able to spare one of His Majesty's regiments for the service of this country.[88]

Perhaps they had heard about the fresh infusion of personnel being added by Craig at the Cape.

The impact of this recruitment drive was certainly evident in the assessment of Richard Wellesley when he arrived in India. Reporting his findings to Dundas, he pointed out that large numbers of European troops in the Company's Bengal Army had recently been recruited from the Cape of Good Hope: 'The recruits from that place form about half of the whole European force of the Company at this presidency, and amount to about nine hundred men.' Wellesley added that 'these are all foreigners of different nations, but chiefly Dutch and German, and almost all were recruited from the prisoners taken on board the Dutch fleet which was captured in Saldanha Bay by Lord Keith'.[89] As Wellesley's comments highlight, then, the Cape was being woven into the wider British Indian Ocean world by virtue of its role as a place from which to transport and recruit troops.

Perhaps reflecting the perceived willingness of European troops to sign up for service in India, there were a number of organised recruitment drives launched from India in subsequent years. With the ever-present spectre of a weak military force combined with tense and febrile local politics, the Company's representatives hoped to profit from the opportunity, as James Craig observed, 'to enlist some good men for India from among the Prisoners of War lately composing this Garrison, who are chiefly Germans'.[90] John Pringle, the East India Company's agent at the Cape of Good Hope, gave an indication of how this was achieved. Pringle informed London that Lieutenant Owen of the Bengal establishment and Lieutenant Malcolm of the Madras establishment were actively engaged in conducting 'a measure highly important to the [East India Company's] service'. He reported that '225 men have been obtained at 5 guineas per man'. Pringle considered these 'very easy terms' for 'such a number of excellent soldiers', before going on to

---

[88] Governor-General and Council of Bengal to Craig, 6 February 1796, *RCC*, vol. I, p. 325.
[89] Wellesley to Dundas, 1 October 1798, *Two Views*, p. 81.
[90] Craig to Dundas, 19 April 1796, *RCC*, vol. I, p. 365.

give details about the logistical arrangements for transferring the new recruits to India:

125 of them are embarked with Lt Owen onboard of the Prince William Henry & Worcester for Bengal. The remainder and 100 men drafted from the St Helena detachment are embarked onboard of the three Bombay ships – some of them would have been sent to Madras but there is no opportunity.[91]

In January 1796, the military commander in Bengal commented that it had been 'represented to me by Lt Owen who is just returned with recruits from the late garrison of the Cape, that there remained from 5 to 600 German soldiers most of whom he believed would be willing to enter into the service of the Company upon the same terms that have been granted to those already entertained'.[92]

The Company's representatives in India were eager to make the most of these opportunities for further strengthening the forces in India from the Cape. Only a month later, John Owen, who had acted as 'Major of Brigade to two Battalions of Seamen at the capture of the Cape', was directed by his superiors in the Bengal Presidency to return there 'accompanied by Lieutenant Mason of the Artillery in the hope of obtaining a further supply of German soldiers from that garrison'.[93] In April 1796, James Craig informed Henry Dundas that Lieutenant Owen had arrived in the *Walsingham*. 'Assisted by another officer', Owen had come 'in the hope of procuring some more recruits for the India Service from the men of the disbanded corps of the late garrison, they have already got about 400 part at Bengal, part at Madras and some to St Helena, I doubt very much of their success being considerable, however they shall have my most cordial assistance in every point in my power'.[94] In spite of Craig's misgivings, however, Owen's recruitment drives proved successful. In September 1796, John Pringle could report that '120 fine recruits mostly Austrians and Poles are embarked by his [Owen's] exertions on your ships, now bound to Madras and Bengal'. And yet more were available: 'The shortness of time would not permit of more being collected but I dare say 200 or 300 will be ready for the next fleet.'[95]

[91] BL, IOR, G/9/6, pp. 7–8, John Pringle to Secret Committee, 14 October 1795, paragraph 3.
[92] BL, IOR, F/4/3, p. 634, Copy of minute of Commander-in-Chief [General Sir Robert Abercromby], 22 January 1796.
[93] BL, IOR, E/4/56, Military Despatches, Fort William, 1 February 1796, paragraph 10.
[94] Craig to Dundas, 19 April 1796, *RCC*, vol. I, p. 365.
[95] BL, IOR, F/4/3, p. 634, Extract of letter from John Pringle, 7 September 1796. Not everyone, however, shared a sanguine view of recruiting from former enemy garrisons. By 1797, the authorities in Calcutta had developed reservations about the process. They informed the Court of Directors in London: 'Not deeming it proper to entertain a greater number of foreigners in your service than those already enlisted, we recalled Captain

The Cape seemed to be a fertile field for recruitment with a plentiful supply of European troops eager and willing to sign up for service in India. The presence of these troops highlights the polyglot nature of British Crown and Company forces in the subcontinent. But it also demonstrates the close links forged by the Company and its military officers between the Cape and India. The example of Owen powerfully illustrates the practical connections that incorporated this region into Britain's Indian Ocean world.

These early recruitment campaigns for the East India Company, undertaken within months of the Cape's falling into British hands, instigated a pattern that was repeated when it was captured again in the first decade of the nineteenth century. As ever, there was a dearth in India. As the Governor and Council at Fort William expressed it to the acting governor at the Cape, Sir David Baird: 'Your Excellency will be apprized by that dispatch that the defective state of our European Force in India urgently requires a reinforcement equal to that which was destined for this country.'[96] And, once again, conditions among European soldiers of the Dutch garrison seemed to augur well for recruitment. The belief was widespread that 'the troops now in garrison at the Cape are mostly Germans, and much disgusted with the Dutch service'.[97] In November 1803, the governor of St Helena, Robert Patton, welcomed John Pringle to the island. Believing his role there would no longer be effective, Pringle decided to leave Cape Town when the Batavian Republic assumed control at the Peace of Amiens.[98] Patton conveyed Pringle's assessment of the colony to Richard Wellesley at Fort William:

By his account, the garrison he left at the Cape was not so formidable as I had been informed; a part of each of the different corps, of which I had received a list, were there, but many of the corps were very incomplete and the German Troops (who formed a large part of the garrison) were discontented and seemed desirous of intimating to him, upon many occasions when an opportunity offered, that they would wish to change masters.

The cause of this unhappiness was clear: 'They were greatly in arrears of pay, money being scarce at the Cape.'[99] By contrast, if the Company was

---

Owen from the recruiting service at the Cape of Good Hope.' See BL, IOR, E/4/57, Military Department, Fort William, to Court of Directors, 28 August 1797, paragraph 184.

[96] Letter from the Governor and Council of Fort William to Sir David Baird, 18 December 1806, *RCC*, vol. VI, p. 67.

[97] 'Instructions to Major General Sir David Baird' [c.July 1805], *RCC*, vol. V, p. 226.

[98] Marcus Arkin, 'John Company at the Cape: A History of the Agency under Pringle (1794–1815)', *Archives Year Book for South African History 1960* (Pretoria: Government Printer, 1961), pp. 177–344, pp. 208–9.

[99] BL, Add. MS 13787, f. 12, Robert Patton to Wellesley, 16 February 1804.

prepared to pay, the implication seemed to be that a significant boost to its military forces could be recruited from Southern Africa.

Once the British hold on the Cape had been secured in 1806, more recruitment schemes for armies in India surfaced. Some of these made explicit reference to previous efforts, such as that of John Owen. Lieutenant-Colonel Lamington Baillie of the Bengal Cavalry, for example, referred specifically to Owen's efforts in the late 1790s when he suggested supplying the Company's armies in India from among Dutch troops at the Cape:

Conceiving it to be probable that the Hon[ourable] the Court of Directors may deem it a desirable object to supply the Company's Artillery and other European Corps in India from among the Dutch troops now at the Cape in the same manner as was so successfully done by Major Owen subsequently to the capture of that place [in the] last war, I humbly beg leave to offer myself for this service.

Baillie's offer to make a material connection between the Indian subcontinent and the southern gateway to the Indian Ocean through the identification and recruitment of troops was based on a personal link. He put himself forward as a suitable person to undertake this task based on 'a long residence in that part of Africa; a general acquaintance with the inhabitants and a knowledge of the Dutch language will appear to you to render me sufficiently qualified to execute this duty to the entire satisfaction of your Hon[ourable] Court'.[100]

Discussions about recruitment for India were not just confined to the East India Company and its armies. Sir David Baird, who was in command of the expeditionary force sent to capture the Cape in 1805, received pleas from the East India Company. But he was also sent instructions which specifically alluded to the possibility of recruiting troops for the king's forces. Reports had reached Lord Castlereagh in London of disaffection among the mainly German garrison in the service of the Dutch in Southern Africa. Baird was one of the army commanders in India who had benefited from reinforcements sent from the Cape by Lord Macartney. As we have seen, soldiers dispatched from the Cape played an active and important role when Baird and his men captured Seringapatam in southern India, the capital of Tipu Sultan of Mysore, in 1799. More than most, then, he was aware of the potential military benefits when he arrived at the Cape in 1806. Baird was instructed to enlist as many men as he could, with Castlereagh encouraging him to 'take the earliest opportunity of inducing them to enter into his Majesty's 60th Regiment'. In this instance, the soldiers were being recruited into the

[100] BL, IOR, E/1/113, p. 153, Baillie to East India Company, 8 April 1806.

Crown forces. However, the process of troop procurement provides a useful window on to the increasingly intertwined and symbiotic relationship between Crown and Company in India. As a result, Baird was given further orders. If, after using his best endeavours to 'procure the whole of these men for the King's service', there were any remaining, Baird was advised to recruit these men for the East India Company's armies. They were to be enlisted 'according to the terms of enlistment usual in the European branch of their army'.[101] When Baird's troops eventually captured Cape Town in 1806, they acquired 370 guns from the city's fortifications, and took 400 soldiers and 270 sailors as prisoners. Most of the soldiers were Waldeckers in the service of the Dutch. Baird agreed they would not be pressed into British service, but he also had to consider Castlereagh's instructions to recruit as many of them as possible. He solved the dilemma by locking them up in the Amsterdam battery on short rations and then offering a bounty of 20 rixdollars each – about £4 sterling – to any of them willing to sign up for service. A total of 270 enlisted, to be spread among all Crown regiments.[102] Rather than retaining these new recruits at the Cape, Castlereagh had instructed Baird to 'attach a considerable proportion of them to the regiments proceeding to India'.[103] Ultimately, then, the service of these men was redistributed from Africa to the Indian subcontinent.

Troops: gateway to the world

Troop movements and exchanges did not just flow in one direction. Although much logistical and organisational effort was expended on getting manpower to India, this reflects only part of the military connection that existed between the southern gateway and the maritime world of which it was a part. In the context of the Indian Ocean in which British power was being increasingly exerted, soldiers also moved in the opposite direction: from India to the South Atlantic. This reciprocal movement highlights the extent to which the oceanic system became integrated, and the part played by places like St Helena and the Cape in facilitating this. One author, writing about St Helena at the beginning of the nineteenth

---

[101] 'Instructions to Major-General Sir David Baird, 25 July 1805', enclosure in Lord Castlereagh to Admiralty, 25 July 1805, in William Gordon Perrin (ed.), *The Naval Miscellany: Volume 3* (London: Naval Records Society, 1928), p. 211.

[102] John Grainger, 'The Conquest of the Cape, 1806', *Army and Quarterly and Defence Journal* 123 (1993), pp. 320–1.

[103] 'Most Secret, Castlereagh to Baird, 10 September 1805', enclosure in Admiralty to Home Popham, 24 September 1805, in Perrin (ed.), *Naval Miscellany*, pp. 221–2.

century, was clear that the island had much to gain from looking east for its military requirements:

Besides, as the troops of the East Indies, instead of knowing their duty, merely from the exercises of parades and field days, are trained up in a scene of perpetual warfare, and under the eye of officers, inured to the most arduous services, there would be a further advantage in recruiting the military establishment of St Helena, from the regiments of India.[104]

Indeed, many 'General Returns' from the island echo that of June 1797 in expressing the hope that the garrison would 'retain a good many discharged soldiers returning from India on the next fleet'.[105]

In contrast to the predominantly European regiments being taken to India, this aspect of the relationship highlights the mobility of indigenous troops and the flexibility and fluidity of British imperial networks. The empire could not rely on European soldiers alone. Much imperial manpower was recruited from non-European sources. This was particularly the case for institutions like the East India Company.[106] By 1808, for example, there were approximately 155,000 sepoys, or Indian soldiers, in the Company's service.[107] Units of the Company's sepoy army were, on several occasions, dispatched overseas in support of its trading activities and to counter the threat posed by hostile powers. This became a regular feature of Indian Army life in the first half of the nineteenth century. And this trend was confirmed, rather than initiated, by a parliamentary select committee report of 1868: it advocated the deployment of Indian, rather than British or locally raised, forces in colonial territories around the Indian Ocean.[108] The realities on the ground had reflected this long before Parliament in London took notice.

Schemes for attacking South America, for instance, often included troops from India. In 1779, the military engineer and East India Company official, John Call, put forward a scheme 'for an expedition to the South Seas'. In doing so, he advocated using troops from India to give 'countenance and support to the inhabitants of Chili and Peru ... to fulfil their disposition and throw off the Spanish Yoke'.[109] The following year, a similar scheme was proposed which enumerated more precisely the

---

[104] Anon., *Island of St Helena*, p. 118.
[105] B'hurst, MS.062/15, General Return, 3 June 1797.
[106] For an examination of the ways in which the East India Company recruited for its Bengal Army, see Alavi, *Sepoys and the Company*.
[107] Omissi, *Sepoy and the Raj*, pp. 1, 3.
[108] Thomas R. Metcalf, *Imperial Connections: India in the Indian Ocean Arena, 1860–1920* (Berkeley, CA: University of California Press, 2007), pp. 13–14, 70.
[109] TNA, HO 42/7, f. 50, Copy of a Paper left with Lord Sydney by Colonel [John] Call [c.1785].

personnel required. William Fullarton estimated that 'a body of 1500 British troops with 2000 Mahomedan Lascar Sepoys' from Madras 'escorted by a detachment from Sir Edward Hughes's Squadron would be sufficient to ensure this undertaking'.[110] Later in the century, troops from even further afield were billeted for deployment in South America. The region's strategic hubs also played a part in facilitating these activities. In 1797, for example, the Admiralty considered using the Cape as a base for a detachment of 'about 500 men which are to be taken from the corps now in New South Wales'. They would join soldiers from Britain already located at the Cape, where the entire enterprise was to be fitted out and provided 'with such military stores as Major General Craig may conceive to be requisite for this service'.[111] A few years later, Henry Dundas's plans for neutralising the Spanish by attacking their interests in South America involved 'a force of between twelve and fifteen thousand troops at the utmost'. But this could not be achieved solely by military units from Europe. As well as a 'black corps', an 'establishment on the coast of Chile ought to be secured by a force to be sent from the Cape of Good Hope, and from India'.[112] And the tiny island of St Helena, with its small but usefully located garrison, could also offer assistance when it came to supplying troops for action in South America.[113] In return for some modifications to St Helena's semaphore system, the governor provided some 200 men from the island's permanent garrison for Home Popham's endeavour.[114]

And it was not just in South America where troops from elsewhere could come in useful. As early as the 1780s, with the East India Company trying to drum up support in government circles for an assault on the Cape, Indian troops were seen as a way of readily reinforcing any future British garrison at the Cape should it require military support. Laurence Sulivan and Sir William James 'humbly conceive that a garrison of three thousand men will be fully sufficient to keep possession of the Cape, and we can and will strengthen it by any number of disciplined sepoys from India, which shall be done, if required, in four months from the date of capture'.[115] Henry Pemberton's plan to establish a settlement at 'Croem

---

[110] BL, IOR, L/PS/1/6, William Fullarton, 'Proposal of an Expedition to South America by India, Laid before the Cabinet by Lord North', 3 June 1780.

[111] TNA, ADM 2/1352, pp. 11, 12, Admiralty to Thomas Pringle, 26 January 1797.

[112] TNA, PRO 30/8/243, pp. 97–8, Dundas, 'Memorandum for the Consideration of HM's Ministers', 31 March 1800.

[113] Patton to Baird, 27 December 1806, RCC, vol. VI, pp. 70–1.

[114] Hugh Popham, A Damned Cunning Fellow: The Eventful Life of Rear-Admiral Sir Home Popham KCB, KCH, KM, FRS, 1762–1820 (Tywardreath: Old Ferry Press, 1991), p. 148.

[115] BL, IOR, H/154, p. 278, Laurence Sulivan and William James to Lord Hillsborough, 25 October 1781.

Riviere Bay' was to be advanced by 'a battalion of seapoys [*sic*] from India (and with whom the country would most likely agree, being sufficiently warm)'.[116] When the Cape eventually came into British hands, some fifteen years later, the new governor revived the idea. Lord Macartney told General Sydenham that the more he saw of the colony, 'the more I am confirmed in my opinion of having an establishment here of 2 or 3 complete battalions of sepoys but that measure must be left to my successor'.[117]

With the prospect of further and more widespread military action in the region in the following decade, Lord Castlereagh also advocated using Indian troops. Prospective assaults on Mozambique and Delagoa Bay required careful planning, not just for the initial capture but in thinking about how best and most efficiently to secure and defend them. Castlereagh suggested that native regiments from India might be used to garrison these places.[118] Around the same time, a British colony on Madagascar was proposed. The advocate was convinced that such an endeavour would only require 'a few people possessed of the useful arts ... to form a colony of the utmost consequence to Great Britain'. But his calculations were predicated on the venture being supported by 'a garrison of sepoys from the East Indies'.[119] And, of course, these men needed supplies. As Robert Farquhar pointed out, 'until we shall have obtained a better knowledge of the resources of Madagascar it is necessary that the native troops should be supplied regularly with all kinds of provisions from India'.[120]

Just as recruiting from the Cape to supply India inspired some specific plans, so the idea of manning the South Atlantic gateway region with Indian troops also encouraged much discussion. On 23 September 1806, for example, Thomas Grenville sent a plan to the Chairman of the East India Company. Grenville, who was First Lord of Admiralty during his brother's short-lived administration, suggested 'putting into practice the very desirable experiment of extending the service of some of the Sepoy troops in India to the defence of the Cape of Good Hope'.[121] Grenville's plan was one of several that advocated employing Indian troops elsewhere in the world. Indeed, many envisaged the deployment of Indian soldiers

---

[116] BL, IOR, G/9/1, p. 22, Pemberton, 'Narrative', p. 22.
[117] RH, MSS.Afr.t.3, Macartney to Major General Sydenham, 12 September 1797.
[118] Castlereagh to Robert Dundas, 13 December 1807, *Londonderry*, vol. VIII, p. 95.
[119] HRO, 38M49/5/61/20, 'Observations on the Island of Madagascar', p. 4.
[120] BL, IOR, H/701, p. 164, Robert Farquhar to Lord Minto, 5 February 1811.
[121] BL, IOR, F/1/3, p. 309, Board of Commissioners for the Affairs of India, 23 September 1806. For a spirited objection to Grenville's plan, see BL, IOR, H/88, pp. 379–97, Dissent of Jacob Bosanquet to the plan proposed by Thomas Grenville, 15 October 1806.

even further afield. In 1804, Robert Percival had published his ideas about the potential contribution that sepoys could make to imperial defence: 'Were any sudden attempt to be made on our West-India Islands, a force from the Cape might in the same manner speedily arrive to their relief; and that mortality be in a great measure prevented which has rendered those colonies the graves of so many Europeans.'[122] And views such as these, perhaps partially influenced by ongoing concerns regarding the raising of black regiments in the Caribbean, gained currency at the very highest echelons of government. Early in 1806, the same year in which Grenville floated his plan, Lord Minto conceived of an even more ambitious arrangement for the strategic deployment of sepoy regiments. Minto was soon to play an important role in the subcontinent, when he was appointed governor general in late 1806. But in the early part of the year, he was President of the Board of Control, with responsibility for oversight of Indian affairs. He wrote to William Windham, War Secretary in Lord Grenville's Cabinet, about a discussion that he had with the Chairman and Deputy Chairman of the Company concerning the employment of sepoy troops. The use of Indian soldiers to reinforce the Cape was perceived as being relatively easy to achieve: 'There seems no reason to doubt that the sepoys will engage very readily in this service.'[123] But the range of Minto's ambitions for the use of sepoy troops did not stop at the Cape:

On considering this matter a good deal I really flatter myself with the hope that this resource may be found available much beyond the limited object of furnishing a garrison to the Cape of Good Hope. The small garrison of St Helena may easily be supplied from India, and I cannot perceive any difficulty in employing any number of sepoys that may be thought advisable at Gibraltar and Malta, or any other service in that quarter.[124]

The use of the gateway as an exit from the Indian Ocean, as much as an entrance to it, was very much part of the political and logistical calculations. The ultimate prize to be gained – the 'great object' from Minto's point of view – was the deployment of Indian troops in the West Indies, an area of the world that required constant infusions of new troops to replace those lost through disease and death. Minto acknowledged the practical difficulties in this part of his plan. Its chances of success were 'more doubtful'. Although 'there seems reason to expect that the climate of the West Indies will prove less fatal to natives of the East Indies than to English troops', Minto conceded that 'it may be found prejudicial even to

[122] Percival, *Account*, p. 336.
[123] BL, IOR, F/2/2, p. 121, Minto to William Windham, 25 May 1806.
[124] BL, IOR, F/2/2, pp. 121–2, Minto to Windham, 25 May 1806.

them'. He thought it 'prudent therefore to make this experiment on a small scale'. His plan involved the deployment of 'about 2 battalions or something less than 2000 sepoys to the West Indies from the Cape of Good Hope after they had been some time, say 6 months at the latter place; some break in the voyage from India to the West Indies is necessary; and that would be obtained in the way I have mentioned'.[125] The sorts of plans advocated by Grenville, Percival and Minto would have, in effect, created a global pool of British military personnel, to be drawn upon by the most needful places, at times when their presence was most required. Sepoys would become what Thomas Metcalf has described as 'an unmatched imperial ready reserve'.[126]

All of these examples are evidence of Britain's aspiration to move military personnel around the world speedily, giving it a strategic flexibility that no other nation could match.[127] This ability also encouraged military commanders, politicians and administrators to think globally about the military forces at their disposal. This is highlighted in the positive reply that Minto received from Windham: 'There can be no doubt that if the point can be carried of inducing the sepoys to embark and to extend their services to stations and settlements out of India, an immense accession will be made to the military strength of the empire.'[128] Picking up on arguments that had, at this stage, become axiomatic, Windham agreed that the Cape would be a useful starting point. Its 'climate is favourable, the voyage not long, and the situation such as would make the communication easy and frequent':

I should think that to the Cape a number not less than 2000 might be sent in the first instance setting free a portion of the European garrison to that amount, who might either be recalled to Europe or sent to the West Indies, or be made to repay directly to India the assistance she had thus furnished.[129]

The plan never seems to have been brought to fruition, perhaps through a lack of need, but also probably due to the particularly febrile political climate at the time, with several changes of administration, and consequently policy, within a very short space of time.[130] But the advantages to be gained from such plans still occupied strategists and commentators. Robert Percival summarised the benefits to be derived from using the Cape as a military springboard for the defence of wider British interests:

---

[125] BL, IOR, F/2/2, pp. 122–3, Minto to Windham, 25 May 1806.
[126] Metcalf, *Imperial Connections*, p. 69.
[127] Davey, 'Repatriation of Spanish Troops from Denmark, 1808', p. 693.
[128] BL, IOR, F/2/2, p. 139, Windham to Minto, 26 May 1806.
[129] BL, IOR, F/2/2, pp. 139–40, Windham to Minto, 26 May 1806.
[130] See John D. Grainger (ed.), *The Royal Navy in the River Plate, 1806–1807* (London: Navy Records Society, 1996), pp. x, 352.

'The facility and expedition with which troops can be sent from it to the East or West-Indies, to South America, or to any part of the coasts of Africa, must enable us to counteract ... every attempt which might be prejudicial to our interests.'[131] Troops, no matter what direction they were travelling, provided the glue for binding together British interests in the wider Indian Ocean region. The example of Mauritius reinforces this point.

Mauritius

A medal commissioned by the East India Company and struck by its mint in Calcutta expresses something of the British reliance on Indian troops in the region, as well as the way in which military personnel connected this oceanic world.[132] Forty-five gold and 2,156 silver versions of this medal were awarded to Bengal troops who brought the defence of Britain's Asian empire to the furthest southern reaches of the Indian Ocean. These soldiers served at the capture of Rodrigues, Ile de Bourbon, and Ile de France. The obverse shows a sepoy standing on the shore with five vessels in the distant harbour. His right arm is raised, waving the Union Flag; in his left, he holds a musket with fixed bayonet. He tramples the prostrate sceptre of France underfoot. The reverse of the medal gives more details, confirming in a Persian inscription that the medal was 'conferred in commemoration of the bravery and accustomed fidelity exhibited by the Sepoys of the English Company in the capture of the Mauritius Islands in the year of Hegira 1226'.[133] The object offers tangible evidence of the ways in which agents moved (or were moved) around the Indian Ocean in support of wider imperial agendas. Indeed, Britain's entire web of oceanic and maritime connections was brought to bear on the operation, demonstrating the way in which the Indian Ocean worked as a connected strategic space bridged by military networks. The capture of Mauritius crystallises many of the key themes about the movement of personnel and the way in which this inscribes a nascent British Empire in the southern gateway to the Indian Ocean world.

Richard Wellesley's strategic priorities for the Royal Navy at the Cape included transporting troops from the Cape to India, supplementing

[131] Percival, *Account*, p. 335.
[132] See MED0014, National Maritime Museum, Greenwich (http://collections.rmg.co.uk /collections/objects/40475.html, accessed 23 July 2015). See also Peter B. Boyden, Alan J. Guy and Marion Harding (eds.), *'Ashes and Blood': The British Army in South Africa, 1795–1914* (London: National Army Museum, 1999), pp. 196–7.
[133] Charles Winter, 'Gold and Silver Medals of the Honourable East India Company', *British Numismatic Journal* 17 (1923/24), pp. 281–7, p. 287.

Admiral Peter Rainier's squadron in the East Indies, and reinforcing John Blankett's naval forces in the Red Sea as Britain prepared to take on Napoleon's armies in Egypt. More than any of these, however, Wellesley concluded that 'the immediate and effectual blockade of the Isle of France' was 'the most important [objective] of all those which I have enumerated'.[134] The intrinsic advantages offered, as well as the danger posed by these islands in the southern Indian Ocean while they remained in the hands of the French, made them an important military objective. Ultimately, securing them depended on troop deployments from both India and the Cape.

Wellesley recognised the complexity of the operation. He attempted to create a grand alliance of troops and military power to descend on this corner of the ocean. He wrote to the Cape, soliciting troop reinforcements in order to assist his schemes to launch a pre-emptive strike on the French islands.[135] On 26 January 1801, he provided Sir Roger Curtis with further details about the prospective assault on the islands. Although Wellesley thought that the force he had assembled at Batavia was large enough to capture Mauritius, he still felt the need to err on the side of caution and request additional support:

It is however advisable that your Excellency should convey from the Cape of Good Hope, for the purpose of cooperating with troops from India, as large a European detachment, particularly of artillery, as may be in the power of His Excellency the Governor of the Cape of Good Hope to afford for that service.[136]

He also wrote to the colony's governor, Sir George Yonge, to request 'every assistance in troops, provisions, and military stores which may be practicable, and which the actual strength of the enemy in the Isle of France at the departure of the expedition from the Cape of Good Hope may appear to require'.[137] He sought artillery and reinforcements for regiments in India. The responses from Sir George Yonge to these requests betrayed a more realistic and pragmatic understanding of the difficulties that would be encountered by any invasion expedition destined for Mauritius. Yonge had discovered details about the state of the island's defences and, as a result, he was not as sanguine about the likelihood of success, as he had consistently pointed out to Wellesley. He acknowledged that if he 'were to listen to what some both in the sea and land service supposed to have some knowledge on the subject suggest

---

[134] BL, Add. MS 13784, ff. 22–3, Richard Wellesley to Roger Curtis, 25 October 1800.
[135] See Raymond D'Unienville and Marina Carter, *The Last Years of the Isle of France (1800–1814)* (Curepipe: La Société de L'Histoire de L'Île Maurice, 2010).
[136] Wellesley to Curtis, 26 January 1801, *RCC*, vol. III, pp. 410–15.
[137] BL, Add. MS 13784, f. 44, Wellesley to Yonge, 26 January 1801.

I would say that this is very easily accomplished'. But Yonge was, in this regard at least, not so easily duped: 'I have thought it my duty to obtain some more accurate information on this point and it is right you should be informed that this enterprise tho' certainly practicable is however not as easy as may be imagined.'[138] He was reticent to send troops and, ultimately, Wellesley's plan did not materialise.

It would be another decade before the neutralisation of the Iles de France and Bourbon was carried out with military assistance from the Cape in the second half of 1810, offering a more comfortable position to Britain in the region. Lord Minto in India received instructions from the Secret Committee of the East India Company to proceed on an expedition against the French Indian Ocean islands. Yet again, the 'reduction' of the French islands would depend on 'troops from Bengal and Fort St George'.[139] The governor of Bombay was instructed to provide two regiments, which were to proceed directly to Rodrigues, an island 350 miles to the east of the Ile de France. This was to be the base for the larger operations. Meanwhile, Lord Minto informed the man who would take over the government of the island in the event of a successful British assault, Robert Farquhar, that the troops for its 'reduction' would be drawn from India, Ceylon and the Cape.[140] The garrison intended for the island after its acquisition was similarly polyglot in nature. Some 3,000 Europeans and 2,000 sepoys would be treated as if they were serving in the subcontinent, even though they were to be 'furnished entirely if possible from the troops of the Cape and of Ceylon'.[141]

Minto's intention to 'purge the eastern side of the globe of every hostile or rival European establishment' is reminiscent of Wellesley. It is also indicative of the way in which the wider Indian Ocean continued to be an important consideration for the British governor general in Calcutta.[142] Minto led an expedition against Java personally. In relation to the French Indian Ocean islands, however, troop movements and reinforcements from within the region were, once more, the crucial means of effecting these objects. Admiral Bertie informed his Admiralty superiors in London of the decision made by Lord Caledon 'to send from the Cape two

---

[138] BL, Add. MS 13785, f. 23, Yonge to Wellesley, 7 February 1800.

[139] NUL, Mi 2F 23, Extract from Bengal Military Consultations relating to the Reduction and Capture of the Isle of France, 8 October 1811.

[140] BL, IOR, H/701, p. 23, Minto to Farquhar, 22 October 1810. For further details, see G. S. Misra, *British Foreign Policy and Indian Affairs, 1783–1815* (London: Asia Publishing House, 1963), p. 89.

[141] BL, IOR, H/701, pp. 28–9, Minto to Farquhar, 22 October 1810.

[142] Quoted in Alan J. Guy, 'British Strategy and the Cape of Good Hope in the Era of the French Revolutionary and Napoleonic Wars', in Boyden, Guy and Harding (eds.), *'Ashes and Blood'*, pp. 32–43, p. 43, n. 33.

regiments to cooperate in the reduction of the Isle of France, upon a requisition being made for that purpose'.[143] Caledon was following a precedent. The following month, the 72nd and 87th regiments were 'ready to embark whenever sufficient tonnage may arrive for their conveyance'.[144] But he was also signalling the further consolidation of the region as part of the British Indian Ocean world.

Projecting and consolidating power: troops in emergency

The relationship between the southern gateway to the Indian Ocean and Britain's interests in the rest of that oceanic world was not solely about providing a regular and healthy supply of troops to India. Local tensions and wider global concerns at times of war meant that there was often a need for immediate reinforcements to bolster the subcontinent's existing contingent of military manpower. The incorporation of the Cape in particular allowed East India Company personnel and government officials alike to call quickly on troops from the region in order to protect, attack or project power as the need arose. Throughout the second half of the eighteenth century, but especially as the French Wars spawned domestic problems, troops simply could not be spared from Europe. As Dundas informed Macartney, 'in the present situation of our forces at home and with the rebellion which unfortunately rages in Ireland, no assistance whatever can be sent from this country'.[145] And, as we have seen, supplies of new recruits from Europe were negligible. Therefore, the southern reaches of the southern Atlantic and Indian oceans became important in offering a staging point for sending troops where they were needed most.

As noted above, plans for attacking South America often relied on personnel from the Cape and St Helena, which could be mobilised quickly and with less risk than taking troops from elsewhere. But it also applied to India itself and underlined the value of holding power in this 'half-way house'. Robert Brooke thought that St Helena could offer some excellent advantages further afield as 'young recruits for India might be trained up with great advantage here, both for the King's and Companies [sic] regiments'. Crucially, Brooke identified that the principal benefit would be in the case of 'critical emergencies', when 'serious aid might be afforded for any expedition distant from Europe'.[146] On his way to take up his appointment at the Cape,

[143] Albemarle Bertie to John Wilson Croker, 12 July 1810, *RCC*, vol. VII, p. 336.
[144] Lieutenant General Grey to Lord Caledon, 25 August 1810, *RCC*, vol. VII, p. 353.
[145] UWits, A88/b47, Dundas to Macartney, 18 June 1798.
[146] BL, IOR, G/32/165, p. 4, Brooke, 'Account of St Helena'.

Macartney had similar thoughts in mind when he asked Brooke about 'the actual state of your strength and force at St Helena'. His curiosity was not entirely disinterested, for Macartney was calculating 'in case of emergency, what part of it [St Helena's military force], if any, and for how long, could be spared if wanted [i.e. needed] to cooperate with me at the Cape?'.[147] Brooke was happy to assure his compatriot that he would be 'ready at an instant's warning to afford some assistance in well trained men and light field pieces'.[148] Macartney's musings were particularly relevant as, only a few years before, troops from the island had assisted at the capture of the Cape. General Craig wrote to Robert Brooke, assuring him that 'no augmentation could be "so inconsiderable as not to be acceptable"'. Ultimately 'nine pieces of field artillery, a complete company of artillery, and three of infantry' were sent, amounting to some 400 men with 'ten thousand pounds in case, and a supply of ammunition and salt provisions'.[149] The following decade, Lord Castlereagh thought that it might make more sense to attempt an assault on South-East Africa by deploying 'a force from the Cape rather than from Bombay'.[150] In all of these cases, military manpower in the South Atlantic was identified as a mobile agent of imperial consolidation or expansion. Having a series of secure bases, and having these manned adequately could prove to be very useful. The way in which troops moved around and within the region in times of emergency demonstrates how adept British strategists, military men and colonial officials had become at shuttling troops around for the maximum advantage abroad.

During times of war, careful planning was paramount: unless recruitment from other sources was a possibility, moving troops to one area generally necessitated their removal from another. Unsurprisingly, given the strategic importance claimed for the region, the potential problem of being left exposed by poorly conceived deployments did not go unnoticed. Lady Anne Barnard alluded to the pervasive fears (or hope, depending on one's political allegiances) of a French invasion sparked by a movement of military personnel, which circulated within the colonial community at the Cape. In a diary entry for 16 June 1799, she recounted the story of one of the Dutch rebels captured at Graaff-Reinet spreading the rumour that 'the French were carrying all before them, that they were going on to take India from us, and that we had sent away all our soldiers from the Cape to defend it, that they would be at the Cape before it was

[147] RH, MSS.Afr.t.3, Macartney to Brooke, 29 March 1797.
[148] B'hurst, MS.062/14, Brooke to Macartney, 1 June 1797.
[149] Brooke, St Helena, p. 310.
[150] Castlereagh to Robert Dundas, 13 December 1807, Londonderry, vol. VIII, p. 95.

long'.[151] Her husband, Andrew Barnard, was also wary about leaving this key strategic base undefended. He was convinced of 'the absolute necessity' of reinforcing the garrison in South Africa 'as we have not at present a force sufficient for the protection of the place'.[152] Nevertheless, in Britain's wider maritime empire, of which this region was becoming an increasingly important part, Indian security generally assumed priority. Richard Wellesley's constant demands, for example, did not brook any reservations from the British authorities in Southern Africa. He made his views abundantly clear that the Cape, and any military personnel there, were an adjunct to British India: they were essentially 'part of the Indian force'.[153] And he hoped that 'the military resources of the Cape of Good Hope will always be applied with the utmost alacrity and judgment to their true object, the preservation of our Empire in the East'.[154]

The strategic advantage of the Cape as the 'Key to India', lauded by so many politicians, travellers and merchants, was frequently tested in practice by a number of military conflicts, mutinies and other upheavals in India. In addition to specific events in India – such as the danger posed by Tipu Sultan in Mysore at the end of the eighteenth century, the Vellore Mutiny of 1806 or the so-called 'white mutiny' three years later – the shadow of potential military emergency loomed large in the thoughts of those advocating the Cape as a military entrepôt and source of troops. As well as providing a base for landing, mustering and deploying troops, the proximity of the Cape to India meant that it could quickly supply troops in the case of military emergency in the subcontinent. Wellesley advised Dundas that, as a depot for 'the maintenance of a military force in India, the Cape is invaluable . . . it would furnish easy means of pouring in troops either upon the coast of Coromandel or of Malabar in such a state of health as to be able to encounter all the inconveniences of an Indian climate'.[155] Robert Percival, admittedly hardly an impartial observer, expressed a common fear but also offered a potential solution:

Were the native princes of India to make such head against us, as that our army there required speedy reinforcements, we could from the Cape convey troops thither in less than half the time in which they could be sent from Europe; and with the additional advantage of their being already seasoned to the climate, and able immediately to act against the enemy.[156]

[151] Margaret Lenta (ed.), *Paradise, the Castle and the Vineyard: Lady Anne Barnard's Cape Diaries* (Johannesburg: Wits University Press, 2006), p. 90.
[152] RH, GB 0162 MSS.Afr.s.1,2, Barnard to Dundas, 20 October 1799.
[153] Wellesley to Dundas, 28 February 1798, *Two Views*, p. 42.
[154] Wellesley to Yonge, 24 October 1800, *RCC*, vol. III, p. 343.
[155] Wellesley to Dundas, 28 February 1798, *Two Views*, p. 41.
[156] Percival, *Account*, pp. 335–6.

Given his forthright views, it is perhaps hardly surprising that, during his time as governor general, Wellesley was one of the most active Indian officials in making use of this pool of potential military personnel, even if he was decidedly more ambivalent about recruiting from soldiers formerly in the service of the Dutch there.[157] For example, when Lord Macartney arrived at the Cape to become the first British civilian governor, he was strongly encouraged by Wellesley immediately to forward a portion of the troops at his disposal to India. The governor general wrote to Macartney and Sir Hugh Christian, the commander of the naval forces in Southern Africa, reminding them of their duty. He was uncompromisingly blunt about 'the necessity of their contributing to the defence of the coast of Malabar'. Although he did permit them to exercise their judgement and to be satisfied that 'the efforts of the French are directed solely to India, and that no attack is to be apprehended against the Cape', there is no question where Wellesley thought Britain's imperial priorities lay and to what use any military force at the Cape should be put: 'I should hope that, under such circumstances, we might expect to receive from the Cape the assistance of several ships of war, and of at least one regiment of European infantry, before the end of the month of February.'[158] Meanwhile, in Southern Africa, Macartney also recognised the fundamental connection between the Cape and Britain's Indian interests. He acknowledged 'the importance of seasoning and preparing our troops at the Cape previous to their serving in India'.[159]

The effectiveness of this connection can be tested by some of the practical demands on personnel precipitated by various crises in India. One of the gravest emergencies in the early years of British rule at the Cape was the increasingly aggressive stance of Tipu Sultan, ruler of Mysore in southern India. Tipu threatened the British position throughout the entire subcontinent, partially through the military prowess of his forces but also as a result of his alliance with the French. He was, as C. A. Bayly has suggested, the first of the '"black" bogeymen' to haunt British consciousness.[160] Stamping out this canker put great strain on the British forces on the ground, comprising both Company and Crown

[157] Wellesley played a crucial part in stopping the recruitment drive in its tracks: 'I have stopped the recruiting at the Cape, and I shall take early steps for getting rid of our foreign Europeans; but I fear it must be a work of a long time unless you can aid us with a large supply of recruits from England, or abolish the Company's European army altogether; which would be of the greatest benefit to the whole service.' See Wellesley to Dundas, 1 October 1798, *Two Views*, p. 81.
[158] BL, Add. MS 13456, f. 97, Wellesley to Dundas, 11 October 1798.
[159] NAS, GD51/1/530/12, Macartney to Dundas, 25 April 1801.
[160] C. A. Bayly, *Imperial Meridian: The British Empire and the World, 1780–1830* (London: Longman, 1989), p. 114.

regiments. But these were given succour by a detachment from the Cape, in one of Lord Macartney's last acts as governor. Macartney was influenced, it seems, by the report that Napoleon intended marching an army of 30,000 men to India.[161] As one of the most perceptive of Britain's officials serving in the Empire, and with considerable experience at Madras, he was keen to help. Macartney dashed off a letter to the governor general in India, assuring him that 'we shall send to Madras ... an efficient force of 1795 rank and file which we flatter ourselves will be able to proceed from hence in the first week of October'.[162] The 84th, which had been raised in York in 1793 and which had always been intended for service in India, arrived at Madras in January 1799.[163] As Macartney wrote to Henry Dundas, he and Dundas's nephew, General Francis Dundas, 'wished on every account to stretch to the utmost the assistance to be now sent to India, and upon calculating the indispensable demands of the service here, we found that there was not a man to spare beyond those we have retained'.[164]

Later, Macartney was able to reflect on the prospects that the Cape offered for precisely this sort of operation:

I had it in my power almost at a moment's notice to send to Madras under the command of Major General Baird above 2000 effective men in the highest health, vigor and discipline who eminently contributed to the capture of Seringapatam and the total subversion of the power of Tippoo.[165]

Meanwhile, Andrew Barnard wrote to India conveying a similarly positive message about the army that was about to embark: 'The whole of the troops are in the highest mettle and spirits and will be no inconsiderable reinforcement to the Madras Army.' Although reinforcements from Europe were always to be welcomed, the health and vigour of troops already acclimatised in South Africa was a great boon. Furthermore, it meant that men who might be 'nearly as much wanted at home' were spared the debilitating journey and climate.[166] As a result of Macartney's foresight, the transport ship, the *Sceptre*, arrived in India on 7 January 1799, with the troops under the command of General Baird. And they rapidly proved their worth to the wider British position, delivering an 'advantage ... in an eminent degree during the war against Tippoo Sultan' when they joined the Grand Army, and formed part of General

[161] Dorothea Fairbridge (ed.), *Lady Anne Barnard at the Cape of Good Hope, 1797–1802* (Oxford: Clarendon Press, 1924), p. 67.
[162] RH, MSS.Afr.t.3, Macartney to Wellesley, 11 September 1798.
[163] Boyden, Guy and Harding (eds.), *'Ashes and Blood'*, p. 192.
[164] RH, MSS.Afr.t.3, Macartney to Dundas, 18 September 1798.
[165] NAS, GD51/1/530/12, Macartney to Dundas, 25 April 1801.
[166] Fairbridge (ed.), *Lady Anne Barnard, at the Cape of Good Hope* p. 67.

Harris's force in the field.[167] Wellesley was sensible of this contribution, as well as Macartney's assistance, writing in appreciation:

This seasonable reinforcement[,] the timely arrival of which must be attributed to the alacrity and vigour of your Lordship's Government[,] has not only placed the safety of these possessions beyond the reach of all immediate danger from the enemy, but will I trust enable me to obtain effectual security from him against any advantages which he might have expected to derive hereafter from his alliance with the French.[168]

And Robert Percival recorded that the regiments were 'partaking in our glorious successes in India, and acting with unabated vigour and energy', offering yet another good reason for Britain to hold on to the Cape.[169]

There were, of course, logistical difficulties in supplying all of these troops speedily. When he was attempting to send reinforcements to take on Tipu, Macartney alluded to the 'very great difficulties in procuring sufficient tonnage for the present embarkation'.[170] He solved these by engaging private transportation. Captain Gilbert Mitchell, commanding the *Prince of Wales*, had arrived at the Cape with stores for the colony. Macartney prevailed upon Mitchell to assist by assuring him that he would 'very strongly' recommend him to Richard Wellesley 'for a Company's freight home'. He ventured to 'solicit' this for Mitchell with Wellesley and hoped that 'on account of the importance of the service he is employed on and his liberal behavior in undertaking it, you will be so good as to effect for him'.[171] Macartney made the same point to Dundas in London:

Our principal difficulty at present is a want of sufficient tonnage, and had it not been for the fortunate arrival of the Thetis, Loyalist, and Prince of Wales, which brought the stores for this Colony, shipped by Mr Davison, which we have taken up as transports for the present service, our means of providing for it would have been totally inadequate.[172]

With the help of these ships, however, Macartney hoped to be able to embark 'about 2229 souls, to be despatched for Madras under the command of Major General Baird' in ten or twelve days.[173] These military networks reveal, therefore, further links and connections.

Francis Dundas, nephew of Henry and Macartney's immediate successor and acting governor, continued the tradition of supplementing British troop resources in India. At the end of January 1799, he remarked

---

[167] Wellesley to Yonge, 24 October 1800, *RCC*, vol. III, p. 343.
[168] BL, Add. MS 13784, ff. 1–2, Wellesley to Macartney, 26 February 1799.
[169] Percival, *Account*, p. 337.
[170] RH, MSS.Afr.t.3, Macartney to Wellesley, 11 September 1798.   [171] *Ibid.*
[172] RH, MSS.Afr.t.3, Macartney to Dundas, 18 September 1798.   [173] *Ibid.*

to Lord Clive, the governor, and his council at Madras that he had 'determined to detain the 51st regiment here until a part of the very considerable reinforcement of troops sent from here should be replaced from Europe'. Since taking that decision, however, Dundas had been apprised of the situation in India and, having been urged by the governor general in Calcutta 'to augment the army of India, I have not hesitated to set aside my own wishes upon the occasion, although the important point gained over the French party in the Carnatic, of which we have since heard, must have very considerably changed the aspect of public affairs in your quarter of the globe'.[174] He followed this up by writing again some weeks later with the news that:

The Scotch Brigade and the 84th regiment embarked here for your presidency and sailed on 4 November under convoy of His Majesty's Ships the *Sceptre* and the *Raisonable*. By the present opportunity you will receive the 10th regiment of infantry from Britain and the 86th regiment from this garrison, together with some hundred recruits, of which the regular embarkation returns will be submitted to you.[175]

There was no doubt about the effect of these reinforcements in India. In 1799, evidence of their beneficial impact was described by the governor general in India: 'We have received [from the Cape] an effective force of 3000 testimony (if any were wanting) to prove the solid advantages of that useful possession.'[176] In Wellesley's eyes, 'the great utility of the Cape of Good Hope is to serve as an outpost to our Indian Empire, and a depot from which seasoned troops may suddenly be drawn for the defence of our possessions in the East in any emergency that may arise'.[177]

Throughout his governorship in India, and as his gubernatorial ambitions grew, Wellesley regarded the supply of troops from the Cape as absolutely requisite for filling the defensive gaps left by the deployment of Indian troops elsewhere. Like Macartney and Barnard at the Cape, he understood that the British position in India needed careful management so as not to be left short. He feared that London-based strategists might plan an attack on the French in Egypt from India, in concert with one from the Mediterranean. He expressed his concerns to Dundas in July 1800 that such an assault would present an 'immediate and imminent hazard to all our most valuable interests in India' by stripping it of its defensive troops. The only way to mitigate this danger, he felt, was 'that additional troops from Europe or from the Cape of Good Hope

---

[174] Francis Dundas to Lord Clive and Council, 31 January 1799, *RCC*, vol. II, p. 352.
[175] Francis Dundas to the Governor in Council, 18 February 1799, *RCC*, vol. II, p. 338.
[176] Wellesley to Dundas, 13 May 1799, *Two Views*, p. 148.
[177] Wellesley to Yonge, 24 October 1800, *Spencer*, vol. IV, p. 163.

should be dispatched instantly in order to replace without a moment of delay any European force which it may be determined to send from hence for this service'.[178] In October 1800, Wellesley wrote to Sir George Yonge, shortly to be replaced as governor of the Cape, requesting 'in the most earnest manner' that Yonge 'dispatch to India with the least practicable delay as considerable a reinforcement of European Infantry as it shall be possible for you to spare from the defence of the colony under your Excellency's Government'.[179] He felt that 'your Excellency will be enabled to send two Regiments of Infantry to India without incurring any considerable hazard during the period which must elapse before those corps can be replaced from England'.[180]

The governor general's objective seemed to be to curry a broad constituency of support in order to apply as much pressure as possible to Sir George. He wrote to the resident colonial secretary at the Cape, Andrew Barnard, requesting his help in obtaining additional troops: 'You will render an essential service to me, and to the public, by enforcing my request, and by expediting the embarkation of the troops. Our exigency is very pressing, and I rely on effectual aid from the Cape.'[181] Wellesley also wrote to Francis Dundas. Wellesley informed Dundas of his application for reinforcements to Sir George, and expressed the hope that Yonge would 'communicate my dispatches to you'. Looking to Dundas for support, he 'earnestly request[ed] the exertions of your talents and activity in accelerating the relief which I have requested from the Government of the Cape'.[182] Wellesley also contacted Sir Roger Curtis, commander of the naval forces in the region, exerting similar pressure on him.[183] Wellesley took it upon himself to proffer 'several suggestions with regard to the employment of HM Squadron under your command, for the purpose of aiding the defence of the British Empire in India in the present crisis of affairs'. He proceeded to enumerate these for Curtis, with the most important consideration helpfully placed at the top of the list:

First, to give convoy to India to any troops which may be embarked from the Cape of Good Hope in consequence of my application to His Excellency Sir George Yonge. I conceive this object to be indispensable and I conclude that one frigate would be sufficient for the purpose.[184]

---

[178] BL, Add. MS 13457, ff. 56–7, Wellesley to Dundas, 13 July 1800.
[179] Wellesley to Yonge, 24 October 1800, *RCC*, vol. III, p. 342.   [180] *Ibid.*, p. 343.
[181] BL, Add. MS 13784, f. 21, Wellesley to Andrew Barnard, 24 October 1800.
[182] BL, Add. MS 13784, f. 20, Wellesley to Francis Dundas, 24 October 1800.
[183] Wellesley to Curtis, 24 October 1800, *RCC*, vol. III, pp. 345–6.
[184] BL, Add. MS 13784, ff. 22–3, Wellesley to Curtis, 25 October 1800.

These demands did not go unnoticed. Andrew Barnard wrote to the previous governor, Lord Macartney – now safely ensconced back in Europe and dividing his time between his London home and his Antrim estates – informing him of Wellesley's demands on Yonge. Barnard's letter strikes a somewhat exasperated tone, acknowledging the advantages to be derived from such movements but also expressing concern at the thin coverage provided by the limited number of British troops in the wider Indian Ocean. Wellesley had urgently requested two regiments as he was 'fearful that the French will soon attempt something against India'. He had written to Barnard too, imploring him 'to press the matter as much as possible'. But the colonial secretary thought it likely that Wellesley's 'request will not be complied with, altho' we have five regiments of infantry and the 8th Dragoons which is more than compleat'. Barnard's assessment of the likelihood of success betrays the limits of Britain's military capabilities across the Indian Ocean, and the important role that carefully planned troop deployment could play in securing the arena:

One regiment I think we might spare, as there is an immediate opportunity of writing home to have it replaced; but I imagine there are good reasons for refusing to comply with His Lordship's request even in part, or else your Lordship's example would have been followed, and the regiments dispatched as fast as possible.[185]

The final decision, of course, rested with the governor of the colony. With that in mind, Wellesley wrote to Sir George Yonge again on the same issue in March 1801, urging immediate action:

In my dispatch of the 24th October 1800, I stated to your Excellency various considerations connected with the security and tranquillity of our Indian possessions which induced me to solicit a reinforcement of two European regiments from the Cape of Good Hope and I have subsequently repeated my request with a degree of earnestness proportional to the exigency of affairs in this country.[186]

The next day, Wellesley followed this up by outlining another service that Southern Africa could offer to the British position in the wider Indian Ocean. The governor general informed Yonge at the Cape that he 'had dispatched an armament from India to the Red Sea to co-operate with HM's and the Turkish forces assembled in the Mediterranean for the purposes of expelling the French from Egypt'. The success of the British troops being deployed depended 'essentially on their being furnished with

[185] Andrew Barnard to Macartney, 12 January 1801, in Fairbridge (ed.), *Lady Anne Barnard, at the Cape of Good Hope* p. 260.
[186] BL, Add. MS 13784, ff. 56–7, Wellesley to Yonge, 1 March 1801.

regular and ample supplies of provisions'.[187] As these could not be procured from India, Wellesley was convinced (or hopeful) that Yonge would 'make every practicable exertion to promote the success of the armament' by dispatching provisions and supplies to Mocha. But again Yonge was decidedly reticent about sending troops. Rehearsing an often-quoted theme, he worried about leaving the Cape exposed to enemy assault, identifying the southern approaches to India as the most important strategic prize to be protected.[188] He elaborated in communication with Henry Dundas – who had been replaced by Lord Hobart before the letter reached London – that the current state of defence at the Cape was simply not up to the task. Of course, in an ideal world, 'such demands would be answered with zeal and pleasure'. But given the circumstances that Yonge was struggling with, he lamented that it was 'full as likely that we might want succours from India, as that we can be equal to the sending any thither'.[189] Yonge held out hope that more troops might be sent from Europe, 'sufficient to form a strength equal to the idea of a military depot'. If that were the case, 'assistance of this kind may be conveniently furnished on extraordinary occasions'.[190]

More general emergencies

Yonge's replacement, Francis Dundas, was more pliant. Dundas sent troops to take part in British operations in Egypt. He hoped that the 'detachment from this garrison of about 1,200 men including officers' would 'reach their place of destination in the healthful state in which they embarked'. He reassured Wellesley that the troops had 'been provided here with every article necessary to enable them immediately to take the field', and that they were 'a very fine body of well disciplined soldiers'.[191] In August 1802, some 3,700 more troops were prepared for India. They would be embarked 'as soon as the ships shall severally arrive meant to convey them to their respective places of destination'. In cases of such large numbers, 'a much more considerable quantity of shipping' was naturally required.[192] Logistics mattered. In conducting his operation a few years earlier, Lord Macartney relied on 'the zeal and activity of the General and Admiral in forwarding every part of this service that depends upon them such as to transcend every praise of mine, and it is a pleasure to me, as well as a duty, to attempt, however imperfectly, to do

[187] Wellesley to Yonge, 2 March 1801, *RCC*, vol. III, p. 436.
[188] BL, Add. MS 13785, ff. 41–3, Yonge to Wellesley, 24 January 1801.
[189] Yonge to Dundas, 20 March 1801, *RCC*, vol. III, p. 447.   [190] *Ibid.*
[191] Francis Dundas to Wellesley, 17 May 1801, *RCC*, vol. III, p. 496.
[192] Francis Dundas to Lord Hobart, August 1802, *RCC*, vol. III, p. 354.

them justice'.[193] In November 1802, Dundas found himself with 417 soldiers still at the Cape. He and Curtis decided to procure whatever shipping they could for 'the conveyance of the regiments to their respective places of destination in India'. To achieve this, they had directed the East India Company's agent at the Cape, John Pringle, to engage the requisite number of transports 'upon the most moderate and reasonable terms'.[194]

Even premeditated movements of troops were often predicated on perceived or real threats to Indian security. The defence of the southern gateway to the Indian Ocean after the capture of the Cape did not prevent Sir David Baird receiving instructions from Lord Castlereagh in 1805, ordering him to supplement any deficiency in Indian armies. These were based on the assumption that British armies in India were under pressure, and that Baird was likely to receive information about this before London. In such circumstances, Baird should proceed, 'without delay, and at the hazard even of reducing your garrison', to 'detach the 38th and 93rd Regiments, consisting of the numbers stated in the margin to the East Indies, transmitting immediate notice thereof to me in order that adequate reinforcements may be sent out to join you'.[195] Castlereagh added up the figures, concluding that 991 men could be expected from the 38th Regiment and 882 from the 93rd Regiment. He continued by informing Baird that the government in London had, in effect, devolved authority to India for directing troop movements:

The same precautionary principles which have induced HM to direct the above instructions to be transmitted to you, have determined HM to give authority to Marquis Cornwallis, or the person in the Chief Command of HM's Troops in India for the time being, to send to the Cape for reinforcements; and you are hereby directed to comply with any requisition you may receive to that effect.[196]

Indeed Baird was warned not to wait for bad news from official channels but to act immediately, taking care to ensure that there were just enough troops to defend the Cape.[197] Sure enough, the Governor and Council at Calcutta requested troops from Baird immediately upon his taking the Cape. As Castlereagh had predicted, they were doing so because of what they perceived as a deteriorating security situation in the south of the subcontinent and the 'defective state of our European Force in India [which] urgently requires a reinforcement'.[198]

---

[193] RH, MSS.Afr.t.3, Macartney to Dundas, 18 September 1798.
[194] Francis Dundas to Hobart, 27 November 1802, *RCC*, vol. III, p. 451.
[195] 'Most Secret, Castlereagh to Baird, 10 September 1805', enclosure in Admiralty to Popham, 24 September 1805, in Perrin (ed.), *Naval Miscellany*, pp. 220–1.
[196] *Ibid.*, pp. 221–2.   [197] *Ibid.*.
[198] Governor and Council of Fort William to Baird, 18 December 1806, *RCC*, vol. VI, p. 67.

The troops travelling to Southern Africa under Baird's command were very much seen as a mobile military force that could be deployed as and when required around the Indian Ocean. During his time in South Africa, Baird received imploring letters from elsewhere. The governor of St Helena, Robert Patton, also looked to the Cape to mitigate a reduction in 'number and strength' of 'our very best men'. These troops were off fighting with Popham and Beresford in South America in support of an action which, as Patton was quick to point out, had been sanctioned by Baird at the Cape.[199]

Emergency infusions of troops continued throughout the period. As he sailed to take up his post as governor general, Lord Minto was also aware of the grave danger to the subcontinent. This time, however, the source of the trouble was domestic: the disaffection of Indian sepoys. He wrote hastily to George Tierney from the Cape. His passage to the subcontinent had been impeded by the need for repairs. But his stop at the Cape also exposed him to 'uncomfortable reports from passengers just arrived on a private trader from Madras'. The anxiety felt by Minto referred to 'the apprehension still prevailing there of disaffection in the native troops': 'No new event is mentioned but the uneasiness on that subject is said still to continue in that presidency, but not in other parts of India. It is said also that an augmentation of British troops is anxiously desired.'[200] Yet again, the forces at the Cape were stretched: 'General Grey could not share a regiment but if any troops are returned to him from La Plata, or sent out to the Cape from England, I flatter myself he will be disposed to forward a regiment to India, and the 83rd as the most complete would no doubt be the fittest.'[201] Minto's correspondent in Britain was less convinced of the urgency: 'What has come to my knowledge is far from comfortable but I am inclined to believe that the state of things is not quite so bad as some would [have] it.'[202] Despite the apparently sanguine reply, however, Tierney had made representations to the highest echelons of the army: 'When I officially [contacted] the Duke of York I availed myself of the opportunity to state to HRH the pressing necessity according to my opinion of further and considerable reinforcements being sent out.'[203]

In 1809, Lord Caledon, governor at the Cape, was eager to help out when another insurrection threatened the Company's possessions in the subcontinent.[204] He was left with 'the most gloomy impression upon my

[199] See Patton to Baird, 27 December 1806, *RCC*, vol. VI, pp. 70–1.
[200] HRO, 31M70/51/a, Minto to George Tierney, 18 May 1807.   [201] *Ibid.*
[202] HRO, 31M70/51/b, George Tierney to Minto, 1 October 1807.   [203] *Ibid.*
[204] See PRONI, D/2431/3/3, Official diary, 23 May 1809–31, March 1810. For more on Caledon's time in South Africa, see John McAleer, '"This *Ultima Thule*": The Cape of

mind for the ultimate fate of British India' when he found out from 'high and sufficient authority that a rebellion' had broken out there.[205] On this occasion, the crisis was precipitated when senior officers on the Madras establishment threatened to defy the orders of the government in protest at what one of the leaders of the movement, Lieutenant-Colonel the Honourable Arthur St Leger, described as the favouring of crown officers over Company officers in 'situations of active trust, responsibility and emolument'. Although the so-called 'white mutiny' spread across southern India, it was quelled with reinforcements of troops from Ceylon and, in the end, troops from the Cape were not required.[206] However, in considering the situation, Caledon was most alarmed 'that a very considerable proportion of the E. I. Company native troops headed by Commanding Officers of the Corps, are in a state of insubordination and mutiny'.[207] Plans were put in place for embarking 2,400 men, together with equipment and provisions.[208]

In situations like this, the interconnectedness of this world was brought home to people like Caledon; so too was its role as a military entrepôt for supplying troops to buttress British interests. Southern Africa may have been thousands of miles away from India, but Caledon knew where his priorities lay. According to one source, he was anxious 'to support the interests of the Company by all practical means'.[209] And John Pringle considered that he 'uniformly and scrupulously maintains in every respect the privileges of the Hon'ble Company' by supporting Indian interests through the transfer of troops.[210] In this, Caledon relied on people like Pringle, whom he praised lavishly for his 'uniform zeal'.[211] Caledon was cognisant that actions taken by him at the Cape might preserve the empire or, conversely, 'our torpor [might give] the last blow to the most valuable possession of the British crown'.[212] John Pringle was equally conversant

Good Hope, Ireland and Global Networks of Empire', *Eighteenth-Century Ireland* 29 (2014), pp. 63–84. For more on the disturbances in India that precipitated such action, see Arkin, 'John Company at the Cape', pp. 231–2.

[205] Henry Alexander to James Luson, 18 April 1809, quoted in Arkin, 'John Company at the Cape', p. 231.

[206] See Wolesley Haig, 'The Armies of the East India Company', in Henry H. Dodwell (ed.), *The Cambridge History of the British Empire: Volume V. The Indian Empire, 1858–1918* (Cambridge: Cambridge University Press, 1932), pp. 153–66, pp. 163–4.

[207] BL, IOR, G/9/10, p. 137, Caledon to Grey, 15 October 1809.

[208] See Arkin, 'John Company at the Cape', pp. 232–4.

[209] Alexander to Luson, 18 April 1809, quoted in Arkin, 'John Company at the Cape', p. 231.

[210] BL, IOR, G/9/7, p. 8, John Pringle to William Ramsay, 4 October 1808.

[211] BL, IOR, H/701, pp. 414–15, Caledon to Secret Committee, 9 November 1810.

[212] BL, IOR, G/9/10, p. 139, Caledon to Grey, 15 October 1809.

with the complexities of the situation, congratulating Henry Grey, the commander of the army in Southern Africa, on his exertions:

The decisive measures [ordered] by you on this most important occasion will, I earnestly hope, effectually contribute to disperse a storm which threatens the very existence of the Empire, and I can with great truth assure you, Sir, that my highest ambition will be to cooperate in all your views and wishes to the utmost extent of my ability.[213]

Writing to Caledon, Pringle was 'fully impressed with the extreme importance' of the situation. He was also aware and appreciative of the 'decided and noble manner in which Your Lordship has acted on an occasion perhaps the most critical for the British Empire that has occurred in this era of extraordinary events'.[214]

Over the next ten years, as British India came under attack from without and within its borders, there were many more solicitations for troop reinforcements. In the mid 1810s, troops stationed at the Cape reinforced the Indian armies on the outbreak of the Nepal War. In June and July 1815, feverish preparations were made to embark the 72nd Regiment as Lord Moira wrote a long, pleading and vaguely threatening letter to the Governor, Lord Charles Somerset.[215] The abject start to the war by the Company's forces, and 'the increasing confidence and means of the enemy', meant that Lord Moira felt obliged 'to direct against the enemy in the ensuing campaign the largest and most efficient force it may be practicable to assemble'.[216] Moira's explanations were building up to his 'solicitation' that Somerset would 'aid the exigencies of this Government from the resources of the colony under your government and command, by sending to India, with the least practicable delay, the largest reinforcements of European infantry which circumstances will admit of your sparing'.[217] Acquiescing in some of these demands, Somerset wrote to the Chairman of the East India Company, William Fullerton-Elphinstone, explaining the position as he saw it:

At the urgent solicitation of the Governor General of India, I have not hesitated to direct the immediate embarkation of HM's 72nd Regiment for Bengal, and regret that the reduced state of the force under my command renders it impracticable for me, at the moment, to give greater aid to the Indian Government under the peculiar situation in which the unfavourable state of affairs in Nepaul [sic] have placed it.[218]

---

[213] BL, IOR, G/9/18, p. 92, Pringle to Grey, 24 October 1809.
[214] BL, IOR, G/9/18, pp. 93–4, Pringle to Caledon, 25 October 1809.
[215] Moira to Somerset, 9 February 1815, RCC, vol. X, pp. 249–51.   [216] Ibid., p. 249.
[217] Ibid., p. 250.   [218] BL, IOR, G/9/4, p. 112, Somerset to Elphinstone, 19 June 1815.

He felt it was his duty, he continued, 'to submit to the judgement of His Majesty's Government at Home the expediency of having an adequate force on this station ready to meet the emergencies from time to time arising in the Eastern Empire'.[219] In outlining his position, Somerset followed terms similar to those laid out by his predecessors over the course of the previous decade of British rule at the Cape: the garrison and troops there were to be drawn upon principally for the sake of preserving Britain's empire in India.

Conclusion

One of the catalysts for the development of the web of British interests in the region was the movements of troops and the consequent drawing of the southern Atlantic and Indian oceans into the orbit of a developing British empire in Asia. The upheavals in India mirrored a wider view of this as an interconnected world: these things, as Lord Moira pointed out, deeply affected 'the national prosperity' but they 'may be deemed more immediately to involve the interests of the East India Company'.[220] The ultimate interconnectedness of this oceanic space was facilitated by the military network, which was one of the regular features of life at the colony. 'Every other thing that I can think of *goes on* pretty much as usual', Lady Anne Barnard wrote to Lord Macartney about the latest developments at the earl's former post, 'except our Regiments – they *go off*, the 86th to India'.[221] The Indian Ocean facilitated a vast web of connections, across which the British tried to assert their influence in the nineteenth century, with varying degrees of success. Even before the days of the telegraph, news travelled quickly and widely, drawing diverse parts of this entangled network together. Strategic troop deployment and recruitment was just one of the ways in which Britain used this 'key to the East' to secure its maritime empire in Asia.

---

[219] *Ibid.*   [220] Moira to Somerset, 9 February 1815, *RCC*, vol. X, p. 251.
[221] Lady Anne Barnard to Macartney, 25 January 1799, in Fairbridge (ed.), *Lady Anne Barnard, at the Cape of Good Hope* pp. 84–5.

6   Conclusions: 'the connection between the settlements becomes more intimate'

The southern reaches of the Atlantic and Indian oceans were often perceived by Europeans to be at 'the very extremity of the earth'.[1] But they were at the heart of Britain's maritime empire.[2] By focusing on the southern gateway to and from the Indian Ocean, this book has attempted to explore and explain the consolidation of the British position in the region, the logistics associated with this, and the reorientation of the British Empire eastwards in the second half of the eighteenth century. The routes of travel, channels of communication and networks of connection facilitated by this region were crucial to the maintenance, development and expansion of Britain's commercial and political interests in Asia. These routes and networks played a vital role in the consolidation and extension of British power in the Indian Ocean, and deeply influenced the nature and exercise of that power.

The multiplicity of functions fulfilled by the region in the development of the nineteenth-century British Empire was encapsulated in a book review penned by Robert Southey, a future poet laureate, in 1805. He recognised that its importance was not reducible to one single consideration. At a time when the Cape was back in Dutch hands and the British position in the region more generally was still unclear, Southey observed that the Cape was 'of importance in many points of view' before elaborating:

The poet figures to his mind on the mention of its name the genius of storms, so sublimely described by Camoens; the naturalist regards it as the favourite point, from which he may explore the animal and vegetable pleasures of Africa; the sailor makes to it for refreshments in his voyages from Europe to the East Indies; and the

---

[1] NUL, Mi 2F 4, 'An Account of Operations off Isles of France and Bourbon' [1809–10], p. 1.

[2] This duality draws on Tony Ballantyne's insights that 'certain locations, individuals or institutions in the supposed periphery, might in fact be the centre of complex networks themselves'. Tony Ballantyne, *Webs of Empire: Locating New Zealand's Colonial Past* (Vancouver: University of British Columbia Press, 2014), p. 46.

statesman considers the manifold advantages it might afford to any European possessor.[3]

Richard Wellesley was, as ever, more direct. He provided perhaps the clearest contemporary assessment of the role to be played by the region in the wider context of the British Empire in Asia. Wellesley considered the acquisition of a territorial or strategic foothold here to be absolutely critical in preserving Britain's interests in India. Writing to Henry Dundas from Cape Town, where he had called on his way to Calcutta, Wellesley mused: 'I doubt whether, with the Cape in the hands of the enemy, it would be possible for you to maintain your Indian trade or empire, unless you could acquire some other settlement on the southern continent of Africa.'[4] His succinct summary of the situation, written to the same correspondent two years later, might equally be applied across the region: 'The importance of the Cape in its relation to India increases every hour; and the connection between the settlements becomes more intimate in every view of our military, political, and commercial interests.'[5] This book has traced the evolution and development of these ideas as well as how such connections worked in practice, as the rhetoric of consolidation in the Indian Ocean was underscored and (sometimes literally) reinforced by the shuttling back and forth of information, intelligence and troops. These examples highlight some of the ways in which we can see the region, in Sir George Yonge's pregnant phrase, as occupying 'the centre of union, correspondence and connexion with every part of the globe'.[6]

This book has demonstrated that the South Atlantic and southern Indian Ocean, as a contiguous maritime space, played a larger rhetorical and practical role in the development of Britain's maritime empire and Indian Ocean world than previously ascribed to it. Narratives of Britain's imperial, colonial, military and commercial links with the wider world, and Asia in particular, in the late eighteenth century have tended to follow Lord Nelson's assessment of places on the route to India. For some historians, as much as for sailors, they are merely 'tavern[s] on the passage' to be passed by as quickly as possible on the voyage to some other historiographical destination.[7] As the previous chapters have shown, however,

---

[3] Robert Southey, 'Review of Robert Percival's *An Account of the Cape of Good Hope*', *Critical Review; or Annals of Literature* 4 (1805), pp. 375–83, p. 375.

[4] Richard Wellesley to Henry Dundas, 28 February 1798, *Two Views*, p. 43.

[5] NAS, GD51/3/2/55, Wellesley to Dundas, 7 October 1800.

[6] BL, IOR, E/1/100/204, Sir George Yonge to Sir Stephen Lushington, 10 May 1799.

[7] House of Lords Debate on the Preliminaries of Peace with France, 3 November 1801, in *The Parliamentary History of England, from the Earliest Period to the Year 1803*, edited by William Cobbett, 36 vols. (London: T. C. Hansard, 1816), vol. 36, p. 185.

contemporaries gave these places careful consideration, and recognised that they were politically and strategically important, as well as being potentially dangerous in the hands of an enemy. And they realised that they might serve positive functions too, supporting all manner of connections and facilitating the circulation of everything from troops and news of colonial unrest, to scientific information and intelligence reports.

To a large degree, then, this book is about information, opinions and the decisions made on the basis of the interaction of these with each other and with external circumstances. It has offered a detailed investigation of the thoughts, words and deeds of those who conceived of the South Atlantic and southern Indian Ocean as Britain's key to India, at a time when the region was coming under sustained political scrutiny by virtue of its strategic importance and, ultimately, under increasing British military and imperial control. The growth of British influence in the region can be seen in Robert Farquhar's assurance to King Radama of Madagascar that 'this happy and powerful and flourishing island of Mauritius is but as one drop of rain compared with the great ocean, when considered as a part of the wealth and power and glory of my Sovereign'.[8] By 1815, St Helena, the Cape and Mauritius formed a chain of British way stations on the route to India, acting as a 'sub-network' within – as well as a gateway to – the Indian Ocean. They were evidence of the increasingly important British connections with Asia and they formed part of what Leitch Ritchie characterised in the first half of the nineteenth century as 'the rapid rise of a British empire in the new southern world'.[9]

Britain's involvement in this region has frequently been viewed in terms of the naval aspects of global conflict or the interrelationship between the trading concerns of the East India Company and the protection offered by the Royal Navy to homeward-bound East Indiamen.[10] Both of these aspects repay attention, of course. But trade and commerce, military prowess, and the growth of Britain's Asian empire were inexorably linked, and contemporaries recognised the careful balancing act required to keep them in equilibrium:

[8] TNA, CO 167/34, p. 85, Robert Farquhar to Radama, 9 August 1817, quoted in Gwyn Campbell, *An Economic History of Imperial Madagascar, 1750–1895: The Rise and Fall of an Island Empire* (Cambridge: Cambridge University Press, 2005), p. 68.

[9] Leitch Ritchie, *The British World in the East: A Guide Historical, Moral and Commercial to India, China, Australia, South Africa, and the Other Possessions and Connexions of Great Britain in the Eastern and Southern Seas*, 2 vols. (London: W. H. Allen, 1846), vol. II, p. 487.

[10] For the former approach, see C. Northcote Parkinson, *War in the Eastern Seas, 1793–1815* (London: Allen & Unwin, 1954). For the role of the Royal Navy in protecting East India Company convoys, see Stephen Taylor, *Storm and Conquest: The Battle for the Indian Ocean, 1809* (London: Faber & Faber, 2007).

If we count the commerce of the world, we must encourage it more than any other nation in the world, and if we entertain a wish to support and increase our maritime power, we must extend our settlements in order to make way for that increase.[11]

This entanglement was mirrored in the geographical interconnectedness that characterised Britain's global interests. Constituent parts of the empire were dependent on each other, particularly during periods of upheaval, war and revolution. As Robert Brooke told Lord Macartney, 'when the absolute existence of the empire seems at stake', it was incumbent on everyone to ensure that no 'branch of British Energy should be unconcerned or idle' in its defence.[12] Exploring the range of possibilities and connections nurtured and sustained by the British presence in the South Atlantic and the southern Indian Ocean offers significant insights into the global ties that helped to bind Britain's geographically dispersed interests together. The role of this gateway region was crucial. Richard Wellesley, for example, believed that 'the great utility of the Cape of Good Hope is to serve as a depot and as an outpost to our Indian Empire'.[13] And one can extend this analysis to cover the adjacent islands in the region. Taken together, they offered revictualling opportunities and strategic advantages, provided ship-based and land-garnered intelligence, and facilitated the movement of commodities and personnel. Assessing the logistical and political considerations involved in the recruitment and deployment of troops from the Cape, for instance, powerfully illustrates how the maritime and military supremacy that Britain increasingly enjoyed at the time materially supported British interests in India. By investigating the movement and deployment of troops between Britain, India and this gateway region, we can observe the projection of power and the use of naval supremacy in the Indian Ocean. And the region also offered other types of connections. For people on St Helena, a 'proposed intercourse' with Africa facilitated by 'two vessels of 220 tons burthen to be kept constantly employed in voyages to and from the island' and Cape Town would be 'expedient and highly beneficial to the Company's interests'.[14]

The story recounted here fits into the wider history of Britain's maritime empire and British power in the East. The places considered in this

---

[11] HRO, 38M49/5/61/20, 'Observations on the Island of Madagascar by Colonel Sir George Young' (n.d., c.1806–7), pp. 7–8.

[12] B'hurst, MS.062/14, Robert Brooke to Lord Macartney, 1 June 1797.

[13] Wellesley to Yonge, 24 October 1800, *RCC*, vol. III, p. 343.

[14] BL, IOR, G/32/163, paragraph 35, Alexander Beatson to Chairman and Directors of the East India Company, 20 August 1813. St Helena's role in the European slave trade had, of course, long connected the island with Africa. See Richard B. Allen, *European Slave Trading in the Indian Ocean, 1500–1850* (Athens, OH: Ohio University Press, 2014).

book were never seriously envisaged as economic powerhouses in themselves or final destinations for vast numbers of migrants leaving Britain. But this region cannot be understood independently from the broader history of empire or the period of warfare that frequently coloured the engagement with the region as it came under British control. This was a time of almost constant conflict, culminating in a generation-long war which pitted Britain against its most bitter European rival, France. The global canvas on which these conflicts were played out meant that geography was a crucial determinant of the course of history. By the end of the long Revolutionary and Napoleonic Wars, Britain had increased its colonial possessions from twenty-six to forty-six colonies. Whether or not this was an 'unforeseen consequence' of the war against Napoleon, it is certainly the case that, as the nineteenth century progressed, the term 'empire' was increasingly equated with (and measured by) large swathes of territorial colonial possessions.[15] But, as Richard Drayton cautions, we should be careful not to look at the British Empire solely through the distorting prism of Victorian imperialism.[16] It was not just about capturing places and securing bases – although that was vital too – it was about the way in which these locations linked people and places, forming webs of connection, interaction and interchange.

At the turn of the nineteenth century, John Barrow declared that 'by the capture of the Cape of Good Hope and of Ceylon, the British language is now heard at the southern extremities of the four great continents or quarters of the globe'.[17] On one level, Barrow enunciated the facts of the late Revolutionary War. But the pairing of these two locations was not coincidental. British control at the southern extremities of the African continent and Indian subcontinent respectively offered much greater security to the country's Asian interests as a whole. And there were other reasons for regarding Ceylon and Southern Africa as analogous. Far from seeing islands, ports or territories in isolation, as so many separate places, Barrow and his contemporaries were apt to consider them as constituent pieces of a lager global mosaic. Possession of one was useful but it was not sufficient to complete the whole picture. In 1806, for example, Robert Craufurd was instructed to consult with William Beresford in order to find 'the means of securing by a chain of ports … an uninterrupted

---

[15] Roger Knight, *Britain against Napoleon: The Organisation of Victory, 1793–1815* (London: Penguin, 2014), p. 474.

[16] Richard Drayton, 'Maritime Networks and the Making of Knowledge', in David Cannadine (ed.), *Empire, the Sea and Global History: Britain's Maritime World, 1763–1833* (Basingstoke, Palgrave Macmillan, 2007), pp. 72–82, p. 73.

[17] John Barrow, *An Account of Travels into the Interior of Southern Africa, in the Years 1797 and 1798*, 2 vols. (London: T. Cadell and W. Davies, 1801–4), vol. I, p. 1.

communication, both military and commercial, between the provinces of Chili and Buenos Ayres'.[18] Similarly, Home Popham often referred to South Africa and South America as being 'contiguous', despite the 3,000 miles of clear blue (and often storm-tossed) ocean separating them.[19] And Sir George Young reminded his readers that Britain's traditional rivals were also keen on creating an interlinked system of ports in the Indian Ocean:

A common chart will then present you with a connected chain of ports in the hands of the enemy, who might at all times interrupt our outward and homeward bound shipping to the Indian Ocean, and however ideal part of this description is, it certainly is in the power of such enterprising enemies to put the whole in practice.

'In such a case', Sir George warned, 'can the Cape guard against the mischief?'.[20] The only rational response, he argued was for Britain to embark on creating its own 'chain'.

As a whole, therefore, the evidence presented in this book contributes to our understanding of how Britain's maritime empire operated in practice and how the region relates to that empire and fits into the British presence in the wider Indian Ocean. It illustrates what it meant, in practice, to attempt to exert control and sustain transoceanic networks in the late eighteenth and early nineteenth centuries. And by focusing on inter- and intra-oceanic connections, and in positing the inevitably inchoate and blurred boundaries of these oceans, this study challenges the division between the Atlantic and Indian oceans. The task of defining the Indian Ocean, its boundaries and Britain's relationship with it, is an ongoing one and something to which this book hopes to contribute. It has attempted to put maritime considerations back into the story of the East India Company and Britain's empire in Asia, splicing the oceanic and the imperial, situating Africa in the centre of the analysis rather than on the margins, and interpolating islands with continents. In this understanding, the sea can be seen as a skein, connecting places in the Indian and Atlantic oceans, and materially influencing what happens on land. Oceans are the ultimate transnational phenomena: the history of any one ocean or sea quickly becomes the history of others. In attempting to write them back into analyses of broader historical patterns, the history of the seas – and the actions of people, institutions and states on those seas – can make

---

[18] BL, Add. MS 37884, p. 227, William Windham to Robert Craufurd, 30 October 1806.
[19] Hugh Popham, *A Damned Cunning Fellow: The Eventful Life of Rear-Admiral Sir Home Popham KCB, KCH, KM, FRS, 1762–1820* (Tywardreath: Old Ferry Press, 1991), p. 148.
[20] HRO, 38M49/5/61/20, 'Observations on the Island of Madagascar', p. 7.

a major contribution to those seeking to understand the mechanisms of globalisation in the early modern world.[21]

The end of the beginning

In many ways, then, the conclusion of this book marks the beginning of a new phase in the region's relationship with the wider British Empire. We began by questioning where to place the Cape and, by implication, the broader maritime region of which it formed a part. The chronological focus of this study necessarily represents a particular stage in the relationship between the southern gateway region and the British presence in the Indian Ocean, after which circumstances in both places altered. There was a change in imperial attitudes and aspirations in Britain too. The consolidation and expansion of the British presence at the southern gateway to the Indian Ocean meant that, perhaps inevitably, people began to envisage other possibilities for the region.[22] After 1815, the Cape in particular increasingly became part of a 'British world' organised around territorial possessions. A process of Anglicisation took place that drew the region further into a wider British 'family' of polities across the globe.[23] In terms of its links with the wider world, the political fact of empire became as significant as the geographical fact of the region's importance for the protection of trade routes. Some people, for instance, recognised that it need not necessarily be inevitably connected to the Indian subcontinent. This was a point articulated by John Bruce as early as 1796 when he argued:

Nor does the importance of the Cape to Great Britain depend only on its situation relatively to our Indian possessions, it results also from the natural fertility of the country and the relation which might be formed between it and America and the West Indies.[24]

---

[21] John Mack, *The Sea: A Cultural History* (London: Reaktion, 2013), p. 20.

[22] See, for example, Edwin A. G. Clark, '"The Spirit of Private Adventure": British Merchants and the Establishment of New Ports and Trades in the Cape of Good Hope, 1795–1840', in Stephen Fisher (ed.), *Innovation in Shipping and Trade* (Exeter: University of Exeter Press, 1989), pp. 111–30.

[23] For example, see B'hurst, MS.507, Printed proclamation, 30 January 1824. For further discussion of this phenomenon, see James Sturgis, 'Anglicization at the Cape of Good Hope in the Early Nineteenth Century', *Journal of Imperial and Commonwealth History* 11 (1982), pp. 5–32; Vivian Bickford-Smith, 'Revisiting Anglicisation in the Nineteenth-Century Cape Colony', *Journal of Imperial and Commonwealth History* 31 (2003), pp. 82–95; Saul Dubow, 'How British was the British World? The Case of South Africa', *Journal of Imperial and Commonwealth History* 37 (2009), pp. 1–27.

[24] B'hurst, MS.060, John Bruce, 'Plans for the Government and Trade of the Cape of Good Hope', pp. 247–8.

This elicited a response – written in the margin and in different (presumably Henry Dundas's) handwriting – that might be seen to encapsulate the changing outlook of the early nineteenth century: 'This requires much consideration'. Henry Colebrooke, a Company administrator in India (and perhaps more famous as a Sanskrit scholar and disciple of Sir William Jones), regarded it as 'an unquestionable point of good policy to promote the prosperity of the Cape by facilitating its intercourse and commercial relations with other British plantations, as well as with the parent country'.[25] There was no doubt that, because the region was 'in the line of communication with the more distant possessions of Great Britain in India and Austral Asia', it was 'especially deserving of encouragement, on grounds of state policy, as materially tending to the aid and support of the British Eastern empire'. And it was certainly a 'convenient intermediate mart'. But Colebrooke also thought more expansively: 'It may become peculiarly important, should Great Britain establish in New Holland a colonizing settlement governed by appropriate colonial laws and distinct from the actual receptacle of convicts at Sidney [*sic*].'[26] Building on these foundations, the connections between Southern Africa and the various fledging colonies of what was to become Australia have attracted scholars seeking to explain the development of the British Empire in the early nineteenth century.[27]

It was not just new connections with the British world that exercised minds. Robert Brooke, for example, foresaw that if Britain were to retain the Cape, there was a chance for people like Macartney to 'create a new Empire in Africa, an Empire populous, happy and advantageous to Great Britain'.[28] Benjamin Stout was among the many people who saw possibilities beyond the victualling or strategic position of a specific location. He prophesied that, as the nineteenth century progressed, the entire region would grow in importance to Britain and become much more than merely 'a half-way house to their settlements in the East Indies'. In fact, Stout was starting the process of turning away from appreciating 'its value in proportion to the accommodation which was given to their shipping' and focusing instead on 'the cultivation of the interior'.[29] A letter, which appeared in *The Times* in 1816, took these ideas further

25 H. T. Colebrooke to Lord Bathurst, 28 January 1818, *RCC*, vol. XI, pp. 455–6.
26 *Ibid.*, p. 455.
27 For example, see Elizabeth Elbourne, 'Between Van Diemen's Land and the Cape Colony', in Anna Johnston and Mitchell Rolls (eds.), *Reading Robinson: Companion Essays to George Augustus Robinson's Friendly Mission* (Clayton: Monash University Publishing, 2012), ch. 5.
28 B'hurst, MS.062/12, Brooke to Macartney, 28 October 1796.
29 Benjamin Stout, *Narrative of the Loss of the Ship Hercules*, edited by A. Porter (1798; revised edition, Port Elizabeth: Historical Society of Port Elizabeth, 1975), p. 14.

still. Written by 'a rough knotted sailor' who had spent some three months the previous year at the Cape, this letter acknowledged the central geographical position of the Cape and its wholesome climatic conditions in much the same terms as many others before him. But this 'Friend' of the region arrived at different conclusions with regard to its value:

The salubrity of the climate is proverbial, and inferior to no other part of the globe. Its centrical situation between the eastern world and the western commands as it were an intercourse with every national flag; and if a liberal line of policy were adapted, it would most certainly very soon become a very desirable place to live at.[30]

Henry Colebrooke offered a similar message. For him, Southern Africa was 'adapted by climate to become beneficial colonies, when peopled by a race retaining British habits, consequently consuming British productions and manufactures'.[31] And a couple of years later – just before the embarkation of five thousand British settlers on an organised migration to the eastern frontier of the Cape Colony – *The Times* lauded the Cape as 'the most precious and magnificent object of our colonial policy'. It acknowledged that 'it is the natural key to India, the bridle of America, and is capable of superseding the whole of Europe in supplying this country with her accustomed articles of importation'. But this encomium was in praise of 'the most fruitful field of adventure to our emigrant population'.[32]

In terms of imperial defence and external threats, the focus of attention was also shifting. Lord Charles Somerset's pronouncement to Lord Bathurst in early 1817 signalled a step change in the attitudes of British administrators towards the Cape Colony: 'The frontiers of this colony will ever afford the most important points to which the attention of a Governor here must be called.'[33] Instead of troops heading off for India or reinforcing British positions elsewhere in the Indian Ocean, they were instead being transported to quell the increasingly fractious colonial frontier. Writing aboard HMS *Favourite* in 1819, Captain Robinson responded to Lord Charles Somerset's 'requisition for the immediate services of His Majesty's Ship under my command in conveying a body of troops to the frontier'.[34] In many ways, the British concern with the borders of the colony symbolises the assurance that maritime

---

[30] *The Times*, 28 September 1816.
[31] Colebrooke to Bathurst, 28 January 1818, *RCC*, vol. XI, p. 455.
[32] *The Times*, 18 June 1819. For more on the 1820s Settlers, see Harold Edward Hockly, *The Story of the British Settlers of 1820 in South Africa* (Johannesburg: Juta, 1957).
[33] Somerset to Bathurst, 23 January 1817, *RCC*, vol. XI, p. 252.
[34] Captain Robinson to Somerset, 15 February 1819, *RCC*, vol. XII, p. 140.

control of the region had bestowed. They could now afford to worry about local difficulties.

Returning to Lord Macartney's statement that we encountered at the outset: this book has demonstrated that the Cape and the wider maritime region of which it was a part did form 'the master link of connection between the western and eastern world'.[35] But this was not a self-evident or straightforward process. It was the product of many people and many discussions about the best way of securing Britain's access to Asia. And the way in which this region operated, practically and logistically, as part of Britain's maritime empire – through the circulation of news, information, ideas and people – also sheds light on the consolidation of its Indian Ocean interests. Indeed, the changing nature of the British presence in the region in the nineteenth century should not diminish or take away from the continued relevance of controlling maritime routes of travel, communication and commerce. As Richard Drayton reminds us, the political map of the British Empire in the late eighteenth and early nineteenth centuries, with its 'secure pink spaces', was a fiction. In reality, the islands, beachheads and coastal hinterlands where British imperial power held sway were held together by maritime networks.[36] The oceanic arc of the South Atlantic and southern Indian Ocean may not have had the terrestrial landmass to make a visual impact on the imperial maps that became such a defining feature of the Victorian and Edwardian empire. But it still offered the key to what lay beyond its shores.

[35] TNA, WO 1/329, p. 17, Macartney to Dundas, 10 July 1797.
[36] Drayton, 'Maritime Networks', pp. 80–1.

Bibliography

Manuscripts and archival sources

Arquivo Histórico Ultramarino, Lisbon

Conselho Ultramarino (CU), Moçambique (Moç.): Papers and correspondence

Bodleian Library of Commonwealth and African Studies, Rhodes House, University of Oxford

GB 0162 MSS.Afr.s.1,2. Letters from the Cape Colony
GB 0162 Micr.Afr.511. George, Lord Macartney correspondence
MSS.Afr.t.2– Afr.t.4*. George, Lord Macartney correspondence

Bodleian Library Special Collections, University of Oxford

MS. Eng.c.2742–4. Howden papers

Brenthurst Library, Johannesburg

MS.052. Henry Dundas correspondence
MS.053. Sir Roger Curtis journals
MS.059. Sir Thomas Reynell journal
MS.060. Francis Dundas memoranda
MS.061. George, Lord Macartney papers
MS.062. Robert Brooke papers
MS.063. George, Lord Macartney papers
MS.310. Home Popham, 'Thoughts of the Naval, Military, Commercial and Colonial Importation of the Cape of Good Hope, with Suggestions for affording Relief to the Distressed and Unemployed Peasantry of Ireland', c.1816
MS.507. Printed proclamation, 30 January 1824

British Library

Add. MS 13456–13457, 13784–13785, 13787. Wellesley papers: Correspondence and papers of Richard Wellesley, 2nd Earl of Mornington; Marquess Wellesley

Add. MS 18126–18127. 'Notes upon the history, geography, religion, etc., of Madagascar, by M. de Froberville'

Add. MS 30097. Memoranda of Sir Robert Wilson, on the Cape of Good Hope, Madeira, St Salvador or Bahia, and St. Helena, with a journal and other papers relating to his services at the Cape of Good Hope, 1805–6

Add. MS 33980. Letters addressed to Sir Joseph Banks

Add. MS 37847, 37884. Windham papers: Official and private correspondence and papers of William Windham, Secretary at War

Add. MS 38226. Liverpool papers: Official correspondence of Charles Jenkinson, Baron Hawkesbury (1786), 1st Earl of Liverpool (1796)

Add. MS 38346. Liverpool papers: Official papers of Charles Jenkinson, Baron Hawkesbury (1786), 1st Earl of Liverpool (1796)

Add. MS 40100–40102. Letters and papers from the correspondence of Henry Dundas, 1st Viscount Melville, Secretary of State, 1791–1801, First Lord of the Admiralty, 1804–5

Add. MS 42071. Hamilton and Greville papers: Correspondence and papers of the Honourable Charles Francis Greville

Add. MS 46119–46120. Thompson papers

Add. MS 47014. Egmont papers: Correspondence and papers of John Perceval, Viscount Perceval, 2nd Earl of Egmont

Add. MS 75834, 75856. Althorp papers: Correspondence and papers of George John Spencer, Viscount Althorp, 2nd Earl Spencer

Egerton MS 3499. Carmarthen-Leeds papers: Correspondence and papers chiefly of Francis Godolphin Osborne, Marquess of Carmarthen, 5th Duke of Leeds, Foreign Secretary 1783–91

Cadbury Research Library, University of Birmingham

LAdd/211–215, 1114–28. Letters Additional Collection

Cumbria Record Office, Carlisle

D HUD. Huddleston family papers
D LONS. Lowther family papers

Department of Historical Papers, William Cullen Library, University of the Witwatersrand, Johannesburg

A24. Sir James Craig papers
A30. Sir Robert Harland correspondence

A51. 'Historie van de Kaap zeer Krachtig 1795'

A124. Sir Charles Tyler journal

A139. W. S. Van Ryneveld, 'Criminal Claim and Conclusion made and demanded by the Fiscal versus Marthinus Prinsloo and his Accomplices', 29 August 1800

A81. J. F. L. Greevestein, 'Journal of the Voyage of the *Zephir* and *Havik*', 1789–93

A88. George, Lord Macartney papers

A154. George Forster correspondence

A162. Sir Albemarle Bertie correspondence

A270. William Edmeades journal

A343. William John Burchell papers

A557. Lady Anne Barnard correspondence

A574. Sir George Yonge correspondence

A666–8. George, Lord Macartney papers

A733–6. George, Lord Macartney correspondence, notebooks

A737. Robert Brooke correspondence

Devon Record Office, Exeter

152 M/C. Addington papers: Political and personal papers of Henry Addington, 1st Viscount Sidmouth

East Sussex Record Office, Lewes

AMS5440. Correspondence from the archive of John Baker Holroyd, Earl of Sheffield

Foyle Special Collections Library, King's College, London, Foreign and Commonwealth Office Historical Collections

DT2042. [John Bruce], 'Sketches of the Political and Commercial History of the Cape of Good Hope', *c.*1796

Hampshire Record Office, Winchester

16M97/2/25. Diary of John White in India and the East, 1801–2

31M70. George Tierney correspondence

38M49/5/61. Wickham family papers

Hertfordshire Archives & Local Studies, Hertford

DE/B472. Family papers of the Calvert family of Furneux Pelham

India Office Records, British Library

D/1–17. Minutes and memoranda of general committees: Minutes of the Committee of Correspondence

E/1. General Correspondence: Home correspondence

E/4. General Correspondence: Correspondence with India

F/1. Board of Control: Board minutes

F/2. Board of Control: Home Correspondence

F/4. General Correspondence: Board's collections

G/9. Factory Records: Cape of Good Hope factory records

G/32. Factory Records: St Helena factory records

G/40. Factory Records: Miscellaneous factory records

H. Home miscellaneous series

L/PS/1. Political and Secret Department: Political and Secret Department Committee minutes

O. Biographical series

P. Proceedings

National Army Museum

1966–02–07. Pay Warrant book, 1807

1998–08–23. George Moore: Correspondence

National Archives, Kew

ADM 1. Admiralty, and Ministry of Defence, Navy Department: Correspondence and papers

ADM 2. Admiralty Board: Out-letters

CO 49/1. War and Colonial Department and Colonial Office: Cape of Good Hope Colony (Cape Colony), entry books

CO 54/22. War and Colonial Department and Colonial Office: Ceylon, original correspondence, despatches

CO 77/25. War and Colonial Department and Colonial Office: East Indies, Secretary of State, original correspondence

CO 167/34. War and Colonial Department and Colonial Office: Missions to Madagascar

CO 267/9. War and Colonial Department and Colonial Office: Sierra Leone, Secretary of State, original correspondence

FO 63/58. Foreign Office: General correspondence, Portugal

HO 42/7. Home Office: Domestic correspondence

PRO 30/8. William Pitt, 1st Earl of Chatham, papers: Correspondence of William Pitt, 1st Earl of Chatham and Lady Hester (Grenville) his wife

SP 89/87/158. Secretaries of State: State Papers Foreign, Portugal

WO 1. Secretary-at-War, Secretary of State for War, and Commander-in-Chief: In-letters and Miscellaneous Papers

National Archives of Scotland, Edinburgh

GD 51. Melville papers

National Library of Scotland, Edinburgh

MSS 11065, 11622, 11683. Minto Papers: Correspondence and papers relating to India and the Far East

National Library of South Africa, Cape Town

MSB 252. Samuel Hudson diaries

National Maritime Museum, Greenwich

CHN. Christian family papers: Sir Hugh Cloberry Christian papers
MID. Middleton papers: Sir Charles Middleton, 1st Baron Barham, papers
SAN. Sandwich papers: Papers relating to John Montagu, 4th Earl of Sandwich (First Lord of The Admiralty), 1718–92
P/16. Thomas Pennant, 'Outlines of the Globe'

Nottingham University Library, Department of Manuscripts and Special Collections

Mi 2 F. Admiral Sir Nesbit Josiah Willoughby papers

Public Record Office of Northern Ireland, Belfast

D572. Macartney papers
D2431–3. Caledon papers
D3030. Castlereagh papers

Royal Botanic Gardens, Kew

FOR. William Forsyth papers
WJB. William John Burchell papers

University of Southampton Library, Special Collections

BR19/1. Broadlands papers
WP1/175/9. Wellington papers

Western Cape Archives and Records Service, Cape Town

A455. Dundas papers
CO 3885. Colonial Office papers

Printed primary sources

Anderson, James, *Correspondence for the Introduction of Cochineal Insects from America, the Varnish and Tallow Trees from China, the Discovery and Culture of White Lac, the Culture of Red Lac. And also for the Introduction, Culture and Establishment of Mulberry Trees and Silk Worms* .... (Madras: Joseph Martin, 1791)

Anon., *A Description of the Island of St Helena* (London: R. Phillips, 1805)

Anon., *A Full and Correct Report of the Trial of Sir Home Popham* (London: Richardson, 1807)

Anon., *Minutes of Court Martial, Holden on board his Majesty's Ship, Gladiator* (London: Longman, Hurst, Rees and Orme, 1807)

Anon., *Thoughts on Improving the Government of the British Territorial Possessions in the East Indies* (London: T. Cadell, 1780)

Baldwin, George, *Political Recollections relative to Egypt* (London: T. Cadell and W. Davies, 1801)

Barrow, John, *An Account of Travels into the Interior of Southern Africa, in the Years 1797 and 1798*, 2 vols. (London: T. Cadell and W. Davies, 1801–4)

Bernardin de Saint Pierre, Jacques-Henri, *A Voyage to the Island of Mauritius (or, Isle of France), the Isle of Bourbon, the Cape of Good Hope* (London: W. Griffin, 1775)

Bickley, Francis (ed.), *The Diaries of Sylvester Douglas, Lord Glenbervie*, 2 vols. (London: Constable, 1928)

Boucher, Maurice and Nigel Penn (eds.), *Britain at the Cape, 1795 to 1803* (Johannesburg: Brenthurst Press, 1992)

Brooke, Thomas H., *A History of the Island of St Helena: From its Discovery by the Portuguese to the Year 1823* (London: Kingsbury, Parbury, and Allen, 1824)
A History of the Island of St Helena: From its Discovery by the Portuguese to the Year 1806 (London: Black, Parry and Kingsbury, 1808)

Bruce, John, *Historical Views of Plans, for the Government of British India and the Regulation of Trade to the East Indies* (London: [s.n.], 1793)

Cleveland, Richard J., *A Narrative of Voyages and Commercial Enterprises*, 2 vols. (Cambridge, MA: John Owen, 1842)

Chambers, Neil (ed.), *The Indian and Pacific Correspondence of Sir Joseph Banks, 1768–1820*, 8 vols. (London: Pickering & Chatto, 2008–14)

Cobbett, William (ed.), *The Parliamentary History of England, from the Earliest Period to the Year 1803*, 36 vols. (London: T. C. Hansard, 1816)

Colquhoun, Patrick, *A Treatise on the Wealth, Power and Resources of the British Empire in every Quarter of the World* (London: Joseph Mawman, 1815)

Corbett, Julian S. and H. W. Richmond (eds.), *Private Papers of George, Second Earl Spencer*, 4 vols. (London: Navy Records Society, 1913–24)

Dalrymple, Alexander, *A Collection of Voyages chiefly in the Southern Atlantick Ocean* (London: J. Nourse, 1775)

Durnford, Charles and Edward Hyde (eds.), *Term Reports in the Court of the King's Bench*, 8 vols. (New York: Collins and Hannay, 1827)

Ellis, William, *History of Madagascar*, 2 vols. (London: Fisher, 1838)

Fairbridge, Dorothea (ed.), *Lady Anne Barnard at the Cape of Good Hope, 1797–1802* (Oxford: Clarendon Press, 1924)

Flinders, Matthew, *A Voyage to Terra Australis ... in the Years 1801, 1802 and 1803*, 2 vols. (London: G. & W. Nicol, 1814)

Gallagher, Robert E. (ed.), *Byron's Journal of his Circumnavigation, 1764–1766* (Cambridge: Hakluyt Society, 1964)

Gillespie, Alexander, *Gleanings and Remarks collected during Many Months of Residence at Buenos Ayres* (Leeds: The Author, 1818)

Grainger, John D. (ed.), *The Royal Navy in the River Plate, 1806–1807* (London: Navy Records Society, 1996)

Greig, James (ed.), *The Farington Diary* (London: Hutchinson, 1924)

Haafner, Jacob, 'Jacob Haafner's Description of Mauritius', in Shawkat Toorawa (ed.), *The Western Indian Ocean: Essays on Islands and Islanders* (Port Louis: Hassam Toorawa Trust, 2007), pp. 77–86

Hamilton, Alexander, *A New Account of the East Indies: Giving an Exact and Copious Description of the Situation*, 2 vols. (1727; London: C. Hitch and A. Millar, 1744)

Historical Manuscripts Commission, *Report on the Manuscripts of J. B. Fortescue, Esq., preserved at Dropmore, Historical Manuscripts Commission*, 10 vols. (London: HMSO, 1892–1927)

Report on the Manuscripts of Mrs Stopford-Sackville, Historical Manuscripts Commission, 2 vols. (London: HMSO, 1904)

Hood, Theodore, *The Life of General the Right Honourable Sir David Baird, Bart.*, 2 vols. (London: Richard Bentley, 1832)

Ingram, Edward (ed.), *Two Views of British India: The Private Correspondence of Mr Dundas and Lord Wellesley, 1798–1801* (Bath: Adams and Dart, 1970)

James, Silas, *Narrative of a Voyage to Arabia, India etc. containing ... A Description of Saldanha Bay* (London: The Author, 1797)

Jones, William, 'Remarks on the Island of Hinzuan or Johanna', in *The Works of Sir William Jones*, edited by Anna Maria Jones, 13 vols. (London: J. Stockdale, 1807), vol. IV, pp. 269–313

Khan, Mirza Abu Taleb, *Travels of Mirza Abu Taleb Khan in Asia, Africa, and Europe, during the years 1799, 1800, 1801, 1802, and 1803*, translated by Charles Stewart (London: Longman, Hurst, Rees, Orme, and Brown, 1814)

Lenta, Margaret (ed.), *Paradise, the Castle and the Vineyard: Lady Anne Barnard's Cape Diaries* (Johannesburg: Wits University Press, 2006)

Lenta, Margaret and Basil Le Cordeur (eds.), *The Cape Diaries of Lady Anne Barnard, 1799–1800*, 2 vols. (Cape Town: Van Riebeeck Society, 1999)

Lewin, Thomas Herbert (ed.), *The Lewin Letters: A Selection from the Correspondence and Diaries of an English Family, 1756–1884*, 2 vols. (London: Archibald Constable & Co., 1909)

Lichtenstein, Henry, *Travels in Southern Africa in the Years 1803, 1804, 1805, and 1806*, translated by Anne Plumptre (London: Henry Colburn, 1812)

Londonderry, Charles William Vane, Marquess of (ed.), *Correspondence, Despatches and other Papers of Viscount Castlereagh, Second Marquess of Londonderry*, 12 vols. (London: William Shoeberl, 1851)

McMaster, John Bach, *The Life and Times of Stephen Girard, Mariner and Merchant*, 2 vols. (Philadelphia: J. B. Lippincott, 1918)

Martin, Robert Montgomery (ed.), *The Despatches, Minutes & Correspondence of the Marquess Wellesley during his Administration in India*, 5 vols. (London: W. H. Allen, 1836–37)

Melliss, John C., *St. Helena: A Physical, Historical, and Topographical Description of the Island* (London: Reeve, 1875)

Milburn, William, *Oriental Commerce, Containing a Geographical Description of the Principal Places in the East Indies, China and Japan, with their Produce, Manufactures and Trade*, 2 vols. (London: Parry, Black and Co., 1813)

Minto, Emma Eleanor Elizabeth, Countess of (ed.), *Lord Minto in India: Life and Letters of Gilbert Elliot, First Earl of Minto, from 1807 to 1814* (London, Longmans, Green, and Co., 1880)

'Miranda and the British Admiralty, 1804–1806', *American Historical Review* 6 (1901), pp. 508–30

Mullett, C. F. (ed.), 'British Schemes and Spanish America in 1806', *Hispanic American Historical Review* 27 (1947), pp. 269–78

Peabody, Robert E., *The Log of the Grand Turks* (London: Duckworth, 1927)

Percival, Robert, *An Account of the Cape of Good Hope* (London: C. & R. Baldwin, 1804)

Perrin, William Gordon (ed.), *The Naval Miscellany: Volume 3* (London: Naval Records Society, 1928)

Philo-Israel [Edward Wheeler Bird], *The Geography of the Gates* (London: Robert Banks, 1880)

Pocock, William Innes, *Five Views of the Island of St Helena from Drawings taken on the Spot* (London: S. and J. Fuller, 1815)

Powell, Anthony (ed.), *Barnard Letters, 1778–1824* (London: Duckworth, 1928)

Prior, James, *Voyage along the Eastern Coast of Africa ... in the Nisus Frigate* (London: Richard Phillips, 1819)

Pyrard, François, *The Voyage of François Pyrard of Laval to the East Indies, the Maldives, the Moluccas and Brazil*, edited by Albert Gray, 2 vols. (London: Hakluyt Society, 1890)

Renshaw, Richard, *Voyage to the Cape of Good Hope and up the Red Sea* (Manchester: J. Watts, 1804)

Ritchie, Leitch, *The British World in the East: A Guide Historical, Moral and Commercial to India, China, Australia, South Africa, and the other possessions and connexions of Great Britain in the Eastern and Southern Seas*, 2 vols. (London: W. H. Allen, 1846)

Robinson, A. M. Lewin (ed.), *The Letters of Lady Anne Barnard to Henry Dundas* (Cape Town: A. A. Balkema, 1973)

Robinson, A. M. Lewin, with Margaret Lenta and Dorothy Driver (eds.), *The Cape Journals of Lady Anne Barnard, 1797–1798* (Cape Town: Van Riebeeck Society, 1994)

Rooke, Henry, *Travels to the Coast of Arabia Felix ... containing a Short Account of an Expedition undertaken against the Cape of Good Hope* (London: R. Blamire, 1783)

Ross, Charles (ed.), *Correspondence of Charles, First Marquis Cornwallis*, 3 vols. (London: John Murray, 1859)

Shields, Nancy K. (ed.), *Birds of Passage: Henrietta Clive's Travels in South India, 1798–1801* (London: Eland, 2009)

'Southern-Ocean: Mauritius', *Naval Chronicle* 29 (1813), p. 130

Southey, Robert, 'Review of Robert Percival's *An Account of the Cape of Good Hope*', *Critical Review; or Annals of Literature* 4 (1805), pp. 375–83

Stout, Benjamin, *Narrative of the Loss of the Ship Hercules*, edited by A. Porter (1798; revised edition, Port Elizabeth: Historical Society of Port Elizabeth, 1975)

[Telfair, Charles], *Account of the Conquest of the Island of Bourbon ... By an Officer of the Expedition* (London: T. Egerton, 1811)

Theal, George McCall (ed.), *Records of the Cape Colony*, 36 vols. (Cape Town: The Government of the Cape Colony, 1897–1905)

Walter, Richard, *A Voyage Round the World, in the Years MDCCXL, I, II, III, IV* (London: Richard Walter, 1748)

Webster, C. K. (ed.), *British Diplomacy, 1813–1815* (London: G. Bell, 1921)

White, William, *Journal of a Voyage performed in the Lion Extra Indiaman, from Madras to Columbo, and Da Lagoa Bay, on the Eastern Coast of Africa* (London: John Stockdale, 1800)

Secondary sources

Abu-Lughod, Janet L., *Before European Hegemony: The World System, A.D. 1250–1350* (New York: Oxford University Press, 1989)

Addison, John and K. Hazareesingh, *A New History of Mauritius* (London: Macmillan, 1984)

Alavi, Seema, 'Introduction', in Seema Alavi (ed.), *The Eighteenth Century in India* (New Delhi: Oxford University Press, 2002), pp. 1–56

The Sepoys and the Company: Tradition and Transition in Northern India, 1770–1830 (New Delhi: Oxford University Press, 2006)

Allen, Brian, 'The East India Company's Settlement Pictures: George Lambert and Samuel Scott', in Pauline Rohatgi and Pheroza Godrej (eds.), *Under the Indian Sun: British Landscape Artists* (Bombay: Marg, 1995), pp. 1–16

Allen, Richard B., *Slaves, Freedmen, and Indentured Laborers in Colonial Mauritius* (Cambridge: Cambridge University Press, 1999)

European Slave Trading in the Indian Ocean, 1500–1850 (Athens, OH: Ohio University Press, 2014)

Alpers, Edward A., 'The Islands of Indian Ocean Africa', in Shawkat Toorawa (ed.), *The Western Indian Ocean: Essays on Islands and Islanders* (Port Louis: Hassam Toorawa Trust, 2007), pp. 1–19

Anderson, Clare, 'Introduction to Marginal Centers: Writing Life Histories in the Indian Ocean World', *Journal of Social History* 45 (2011), pp. 335–44

Anderson, Clare, *et al.*, 'Review of Kerry Ward's *Networks of Empire*', *International Journal of Maritime History* 21 (2009), pp. 297–340

Arkin, Marcus, 'John Company at the Cape: A History of the Agency under Pringle (1794–1815)', *Archives Year Book for South African History 1960* (Pretoria: Government Printer, 1961), pp. 177–344

'Supplies for Napoleon's Gaolers: John Company and the Cape-St Helena Trade during the Captivity, 1815–21', *Archives Year Book for South African History 1964* (Cape Town: Government Printer, 1965), pp. 167–225

Storm in a Teacup: The Late Years of John Company at the Cape, 1815–36 (Cape Town: Struik, 1973)

Armitage, David and Michael J. Braddick (eds.), *The British Atlantic World, 1500–1800* (Basingstoke: Palgrave Macmillan, 2002)

Atkins, Keletso, 'The "Black Atlantic Communication Network": African American Sailors and the Cape of Good Hope Connection', *Issue: A Journal of Opinion* 24 (1996), pp. 23–25

Auber, Jacques, *Histoire de l'Océan Indien* (Antananarivo: Société Lilloise d'imprimerie de Tananarive, 1955)

Austen, H. C. M., *Sea Fights and Corsairs of the Indian Ocean: Being the Naval History of Mauritius from 1715 to 1810* (Port Louis: R. W. Brooks, 1935)

Bailey, Craig, 'Metropole and Colony: Irish Networks and Patronage in the Eighteenth-Century Empire', *Immigrants & Minorities* 23 (2005), pp. 161–81

Bailyn, Bernard (ed.), *Atlantic History: Concept and Contours* (Cambridge, MA: Harvard University Press, 2005)

Ballantyne, Tony, 'Races and the Webs of Empire: Aryanism from India to the Pacific', *Journal of Colonialism and Colonial History* 2 (2001), pp. 1–36

Orientalism and Race: Aryanism in the British Empire (Basingstoke: Palgrave, 2002)

Webs of Empire: Locating New Zealand's Colonial Past (Vancouver: University of British Columbia Press, 2014)

Bauss, Rudy, 'Rio de Janeiro: Strategic Base for Global Designs of the British Royal Navy, 1777–1815', in Craig L. Symonds *et al.* (eds.), *New Aspects of Naval History* (Annapolis, MD: Naval Institute Press, 1981), pp. 75–89

Bayly, C. A., *Imperial Meridian: The British Empire and the World, 1780–1830* (London: Longman, 1989)

Empire and Information: Intelligence Gathering and Social Communication in India, 1780–1870 (Cambridge: Cambridge University Press, 1996)

The Birth of the Modern World, 1780–1914 (Oxford: Blackwell, 2004)

Bender, Thomas, Laurent Dubois and Richard Rabinowitz (eds.), *Revolution! The Atlantic World Reborn* (New York: Giles, 2011)

Bentley, Jerry H., 'Sea and Ocean Basins as Frameworks of Historical Analysis', *Geographical Review* 89 (1999), pp. 215–24

Bentley, Jerry H., Renate Bridenthal and Kären Wigen (eds.), *Seascapes: Maritime Histories, Littoral Cultures, and Transoceanic Exchanges* (Honolulu: University of Hawai'i Press, 2007)

Bew, John, *Castlereagh: Enlightenment, War and Tyranny* (London: Quercus, 2011)

Bickford-Smith, Vivian, 'Revisiting Anglicisation in the Nineteenth-Century Cape Colony', *Journal of Imperial and Commonwealth History* 31 (2003), pp. 82–95

Booth, Alan R., *The United States Experience in South Africa, 1784–1870* (Cape Town: A. A. Balkema, 1976)

Bose, Sugata, *A Hundred Horizons: The Indian Ocean in the Age of Global Empire* (Cambridge, MA: Harvard University Press, 2006)

Boswell, Rosabelle, 'Islands in the (Global) Stream: The Case of Mauritius and Seychelles', in Pamila Gupta, Isabel Hofmeyr and Michael Pearson (eds.), *Eyes Across the Water: Navigating the Indian Ocean* (Pretoria: UNISA Press, 2010), pp. 286–303

Bowen, H. V., *Revenue and Reform: The Indian Problem in British Politics, 1757–1773* (Cambridge: Cambridge University Press, 1991)

The Business of Empire: The East India Company and Imperial Britain, 1756–1833 (Cambridge: Cambridge University Press, 2006)

'Mobilising Resources for Global Warfare: The British State and the East India Company, 1756–1815', in H. V. Bowen and Augustín González Enciso (eds.), *Mobilising Resources for War: Britain and Spain at Work during the Early Modern Period* (Pamplona: EUNSA, 2006), pp. 81–110

'Britain in the Indian Ocean Region and Beyond: Contours, Connections and the Creation of a Global Maritime Empire', in H. V. Bowen, Elizabeth Mancke and John G. Reid (eds.), *Britain's Oceanic Empire: Atlantic and Indian Ocean Worlds, c.1550–1850* (Cambridge: Cambridge University Press, 2012), pp. 45–65

Bowman, Larry W., 'The United States and Mauritius, 1794–1994: A Bicentennial Retrospective', *American Neptune* 56 (1996), pp. 145–62

Boyden, Peter B. and Alan J. Guy (eds.), *Soldiers of the Raj: Indian Army, 1600–1947* (London: National Army Museum, 1998)

Boyden, Peter B., Alan J. Guy and Marion Harding (eds.), *'Ashes and Blood': The British Army in South Africa, 1795–1914* (London: National Army Museum, 1999)

Bradley, Margaret, *Daniel Lescallier, 1743–1822, Man of the Sea or Military Spy? Maritime Developments and French Military Espionage* (Lewiston, NY: Mellen, 2005)

Braudel, Fernand, *The Mediterranean and the Mediterranean World in the Age of Philip II*, 2 vols. (London: Collins, 1972–73)

Broeze, Frank, *Gateways of Asia: Port Cities of Asia in the 13th–20th Centuries* (London: Routledge, 1997)

Bryant, Gerald J., *The Emergence of British Power in India, 1600–1784: A Grand Strategic Interpretation* (Woodbridge: Boydell & Brewer, 2013)

'Officers of the East India Company's Army in the days of Clive and Hastings', *Journal of Imperial and Commonwealth History* 6 (1978), pp. 203–27

Burton, Antoinette, 'Who needs the Nation? Interrogating "British" History', *Journal of Historical Sociology* 10 (1997), pp. 227–48

'Sea Tracks and Trails: Indian Ocean Worlds as Method', *History Compass* 11 (2013), pp. 497–502

Buschmann, Rainer F., 'Oceans of World History: Delineating Aquacentric Notions in the Global Past', *History Compass* 2 (2004), pp. 1–5

Oceans in World History (New York: McGraw-Hill, 2007)

Campbell, Gwyn, 'Imperial Rivalry in the Western Indian Ocean and Schemes to Colonise Madagascar (1769–1826)', in Laurence Marfaing and Brigitte Reinwald (eds.), *Afrikanische Beziehungen: Netzwerke und Räume* (Hamburg: LIT Verlag, 2001), pp. 111–30

An Economic History of Imperial Madagascar, 1750–1895: The Rise and Fall of an Island Empire (Cambridge: Cambridge University Press, 2005)

Carter, Marina, *Companions of Misfortune: Flinders and Friends at the Isle of France, 1803–1810* (London: Pink Pigeon Press, 2003)

Chambers, David Wade and Richard Gillespie, 'Locality in the History of Science: Colonial Science, Technoscience, and Indigenous Knowledge', in Roy MacLeod (ed.), 'Nature and Empire: Science and the Colonial Enterprise', *Osiris* 15 (2000), pp. 221–40

Charters, Erica, *Disease, War, and the Imperial State: The Welfare of the British Armed Forces During the Seven Years' War* (Chicago: University of Chicago Press, 2014)

Chaudhuri, K. N., *The Trading World of Asia and the English East India Company, 1660–1760* (Cambridge: Cambridge University Press, 1978)

Trade and Civilisation in the Indian Ocean: An Economic History from the Rise of Islam to 1750 (Cambridge: Cambridge University Press, 1985)

Asia before Europe: Economy and Civilisation of the Indian Ocean from the rise of Islam to 1750 (Cambridge: Cambridge University Press, 1990)

Christopher, Emma, *A Merciless Place: The Fate of Britain's Convicts after the American Revolution* (Oxford: Oxford University Press, 2010)

Clark, Edwin A. G., '"The Spirit of Private Adventure": British Merchants and the Establishment of New Ports and Trades in the Cape of Good Hope, 1795–1840', in Stephen Fisher (ed.), *Innovation in Shipping and Trade* (Exeter: University of Exeter Press, 1989), pp. 111–30

Conway, Stephen, 'Continental European Soldiers in British Imperial Service, c. 1756–1792', *English Historical Review* 129 (2014), pp. 79–106

Cooper, Frederick and Ann Laura Stoler (eds.), *Tensions of Empire: Colonial Cultures in a Bourgeois World* (Berkeley, CA: University of California Press, 1997)

Cotton, Evan and Charles Fawcett, *East Indiamen: The East India Company's Maritime Service* (London: Batchwood Press, 1949)

Crosby, Alfred W., 'American Trade with Mauritius in the Age of the French Revolution and Napoleon', *American Neptune* 25 (1965), pp. 5–17

Cullinan, Patrick, *Robert Jacob Gordon, 1743–1795: The Man and his Travels at the Cape* (Cape Town: A. A. Balkema, 1992)

D'Unienville, Raymond and Marina Carter, *The Last Years of the Isle of France (1800–1814)* (Curepipe: La Société de L'Histoire de L'Île Maurice, 2010)

Davey, James, 'The Repatriation of Spanish Troops from Denmark, 1808: The British Government, Logistics, and Maritime Supremacy', *Journal of Military History* 74 (2010), pp. 689–707

 In Nelson's Wake: The Navy and the Napoleonic Wars (London: Yale University Press, 2015)

Davies, Timothy, 'English Private Trade on the West Coast of India, *c.*1680–*c.*1740', *Itinerario* 38 (2014), pp. 51–73

De Kiewiet, C. W., *A History of South Africa: Social and Economic* (Oxford: Clarendon Press, 1941)

De Silva, Colvin R., *Ceylon under British Occupation, 1795–1833*, 2 vols. (Colombo: Colombo Apothecaries' Company, 1953–62)

Dodds, Klaus, *Pink Ice: Britain and the South Atlantic Empire* (London: I. B. Tauris, 2007)

Dozier, Robert R., *For King, Constitution, & Country: The English Loyalists and the French Revolution* (Lexington, KY: The University Press of Kentucky, 1983)

Drayton, Richard, *Nature's Government: Science, British Imperialism and the Improvement of the World* (New Haven: Yale University Press, 2000)

 'Maritime Networks and the Making of Knowledge', in David Cannadine (ed.), *Empire, the Sea and Global History: Britain's Maritime World, 1763–1833* (Basingstoke: Palgrave Macmillan, 2007), pp. 72–82

Dubow, Saul, 'How British was the British World? The Case of South Africa', *Journal of Imperial and Commonwealth History* 37 (2009), pp. 1–27

Duffy, Mike, *Soldiers, Sugar and Seapower: The British Expeditions to the West Indies and the War against Revolutionary France* (Oxford: Oxford University Press, 1987)

Durey, Michael, 'William Wickham, the Christ Church Connection and the Rise and Fall of the Security Service in Britain, 1793–1801', *English Historical Review* 121 (2006), pp. 714–45

Elbourne, Elizabeth, 'Between Van Diemen's Land and the Cape Colony', in Anna Johnston and Mitchell Rolls (eds.), *Reading Robinson: Companion Essays to George Augustus Robinson's Friendly Mission* (Clayton: Monash University Publishing, 2012), ch. 5

Endersby, Jim, *Imperial Nature: Joseph Hooker and the Practices of Victorian Science* (Chicago: University of Chicago Press, 2008)

Esdaile, Charles, *Napoleon's Wars: An International History 1803–1815* (London: Allen Lane, 2007)

Fichter, James R., 'The British Empire and the American Atlantic on Tristan da Cunha, 1811–16', *Journal of Imperial and Commonwealth History*, 36 (2008), pp. 567–89

 So Great a Profitt: How the East Indies Trade transformed Anglo-American Capitalism (Cambridge, MA: Harvard University Press, 2010)

Fleischer, Alette, 'The Company's Garden and the (Ex)change of Nature and Knowledge at Cape of Good Hope (1652–1700)', in Lissa Roberts (ed.), *Centres and Cycles of Accumulation in and around the Netherlands during the Early Modern Period* (Zurich: LIT, 2011), pp. 101–27

Fletcher, Ian, *The Waters of Oblivion: The British Invasion of the Rio de la Plata, 1806–1807* (Tunbridge Wells: Spellmount, 1991)

Frost, Alan, *The Global Reach of Empire: Britain's Maritime Expansion in the Indian and Pacific Oceans, 1764–1815* (Carlton: Miegunyah Press, 2003)

Fry, Michael, *The Dundas Despotism* (Edinburgh: Edinburgh University Press, 1992)

Frykman, Niklas, 'Connections between Mutinies in European Navies', *International Review of Social History* 58 (2013), pp. 87–107

Frykman, Niklas, Clare Anderson, Lex Heerma van Voss, and Marcus Rediker, 'Mutiny and Maritime Radicalism in the Age of Revolution: An Introduction', *International Review of Social History* 58 (2013), pp. 1–14

Furber, Holden, *Henry Dundas, First Viscount Melville, 1742–1811* (Oxford: Oxford University Press, 1931)

Ghosh, Devleena and Stephen Muecke (eds.), *Cultures of Trade: Indian Ocean Exchanges* (Newcastle-upon-Tyne: Cambridge Scholars Press, 2007)

Ghosh, Durba and Dane Kennedy (eds.), *Decentring Empire: Britain, India and the Transcolonial World* (London: Sangam Books, 2006)

Gilbert, Arthur N., 'Recruitment and Reform in the East India Company Army, 1760–1800', *Journal of British Studies* 15 (1975), pp. 89–111

Giliomee, Hermann, *Die Kaap Tydens die Eerste Britse Bewind, 1795–1803* (Cape Town: H.A.U.M., 1975)

Gillis, John R., 'Islands in the Making of an Atlantic Oceania, 1500–1800', in Jerry H. Bentley, Renate Bridenthal and Kären Wigen (eds.), *Seascapes: Maritime Histories, Littoral Cultures, and Transoceanic Exchanges* (Honolulu: University of Hawai'i Press, 2007), pp. 21–37

Glaisyer, Natasha, 'Networking: Trade and Exchange in the Eighteenth-Century British Empire', *Historical Journal* 47 (2004), pp. 451–76

Gosse, Philip, *St Helena, 1502–1938* (London: Cassell, 1938)

Gough, Barry M., 'Sea Power and South America: The "Brazils" or South American Station of the Royal Navy, 1808–1837', *American Neptune* 50 (1990), pp. 26–34

  The Falkland Islands/Malvinas: The Contest for Empire in the South Atlantic (London: Athlone Press, 1992)

  Pax Britannica: Ruling the Waves and Keeping the Peace before Armageddon (Basingstoke: Palgrave Macmillan, 2014)

Gould, Eliga H., 'Entangled Histories, Entangled Worlds: The English-Speaking Atlantic as a Spanish Periphery', *American Historical Review* 112 (2007), pp. 764–86

Graham, Gerald S., *Great Britain in the Indian Ocean: A Study of Maritime Enterprise, 1810–1850* (Oxford: Clarendon Press, 1967)

  The Politics of Naval Supremacy (Cambridge: Cambridge University Press, 1965)

Grainger, John, 'The Conquest of the Cape, 1806', *Army and Quarterly and Defence Journal* 123 (1993), pp. 320–1

Green, Nile, 'Maritime Worlds and Global History: Comparing the Mediterranean and Indian Ocean through Barcelona and Bombay', *History Compass* 11 (2013), pp. 513–23

Groenewald, Gerald, 'Entrepreneurs and the Making of a Free Burgher Society', in Nigel Worden (ed.), *Cape Town between East and West: Social Identities in a Dutch Colonial Town* (Hilversum: Uitgeverij Verloren, 2012), pp. 45–64

'Southern Africa and the Atlantic World', in D'Maris Coffman, Adrian Leonard and William O'Reilly (eds.), *The Atlantic World* (Abingdon: Routledge, 2015), pp. 100–16

Grove, A. T., 'St Helena as a Microcosm of the East India Company World', in Vinita Damodaran, Anna Winterbottom and Alan Lester (eds.), *The East India Company and the Natural World* (Basingstoke: Palgrave Macmillan, 2014), pp. 249–69

Grove, Richard, *Green Imperialism: Colonial Expansion, Tropical Island Edens and the Origins of Environmentalism, 1600–1860* (Cambridge: Cambridge University Press, 1996)

Gupta, Pamila, 'Island-ness in the Indian Ocean', in Pamila Gupta, Isabel Hofmeyr and Michael Pearson (eds.), *Eyes Across the Water: Navigating the Indian Ocean* (Pretoria: UNISA Press, 2010), pp. 275–85

Gupta, Pamila, Isabel Hofmeyr and Michael Pearson (eds.), *Eyes Across the Water: Navigating the Indian Ocean* (Pretoria: UNISA Press, 2010)

Guy, Alan J., 'British Strategy and the Cape of Good Hope in the Era of the French Revolutionary and Napoleonic Wars', in Peter B. Boyden, Alan J. Guy and Marion Harding (eds.), *'Ashes and Blood': The British Army in South Africa, 1795–1914* (London: National Army Museum, 1999), pp. 32–43

Haig, Wolesley, 'The Armies of the East India Company', in Henry H. Dodwell (ed.), *The Cambridge History of the British Empire: Volume V. The Indian Empire, 1858–1918* (Cambridge: Cambridge University Press, 1932), pp. 153–66

Haight, Mabel V. Jackson, *European Powers and South-East Africa: A Study of International Relations on the South-Eastern Coast of Africa, 1796–1856* (London: Routledge & Kegan Paul, 1967)

Hall, Christopher D., *British Strategy in the Napoleonic War, 1803–15* (Manchester: Manchester University Press, 1992)

Hamilton, Douglas, 'Local Connections, Global Ambitions: Creating a Transoceanic Network in the Eighteenth-Century British Atlantic Empire', *International Journal of Maritime History*, 23 (2011), pp. 1–18

Hancock, David, 'The Trouble with Networks: Managing the Scots' Early Modern Madeira Table', *Business History Review* 79 (2005), pp. 467–91

Harding, Richard, *The Emergence of Britain's Global Naval Supremacy: The War of 1739–1748* (Woodbridge: Boydell, 2013)

Harlow, Vincent T., *The Founding of the Second British Empire, 1763–1793*, 2 vols. (London: Longmans, 1952–64)

Harris, Steven J., 'Long-Distance Corporations, Big Sciences, and the Geography of Knowledge', *Configurations* 6 (1998), pp. 269–304

Henshaw, Philip, 'The "Key to South Africa" in the 1890s: Delagoa Bay and the Origins of the South African War', *Journal of Southern African Studies* 24 (1998), pp. 527–44

Hockly, Harold Edward, *The Story of the British Settlers of 1820 in South Africa* (Johannesburg: Juta, 1957)

Hofmeyr, Isabel, 'South Africa's Indian Ocean – Notes from Johannesburg', *History Compass* 11 (2013), pp. 508–12

Howard, Richard A., 'The St Vincent Botanic Garden: The Early Years', *Arnoldia* 57 (1997), pp. 12–21

Huigen, Siegfried, *Knowledge and Colonialism: Eighteenth-century Travellers in South Africa* (Leiden: Brill, 2009)

Hyam, Ronald, 'British Imperial Expansion in the Late Eighteenth Century', *Historical Journal* 10 (1967), pp. 113–24

Igler, David, *The Great Ocean: Pacific Worlds from Captain Cook to the Gold Rush* (Oxford: Oxford University Press, 2013)

Ingram, Edward, *The Beginning of the Great Game in Asia, 1828–1834* (Oxford: Clarendon Press, 1979)

    Commitment to Empire: Prophecies of the Great Game in Asia, 1797–1800 (Oxford: Clarendon Press, 1981)

    In Defence of British India: Great Britain in the Middle East, 1774–1842 (London: Cass, 1984)

    Britain's Persian Connection, 1798–1828: Prelude to the Great Game in Asia (Oxford: Clarendon Press, 1992)

Johnson, David, *Imagining the Cape Colony: History, Literature, and the South African Nation* (Edinburgh: Edinburgh University Press, 2012)

Johnson, Nuala C., *Nature Displaced, Nature Displayed: Order and Beauty in Botanical Gardens* (London: I. B. Tauris, 2011)

Joseph, Betty, *Reading the East India Company, 1720–1840* (Chicago: University of Chicago Press, 2004)

Kearney, Milo, *The Indian Ocean in World History* (London: Routledge, 2004)

Keay, John, *The Honourable Company: A History of the English East India Company* (London: Harper Collins, 1993)

Kinahan, Jill, 'The Impenetrable Shield: HMS *Nautilus* and the Namib Coast in the Eighteenth Century', *Cimbebasia: Journal of the State Museum, Windhoek* 13 (1990), pp. 23–67

    By Command of Their Lordships: The Exploration of the Namibian Coast by the Royal Navy, 1795–1895 (Windhoek: Namibia Archaeological Trust, 1992)

Klein, Bernard and Gesa Mackenthun (eds.), *Sea Changes: Historicizing the Ocean* (New York: Routledge, 2004)

Knight, Roger, *Britain against Napoleon: The Organisation of Victory, 1793–1815* (London: Penguin, 2014)

Kocka, Jürgen, 'Comparison and Beyond', *History and Theory* 42 (2003), pp. 39–44

Lambert, David, Luciana Martins and Miles Ogborn, 'Currents, Visions and Voyages: Historical Geographies of the Seas', *Journal of Historical Geography* 32 (2006), pp. 479–93

Lawson, Philip, *The East India Company: A History, 1600–1857* (London: Longmans, 1993)

Lester, Alan, 'British Settler Discourse and the Circuits of Empire', *History Workshop Journal* 54 (2002), pp. 24–48

Lightman, Bernard, Gordon McOuat and Larry Stewart (eds.), *The Circulation of Knowledge between Britain, India and China: The Early-Modern World to the Twentieth Century* (Leiden: Brill, 2013)

Liss, Peggy K., *Atlantic Empires: The Network of Trade and Revolution, 1713–1826* (Baltimore and London: Johns Hopkins University Press, 1983)

Lloyd, Christopher, *Mr Barrow of the Admiralty: A Life of Sir John Barrow, 1764–1848* (London: Collins, 1970)

Lynch, John, 'British Policy and Spanish America, 1783–1808', *Journal of Latin American Studies* 1 (1969), pp. 1–30

McAleer, John, *Representing Africa: Landscape, Exploration and Empire, 1780–1870* (Manchester: Manchester University Press, 2010)

'"In Trade as in Warfare": Conflict and Conquest in the Indian Ocean, 1600–1815', in H. V. Bowen, John McAleer and Robert J. Blyth, *Monsoon Traders: The Maritime World of the East India Company* (London: Scala, 2011), pp. 126–57

'"The Key to India": Troop Movements, Southern Africa and Britain's Indian Ocean World, 1795–1820', *International History Review* 35 (2013), pp. 294–316

'Plants, Patronage and Promotion: Lord Caledon's Connections at the Cape of Good Hope', *Bulletin of the National Library of South Africa* 68 (2014), pp. 53–68

'"This *Ultima Thule*": The Cape of Good Hope, Ireland and Global Networks of Empire', *Eighteenth-Century Ireland* 29 (2014), pp. 63–84

'Atlantic Periphery, Asian Gateway: The Royal Navy at the Cape of Good Hope, 1785–1815', in John McAleer and Christer Petley (eds.), *The Royal Navy and the Atlantic World in the Eighteenth Century* (Basingstoke: Palgrave Macmillan, 2016), pp. 183–206

McAteer, William, *Rivals in Eden: The History of Seychelles, 1742–1827* (Mahé: Pristine Books, 2002)

McCracken, Donal M., *Gardens of Empire: Botanical Institutions of the Victorian British Empire* (London: Leicester University Press, 1997)

McCracken, J. L., 'The Cape of Good Hope, 1796–98', in Peter Roebuck (ed.), *Macartney of Lisanoure, 1737–1806* (Belfast: Ulster Historical Foundation, 1983), pp. 266–77

Machado, Pedro, *Ocean of Trade: South Asian Merchants, Africa and the Indian Ocean, c.1750–1850* (Cambridge: Cambridge University Press, 2014)

Mack, John, 'The Land viewed from the Sea', *Azania* 42 (2007), pp. 1–14

The Sea: A Cultural History (London: Reaktion, 2013)

McKenzie, Kirsten, *The Making of an English Slave-owner: Samuel Eusebius Hudson at the Cape of Good Hope, 1796–1807* (Rondebosch: University of Cape Town Press, 1993)

Scandal in the Colonies: Sydney and Cape Town, 1820–1850 (Carlton: Melbourne University Press, 2004)

'Social Mobilities at the Cape of Good Hope: Lady Anne Barnard, Samuel Hudson, and the Opportunities of Empire, *c.*1797–1824', in Tony Ballantyne and Antoinette Burton (eds.), *Moving Subjects: Gender, Mobility, and Intimacy in an Age of Global Empire* (Urbana, IL: University of Illinois Press, 2008), pp. 274–95

Mackesy, Piers, *The War for America, 1775–1783* (London: Longman, 1964)
  The British Victory in Egypt, 1801: The End of Napoleon's Conquest (Abingdon: Routledge, 1995)
MacLeod, Roy, 'On Visiting the "Moving Metropolis": Reflections on the Architecture of Imperial Science', in Nathan Reingold and Marc Rothenberg (eds.), *Scientific Colonialism: A Cross-Cultural Comparison* (Washington DC: Smithsonian Institution Press, 1987), pp. 217–49
McPherson, Kenneth, *The Indian Ocean: A History of People and the Sea* (Oxford: Oxford University Press, 1993)
Mapp, Paul W., *The Elusive West and the Contest for Empire, 1713–1763* (Chapel Hill, NC: University of North Carolina Press, 2011)
Margariti, Roxani, 'An Ocean of Islands: Islands, Insularity, and Historiography of the Indian Ocean', in Peter N. Miller (ed.), *The Sea: Thalassography and Historiography* (Ann Arbor, MI: University of Michigan Press, 2013), pp. 198–229
Marnitz, P. W. and H. D. Campagne, *The Dutch Surrender of the Cape of Good Hope, 1795* (Cape Town: Castle Military Museum, 2002)
Marshall, P. J. 'The Eighteenth-Century Empire', in Jeremy Black (ed.), *British Politics and Society from Walpole to Pitt, 1742–1789* (Basingstoke: Macmillan, 1990), pp. 177–200
  'A Free though Conquering People': Eighteenth-Century Britain and its Empire (Aldershot: Ashgate, 2003)
  The Making and Unmaking of Empires: Britain, India. and America c. 1750–1783 (Oxford: Oxford University Press, 2007)
  Remaking the British Atlantic: The United States and the British Empire after Independence (Oxford: Oxford University Press, 2012)
  (ed.), *The Oxford History of the British Empire. Volume II: The Eighteenth Century* (Oxford: Oxford University Press, 1998)
Martins, Luciana and Felix Driver, '"The Struggle for Luxuriance": William Burchell collects Tropical Nature', in Felix Driver and Luciana Martins (eds.), *Tropical Visions in an Age of Empire*, (Chicago: University of Chicago Press, 2005), pp. 59–74
Masson, Madeleine, *Lady Anne Barnard: The Court and Colonial Service under George III and the Regency* (London: Allen & Unwin, 1948)
Matheson, Cyril, *The Life of Henry Dundas, First Viscount Melville, 1742–1811* (London: Constable, 1933)
Metcalf, Thomas R., *Imperial Connections: India in the Indian Ocean Arena, 1860–1920* (Berkeley, CA: University of California Press, 2007)
Miller, David Philip, 'Introduction', in D. P. Miller and P. H. Reill (eds.), *Visions of Empire: Voyages, Botany and the Representations of Nature* (Cambridge: Cambridge University Press, 1996), pp. 1–18
Misra, G. S., *British Foreign Policy and Indian Affairs, 1783–1815* (London: Asia Publishing House, 1963)
Mitchell, B. R., *Abstract of British Historical Statistics* (Cambridge: Cambridge University Press, 1971)
Morris, James, *Pax Britannica: The Climax of an Empire* (Harmondsworth: Penguin, 1979)

Neale, Jonathan, 'The Influence of 1797 upon the Nereide Mutiny of 1809', in Ann Veronica Coats and Philip MacDougall (eds.), *The Naval Mutinies of 1797: Unity and Perseverance* (Woodbridge: Boydell & Brewer, 2011), pp. 264–79

Omissi, David, *The Sepoy and the Raj: The Indian Army, 1860–1940* (Basingstoke: Macmillan, 1994)

O'Neill, Lindsay, *The Opened Letter: Networking in the Early Modern British World* (Philadelphia: University of Pennsylvania Press, 2015)

Panikkar, Kavalam Madhava, *India and the Indian Ocean* (London: Allen & Unwin, 1945)

Parkinson, C. Northcote, *Trade in the Eastern Seas* (Cambridge: Cambridge University Press, 1937)

War in the Eastern Seas, 1793–1815 (London: Allen & Unwin, 1954)

Pearson, Michael, *The Indian Ocean* (London: Routledge, 1992)

Peers, Douglas M. and Nandini Gooptu (eds.), *India and the British Empire* (Oxford: Oxford University Press, 2012)

Penn, Nigel, 'Soldiers and Cape Town Society', in Nigel Worden (ed.) *Cape Town between East and West: Social Identities in a Dutch Colonial Town* (Hilversum: Uitgeverij Verloren, 2012), pp. 176–93

Penrose, Boise, 'Some Jacobean Links between America and the Orient', *Virginia Magazine of History and Biography* 48 (1940), p. 289

Philips, C. H., *The East India Company, 1784–1834* (Manchester: Manchester University Press, 1940)

Pineo, Huguette Ly-Tio-Fane, *In the Grips of the Eagle: Matthew Flinders at Ile de France, 1803–1810* (Moka, Mauritius: Mahatma Gandhi Institute, 1988)

Polasky, Janet, *Revolutions without Borders: The Call to Liberty in the Atlantic World* (London: Yale University Press, 2015)

Popham, Hugh, *A Damned Cunning Fellow: The Eventful Life of Rear-Admiral Sir Home Popham KCB, KCH, KM, FRS, 1762–1820* (Tywardreath: Old Ferry Press, 1991)

Price, Richard, *Making Empire: Colonial Encounters and the Creation of Imperial Rule in Nineteenth-Century Africa* (Cambridge: Cambridge University Press, 2008)

Purcell, Nicholas, 'Tide, Beach, and Backwash: The Place of Maritime Histories', in Peter N. Miller (ed.), *The Sea: Thalassography and Historiography* (Ann Arbor, MI: University of Michigan Press, 2013), pp. 84–108

Raven-Hart, Rowland (ed.), *Before Van Riebeeck: Callers at South Africa from 1488 to 1652* (Cape Town: Struik, 1967)

Richards, Thomas, *The Imperial Archive: Knowledge and the Fantasy of Empire* (London: Verso, 1993)

Richmond, Herbert, *The Navy in India, 1763–1783* (London: Ernest Benn, 1931)

Rivière, Marc Serge, 'From Belfast to Mauritius: Charles Telfair (1778–1833), Naturalist and a Product of the Irish Enlightenment', *Eighteenth-Century Ireland* 21 (2006), pp. 125–44

Roberts, Lissa, 'Centres and Cycles of Accumulation', in Lissa Roberts (ed.), *Centres and Cycles of Accumulation in and around the Netherlands during the Early Modern Period* (Zurich: LIT, 2011), pp. 3–27

'Accumulation and Management in Global Historical Perspective: An Introduction', *History of Science* 52 (2014), pp. 227–46

' "*Le centre de toutes choses*": Constructing and Managing Centralization on the Isle de France', *History of Science* 52 (2014), pp. 319–42

Roberts, P. E., *India under Wellesley* (London: G. Bell and Sons, 1929)

Robinson, Tim, *William Roxburgh: The Founding Father of Indian Botany* (Chichester: Phillimore, 2008)

Rodger, N. A. M., 'Seapower and Empire: Cause and Effect?', in Bob Moore and Henk Van Nierop (eds.), *Colonial Empires Compared: Britain and the Netherlands, 1750–1850* (Aldershot: Ashgate, 2003), pp. 97–111

Rose, J. Holland *The Life of William Pitt. Volume 2: William Pitt and the Great War* (London: G. Bell, 1934)

Ross, Robert, 'Cape Town (1750–1850): Synthesis in the Dialectic of Continents', in Robert Ross and Gerard J. Telkamp (eds.), *Colonial Cities: Essays on Urbanism in a Colonial Context* (Dordrecht: Martinus Nijhoff, 1985), pp. 105–21

Ross, Robert and Alicia Schrikker, 'The VOC Official Elite', in Nigel Worden (ed.) *Cape Town between East and West: Social Identities in a Dutch Colonial Town* (Hilversum: Uitgeverij Verloren, 2012), pp. 26–44

Rothschild, Emma, 'The Atlantic Worlds of David Hume', in Bernard Bailyn and Patricia L. Denault (eds.), *Soundings in Atlantic History: Latent Structures and Intellectual Currents, 1500–1830* (Cambridge, MA: Harvard University Press, 2009), pp. 405–48

Royle, Stephen A., 'Perilous Shipwreck, Misery and Unhappiness: The British Military at Tristan da Cunha, 1816–1817', *Journal of Historical Geography* 29 (2003), pp. 516–34

The Company's Island: St Helena, Company Colonies and the Colonial Endeavour (London: I. B. Tauris, 2007)

Samkin, Grant, 'Trader Sailor Spy: The Case of John Pringle and the Transfer of Accounting Technology to the Cape of Good Hope', *Accounting History* 15 (2010), pp. 505–28

Schaffer, Simon, 'Visions of Empire: Afterword', in D. P. Miller and P. H. Reill (eds.), *Visions of Empire: Voyages, Botany and the Representations of Nature* (Cambridge: Cambridge University Press, 1996), pp. 335–52

Schiebinger, Londa, 'Scientific Exchange in the Eighteenth-Century Atlantic World', in Bernard Bailyn and Patricia L. Denault (eds.), *Soundings in Atlantic History: Latent Structures and Intellectual Currents, 1500–1830* (Cambridge, MA: Harvard University Press, 2009), pp. 294–328

Seed, Patricia, *Ceremonies of Possession in Europe's Conquest of the New World, 1492–1640* (Cambridge: Cambridge University Press, 1995)

Sicking, Louis, 'Islands and Maritime Connections, Networks and Empire, 1200–1700: Introduction', *International Journal of Maritime History* 26 (2014), pp. 489–93

Sivasundaram, Sujit, 'Sciences and the Global: On Methods, Questions and Theory', *Isis* 101 (2010), pp. 146–58

Islanded: Britain, Sri Lanka and the Bounds of an Indian Ocean Colony (New Delhi: Oxford University Press, 2013)

Smith, Kenneth Wyndham, *From Frontier to Midlands: A History of the Graaff-Reinet District, 1786–1910* (Grahamstown: Institute of Social and Economic Research, Rhodes University, 1976)

Sörlin, Sverker, 'National and International Aspects of Cross-Boundary Science: Scientific Travel in the 18th Century', in Elizabeth Crawford, Terry Shinn and Sverker Sörlin (eds.), *Denationalizing Science: The Contexts of International Scientific Practice* (Dordrecht: Kluwer Academic Publishers, 1993), pp. 43–72

Sparrow, Elizabeth, 'Secret Service under Pitt's Administration, 1792–1806', *History* 83 (1998), pp. 280–94

Spray, William A., 'British Surveys in the Chagos Archipelago and Attempts to form a Settlement at Diego Garcia in the Late Eighteenth Century', *Mariner's Mirror* 56 (1970), pp. 59–76

Stafford, Robert A., 'Scientific Exploration and Empire', in Andrew Porter (ed.), *The Oxford History of the British Empire, Volume 3: The Nineteenth Century* (Oxford: Oxford University Press, 1999), pp. 294–319

Steinberg, Philip E., 'Of Other Seas: Metaphors and Materialities in Maritime Regions', *Atlantic Studies* 10 (2013), pp. 156–69

Stern, Philip J., 'Politics and Ideology in the Early East India Company-State: The Case of St. Helena, 1673–1696', *Journal of Imperial and Commonwealth History* 35 (2007), pp. 1–23

The Company-State: Corporate Sovereignty and the Early Modern Foundations of the British Empire in India (Oxford: Oxford University Press, 2011)

Sturgis, James, 'Anglicization at the Cape of Good Hope in the Early Nineteenth Century', *Journal of Imperial and Commonwealth History* 11 (1982), pp. 5–32

Subrahmanyam, Sanjay, 'Connected Histories: Notes towards a Reconfiguration of Early Modern Eurasia', *Modern Asian Studies* 31 (1997), pp. 735–62

'Seths and Sahibs: Negotiated Relationships between Indigenous Capital and the East India Company', in H. V. Bowen, Elizabeth Mancke and John G. Reid (eds.), *Britain's Oceanic Empire: Atlantic and Indian Ocean Worlds, c. 1550–1850* (Cambridge: Cambridge University Press, 2012), pp. 311–39

Tabler, E. C., 'Loss of the Ship *Hercules*', *Africana Notes and News* 17 (1966), p. 88

Tarling, Nicholas, *Anglo-Dutch Rivalry in the Malay World, 1780–1824* (Cambridge: Cambridge University Press, 1962)

Taylor, Stephen, *Storm and Conquest: The Battle for the Indian Ocean, 1808–10* (London: Faber & Faber, 2007)

Thomas, Adrian T., 'The Establishment of Calcutta Botanic Garden: Plant Transfer, Science and the East India Company, 1786–1806', *Journal of the Royal Asiatic Society* 16 (2006), pp. 165–77

Thomas, James H., 'The Isle of Wight and the East India Company, 1700–1840: Some Connections Considered', *Local Historian* 30 (2000), pp. 4–22

Toussaint, Auguste, *History of the Indian Ocean*, trans. June Guicharnaud (London: Routledge & Kegan Paul, 1966)

La Route des Iles, contribution à l'histoire maritime des Mascareignes (Paris: SEVPEN, 1967)

(ed.), *Early American Trade with Mauritius* (Port Louis: Esclapon, 1954)

Tracy, Nicholas, 'Parry of a Threat to India, 1768–1774', *Mariner's Mirror* 59 (1973), pp. 35–48

Navies, Deterrence, and American Independence: Britain and Seapower in the 1760s and 1770s (Vancouver: University of British Columbia Press, 1988)

Turner, L. C. F., 'The Cape of Good Hope and the Anglo-French Conflict, 1797–1806', *Historical Studies. Australia and New Zealand* 9 (1961), pp. 368–78

'The Cape of Good Hope and Anglo-French Rivalry, 1778–1796', *Australian Historical Studies* 12 (1966), pp. 166–85

Ulrich, Nicole, 'International Radicalism, Local Solidarities: The 1797 British Naval Mutinies in Southern African Waters', *International Review of Social History* 58 (2013), pp. 61–85

Vaughan, Megan, *Creating the Creole Island: Slavery in Eighteenth-Century Mauritius* (London: Duke University Press, 2005)

'Foreword', in Shawkat Toorawa (ed.), *The Western Indian Ocean: Essays on Islands and Islanders* (Port Louis: Hassam Toorawa Trust, 2007), pp. xv–xix

Villiers, Alan, *The Western Ocean: Story of the North Atlantic* (London: British Museum Press, 1957)

Vink, Markus, 'Indian Ocean Studies and the "New Thalassology"', *Journal of Global History* 18 (2007), pp. 41–62

Wald, Erica, *Vice in the Barracks: Medicine, the Military and the Making of Colonial India, 1780–1868* (Basingstoke: Palgrave Macmillan, 2014)

Ward, Kerry, '"Tavern of the Seas"? The Cape of Good Hope as an Oceanic Crossroads during the Seventeenth and Eighteenth Centuries', in Jerry H. Bentley, Renate Bridenthal and Kären Wigen (eds.), *Seascapes: Maritime Histories, Littoral Cultures, and Transoceanic Exchanges* (Honolulu: University of Hawai'i Press, 2007), pp. 137–52

Networks of Empire: Forced Migration in the Dutch East India Company (Cambridge: Cambridge University Press, 2008)

Ward, Peter A., *British Naval Power in the East, 1794–1805: The Command of Admiral Peter Rainier* (Woodbridge: Boydell & Brewer, 2013)

Washbrook, David, 'The Indian Economy and the British Empire' in Douglas M. Peers and Nandini Gooptu (eds.), *India and the British Empire* (Oxford: Oxford University Press, 2012), pp. 44–74

Wigen, Kären, 'Introduction', in Jerry H. Bentley, Renate Bridenthal and Kären Wigen (eds.), *Seascapes: Maritime Histories, Littoral Cultures, and Transoceanic Exchanges* (Honolulu: University of Hawai'i Press, 2007), pp. 1–18

Williams, Glyndwr, '"The Inexhaustible Fountain of Gold": English Projects and Ventures in the South Seas, 1670–1750', in John E. Grant and Glyndwr Williams (eds.), *Perspectives of Empire: Essays presented to Gerald S. Graham* (London: Longman, 1973), pp. 27–53

Winch, Donald, *Classical Political Theory and Colonies* (Cambridge: Harvard University Press, 1965)

Winter, Charles, 'Gold and Silver Medals of the Honourable East India Company', *British Numismatic Journal* 17 (1923/24), pp. 281–7

Worden, Nigel, 'VOC Cape Town as an Indian Ocean Port', in Himanshu Prabha Ray and Edward A. Alpers (eds.), *Cross Currents and Community Networks: The History of the Indian Ocean World* (Oxford: Oxford University Press, 2007), pp. 142–62

'VOC Capetown as an Indian Ocean Port', in Devleena Ghosh and Stephen Muecke (eds.), *Cultures of Trade: Indian Ocean Exchanges* (Newcastle-upon-Tyne: Cambridge Scholars Press, 2007), pp. 31–46

(ed.), *Contingent Lives: Social Identity and Material Culture in the VOC World* (Cape Town: University of Cape Town Press, 2007)

Worden, Nigel, Elizabeth van Heyningen and Vivian Bickford-Smith, *Cape Town: The Making of a City* (Cape Town: David Philip, 1998)

Zahlan, Rosemarie Said, 'George Baldwin: Soldier of Fortune?', in Paul Starkey and Janet Starkey (eds.), *Travellers in Egypt* (London: I. B. Tauris, 1998), pp. 24–38

Unpublished secondary sources

Bryant, Gerald J., 'The East India Company and its army', Ph.D. thesis, University of London, 1975

Coetzee, Colin, 'Die Stryd om Delagoabaai en die suidooskus, 1600–1800', Ph. D. thesis, University of Stellenbosch, 1954

Day, John Frederick, 'British Admiralty control and naval power in the Indian Ocean, 1793–1815', Ph.D. thesis, University of Exeter, 2012

Field, A. G., 'The expedition to Mauritius and the establishment of British control', MA thesis, University of London, 1931

Geber, Jill, 'The East India Company and Southern Africa: a guide to the Archives of the East India Company and the Board of Control, 1600–1858', Ph.D. dissertation, University of London, 1998

Schulenburg, Alexander H., 'Transient observations: the textualizing of St Helena through five hundred years of colonial discourse', Ph.D. thesis, University of St Andrews, 1999

Smith, Alan Kent, 'The struggle for control of southern Mozambique, 1720–1835', Ph.D. thesis, UCLA, 1970

Twidle, Hedley, 'Prison and garden: Cape Town, natural history and the literary imagination', Ph.D. thesis, University of York, 2010

Ward, Peter, 'Admiral Peter Rainier and the command of the East Indies Station, 1794–1805', Ph.D. thesis, University of Exeter, 2010

Wastell, R. E. P., 'British imperial policy in relation to Madagascar, 1810–1896', Ph.D. thesis, University of London, 1944

Williams, Siân, 'The Royal Navy in the Caribbean, 1756–1815', Ph.D. thesis, University of Southampton, 2014

Index